DESIGN FOR
MOUNTAIN
COMMUNITIES

DESIGN FOR MOUNTAIN COMMUNITIES

A Landscape and Architectural Guide

Sherry Dorward, ASLA

VNR VAN NOSTRAND REINHOLD
_____ New York

Library of Congress Catalog Card Number 89–56021
ISBN 0-442-22095-2

Printed in the United States of America

Van Nostrand Reinhold
115 Fifth Avenue
New York, New York 10003

Van Nostrand Reinhold International Company Limited
111 New Fetter Lane
London EC4P 4EE, England

Van Nostrand Reinhold
480 La Trobe Street
Melbourne, Victoria 3000, Australia

Nelson Canada
1120 Birchmount Road
Scarborough, Ontario
Canada M1K 5G4

16 15 14 13 12 11 10 9 8 7 6 5 4 3 2 1

Library of Congress Cataloging-in-Publication Data

Dorward, Sherry
    Design for mountain communities: a landscape and archi-
    tectural guide / by Sherry Dorward.
        p. cm.
    Bibliography: p.
    Includes index.
    ISBN 0-442-22095-2
    1. Hillside landscape architecture. 2. Hillside architecture.
    3. Mountain ecology.
I. Title: Mountain communities.
SB475.9.H54D67   1990
712--dc19   89-5602
                                                    CIP

Contents

Preface

A decade ago, when I was in graduate school in landscape architecture, it seemed that classmates who were most comfortable with the science of ecology opted for the seminar rooms to study environmental planning. Those who preferred design headed for the studios, where a decidedly urban perspective held sway. When we occasionally reunited after this parting of the ways, one group, having learned the language of ecoscience, spoke about issues of regional import; the other, magic markers in hand, spoke in graphics about smaller areas on a site map. We were not terribly fluent in each other's language.

From a designer's perspective, information about ecological processes often seemed either too broad or too technical to be truly meaningful for design. This wasn't much help for a designer whose nonurban focus was on smaller communities, where the natural environment was still the major force to be reckoned with and where the bonds between nature and people were more nearly intact.

Out of this observation came the idea for a book. It began as a master's thesis, in which I sought to reinject ecology into community design in the environment I care about most, the mountains.

I have lived virtually my entire life near mountains. They invigorate my spirit, soothe my soul. To a less passionate extent, so do livable communities. Can't we overlay the one upon the other more gently than we have? Protect the natural community while animating the human community with its spirit? Knit the two into a fabric of incomparable quality?

I am saddened by the disregard that some developments display, not only toward their mountain surroundings but also toward the people who must endure the shoddiness of what has been built. The failure to realize the potential of such special places is a disappointment to me, but I am heartened by the many projects that show respect for place and for people. A myriad of lessons lie hidden there.

This book fills a void by offering these lessons as guidance to those who, until now, have been left alone to repeat the mistakes of others. My intention has been to forge more sensitive precepts for design in the mountains by reviewing the experience of high-country residents, developers, contractors, and scientists and by gathering together their wisdom in all facets of mountain ecology.

The resulting design guidelines do not represent the only right way to build in the mountains. Although the book assumes a framework of values to govern design in a natural place, it offers mainly guidance, not gospel. I recognize that other opinions, other experiences, the peculiarities of specific sites, and factors unrelated to design theory or ecology will influence how each designer or builder responds to the mountain environment. Indeed, it has been my

own experience working in the mountains that special circumstances always seem to make it difficult, if not impossible, to adhere in every instance to ideal guidelines. In this environment of constraints and extremes, design is an evolving art and a collaborative effort. But although the finished product cannot be perfect, surely we can improve on the status quo.

It has not been my intention to make exhaustive critiques. In many cases, the projects mentioned here that have fallen short of expectations preceded current environmental legislation and were products of ecological naïveté, not wanton disregard. Knowledge and regulation have progressed measurably in the past fifteen years, and many of these projects would almost certainly be different if they were built today. My only motive in evaluating these examples has been, therefore, to extract useful lessons for future application.

Design for Mountain Communities concerns only design, not planning. It does not attempt to address the pressing environmental issues that complicate development in the mountains. It does not pretend that sensitive design can justify ill-advised development. Design is only part of a broader process of understanding, restraint, growth, and adjustment. I am hopeful, however, that by regaining a sensitivity to the natural environment, design by itself can contribute to livable communities that exist in harmony with the fragile and beautiful mountain setting.

Purpose. This book explores landscape and architectural design in mountain communities, illustrating how built forms can be made compatible with their natural setting, respectful of their context, and evocative of place. It is written in the belief that design that delights people and best serves their needs flows from a reverence for the beauty, ecology, and limitations of the mountain environment.

Design for Mountain Communities is written not just for designers and builders but for all people who care about the mountains as an enduring resource. It is a guidebook that applies concepts of ecological common sense, human sensitivity, and aesthetic quality to the process of designing places for people in mountain landscapes, where these values are sorely needed.

Which Mountains? The mountain environment that is the focus of this book does not include all mountainous or hilly regions. Rather, the mountains explored here are characterized by rugged terrain and a harsh winter climate. They are high enough that visitors notice the elevation, and they are relatively remote and sparsely populated. These are the scenic mountains of summer vacations, the romantic mountains of nineteenth-century naturalist painters, the snow-covered mountains on Christmas greeting cards. These mountains of the middle latitudes—and the communities that have traditionally been associated with them—project images uniquely their own, images that provide clues to designing a new development that is quintessentially mountain in character.

A Three-part Exploration. This book is divided into three parts. Part I consists of a pair of background chapters, one on historical patterns of settlement in the mountains and the other on the singular aesthetics of mountain landscapes.

Part II reviews the environmental factors that have implications for design: climate and elevation, topography and geology, vegetation and soils. It suggests design guidelines for responding to these and outlines a process for designing in any mountain situation (indeed, in any natural context).

Part III focuses on the products of design, from entire communities to buildings and site details. Examples are taken from existing mountain towns and resorts in the Rockies, Sierras, New England, and British Columbia. The chapters in this section discuss decisions about community form, design of the community core, landscape themes, architectural styles, and detailing for snow and ice.

A constant theme prevails in all three parts: Design concepts and forms appropriate to mountain environments have their underpinnings in the physical constraints imposed by natural systems and in the special sensory character of the landscape. In the mountains, natural factors are the best source of community identity and the strongest determinants of form.

Acknowledgments

Scores of people have given freely of their time and expertise in interviews for this project. I am grateful to them for their willingness to share what they have learned working in the mountains. I have benefitted especially from insights about design and the sense of place that I have gained in conversations with architects Buff Arnold, Fritz Benedict, Cab Childress, Bruno Freschi, Pam Hopkins, Bob Odermatt, Antoine Predock, Ron Rinker, Fitzhugh Scott, William Turnbull, and Larry Yaw; with landscape architects Dick Berridge, Gage Davis, John Exley, Burt Litton, Joe Porter, and Jeff Winston; and with planners Gerry Engle, Terry Minger, Peter Patten, Miles Rademan, and Mike Vance.

I am also indebted to colleagues who have reviewed portions of the manuscript related to their professional specialties: architects Henrik Bull, George Hoover, and George Rockrise; geotechnical engineer Ken Myers; climatologist David Greenland; fluvial geomorphologist Robert O'Brien; soil scientists Hayes Dye and Gib Bowman of the Soil Conservation Service; plant ecologist David Cooper; tundra ecologist Betty Willard; and wetland specialist Brad Miller at the Environmental Protection Agency.

Many design offices and project developers have contributed to the book, and I have credited their work where it appears. My thanks to all of them for their generous cooperation, especially Winston Associates in Boulder, Colorado, Design Workshop Inc. in Denver and Aspen, and Ms. Jerry Arnold of Vail Associates Inc., for helping me locate drawings that reconstruct a picture of how design concepts evolve.

I also wish to thank the Berkeley Professional Studies Program in India, which in 1979–80 sponsored me as a research fellow for a study of land use and environmental problems in the Valley of Kashmir. That year of exposure to high-altitude ecology and to remote Himalayan villages was the genesis for many ideas in this book.

To make the book a visual reality, I am fortunate to have had the help of two incredibly talented friends. Denver architect Jim Leggitt, of Leggitt Design, did the graphic design for the book, the cover illustration and all of the pen-and-ink sketches. His accomplished hand and keen eye have made the book as appealing visually as the landscape it depicts. Landscape architect Craig Schreiber, based in Leadville, Colorado, drew all the guidelines and diagrams, his mountain origins showing at every stroke of the pen. My appreciation for their work and their enthusiasm for the project goes far beyond words.

I am also grateful to Cheryl Wright Green, who donated much of her summer locating archival photos and background material, and to Jim Beebe, who did the darkroom work for over a hundred of my black-and-white photographs.

Most of all, to Eldon Beck, my thesis adviser at the University of California, Berkeley, I extend my deepest thanks. The idea for this project would never have taken root had it not been for his wisdom and inspiration. Throughout the long process of transforming my thesis into a book, he has stayed involved, generously taking time away from his own landscape architecture practice to review the drafts. His unequaled sensitivity to the landscape has had an enormous influence on me and on my book.

No amount of inspiration could have brought this project to fruition without the encouragement of Chip Newell. For his enduring patience and support, thanks hardly suffice.

Brooks Range

Ogilvie Range
Mackenzie Mts.
Selwyn Mts.

Alaska Range

NORTHERN ROCKIES
Hart Range
Cariboos
Continental Range
Monashees
Selkirks
Purcell Mts.

PACIFIC COAST MTS.

CANADA
U.S.A.

NORTHERN CASCADES

Bitterroot Mts.
Sawtooth Mts.
Tetons

Olympic Range

SOUTHERN CASCADES

CENTRAL ROCKIES
Wind River Mts.
Uinta Mts.
Wasatch Range
Front Range

COAST RANGES

SOUTHERN ROCKIES
Sangre de Cristos
San Juans

SIERRA NEVADA

Great Basin Ranges

MEXICO

SIERRA MADRE

MOUNTAINS OF NORTH AMERICA

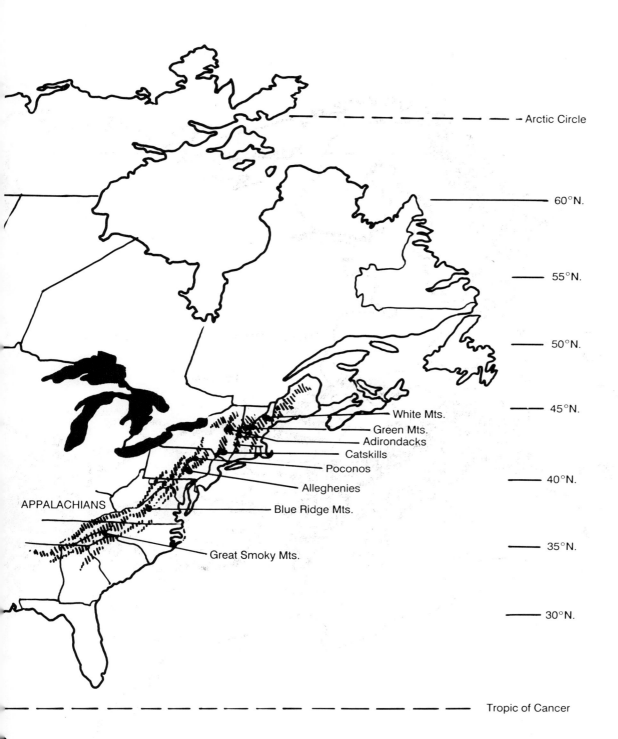

Arctic Circle

60°N.

55°N.

50°N.

45°N.

White Mts.

Green Mts.

Adirondacks

Catskills

Poconos

40°N.

Alleghenies

APPALACHIANS

Blue Ridge Mts.

35°N.

Great Smoky Mts.

30°N.

Tropic of Cancer

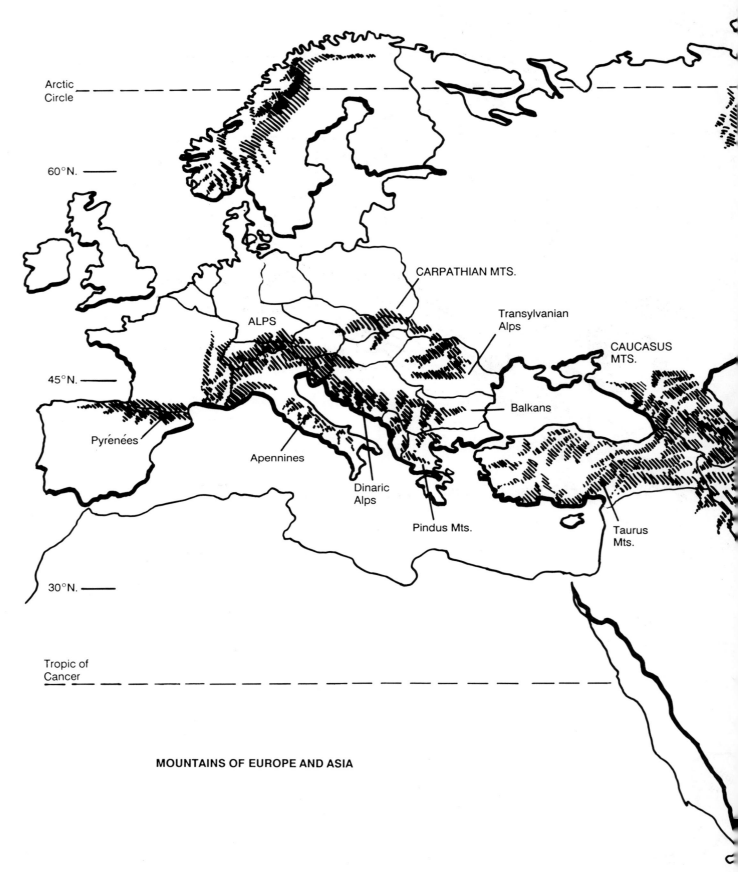

Arctic
Circle

60°N.

45°N.

30°N.

Tropic of
Cancer

CARPATHIAN MTS.

Transylvanian
Alps

CAUCASUS
MTS.

ALPS

Balkans

Pyrénées

Apennines

Dinaric
Alps

Pindus Mts.

Taurus
Mts.

MOUNTAINS OF EUROPE AND ASIA

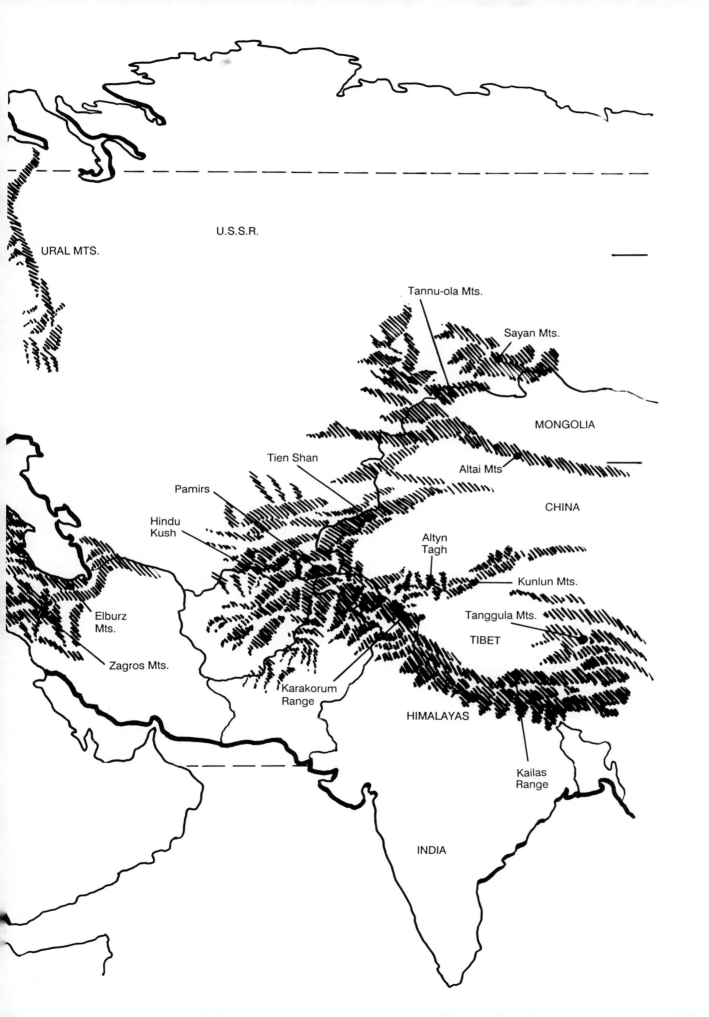

URAL MTS.

U.S.S.R.

Tannu-ola Mts.

Sayan Mts.

MONGOLIA

Tien Shan

Altai Mts

Pamirs

CHINA

Hindu
Kush

Altyn
Tagh

Kunlun Mts.

Elburz
Mts.

Tanggula Mts.

TIBET

Zagros Mts.

Karakorum
Range

HIMALAYAS

Kailas
Range

INDIA

PART I

Attitudes, History, and Landscape Aesthetics

Climb into the mountains and get their good tidings. Nature's peace will flow into you as sunshine into trees. The winds will blow their own freshness into you, and storms their energy, and cares will drop off like autumn leaves.
—John Muir

If among the objects of the world of the spirit there is something fixed and unalterable, great and illimitable, something from which the beams of revelation, the streams of knowledge pour into the mind like water into a valley, it is to be symbolized by a mountain.
—al-Ghazali (1058–1112), The Niche for Lights

A turn-of-the-century poster romanticizing an early motor route through the French Alps. Painted by Emile Brun, 1912; Ateliers F. Hugo d'Alési, Paris. Gorsuch Collection, Vail, Colorado.

1
ECOLOGY, COMMUNITY, AND DESIGN IN THE MOUNTAINS

A FRONTIER OF VIVID IMAGES

Mountains form a landscape of commanding presence and splendid visual character. No longer the decisive physical barrier they once were, high mountains still remain a magnetic frontier for our collective spirit. Majestic, echoing with wildness and adventure, indomitable yet fragile, the mountain landscape calls up potent sensory images that can be mistaken for no other environment on earth.

Such landscapes present tremendous opportunities for environmental design. Over generations, perceptions of the mountain landscape—its grand scale, layered vistas, rushing waters, dark forests, and unspoken dangers—have intermingled to create a vivid sense of place and equally distinctive patterns of building (Fig. 1-1).

The physical environment—climate, terrain, geology—always plays a role in shaping the built environment, but its influence on the patterns of human settlement is most apparent in extreme environments and dramatic landscapes (Fig. 1-2). The natural forces that shaped high mountain landscapes are dominant and unforgiving, and they have clearly influenced the form of mountain communities.

Traditional alpine villages have always been appealing, manifesting environmental wisdom, ingenuity with limited resources, and emotional attachment to place. They counter the vastness of nature with the security and comfort of human scale. They are not composed of monuments to power or fancy; they are practical responses to the rigors and

Figure 1-1. *A Storm in the Rocky Mountains—Mt. Rosalie (1866), by Albert Bierstadt (American, 1830–1902). One art critic described the huge painting as a "visual celebration of the sublime natural wonders of the New World on a scale commensurate with the vastness of the land itself.· . . . It is the apogee of American landscape painting at its most intense and rapturous." (Denver Post Roundup, July 25, 1976, p. 25) Oil on canvas, 83″ × 142¼″. Courtesy of The Brooklyn Museum, 76.79.*

Figure 1-2. *Settlement shaped by its dramatic landscape: Anasazi cliff dwelling, Mesa Verde National Park, Colorado.*

simple pleasures of mountain life. For many people, alpine villages represent an ideal of harmony with nature and protection from its perils.

Newer mountain communities, however, less often exhibit the wisdom that taught earlier generations respect for natural processes and environmental limits (Fig. 1-3). Indeed, accessible mountain areas today are in the vortex of two frequently conflicting forces: the pressure for development and the effort to preserve the quality of the natural environment. One side argues for progress while the other pleads for restraint.

Although these two cannot always be reconciled, it is possible now, as in the past, to build in ways that respond far more sensitively to the unique qualities of a mountain setting. That is, it is possible to create appealing mountain communities by translating the sensory qualities of the landscape into built forms and to develop more economically viable, functionally diverse mountain communities without violating natural limits. Success requires better understanding of the mountain environment, how it affects design and how design affects people.

Figure 1-3. *Dillon Valley, Colorado, and Interstate 70 looking west toward the Continental Divide from an elevation of roughly 9100 feet (2775 m).*

ROOTS OF POOR DESIGN

Why has so much been built in the mountains that makes no reference to the landscape and fails to capitalize on obvious natural clues? New construction in the mountains has begun to look the same as that in any other place (Fig. 1-4). This trend is accelerating despite the visually dominant setting and the distinct images that most people have of mountain building styles.

A lack of familiarity with the mountains and a lack of sensitivity to the landscape are part of the problem. The potential for unique regional character is undermined by the force and momentum of modern generic styles, by insufficient appreciation for the qualities of the landscape, by an incomplete understanding of the reasons that people come to the mountains, and by greed.

Missed Signals. The western mountains in particular suffer from a dearth of long-established cultural legacies and home-grown architectural styles. These areas were settled fairly recently, often by people from a variety of backgrounds whose reasons for coming and ideas of how a community should look differ greatly.

Differences in life-styles, economic goals, views on nature and wilderness, and duration of stay in the mountains are often reflected locally in a mercurial mix of politically inexperienced people who lack a common dialogue. Under these circumstances, the shared respect for the natural landscape that is essential to the special character of a mountain community rarely coalesces in an effective design process.

Where there are many property owners, individuals often fail to consider—or refuse to be responsible for—the aggregate impact of their projects on a community. Lack of coordination among clients and developers, engineers and ecologists, and design and planning consultants is not uncommon. As a result, design concepts may be based on inadequate data, may be lost in implementation, or may ignore the plans of others. And thus opportunities to contribute to the physical or social sense of community are lost.

Many mountain towns and counties, especially in the West, have been hesitant to adopt any sort of design control. Even in those places where design standards and review processes have been instituted, their effectiveness has been uneven, whether because visual objectives are not shared or not clearly articulated, because review board members are inexperienced or have conflicting interests, or because needed regulatory and environmental expertise from sources outside the community has not been made available.

Regional land-use planning issues have generally determined how natural factors information is gathered and analyzed. Environmental research, used primarily to identify project constraints, has not often

Figure 1-4. *An apartment building in the Colorado Rockies that could be anywhere.*

***Figure* 1-5.** *Development at the base of an active mudflow and avalanche track, Vail, Colorado.*

been packaged in a form useful to designers, especially in rural communities. Its contribution to design has therefore not yet been fully realized.

In nonurban areas, this information gap can be a serious impediment to sensitive design. If nature is truly the dominant design rationale in the mountains, designers will have to utilize environmental information to a much greater degree than they have in the past.

The lack of communication and experience in mountain environments also contributes to technical deficiencies in design and construction. What is built too often underestimates the problems of snow, ice, and slope and overestimates the resilience of mountain ecosystems. Drainage systems, grade changes, microclimate control, and revegetation efforts are frequently inadequate. And there are too few old-timers around who can pass along time-tested knowledge of what works and what doesn't.

Mounting Pressures. Mountain development has not yet been forced to confront its collective impact on the fragile mountain environment, but the degradation of mountain ecosystems is a worldwide problem. In the less developed mountain regions of

Europe, Asia, and Latin America, accelerating population pressures have led to a litany of ills: overgrazing, deforestation, endangered wildlife, flooding, soil erosion and loss of soil fertility, marginally productive agriculture, and disruption of traditional ways of life in mountain villages.

In the mountains of the United States, though sparsely populated until recent decades, some of the same problems have begun to be evident: The rush to develop vacation properties, roads, and infrastructure has led in some areas to spurts of uncontrolled and unplanned growth. The environmental consequences —air and water pollution, wildlife displacement, erosion, and increasing exposure to geological hazards —have become serious concerns (Fig. 1-5). Burgeoning concentrations of people in confined valleys, as well as the considerable sums available for investment in mountain resorts and mining, exacerbate the threat.

In many mountain regions, aesthetic quality has fallen prey to spreading urbanization. The most accessible places are suffering the loss of indigenous character, the spread of poorly conceived and scattered development, and the proliferation of eyesores and scars upon the landscape (Fig. 1-6).

Figure 1-6(a). *Sloping site was leveled to make a flat building pad for a standard motel plan (Summit County, Colorado).*

Figure 1-6(b). *Trailer housing for locals and a bankrupt high-rise condominium building mark the fringes of a major mountain resort in Colorado.*

Figure 1-6(c). *Standard layout of parking and buildings in an auto-oriented convenience shopping center consumes the gentler terrain below Dillon Dam, Colorado.*

Figure 1-6(d). *A Colorado subdivision at 9100 feet (2775 m) illustrates the visual impacts of development in a high-altitude environment.*

Aesthetic degradation may seem less urgent than damage to the environment, but it is intimately tied to attitudes and practices inimical to the landscape's ecological health.

Poor design also has financial implications that compound the negative impacts of development pressures. Projects that misunderstand the market, destroy the natural setting, reinforce lopsided seasonality in business, or incur excessive costs may fail, and indeed, design is as often at fault as development strategies.

In mountain towns, there are, of course, other factors at work besides shortcomings of design. Escalating land prices argue for excessive density. The single-industry, single-season economy imposes financial constraints and restricts the supply of skilled labor. High living costs prevent potential long-term residents from entering the market and discourage the evolution of genuinely heterogeneous communities.

Design quality alone cannot remedy all the deficiencies in modern mountain development, but it is surely an indispensable part of the solution.

Figure 1-7. *The mountain man. Photo from the Colorado Historical Society.*

THINKING ABOUT COMMUNITY

Isolation or Interaction? Although many of the design guidelines in this book can be applied to small developments in remote locations, the book's underlying focus is the concept of community. This may seem a contradiction, for it is a common presumption that people go to the mountains for solitude, to commune with nature in rustic isolation and to leave the urban world far behind.

To the contrary, true wilderness can be a daunting place. It is likely that few visitors genuinely seek to emulate the self-sufficient nineteenth-century mountain man (Fig. 1–7). The search for solitude may be partially responsible for drawing people to the mountains, but even in the backwoods, most of them welcome friendly interaction and a measure of convenience. Given their choice, most people prefer a real community.

Still, the perception lingers that community is not as important to places surrounded by wilderness as it is to more populous locations. This misconception has encouraged years of inattention to issues of community vitality in mountain development. In many resort areas in fact, the single-minded drive to capture seasonal visitors has taken priority over the

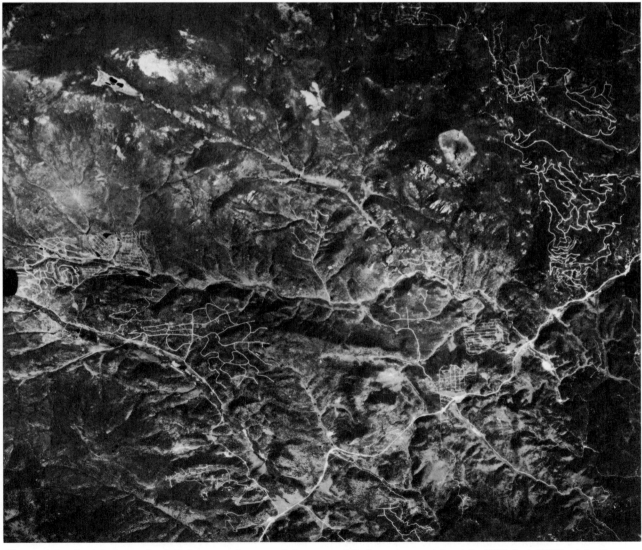

Figure 1-8. *Aerial photo of subdivision roads around the town of Bailey, at approximately 8500 feet (2590 m) in the foothills near Denver, Colorado. Photo by Soil Conservation Service.*

development needs of year-round communities.

The negative consequences of this shortsightedness are all too apparent. As evidence, consider the second-home subdivisions of cookie-cutter lots with difficult access (Fig. 1-8); the exclusive condominium developments completely disconnected from neighbors; the redundant strip shopping centers lining through-town highways; the absence of adequate pedestrian linkages and hospitable places to linger; and the scattered public facilities, unable to attract a critical mass of people. The new "village centers" adjacent to old towns too often resemble movie sets for tourists, which drain off energy essential to the rebirth of established main streets. The numbing inactivity of the off-season is an inevitable result.

Designing for Community Cohesion. Among the nicest places to live or visit are those that have the basic attributes of healthy communities: a reasonably diverse economy; high resident participation and consensus; an institutional base that functions, among other things, to regulate quality; and traditions and well-developed building prototypes that codify community expectations.

The national parks excepted, memorable places for people rarely evolve without a local citizenry. A stable base of happy long-term residents both depends on and helps foster a sense of community. This in turn enhances a place's ability to attract visitors and to maintain itself economically. The vitality of most year-round communities contrasts with the monotony of developed areas, however scenic, where most properties are second homes and most property owners are absentees.

Design decisions on virtually every level, public and private, affect the community fabric, either strengthening or detracting from the perception of cohesiveness. The public process of urban design, by which a community's physical framework is coordinated and shaped, promotes the community's functional, social, and economic diversity.

In *A Pattern Language*, their exhaustive inventory of archetypal patterns in architecture, Professor Christopher Alexander and his coauthors write: "When you build a thing you cannot merely build that thing in isolation, but must also repair the world around it, and within it, so that the larger world at that one place becomes more coherent, and more whole; and the thing which you make takes its place in the web of nature, as you make it" (1977, p. xiii). Building that is inspired by this value system is a force for positive change in the quality of life in any environment.

The issue of community adds another dimension to the environmental and aesthetic sensitivity required for appropriate design in the mountains. It means that another measure of quality is design that enriches human social dynamics and the quality of mountain life.

There is an urgent need in mountain design to turn our attention to communities, because it is there that the potential development impacts on people and the environment are greatest. We need reasonable alternatives to the trend toward scattered mountain development for seasonal use. The long-term, year-round viability of resort villages has become a necessity. But only when planned and designed with foresight can these single-purpose developments emerge as stable year-round communities, as they must to survive.

Town, Community, Village, and Resort

Throughout the book, I shall use the terms *town, community, village,* and *resort* to describe aggregations of people living in or visiting a place. They do not all mean the same thing but represent instead gradations of population size, diversity, and permanence (Fig. 1-9).

Although a town is generally larger and more diverse than a community, I use both terms to describe a cluster of residences, civic facilities, and commercial enterprises identified by a place name as a distinct geographical entity. Both terms assume an interacting population of permanent residents living in a common location and having a variety of interests. Both have connective ingredients, space devoted to public amenities, and certain basic public services and physical systems, like public transportation. A community, if part of a larger town, may or may not have a diverse economic base within its boundaries.

There is no hard and fast rule regarding the number of people it takes to make a community or regarding the point at which public services begin to be duplicated and one community becomes several to form a town. The authors of *A Pattern Language* consider a population of 500 to 10,000 people the

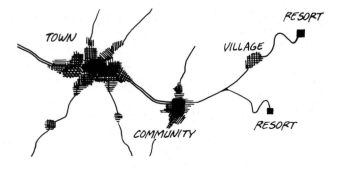

Figure 1-9. *Aggregations of human settlement exist across a spectrum of size and diversity.*

Figure 1-10. *In similar landscapes, contrasts in scale and form distinguish (a, left) a traditional Swiss village from (b, right) a new resort "village."*

optimal range for self-contained communities and rural towns. Their studies suggest that in a community larger than 5,000 to 10,000 people, individuals have no effective way to participate in a dialogue on the issues that concern them: land use, schools and housing, recreation and parks, streets and maintenance, police and safety (Alexander et al. 1977, pp. 35, 71). The authors thus recommend using natural geographical and historical boundaries to define and separate individual communities and to keep them from growing beyond that workable range.

Except along the American East Coast, where *village* is the proper term for the center of a township, the word generally denotes more primitive or vernacular settlements (Fig. 1-10a). In this traditional sense, small size alone is not what sets villages apart from towns. Rather, their primary distinguishing features are their homogeneity and simplicity, their one-dimensional economy (traditionally agriculture), and the absence of many of the public services found in larger settlements. When a more recently developed place in a scenic setting is called a village today, it usually signals what is in fact only a resort or a residential compound (Fig. 1-10b) without the year-round population and community cohesiveness of a true village.

A resort is a place dominated by temporary lodgings and visitors who come for recreation and entertainment. It lacks the network of systems, services, and governance needed in a community. Many wilderness resorts are just isolated hotels, but

some aspire to be villages. A resort village has few permanent residents, little political life, and a single source of income. Some evolve into self-governing resort communities, however, and as this transition takes place, more attention must be given to providing the services needed by a growing population of local residents.

Resorts and villages, communities and towns coexist on a spectrum of growth and maturation. The process of design in the mountains thus needs both the vision to see that attractive resorts can one day become exceptional communities and the foresight to help that transition take place.

Mountain Resorts As Community Design Prototypes

Many older mountain towns were founded for reasons other than tourism (such as frontier defense, mining and ranching centers, and railheads), but few survive today without the impetus of tourism and resort development. Most current planning and design energy in the mountains—not to mention most of the recent population growth—has been concentrated in areas attractive to visitors and weekenders. It is not unreasonable, then, to use resorts and resort towns as a primary source of case studies in mountain design.

Even though they are not full-service communities, resorts are useful as models for community design. Resorts spring up where urban and rural patterns of

Figure 1-11. *Infill, styling, uses, and pedestrian spaces are among the differences that distinguish(a, left) a commercial street in a major resort town, Aspen, Colorado, from (b, right) the main street of a nonresort mountain town, Idaho Springs, Colorado.*

life converge, and in that convergence are many lessons for the planning and design of new towns and suburbs anywhere, not just in the mountains.

Design Quality. Comprehensively planned resort developments have often led the way in instituting design quality standards. When resorts are in scenic areas, there is typically a strong interest in retaining the visual quality of the natural landscape in order to preserve a unique sense of place.

The value placed on the quality of the resort visitor's experience leads to a greater willingness to provide for the pedestrian, to consider public transportation, and to try innovative methods of dealing with cars, undoubtedly one of the most formidable problems in the mountains (Fig. 1-11a). To some extent, the lessons learned from these efforts can be applied to small communities everywhere that suffer the vagaries of boom–bust cycles and single-resource economies.

Another factor that underscores the relevance of resorts to design in mountain communities in general is the accelerated growth they often spark in adjacent regions. Development outside a resort's boundaries, where it is less carefully controlled, often threatens to degrade the character of the region of which the resort is a part. To encourage higher-quality design and planning on a broader scale, resorts—along with the Forest Service and other public officials—are initiating processes to examine aggregate impacts, community dynamics, and regional linkages.

Provisos. There are admittedly some dangers in adapting lessons from resorts to communities neither founded for recreation nor well situated for tourism. That is, the "normal" town and the resort town have some significant differences that invariably influence their respective courses of development. For example, in a resort, in contrast with a nonresort town, people generally have higher income levels and different reasons for being there. The resort population, being transient, seasonal, and more homogeneous, typically holds different attitudes toward autos and different expectations for recreational facilities, scenic quality, building styles, employment, housing, and shopping alternatives. The physical scale of a resort village may also be different. Good access and an understandable framework are essential to serving visitors well. The sense of community may be less important, but a villagelike structure that encourages social interaction often contributes to a resort's popularity.

In a nonresort town, activity centers have a different focus; employment opportunities are a concern; and automobiles tend to be more prominent in daily life (Fig. 1-11b). Leisure-oriented municipal improvements thus are often hard to justify and harder to finance. As a result, some design concepts that suit resort towns are inappropriate or unaffordable in nonresort towns.

In Defense of the Transition. Using resorts as models focuses attention on design strategies that facilitate their evolution along the spectrum toward community.

For example, community-oriented design can play a sensitizing role, bringing to light the long-term implications of different development philosophies. Many mountain resorts are the product of corporate developers and were never intended to offer the variety and services of a genuine community. In these resorts, developers are the sole determinants of design quality and purpose. Whether communities will ever evolve from their creations depends on the developers' philosophy of development, their budget and program, and the length of their planned involvement. The quality of public amenities depends on their corporate goals: whether the quality of experience is as important as the completion of a product, whether user satisfaction is as important as cash flow and earnings. Design quality depends on their corporate attitudes toward architecture in relation to its regional context and to nature in general.

The design of most resort villages discourages permanent residency within its boundaries but often encourages it in the vicinity beyond. Attracting and retaining residents as the support base for a resort requires affordable housing and community facilities that cater to their needs, increase their skills, and keep them stimulated. It requires recreational and educational facilities, adequate circulation systems, and open space. These needs compete for limited funds with facilities for tourists. Where resorts are evolving into communities, the conflict surfaces in public debates over the allocation of resources and in how such issues as parking, recreation, nightlife, and family concerns are handled. Community-oriented design may help mediate such conflicts.

At some point, resorts that attract permanent residents to the vicinity—and most of them do—consider municipal incorporation. The public sector plays an important role in design by adding a forum for citizen participation. It can set standards of quality and pursue measures that encourage social diversity. It provides a vehicle through which important community concerns can be addressed, such as housing, traffic congestion, public amenities, design control, economic vitality, environmental compatibility, impact mitigation, and protection of place-making natural features in the community. The public sector also provides the mechanism for funding and implementation. How much smoother the transition to self-governance would be if design had already anticipated the physical framework needed to accommodate it.

Progress toward community is often hindered by the reluctance of conservative financing institutions to underwrite innovative design. Their predilection for safe, proven, and easily marketable patterns of building can be an unyielding constraint and an easy excuse for mediocre quality. But design that can be justified by its potential for positive community impacts may reassure institutions traditionally less willing to take risks.

Few mountain resorts can expect to become communities in the fullest sense, for developing mountain areas will likely continue to rely heavily on seasonal tourism. Because of their relative remoteness and the inadequacy of nearby resources to support other enterprises, they are limited in their potential for economic diversification and in their ability to pay for a full range of community services. Nevertheless, there are clear advantages for residents and visitors alike in pursuing that goal.

Nature-based Standards for Design Quality

Are the mountains really so different a place in which to build? If so, too few builders have noticed.

Why won't designs that work in towns on the plains or in the dry coastal hills work in the mountains? The answer lies in the natural environment. Design quality correlates with the degree of sensitivity to contextual forces. In the mountains, quality design demands creative solutions to the physical constraints of ecology and climate. It demands responses that satisfy people's needs without degrading essential ecosystems or diminishing the natural beauty that brought them there.

Of those who build in the mountains, too few have asked themselves the questions required of sensitive designers: How can natural factors fortify the cohesiveness of a community and its sense of place? How should the character and constraints of mountain environments be reflected in built forms? How do we judge what is appropriate to the mountains in terms of siting, site planning, landscape development, and architecture? *Design for Mountain Communities* answers these questions with an approach to design that regards the natural environment as its central rationale for form.

REFERENCES

Alexander, Christopher. 1979. *The Timeless Way of Building.* New York: Oxford University Press.

Alexander, Christopher, et al. 1977. *A Pattern Language.* New York: Oxford University Press.

The image of an ideal Alpine village: Mürren, Switzerland, near Lauterbrunnen.

2
HISTORICAL PATTERNS
IN MOUNTAIN SETTLEMENT

Ask people what comes to mind as their ideal mountain town. Chances are they will describe an Alpine village, nestled in a meadow of wildflowers beneath snowcapped peaks. It is no coincidence that American ski towns are full of Swiss chalets, Bavarian clock towers, and inns with names like St. Moritz and Kitzbühel, Edelweiss and Alpenhof. They are there because it's thought that's what the public expects to find and because the image is appealing.

Is it simply the Alpine style of building to which people are attracted? Perhaps not, for the image is so persistent that one suspects a deeper significance. The Alpine village may symbolize a sense of community and a small scale for which we long. People may see in it a measure of intimacy, security, and nearness to nature that is hard to find in newer communities and larger towns.

This suggests that it is not enough simply to replicate the superficial elements of the Alpine style. The deeper appeal lies in the physical organization and scale of the village and in the social meaning of its forms. In this respect, there are instructive prototypes to be found not just in the Alps but also in other primitive mountain cultures, as well as in early American mining towns and even in postwar recreation developments.

PATTERNS IN PRIMITIVE MOUNTAIN VILLAGES

In the difficult physical environment of most mountain areas, climate and terrain are more powerful than sociocultural influences as determinants of vernacular form. As a result, certain characteristics of traditional mountain styles in the Alps, Himalayas, and Andes consistently reappear despite marked cultural and religious differences. Although modern development and tourism have begun to erode these patterns in some areas, the ancestral traditions of building are still largely intact in more primitive areas, where the remoteness of high valleys has restricted the spread of newer styles.

These traditional views about how village life should be arranged reveal the villagers' intuitive and spontaneous responses to the interrelatedness of

Figure 2-1. *Extensive terracing in the central Himalayas makes possible the cultivation of steep slopes.*

These towns do not diminish the landscape, they enhance it — they are themselves crystallized landscape, growing out of the natural materials and rhythms of the place.
—*Norman Carver,* Italian Hilltowns

people and nature. Some vernacular patterns relate well to specific design decisions that modern builders confront, such as village siting, responses to climate, overall village form and appearance, size and scale, and the treatment of special landscape features.

Siting and Climatic Responses

Settlements universally are located near the resource that supports them. In the mountains, this resource for centuries has been scarce farming and grazing land. From the Andes and the mountains of Europe, through the Himalayas and into China, villagers have traditionally mixed farming with herding as a matter of survival. To exploit the productive capacity of each elevation zone, they have moved their herds seasonally from the warmer valley floors to high summer pastures, and they have made intricate mosaics of different crops ascending the hillsides (Fig. 2-1). Their main villages, however, are always located at the lower elevations, where the growing season is longer and the soil supports fields and small gardens.

The most fertile land, usually the flattest, was never used for building (Fig. 2-2). To avoid consuming valuable agricultural bottomlands (and in some cases for defensive purposes), villages and roads were often sited on ridge lines, old moraine deposits, or ledges and alluvial terraces on the lower slopes, just above the more fertile valley floor.

Both in choosing the village site and orienting individual structures, there was a remarkably precise adaptation to climate. Villages in the Northern Hemisphere are most often arrayed on south-facing slopes to catch the sun (Fig. 2-3). For warmth, entry facades face south; buildings are typically clustered and often connected. Rows of buildings along the contours and solid uphill walls protect pathways and interiors from cold downslope winds.

Spiritual beliefs and mythologies of indigenous cultures, even when quite different from one another, sometimes validate similar ecologically sensible patterns of village development. Consider, for example, the Chinese sacred art of *feng shui,* in which buildings (as well as rooms and furniture) are sited and arranged for the most beneficial relationship with nature.

In the Chinese mind, mountains and water are interdependent, eternal yin–yang symbols of natural harmony and beauty (Fig. 2-4). They also are the preeminent landscape features in *feng shui.* Mountain shapes are studied carefully for their resemblance to animal forms, for they are thought to possess the same powers and attributes. The dragon is the most common mountain simile, embodying in the peaks and ridges of its body the force and unpredictability of nature. The dragon can be a village's protector,

Figure 2-2. *A road in the Khatmandu Valley, Nepal, follows a moraine to avoid consuming fertile farmland.*

unless one builds on its tail or near its mouth or where it does not have enough water to drink.

Mythological animals in *feng shui* are metaphors in a system of site selection giving priority to proper orientation, ventilation, sun, and trees. The most auspicious places for building are above the valley floor on south- and east-facing slopes, where there is more abundant vegetation and where encircling hills and ridges offer protection from the wind (Fig. 2-5). Riverless plains and featureless landscapes are considered the worst possible sites.

Vast climatic and cultural differences separate the *feng shui* practitioner from the Alpine farmer-herdsman, but their respective systems of belief have led them to adopt similar views on the most desirable sites. The question confronting us today is how to respect ecological and climatic wisdom in modern siting decisions in which densities are far greater and the best village site may not be convenient to the resource, such as north-facing ski slopes, that supports it.

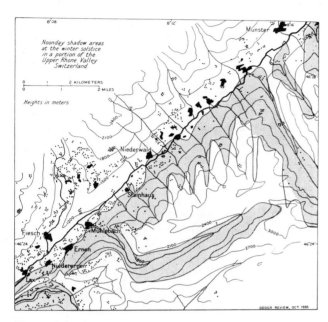

Figure 2-3. *Swiss villages in the Upper Rhône Valley are sited with a consistent preference for sunny exposures. Shaded areas are those in noonday shadow during winter. A. Garnett,* Geographical Review, *1935.*

Figure 2-4. *The Chinese express the English word* landscape *with two characters, mountain (shan, top) and water (shui). In the Taoist concept of natural harmony, the mountain is the passive center (yin), and water is the active counterbalance (yang). Calligraphy by C. C. Wang.*

Figure 2-5. *Small villages are part of the idealized Chinese mountain landscape, shown in this handscroll (left half),* Summer Mountains, *by Ch'u Ting (active circa 1023–1056). Ink and light color on silk 17¾″ × 45¼″. Courtesy of The Metropolitan Museum of Art, Gift of the Dillon Fund (1973.120.1).*

Village Form and Appearance

Primitive mountain villages are usually compact in form, their edges clearly demarcated by walls, pathways, spiritual precincts, or cultivated fields (Fig. 2-6). "The tendency to build on sites of difficult access can be traced no doubt to a desire for security but perhaps even more so to the need of defining a community's borders" (Rudofsky 1964, p. 48).

The three-dimensional form of the primitive community reiterates the topography. Buildings fit

19

Figure 2-6. *Traditional villages, like Romont, Switzerland, are typically compact and have distinct edges.*

Figure 2-8. *The coarsely textured, repetitive forms of an Italian hilltown cloak an Apennine slope.*

Figure 2-7. *Houses in Namche Bazaar, Nepal (elevation 11,283 ft., 3440 m), show typical Sherpa buildings aligned lengthwise across the slope.*

the slope. For example, in the Sherpa villages of Nepal (Fig. 2-7), rows of buildings, as well as the lengthwise axis of individual structures, are parallel to the contours. Buildings usually cut into the slope in the rear; they are rarely built on fill (Sestini and Somigli 1978).

The repetitive basic forms and highly textural materials of vernacular architecture are a source of visual unity and a vivid connection with the landscape (Fig. 2-8). The richness of the whole derives from the rhythmic pattern of the village on the terrain, numerous small site-specific adaptations to the landform, occasional punctuation by exceptional buildings like temples and castles, and abundant symbolic and traditional decorative ornamentation. The picturesque quality that results is "logically derived from a sensitive adaptation to the site or from a forthright use of materials and building techniques" (Carver 1979, p. 48).

Primitive transportation and technical knowledge demanded both the use of simple construction methods, openly revealed in form, and the use of local materials, such as wood, stone, and mud. These, too, are important to the visual integration of the village with its setting. The limitations of simple building techniques also meant that the presence of a village rarely had a negative visual impact on the site. It was not mechanically feasible to make significant alterations in the landform. Traditional villages drape gently over the slopes and enhance the landscape with a rich, unified layer of texture and detail.

Village form was influenced by a complex mix of forces: cultural forces unique to the place and time, as well as physical forces common to a mountain landscape—a rugged site, harsh climate, and limited materials for building. Because growth was slow and there was no comprehensive concept of village composition, workable forms evolved over long periods of time, "motivated by real needs restrained by limited means and by the forces of tradition" (Carver 1979, p. 27).

Village Organization, Size, and Scale

Observing Italian hilltowns, author/architect Norman Carver noted (1979, p. 29) that traditional villages rarely grew beyond a limited, comprehensible size and a consistently human scale. Similarly, in the Nepali Himalayas, it is striking to observe the relatively even distribution of like-sized villages, even in the more heavily populated areas. There seems to be an instinctive understanding both of the physical limits to the number of people that a given site can support and of the optimal size of a social unit. This is of interest today because the political control of growth

has become one of the most pressing issues in rural development. Virtually every successful resort community has violated realistic natural constraints on its site, but ecosystem limits have proved extremely difficult to define.

In primitive villages, a tangent benefit of limited size was the preservation of clear linkages with nature beyond the village precinct. Building clusters reached out in fingers to connect with the landscape, and tilled or terraced fields pushed inward, harmoniously balancing the human-dominated world and the natural world.

The streets and outdoor spaces of a primitive village, not just buildings, are scaled for human size and comfort. Its pathway network, although designed entirely for pedestrian and animal traffic, is of interest not just for its scale but also for the hierarchy in its layout. The wider major pathways are almost always parallel to the contours, and narrow lanes and steps connect them at right angles up and down the slope. If a village has shops or travelers' amenities like tea houses or inns, they will generally be found on the main path through town, accessible to all residents and easily found by visitors. There is no obvious segregation of uses; functions exist side by side and often under the same roof. Legibility in the pathway system unites them.

Most villages have a focal element—a church, castle, or town hall—that is larger in scale and proportion than the buildings for domestic use (Fig. 2-9). This focal element is often located in a visually prominent place near the main road into the village or at the highest point on the village site, symbolically anchoring its linkage with nature and its claim to the site.

Most villages also have a communal activity space somewhere outdoors, whose exact form was largely determined by religious and cultural factors (Fig. 2-10). It may coincide with the village's water source (a well or a slow-moving section of a stream through the village), a sacred tree, a tea house, the market area, or a ceremonial plaza. Places in which to congregate seem to be more deliberate and formalized in villages that are dependent on trade rather than agriculture or in which religious ceremony plays a major role in daily life.

These central outdoor spaces reflect both accidental patterns and conscious efforts to provide for the community's social and spiritual needs. The activity center, whether or not it is formalized as a village square or plaza, is an essential element in the physical composition of a community. J. B. Jackson, a keen observer of vernacular patterns, wrote that "modern communities still need the public space, but need to understand how to revise traditional forms to reflect new present-day uses" (1984, p. 18).

Figure 2-9. *Focal buildings are prominent in distant views of traditional villages. A church at the upper end and a castle below anchor the edges of the Italian hilltown of Revello.*

Figure 2-10. *The central plaza in Bhadgaon, Nepal, is the focal point for a multitude of activities: drying grain and pottery, trading goods, socializing, and drawing water from the village well.*

Special Landscapes and Spiritual Necessities

Most mystic experience tends to occur outdoors. The traditional predilection of religious devotees for mountaintops and desert places may not be merely a desire to get away from the distractions of the social world, but a movement to a place where experiences of enhanced depth are possible. The traditional association of mountaintops with the abode of the Deity may be less because they are higher than the areas around them than because they make possible those experiences of expanded depth in which the self can invest itself in the world around it. . . .
— *William James*

Westerners often miss the pervasive spiritual symbolism in a primitive village. Special landscape features and scenic vantage points often become places of spiritual importance and are revered, protected, and embellished with symbols of shared meaning (Fig. 2-11).

In the Buddhist and Hindu Himalayas, where religion is an integral and mystical part of daily life, promontories are graced with small monuments and prayer flags, beautiful sections of trails with rest benches or prayer walls, and unusual rock formations with carved inscriptions. Spiritually important places are sometimes, though not always, sited symbolically and reached by a sequence of progressively narrower and more difficult pathways that offer carefully chosen views of the destination.

Among the best examples of spirituality fully integrated into the physical organization of a mountain community are the pueblos of the American Southwest. To Native Americans, humans and other living things are one with nature; nothing is inanimate or separate. Shelters, structures, and mountains all are the same, joined together in a divine system.

Pueblo village composition and architecture, described in detail in Vincent Scully's book *Pueblo: Mountain, Village, Dance,* illustrate this union:

Looking like natural rock outcrops on the crowns of their mesas, [Pueblo buildings] are not exactly engaged in "fitting in" with nature, as so many Western romantic buildings have tried to do. They are nature, pure and simple, but their resemblance to the shapes of the earth is not accidental entirely either. It is . . . at once an act of reverence and a natural congruence between two natural things. (1972, pp. 9–10)

The intricate ceremonial life of the Pueblo Indians evolved as an attempt to affect the universe and to counter the progressive aridity of their land, concerns that dominated the structure of their settlements. Pueblos are always related to specific sacred mountains or ceremonially functional landscapes,

Figure 2-11. *Looking toward Ama Dablam (22,488 ft., 6856 m), prayer flags and a chorten grace a spectacular vantage point at Thyangboche monastery (12,464 ft., 3800 m), Nepal.*

with their architecture creating the stage setting for their ceremonial system (Fig. 2-12).

The dominant concern of Pueblo architects from the ancient Anasazis onward was not to create individually distinctive structures or interior uses but, rather, to design buildings that as a group "frame a plaza in which ritual dances can be performed and from which they could be watched. . . . The human scale is precise. . . . The environment frames the act" (Scully 1972, p. 14). Stepped building profiles reiterate the mountain form and unite it with the sky, but they are essentially functional: The architectural pattern is complete only when people line the roofs and dancers fill the plaza.

Taos Pueblo in the Sangre de Cristo Mountains of northern New Mexico is the epitome of a community totally at one with its natural surroundings (Fig. 2-13). Scully observed:

[It is] a place of special power. . . . Its splendid, sweeping plaza is [an] imperial container. . . . It grandly receives the full force of looming Taos Mountain. . . . The plaza taps the mountain's water, and the buildings to the north and south open outward as if dancing to celebrate its flow. . . . Together [the plaza and buildings] organize an articulated mass which echoes the mountain and abstracts it to the measure of human units. . . . (1972, p. 39)

23

Figure 2-12. *Buildings are the grandstand for a dance festival at Taos Pueblo on San Geronimo Day, early 1900s. Photo from the Museum of New Mexico.*

Figure 2-13. *The Taos Pueblo echoes the form of the Sangre de Cristo Range beyond.*

The pueblos are the product of a particular spiritual view of the universe. Although they cannot be replicated with the same intense meaning in secular cultures and other landscapes, they do offer some important lessons. First is the place of the Pueblo village in the landscape. Its siting at the edge of a mountain slope and its obvious orientation to the most prominent (sacred) mountain make it part of a natural, ordered sequence from mountains to plains. An expression of harmony is the result.

Second is the gentle, modest architecture, the refusal to make a statement with individual dwellings and the reticence to compete with the natural setting. The hand-shaped adobe structures suggest, rather than oppose, the mountain forms. The concern for the whole celebrates unity and interaction with earth and sun, with an effect that is calming, comforting, and joyful.

Modern communities, like folk cultures, need to reveal in their physical form some veneration for the special aspects of place and the meaningful symbols of their culture. Exceptional natural landscapes offer many opportunities, spiritual as well as visual, that we should not ignore.

Judging from the wealth of mystical and spiritual traditions born in the world's high mountains, high-altitude landscapes are especially potent with symbolic associations and psychological effects. Finding ways to resurrect and express symbols of our culture and to provide for the meditative needs of a fast-paced society are among the hardest design tasks, but the dramatic mountain landscape makes it easier to do.

MOUNTAIN MINING TOWNS OF WESTERN AMERICA

The first people to penetrate America's wildest mountains were the Native Americans, who, like Asian and medieval Alpine villagers, regarded the high country as a haunted and spiritual realm. The first Europeans to explore the American West were nineteenth-century dreamers, artists, and adventurers, and their journals and paintings were filled with romantic preconceptions of a vast and heroic mountain wilderness (see Chapter 3). But those who first settled the West had a more functional disposition that biased their approach to town building.

The America of the early 1800s was a young, energetic nation, anxious to exploit its resources and conquer the wilderness. Its curiosity about the frontier was colored by the Western world's cultural tendency to view land as something to be possessed and tamed, to be made productive. It was not surprising, then, that although the nation's fascination with the wilderness landscape persisted in art, the spiritual aura of the mountains was soon overtaken by the secular celebration of America's westward progress.

In this cultural context, the western mountains were seen as an unwanted and threatening impediment to communication between the East and the Pacific Coast. Indeed, the mapping expeditions of Lewis and Clark in the Northwest from 1804 to 1806 and Zebulon Pike in Colorado from 1806 to 1807 for the fledgling U.S. Geological Survey were largely motivated by the desire to find easier routes through the ranges.

The Sierras remained a barrier until long after Jedediah Smith first crossed them in the October snows of 1827. But even more decades passed before the range was more widely explored. John Fremont discovered Lake Tahoe in 1844; Yosemite Valley and the giant sequoias did not become well known until after 1850. Not until 1863 did the California State Geological Survey launch a scientific exploration of the Sierras. Shortly after 1869, when John Muir began to publish journals of his Sierran visits, summertime mountain recreation first began to take hold.

The Gold Rushes. The discovery of gold in the Sierra foothills in 1849 did much to open the western frontier but little to settle the higher Sierras. Miners at the lower elevations of the California Mother Lode communities (2000 to 3000 ft., 600 to 900 m) were only vaguely aware of the lofty range to the east.

In contrast, gold mining was the primary catalyst for town building at higher elevations in the continent's central mountains. The Rocky Mountain "Pikes-Peak-or-bust" gold rush in 1858 was the impetus for the construction in 1870 of a railroad connection from Denver to the main east–west Union Pacific line in Cheyenne, Wyoming, as well as a network of narrow-gauge mountain lines in place by the late 1870s.

High mountain basins, known as *parks*, in Colorado (the North, South, and Middle Parks and the San Luis Valley) and around Jackson Hole in the Tetons of northwestern Wyoming also played an important role in mountain settlement. Their rich grasslands supported game and a cattle-growing industry that provided much of the food for the gold-mining camps.

Explosive growth fueled by gold fever enabled Colorado, boasting a population of 25,000, to become a federal territory in 1861, just three years after the Rocky Mountain gold rush had begun. By 1890, successive gold and silver booms had pushed the state's population to 415,000. Unlike the current population distribution in the Rocky Mountain states, which favors the plains, most of this number was in the mountains, clustered in boomtowns like Leadville, Cripple Creek, Central City (Fig. 2-14), Creede, Silverton, and Georgetown in Colorado; Carson City and Virginia City in Nevada; Idaho City in Idaho; and Butte in Montana.

Gold fever made town building in the mountains a raucous and haphazard process. Not all western-mountain mining settlements developed into full-fledged communities. Indeed, some, in poor mining districts or remote areas, never made it beyond the tent and crude log cabin phase (Fig. 2-15). Others went as far as laying out streets and utilities and erecting primitive wooden commercial buildings before the veins played out. But a more permanent town became established only where a mining camp worked major lodes or where location made it an important supply depot. Though the mining camps were often in precipitous locations, the larger supply towns were sited more commodiously in less rugged valleys among the mines they supplied (Fig. 2-16).

The Village, Americanized. Town-building patterns in the mountains did not differ greatly from settlement patterns elsewhere in America. In *Common Landscape of America*, John Stilgoe observed, "Only in New England was there a strong tradition in favor

Figure 2-14.   *Central City, Colorado — at 8300 feet (2530 m) the center of one of the West's richest mining districts — has an uncharacteristically organic plan that conforms to the topography of its site. Illustration from an 1878 publication, Denver Public Library, Western History Department.*

Figure 2-15.   *At 9300 feet (2835 m), the mining settlement of Keystone, Colorado, never made it beyond the crude log cabin phase. Its few remaining log structures are preserved within the limits of Keystone Resort. Photo by Peter Witter.*

*Every valley shall be exalted, and every mountain and
hill shall be made low.*

Isaiah 40:4

of compact rural villages. Elsewhere, settlement was
dispersed and haphazard; roads did not converge on
villages, only on other roads." The old European
order had been organized around a core, marked by
nestled "steads" and the church and surrounded by
common fields and woodlots. But American pioneers
preferred scattered settlements: detached houses
surrounded by land. Rural America "lacked
intersections of combined economic, ecclesiastical,
political, and social order. European travelers . . .
sought church spires in expectation of nearby inns,
and found only churches . . ." (1982, pp. 211, 219).

Like other settlements outside New England, towns
on the western frontier were incomplete social
microcosms. They were almost exclusively mercantile
centers whose residents depended on outlying miners,
farmers, and ranchers for their livelihood. Suppliers,
storekeepers, blacksmiths, assayers, and tavern
keepers fed on the prosperity of a much larger
neighborhood, and they grouped their services along
the armature that came to be called Main Street.

Virtually all of the mountain mining towns used a
rigid grid for their street layout. Typical of town
development in America at the time, the grid also
made the speculators' job easier in the expansive
landscape of the West (Fig. 2-17). If the valley was so
confined by mountains that the town fathers had to
contend with streams and slopes, the grids were
reluctantly modified. Where the terrain allowed,
streets as wide as 60 feet were common, so as to allow
horse-drawn freight wagons and pack trains to turn
around.

C. Eric Stoehr, a mining town historian, describes
how they were organized:

*One or two main streets usually went down the center of
town. Almost all commercial enterprises, such as hotels,
stores, shops and offices, were located along these
thoroughfares. Generally, livery stables, industries, and
other undesirable commercial ventures were located at
the edge of town. Residential areas were located behind
one side or both sides of the main street. The main
street of a camp in a hilly location would traverse the
slope, dividing the camp into an upper and a lower
section. Schools, churches, and the more desirable
residential lots were likely to appear on the upper levels
of the town. The less desirable saloons, as well as
gambling halls, the red-light district, and inexpensive
housing, would be found on the lower levels, closer to the
creek, river, or railroad tracks. In a town located on a
flat site, the creek, river or railroad side of the main
street was generally seen as the least desirable area.
(1975, p. 13)*

The main street, defined by adjoining flush-fronted,
two-storied buildings in parallel rows, was the
primary public space, shared by pack animals,

Figure 2-16. *The Silver Queen mine on Ajax Mountain made Aspen, Colorado, an important population center in the
late 1800s. Photo circa 1880, Denver Public Library, Western History Department.*

It is in the midst of a wild and rugged country where nothing but rich mines would ever induce a human being to live longer than absolutely necessary.
          —Letter from an unknown Easterner visiting the San Juan Mountains in Silverton, Colorado, 1883

Figure 2-17. *The gridded streets of Silverton, Colorado, were typical of most western mountain towns. Photo circa 1900, Denver Public Library, Western History Department.*

wagons, and pedestrians alike (Fig. 2-18). Building styles in more prosperous towns were basically Victorian, with touches of western vernacular, like false fronts, that were unknown in the East. "Main street verticality resulted from businessmen's desires to imitate the dynamic enclosure of city streets, of course, and many entrepreneurs built two-story facades on one-story shops in order to make their places of business seem significant" (Stilgoe 1982, p. 260).

Buildings in the center of town were erected on top of one another, prompting one quid-chewing miner to complain that "no man dare to spit out his front door for fear of hitting his neighbor's chimney and putting out the fire" (Stoehr 1975, p. 16). Beyond the center of town, however, any pretenses of compact development fell away. Real estate speculation was big business, and lots were sold as fast as they could be platted.

Platting was often done by engineers in the East who had never seen the site and were woefully ignorant of the topography. Typical of many mining town of the period, the streets in Park City, Utah, for example, were platted in a strict grid, but although rights-of-way still exist, some of the streets have never been constructed because the grades cannot be negotiated (see Fig. 9-16).

Mining towns grew with no plan whatsoever. "The mining camp represents something different and . . . new in the American frontier experience: urbanization. . . . Urbanization meant that the problems which faced the settled regions were transported to the frontier and placed in an entirely new environment" (Stoehr 1975, p. 16). Mountain towns still must grapple with this dilemma.

In 1893, American abandoned silver as a monetary standard, and the mining boom faded overnight. The narrow gauges stopped running. Camps and less accessible towns died quickly. Though shrunken and depressed, some of the more important supply towns survived, however, their lives prolonged by coal and other mining.

Mining Town Legacies. The obvious problems with the mining town as a modern design prototype are its insensitivity to the natural environment, its lack of any spiritual connections with nature or a sense of permanence, and its failure to integrate the landscape's natural assets into the core of the town. The get-rich-quick mentality of the boomtown preempted any coherent attention to needs of the community at large.

These drawbacks aside, the mining town's main street is still a viable concept, provided that any conflicts with vehicular traffic can be overcome. Indeed, main street and the compact mixed-use commercial district it anchored are perhaps the most significant prototypes to come from these once-vibrant boom–bust towns. Among their most conspicuous assets are the buildings' small scale, the uniform spacing between the buildings, the transparent facades of storefront commercial buildings

at the street level, and the consequent fine texture of the town's commercial core (Fig. 2-19).

These old main streets are models for design integrity, unity, and cohesiveness. The period architecture, which remains today as a major source of community pride and affection, is not the only reason for their appealing image. Perhaps more important is that they reinforce our culture's traditional preference for pedestrian-scaled space. The conformity in the size, shape, and width of the structures, as well as more subtle features, such as the horizontal alignment of building cornices, moldings, windows, and arcades, further strengthen this image (Fig. 2-20). It is the unity of the core's fabric that seems to count most.

Most of these towns were anything but opulent; they were working class communities, and their simple, functional architecture was a straightforward reflection of individual and social needs. The lesson in this, as in all vernacular styles, may be that people do not need monuments or grand statements in architecture to feel like a unified community. Much more important to people is the humaneness, scale, and sociability of the place as a whole.

Figure 2-18. *Chestnut Street was once one of the main commercial thoroughfares in Leadville, Colorado. Photo circa 1880, Denver Public Library, Western History Department.*

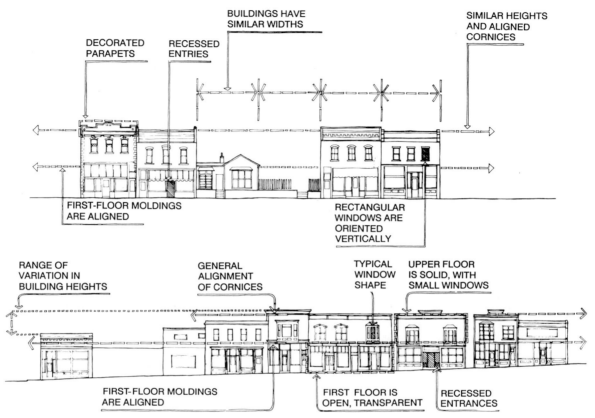

DECORATED
PARAPETS

RECESSED
ENTRIES

BUILDINGS HAVE
SIMILAR WIDTHS

SIMILAR HEIGHTS
AND ALIGNED
CORNICES

FIRST-FLOOR MOLDINGS
ARE ALIGNED

RECTANGULAR
WINDOWS ARE
ORIENTED
VERTICALLY

RANGE OF
VARIATION IN
BUILDING HEIGHTS

GENERAL
ALIGNMENT
OF CORNICES

TYPICAL
WINDOW
SHAPE

UPPER FLOOR
IS SOLID, WITH
SMALL WINDOWS

FIRST-FLOOR MOLDINGS
ARE ALIGNED

FIRST FLOOR IS
OPEN, TRANSPARENT

RECESSED
ENTRANCES

Figure 2-19. *Sketch elevations in two Colorado mining towns—Telluride (top) and Durango (bottom)—highlight the architectural elements that unify their Victorian-era main streets. Drawings by Noré V. Winter, courtesy of the Colorado Historical Society.*

Figure 2-20. *Main Street, Central City, Colorado. Photo taken in the early 1900s, Denver Public Library, Western History Department.*

RECREATION AND REBIRTH

Ski Villages in Europe

Before the nineteenth century, travelers' accommodations in the Alps were limited to the homes of friends, houses rented from farmers who were away in the high pastures for the summer, or small taverns and *auberges* along the roads to shrines and other important destinations. In the early 1800s, however, this began to change. A romantic passion for mountain climbing—the same passion that marked the dark landscape painting and the angst-ridden Germanic literature of the era—began to lure upper-class lowlanders into the high country. Demand grew for the development of mountain resorts for health cures and leisure, such as spas at St. Moritz and Baden-Baden; tuberculosis treatment centers at Leysin, St. Vallier, and Menton; and summer hospices in Chamonix, Zermatt, and Garmisch. Chamonix gained additional prominence as a ski resort when it was expanded for the 1920 Olympic Games.

These "first-generation" tourist resorts of the early 1900s were integrated parts of traditional villages (Fig. 2-21). Houses were turned into pensions, hotels were built, and a "suburban" zone of larger buildings grew up at the periphery of the village. Resort location was determined by ease of access; limitations on year-round road travel at elevations above 4000

feet (1200 m) restricted resort development to lower villages. Although skiing had become a recreational pastime by the 1890s, the inadequacy of snow cover at these lower elevations and the lack of ski lifts limited its appeal and forced a ski season of very short duration.

The Rise of Skiing. Skiing did not become widely popular in Europe until the 1930s, when several factors coalesced: The ski season was prolonged by the introduction of mechanical ski lifts; dissatisfaction grew as existing villages expanded disjointedly beyond their capacities; and the first fully planned, self-contained seaside and ski resorts appeared. This launched the "second generation," which spanned the years from about 1930 until World War II. Two Italian ski villages, Cervinia and Sestriere—the latter financed by Fiat for its employees—were the first to be constructed in previously unexploited mountain areas, followed soon after by Alpe d'Huez and Val d'Isère in France (Fig. 2-22).

It was the practice in this period to build the new Alpine resorts at higher elevations—5400 to 6400 feet (1600 to 1900 m)—but to stay within reasonable proximity of existing villages in order to take advantage of established services and facilities in the early stages of development. This led in time to a buildup of the local work force and a slight shift away from agrarian to resort-based employment. Development during this prewar period was typically

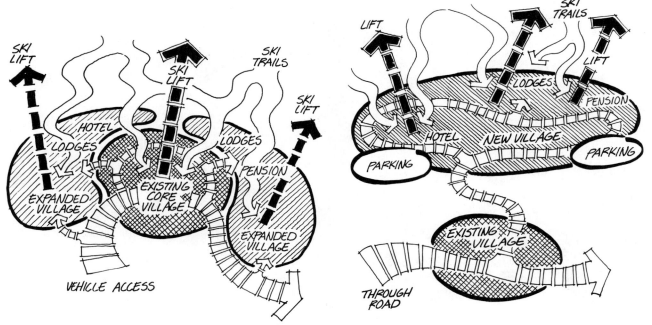

Figure 2-21. *First-generation alpine tourist facilities generally stayed within existing villages (left). Second-generation ski resorts were sited nearby to utilize village services (right).*

Figure 2-22. *In Alpe d'Huez, France, second-generation lodgings were developed adjacent to the traditional village (lower left corner). Photo from the French Government Tourist Office.*

funded privately and was not coordinated with any village or regional interests.

After World War II, plans for the rehabilitation of France included an extensive regional planning process which, among other goals, targeted resort development in the French Alps (Juul 1979, p. 23). A major campaign was launched to promote winter tourism in the Alps, and skiing became firmly established as a popular recreational sport in western Europe. Entirely new "third-generation" towns such as Courchevel and Mottaret (Fig. 2-23) were created, using public funds and low-interest government loans as incentives to developers.

The main design program components for these resort villages were centralized, self-contained services and support facilities; the segregation of cars from pedestrians and skiers; and the ability of skiers to reach their lodgings on skis. These parameters necessitated base elevations above 5400 feet (1600 m) and site plans that maximized ski slope frontage.

Buildings were arranged either in north–south rows up the slopes, separated by skiable corridors, or in one long east–west block across the contours, separating the ski slopes from the parking lots (Fig. 2-24). Skiable terrain adjacent to the site was the main determinant in site selection, not proximity to existing villages or access roads.

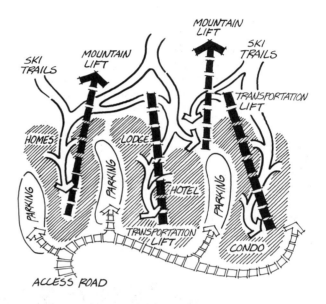

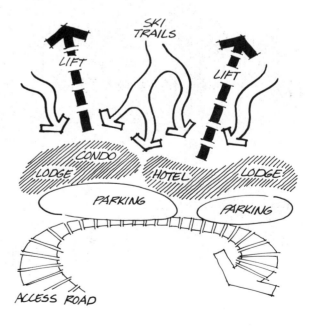

Figure 2-24. *Postwar French ski resorts valued segregated parking and direct access from lodging to ski slopes. Buildings either framed skiable corridors (top) or defined the ski slope runout (bottom), in both cases separating skiers from cars.*

Figure 2-23. *Mottaret, near Courchevel and Meribel in Savoie, is a self-contained third-generation French ski resort. Photo by H. Peter Wingle.*

33

***Paquebots sur la Neige* ("Steamships on the Snow").** By the late 1950s, the French government was assembling package deals in which a financial institution would invest in a new town and pay for the infrastructure. The resort town designs of this period, like Flaine, designed by Marcel Breuer (Fig. 2-25), La Plagne (1962), and Les Menuires (1965), were connected to neither the landscape nor the existing social fabric (Fig. 2-26).

These megastructure "snow cities" were comprehensively planned, stark, massive, urban, and isolated. They offered under one roof every convenience to skiers. Panoramic windows made up for the inhospitable siting above the tree line at the base of a north-facing slope. But this concept was not well accepted. Villages in name only, they served only one purpose, had no permanent residents, and languished for eight months of the year. Design strategies were reconsidered.

Currently in Europe, there is a back-to-basics trend in Alpine development and a renaissance in the remaining small villages. New "fourth-generation" resort villages such as Val Morel (Fig. 2-27) are being developed as part of a planning process that views the town and valley as an integrated social and economic unit. New structures, though still modernistic in style, are more villagelike in scale and layout and show a somewhat stronger emphasis on integration with the natural environment. There is also renewed attention to existing villages and a search for ways to revitalize and repopulate them as viable year-round support communities.

Figure 2-25. *Les Menuires is one of France's most modernistic postwar alpine resorts. Photo by John R. Smith.*

Figure 2-26. *The postwar French ski resort of Flaine was designed by Marcel Breuer. Photo by John R. Smith.*

Figure 2-27. *Val Morel, France, is a fourth-generation resort that heralded a return to village scale. Photo by H. Peter Wingle.*

Mountain Resorts in America

The comprehensive planning of mountain resorts came later in the United States and has never been pursued with the intensity of federal government involvement that it was in France. Very little happened in the early postwar years.

In the eastern mountains—the Adirondacks, Catskills, and Alleghenies—tourism remained primarily a summer business, and resort hotels were similar to those of France's first generation, not yet completely self-contained. As skiing grew more popular, Lake Placid, New York, and Stowe, Sugarbush, Killington, and Mt. Snow, Vermont, emerged early as popular destinations, although only Lake Placid and Stowe have the attributes of more mature communities.

In the central mountain states until the late 1960s, it was more common to see the repositioning of existing mining and ranching towns to capture tourist business. Because mining town sites were typically at high elevations, ski lifts could be brought into or very near the town. Sun Valley, Idaho, a resort built by the Union Pacific Railroad in the mid-1930s, was the

first in the Rockies to be built from scratch, although the ski lifts are in the neighboring town of Ketchum. Aspen, Colorado, formerly a mining town, opened for skiing in 1947 (Fig. 2-28).

Other old mountain towns have since returned from oblivion to eminence as ski, and later as summer, resorts. The mining towns of Crested Butte, Breckenridge, and Telluride in Colorado and Park City in Utah, as well as the ranching communities of Steamboat Springs, Colorado, and Jackson Hole, Wyoming, have taken the plunge into tourism. Even venerable Leadville, Colorado, kept alive by molybdenum until the mine closed in 1982, hopes to encourage tourism through the private redevelopment of its historic buildings.

In these towns, resort life has been laid over a rich and appealing frontier past, providing an ambience unavailable anywhere else in the world. As the French have already discovered, however, even in the same culture and place, there are obstacles that frustrate the adaptation of the town form of one era for another time and a different use.

A major disadvantage is the inability of the old town center to accommodate the larger population

The American small town, like the bald eagle, is vanishing from our landscape and our minds. . . . The decline from proud and quirky to quaint and cute is part of the process that turns a town into a commodity.
—Peggy Clifford, Aspen/Dreams and Dilemmas:
Love Letters to a Small Town

Figure 2-28. *A decimated mining town, Aspen opened for skiing in 1947. Compare with recent photo, Fig. 10-19. Photo by Elmar Baxter, collection of Aspen Skiing Co.*

now imposed on it. Larger crowds mean a larger scale, but new buildings are not easily intermixed with the old. A visitor public demands easier access, which means intrusive highways, parking lots, and sometimes airports. Pedestrians cannot compete with the automobiles now clogging the streets. Main street's parallel facades leave few openings for pedestrian spaces, and old buildings designed for other uses are difficult to retrofit to serve new, more leisure-oriented needs. Above all, it is hard to inject a sense of the landscape into forms from an era that did not put as high a priority on scenic and ecological values.

New Ski Villages. Partially in response to these difficulties, the past two decades have witnessed the development of completely new resort communities in the North American mountains to capitalize on the boom in skiing and tourism. Comprehensively

planned, often by a single private developer, they were intended to avoid the redevelopment problems and lack of control faced by developers in existing towns and to address more specifically the needs of the leisure-seeking market.

In the western states, this trend has produced a string of new resort villages: in California, a large base village at Squaw Valley for the 1960 Winter Olympics and two new resorts in the early 1970s, Northstar (Fig. 2-29) and Kirkwood Meadows, near Lake Tahoe; in Utah, Snowbird (1971) and Deer Valley at Park City (1981); and in Colorado, Vail Village (1962) and its satellite, LionsHead (1967), Snowmass at Aspen (1967), Keystone Resort (1970), Copper Mountain (1972), Beaver Creek Resort near Vail (1981), and Purgatory Village Center (1983–1984). Of these, only Vail/LionsHead and Snowmass have since incorporated as towns; the rest are still owned and controlled by single development entities. (See

Appendix A for comparative statistics on most of these.)

In the eastern United States, Stratton, Vermont, recently completed a new pedestrian core (Fig. 2-30). The area opened for skiing in the winter of 1961 near the site of a village, chartered in 1761, that had fallen into near total decline. Waterville Valley, an incorporated new town near skiing in New Hampshire, has been slowly adding community facilities since its master planning began in the late 1960s. In British Columbia, Whistler Resort Village, where construction began in 1979, is the preeminent model of a planned mountain community in Canada. All of these resorts exhibit both the achievements and the shortcomings common to master-planned developments built as a single package.

LESSONS FROM THE PAST

Each of the following issues in community design, some of them environmental and some behavioral, is essential to the creation of a mountain place, a community, where people wish to spend time.

Climate. The first consideration for building in the mountains is respect for an extremely harsh climate. Traditional villages exhibit time-tested, appropriate responses to cold temperatures, wind, snow, and rain. Perhaps they do so because their inhabitants intended to live there for a lifetime, not just to make a fortune in gold and leave. In this respect, American mining towns—our nearest historical parallel to traditional

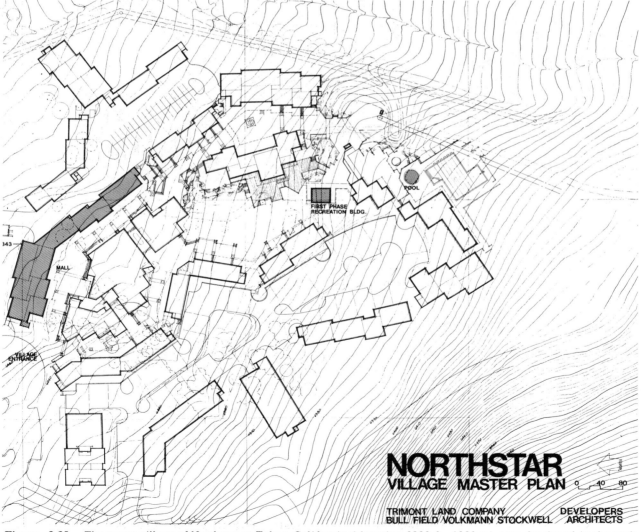

Figure 2-29. *The resort village of Northstar-at-Tahoe, California (elevation 6330 ft., 1930 m), was developed in the early 1970s by Trimont Land Company dba Northstar. First-phase master plan by Bull Volkmann Stockwell, San Francisco, architecture and planning, and EDAW, San Francisco, landscape architecture.*

Figure 2-30. *The first phase in a major expansion of Stratton Mountain Village, Vermont, was begun in 1987. Developer, The Stratton Corporation. Hull-Mozley & Associates, Atlanta, Georgia, master planning; William Cox, Coral Gables, Florida, architecture; The Cavendish Partnership, Ludlow, Vermont, phase I landscape architecture. Photo by Hubert Schreibl.*

mountain villages—are among the least suitable models for ecologically sensitive design. Elsewhere in mountainous regions, compactness of form for heat efficiency, wind shielding, and efficient use of buildable land is an almost universal indigenous response.

Topography. The terrain of a mountain village site may be both a limiting factor and one of the site's greatest place-making assets. Vernacular communities and some planned resorts have shown how to turn the constraints of topography into scenic opportunities. In the most memorable mountain villages, respect for topography is evident in sensitive siting, compatible overall form and scale, distribution of densities, and layout of circulation networks. Slopes are not avoided; rather, where feasible, they are utilized for maximum visual advantage, and the flatter areas are dedicated to higher-density uses or public open space.

The major shortcoming in most heavily visited

mountain communities is a circulation pattern that does not work well with the topography or with the volume of traffic imposed on it. In the most appealing resorts, cars, which pose an enormous challenge in rugged terrain, are excluded from areas of concentrated pedestrian activity.

A mountain town completely free of autos is by far the solution most respectful for the natural environment, but the exclusion of cars may not be politically or functionally practical in every case. However, it is a solution that must not be rejected out of hand. Somewhere between the extremes, more efficient, less destructive mountain circulation systems must be created in both resorts and working mountain towns. At the least, this may require excluding cars from central zones where they would conflict with people and terrain.

Aesthetic Quality. In the mountains, scenery has proved to be more valuable than constructed elements in the process of place making. Simplicity of built form, richness of detail, unity of the whole, and respect for history and natural beauty at all scales can, without contrivance, produce a community of rare quality in a majestic setting. On this point, the postwar European ski "village" is an equally unsuitable model.

Size and Scale. Where people circulate mainly on foot, there are finite limits to expansion. The human scale and pedestrian orientation of traditional mountain villages have clear and positive social implications. The small scale of most vernacular structures is particularly comforting in a setting in which the scale of the natural landform may be overpowering.

Urbanity versus Wilderness. The mountain community is essentially an urban organism in a natural arena. The interplay between the two domains creates a certain amount of psychological tension that can either sap or buoy the spirit. In a primal sense, the definite boundaries of a primitive village were symbols of the need to establish the village precinct as a place where people were, if not in control over nature, at least capable of lessening their exposure to it. Vernacular architecture has instinctively met this need through careful siting and orientation, by providing space within the boundaries for social and ceremonial needs, by designing transitions from the "natural" outside to the "urban" inside the boundaries, and by letting nature—in untouched or in symbolic form—penetrate to the heart of the village.

Real Town versus Resort. People quickly sense authenticity or artifice. Notwithstanding the popularity of the Disney theme parks, people are attracted to "real" communities, even for their vacations, because resort communities always lack to some degree the diversity of people and activities found in a real community. Only a few newer resort villages, like Vail, Colorado, have grown to seem more genuine, but these successes show that, with time, it is possible.

Authenticity derives from evidence of age and the passage of time, from straightforwardness of form and function, and from eclecticism and individuality. These urban design issues are relevant to virtually any setting where people congregate, and so it is shortsighted to deem them less important to a community surrounded by wilderness.

REFERENCES

Carver, Norman F., Jr. 1979. *Italian Hilltowns.* Kalamazoo, Mich.: Documan Press.

Jackson, J. B. 1984. *Discovering the Vernacular Landscape.* New Haven, Conn.: Yale University Press.

Juul, Tore. 1979. *The Architecture and Planning of Ski Resorts in France.* Norfolk, England: Page Bros. (Norwich).

Rossbach, Sarah. 1983. *Feng Shui: The Chinese Art of Placement.* New York: Dutton.

Rudofsky, Bernard. 1964. *Architecture Without Architects.* New York: Doubleday.

Scully, Vincent. 1972. *Pueblo: Mountain, Village, Dance.* New York: Viking.

Sestini, Valerio, and Enzo Somigli. 1978. *Sherpa Architecture.* Geneva, Switzerland: UNESCO.

Stilgoe, John. 1982. *Common Landscape of America, 1580 to 1845.* New Haven, Conn.: Yale University Press.

Stoehr, C. Eric. 1975. *Bonanza Victorian: Architecture and Society in Colorado Mining Towns.* Albuquerque: University of New Mexico Press.

Moonrise over Mt. Everest (elevation 29,021 ft., 8848 m). Photo from summit of Cho Oyu by Mark Udall, Colorado Outward Bound School.

3
THE SINGULAR AESTHETICS OF MOUNTAIN LANDSCAPES

Environmental design is the art of manipulating the formation of landscape images: enhancing perceptions, revealing natural functions and content, reinforcing symbols, expressing meaning. The art demands more than a rational basis for built form; clues from context, ecology, and climate are necessary but not enough. Also required are intuition and a grasp of the aesthetic significance of a landscape, its scenic beauty, its imageability, the nearness of nature, and the meanings and seasonal rituals with which it is associated.

PHYSICAL COMPONENTS OF LANDSCAPE CHARACTER

The aesthetic character of any natural landscape is a tapestry of four physical components: landform, water, vegetation, and rock. Under the influence of climate and time, these interact and combine in an infinite variety of visual and sensory images. To identify the qualities of the composition they form in any given place is to define the natural landscape in a way that has meaning for design.

Landform.   Landform is the basic three-dimensional armature of the mountain landscape (Fig. 3-1). It is unquestionably the dominant element, in both scale and mass. As a visual backdrop, the mountain profile dwarfs any built environment.

Angular landform profiles are common in mountain landscapes. The dominant components of a mountain scene are the steep mountainsides and the more gently sloping base that forms the transition to the valley floor. The ridge tops, often sharp, are likely to read as edges rather than area and to mark a sharp line of contrast with the sky. Similarly, the valley bottomlands, most often rather narrow as well, are generally less significant than the slopes in the overall view. In a geologically more mature mountain landscape, the hills are softer and more curvilinear, and the valley's directional qualities are less distinct.

Researchers developing methodologies for rating landscape quality have found that surface relief with greater variation and complexity usually correlates with landscapes that are high in scenic quality and visual interest (Litton 1984, p. 13). This helps explain the appeal of the mountain landscape and underscores the importance of landform in creating mountain landscape images.

Figure 3-1.   *Landform.*

Attraction to the mountain landscape goes far deeper, however, than visual stimulus. For centuries, religions have recognized the spirituality of mountain summits by making high peaks into symbols of ascension, abodes of gods, and objects of sacred journeys. Altitude is a universal symbol of an uplifted spirit, and the mountain itself is a symbol of enlightenment.

Although mountain masses are solid and unmoving, there is a suggestion of movement in the ascending lines and receding layers of peaks and ridges (Fig. 3-2). This perception is not the only kinetic property of mountain landforms; real movement through the landscape is equally influential in shaping the perceived character of mountain regions. Traveling up, down, and through the mountains reveals landforms in endlessly changing relationships to one another. Movement opens exhilarating views and hides them again. It persistently engages the senses, fascinates, and forces response.

The journal of a traveler in Alaska expressed these feelings:

Just go on and on. . . . Do you see the mountain ranges there, far away? One behind another. They rise up. They tower. That is my deep, unending inexhaustible kingdom.

—Henrik Ibsen, The Master Builder

Figure 3-2. *Layered ridge lines give a kinetic quality to the mountain view. (View looking north to the high peaks from the Himalayan foothills.)*

Like no other wilderness, mountains demand the eye, beg us to fantasize and speculate in advance of contact. The sea, by contrast, seems all of a piece, like the desert or the jungle: one edges timidly into it, fearing not worse, but too much of the same—the terror of ordinariness, of getting lost. In the mountains the urge is to be ensconced, to find and reach the heart of difficulty; the corresponding fear is being stranded there. . . . (Roberts 1979, p. 63)

No other type of landform so effectively communicates three-dimensionality, depth, and distance. In the visual and ecological changes that occur with increasing elevation in the mountain landscape is nature's metaphor for sequence, progression, and transformation.

Water. "Other than motion, water is the strongest attraction" (K. Lynch 1971, p. 356) (Fig. 3-3). Water is perhaps the only element in the mountain setting that can compete visually with the landform. Water has aesthetic meaning in its dynamic, kinetic character and its seasonal metamorphoses. It has sound, motion, viscosity, light, reflectivity, depth, and the ability to distort vision. It has meaning in its connection with the land, its contrast with the landform, and the character of its edges. Because water edges are limited in mountain environments, they are particularly valuable image-making elements.

Streams, with their cascades and waterfalls, deep pools and rapids, are the gems of this landscape, but ponds and lakes are important as well.

Not only is impounded water the only truly flat and potentially simplest surface to be expected in the landscape; its changing response to light and water give it what might be termed a life of its own. . . . Its edge, as the junction between liquid and solid materials, delineates an extremely strong and lucid shape or floor configuration. (Litton 1968, p. 15)

In the mythic tradition the Mountain is the bond between Earth and Sky. Its solitary summit reaches the sphere of eternity, and its base spreads out in manifold foothills into the world of mortals.
  —*René Daumal,* Mount Analogue

Figure 3-3. *Water.*

Rock. "Rocks are the bones of the earth," says a Chinese proverb (Fig. 3-4). Rock is an abundant, highly visible element in the mountain landscape. The delineator and embellisher of natural spaces, rock gives character by means of its spatial power and its variable textures, shapes, and colors. Its traits are site specific; even rock of the same composition can exhibit a variety of forms and textures depending on its origin and manner of occurrence. Rock conveys permanence and reveals the process of geological change. Even where it is a physical barrier, it is a connection with time and natural history.

Figure 3-4. *Rock.*

Vegetation. A more placid and visually delicate element, vegetation is the soft glove over a rock-faceted surface (Fig. 3-5). Though less imageable than

landform or water, vegetation has abundant aesthetic meaning in its mosaics of color and texture, its edges, its seasonal changes, the sensuous qualities with which its lifeforms and ecosystems are associated, and the role it plays in connecting the disparate pieces of the alpine landscape. At any viewing distance, vegetation is a key component in the locally recurring patterns and shapes that distinguish the scenery of one region from that of another.

Vegetation can be an important variable in softening the visual impacts of change, but the clearing of vegetation is one of the first things that happens in development. Forest disturbances are especially noticeable from a distance, where the lack of species diversity gives rise to textural uniformity that is easily interrupted.

Figure 3-5. *Alpine vegetation.*

Atmospherics. These four components of the landscape—landform, water, rock, and vegetation— are by themselves strong determinants of aesthetic character, but they also interplay with an important ephemeral factor that we can call *atmospherics*: the season, the weather, the time of day, and the quality of light and reflected images (Fig. 3-6).

The seasonal metamorphosis in the color of a mountain landscape, from a blanket of deep matte green to a mantle of gleaming white, could hardly be a more dynamic variable. The thin, clear air of the high elevations has a more subtle influence: Sunlight is intense, shadows are noticeably chilling, and dizzyingly long views can be astounding in their clarity. The quality of light changes constantly during the day and throughout the seasons, from clear to

I love the mountains passionately. I have signed a sort of contract with them, and in them I will live out my life. I love other things, too, but the mountains are where nature offers her most beautiful contrasts.
—*Walter Bonatti, mountaineer*

Figure 3-6. *Clouds hide a wall in the Khumbu Himalayas, northeastern Nepal.*

hazy and from delicate to intense. Colors follow suit, changing from crystalline brilliance to muted monochromes. The quality of light and color also depends on the distance from which landscape elements are viewed. Foreground colors are more vivid, and dust and moisture in the air mute them at a distance.

Weather patterns in the mountains constantly enmesh earth with sky. Clouds are impaled on peaks, snared in valleys; they creep over ridges and fill the valleys. While one stands in sunshine, rain shafts strafe distant slopes. When snowstorms close in, they shutter out the view, and when they clear, snowdrifts in wind-blown fantasy forms have transformed every protruding object.

In truth, it may well be the air, the light, and the clouds playing upon the mountain landscape that make its depth and scale so palpable and that create such enduring impressions of place.

EMOTIONAL RESPONSES TO THE MOUNTAIN LANDSCAPE

Mountains are perceived and remembered differently from images of other landscapes. Those who wish to build in the spirit of the mountains must understand the source and emotional power of their mystique.

References to landscape in literature reveal vastly different sensory perceptions of mountains, compared with those of the sea and the plains. Early explorers consistently noted in their journals the mountains' overwhelming scale, their dark and threatening forms, the exhilaration of precipitous verticality and infinite views, the fear of what could not be seen, and the agelessness and divinity of the landscape. As artist George Catlin wrote at the mouth of the Yellowstone River in 1832:

. . . I am surrounded by living models of such elegance and beauty, that I feel an unceasing excitement of a much higher order—the certainty that I am drawing knowledge from the true source. No man's imagination, with all the aids of description that can be given to it, can ever picture the beauty and wildness that may be daily witnessed in this romantic country. (Gussow 1971, p. 71)

Paintings of mountain landscapes depict many of the same reactions (Fig. 3-7, 3-8). Romantic painters of the nineteenth-century American West, for example, relied on dark colors to depict the undertone of fear in a strange and intimidating landscape. But they also expressed the excitement and drama of the mountains and of the great distances revealed from the summits (Fig. 3-9). Their paintings were often enormous, the

Figure 3-7. The Passage of Mount St. Gothard (1804), by J. M. W. Turner (English, 1775–1851), reflects the fear and awe with which the high mountains were regarded in his time (compare with Fig. 2-5). Watercolor, 985 mm × 685 mm. Abbot Hall Art Gallery, Kendall, Cumbria, England.

Figure 3-8. *The embellished landscape:* Estes Park, Long's Peak (1877). *Painter Albert Bierstadt took considerable liberties with the topographical scale to dramatize and romanticize the alpine landscape. Oil on canvas, 62″ × 98″.* Denver Public Library, Western History Department.

Figure 3-9. *The real landscape:* Long's Peak, Estes Park *(right plate of a stereoscopic pair). The same view that Bierstadt painted was captured by photographer W. G. Chamberlain around 1875. Denver Public Library, Western History Department.*

*The sense of relation between nature and man in some
form has always been the actuating spirit of art.*
    —*John Dewey,* Experience and Nature

tiny details of the scenery contrasting with the
immensity of the landscape. These painters' emotional
responses are evident in the inflated scale, in the
surreal storm clouds and sunsets of mythical
grandeur, and in the allegorical scenes they often
superimposed on the landscape. Their themes are
meditations on the spirituality, beauty, timelessness,
and terror of the wilderness, themes, though muted,
that can still be found in contemporary responses to
the alpine landscape.

DESIGN GUIDELINES

The mountain landscape appeals to both the senses
and the emotions. The designer's job is to enhance
those sensory perceptions and encourage response, to
create places and sequences of experience that
involve people in the landscape's singular character.
Good design in a natural landscape preserves and
plays up its details and variety. To take advantage of
the aesthetic qualities of the mountain landscape,
designers are encouraged to keep in mind the
following guidelines.

1. Respect the landscape's spiritual character.
The elements that make a landscape special extend
beyond the visual, as they are often intangible
confluences of sensory appeals, cultural traditions,
and personal histories. Sensitivity to what is
meaningful about a place helps keep it that way.

2. Counteract intimidating scale. Somewhere in
the mountain community should be both natural and

built spaces that seem sheltering, warm, and intimate.
Canopies, screens, enclosures, softening contrasts, and
elements that frame and direct views can serve an
essential spatial function by moderating the
superhuman proportions of mountain-defined spaces.

*The inhuman dimensions of the mountains both exalt
and dwarf [man's] individuality. He stands, often in
precarious verticality, at the cleft or narrows, not in the
open agora. . . . His horizon is a wall, where the sea is
a gate flung open by the light.*

    —*George Steiner, ''Cairns''*

3. Take advantage of views and view lines.
Views help orient people to their regional
surroundings and reinforce the place-making
contribution of natural features. Vantage points can
become places with ceremonial quality, depending on
how well they are sited and connected with other
landscape elements.

In the formation of images, views of a place are as
important as views from it. Taking advantage of
views is an issue not only of siting but also of
establishing and protecting view corridors. In
mountain landscapes, three-dimensional control is a
necessity.

Certain places in the landscape, exceptional or not,
are more conspicuous where lines of sight converge
or coincide with natural axes, like a river reach.
Places where views terminate should be identified,
and care should be taken to ensure that any alteration
planned there will not degrade the view.

No two hills are alike, but everywhere on earth plains are one and the same.
—*Jorge Luis Borges,* Utopia of a Tired Man

4. Respect visually sensitive scenery. Dominant natural features—special landforms, rock outcrops, trees, or water features—stand out because of their compositional qualities (line, form, color, texture), the contrast with their surroundings, and variables that affect how they will appear (motion, light and atmospheric conditions, season).

Physical character alone, however, is not the measure of visual sensitivity. The relative visual importance of a particular landscape or a dominant feature also depends on how it is viewed: the number of viewers, their expectations of scenic character, their distance from the area, their angle and duration of view, and the number of other focal points competing for their attention. For example, an area that is visible from a heavily visited vantage point is more important to the impression of scenic quality than an area that can be seen only for a moment from a high-speed highway.

The vulnerability of a landscape—its ability to absorb change without losing its visual character—depends on the degree of diversity in its vegetation, rock outcrops, and water features; the extent to which landform and vegetation can screen changes; and the ability of its vegetation to recover from disturbances. Measurements of vulnerability and visual sensitivity can be mapped to show where development would be least intrusive.

Certain landscapes are both visually sensitive and highly vulnerable to change. For example, shorelines and ridge lines silhouetted against the sky can be hurt by breaks in the forest edge and the intrusion of built forms. Lower ridge lines silhouetted against other landmasses and vegetative edges (ecotones) are also sensitive to change, although contrasts of color and texture are not as great. Muted terrain edges are more important where several overlapping lines of ridges converge.

Exceptionally scenic features require special design attention, as they have a "sphere of influence that needs to remain intact or that can tolerate only certain changes without deterioration" (Litton 1968, p. 26). The first step in deciding how much change

can be allowed, if any, in their vicinity is to plot the limits of the sphere and then to identify a range of compatible design possibilities.

5. Manipulate the observer's vertical position in the landscape. Most people see mountain scenery from the base looking up, thereby exaggerating the already sizable contrast between human scale and the mountain. This viewpoint also makes it difficult to judge size, extent, distances, and heights.

People love places with views. Pathways, roads, and buildings can incorporate elevation changes in ways that can extend viewing opportunities to less vigorous people. And by elevating viewing positions where possible, the novelty of a mountain experience is enhanced.

6. Recognize the importance of both movement through the landscape and sequences of experiences and views. The three-dimensionality of mountain scenery cannot be fully appreciated from a static position. Much more effective in communicating the breadth of the landscape are sequential experiences, "the progressive interplay of forms, distances, spaces, lighting, and observer position" (Litton 1968, p. 22). Visual images of the landscape and the features within it vary according to the distance from which they are viewed, for distance alters the perception of color, texture, detail, scale, and proportion.

7. Attend to the foreground. The peaks in the distance may be stunning, but people still look to the scenery close at hand to provide humanly scaled shelter and sensory stimulus. Texture and detail register best at close range. Streams, boulders, trees, wildflowers, and other carefully scaled and detailed elements all help bring down the setting to a more comfortable scale. Foreground details that are representative of the overall landscape pattern also exemplify the essence of place and are thus design tools with symbolic importance.

9. Preserve natural water features and add more. Water in its many manifestations—brooks, streams, ponds, glacial lakes, marshy meadows, cascades, torrential runoff, snow, and ice—is both a precious commodity and a seasonal life cycle metaphor for mountains. Neglecting it guarantees practical problems, and using it sensitively as a design tool ensures greater enjoyment. Weaving it throughout a mountain community establishes another linkage with the place, the ecosystem, and the passage of time.

8. Protect the continuity of the ground plane. When one views a landscape from the lowest points in it, the ground plane becomes a major factor in the scene's continuity. Uneven, rangy understory vegetation or dense forest are natural barriers to the continuity of the sight line and to movement. In contrast, lakes, ponds, meadows, and small forest clearings are among the most valued elements in most mountain landscapes, for they allow visual penetration at the ground level.

If such areas are developed, these features will often be the first to be affected. Continuity can be lost by such changes as structures that are too broad; development that is too extensive for the site; the loss of important cones of vision; ground plane materials and forms that are not natural to the site; or the filling up of clearings with buildings because they seem to be the easiest places in which to build.

10. Interpret time, natural processes, and change. Familiarity with the site is a designer's best means to communicate its natural history. Streams, rock formations, and outcrops are especially good illustrations of formative processes and geological time. Design on any scale, from town site planning to detailing, should highlight geomorphically significant features or areas in which active processes are evident.

11. Understand the visual impacts of slope.
Builders tend to confine their thinking about slope to
practical limitations, but there are aesthetic
considerations as well. On steeper slope gradients,
more surface area can be seen. Conversely, on gentler
slopes and bottomlands, less surface area is visible
because of perspective foreshortening. The gentler the
slope gradient, the greater the potential for vegetation
to provide screening.

This means that on slopes, building masses and
access roads are more visible. Sites high on a slope
are more visible than those nearer the base because
there are fewer things to block the view of them and
more spots from which they can be seen. Depending
on the viewer's position, roof lines can become more
visually dominant. Also more noticeable on slopes are
repeated shapes and patterns in the native vegetation.
Understanding how these patterns correlate with
variations in landform and relating new shapes to
naturally occurring ones will help reduce visual
impacts on slopes.

To anticipate visual impacts, the designer must
understand how the land flows, how slope controls
drainage patterns, and how and where to drop in
buildings and roads. In sum, to design effectively for
sloping terrain requires more practiced vision in the
vertical as well as the horizontal plane.

**12. Take clues to structural forms from the
landform.** When a structure seems out of place in its
natural setting, a common problem is its failure to

conform with the terrain. Commonality in form or
angle, mass or scale, color or material helps draw a
clearer relationship between communities and the
character of the surrounding landscape.

13. Remember the change of seasons.
Temperature is not the only thing that changes
radically from summer to winter in the mountains.
Colors and aromas are also signals of the season and
sensory symbols of place. The odors of pine and wet
fallen leaves, for example, may readily trigger recall
of one's past experiences in similar landscapes and
make a subtle linkage between place and one's own
personal history. Astute designers perceive and refer
to the elements that contribute to a site's sensory
character in each season, especially those elements
that change dramatically, like deciduous vegetation.

14. Create fantasy by means of snow. Wind and
snow are nature's overnight sculptors, and landscape
elements are the underlying armature. The first clear
morning after a snowstorm is one of sparkling
fantasy, unveiling the shapes the snow has wrought
from ordinary rocks, trees, posts, and walls. Such
effects need not always be unplanned.

15. Take advantage of the sense of hearing.
Asked to describe memories of a mountain experience, people often mention the sounds: the babbling stream, a waterfall, the wind through the pines, the crack of falling rocks or breaking ice, birds singing, echoes, and even the peerless winter silence. A perceptive designer recognizes the importance of sound in experiencing the landscape and uses it to create a special outdoor space, lay out a trail, or locate interior uses and windows so that the outdoors can be heard.

16. Take advantage of the sense of touch.
Materials and textures are more than just agents of color and tools of composition. In the communication of permanence and continuity, they express a more transcendent meaning. People instinctively reach out to touch rock, to feel its hardness and texture. They want to feel the water, to gauge its velocity and coolness. By making these materials accessible, design more fully involves people in the landscape.

When people appreciate a landscape, the images they retain are a composite of their preconceptions and their experience, what and how much they see and for how long. "Images are not formed from static pictures, but are abstracted from a series of vignettes perceived over time" (Twiss and Litton 1965, p. 81).

Images are as much a product of the setting as of its individual features. That is, the total landscape, with its connective elements and its combinations of unremarkable as well as spectacular scenery, is as important to its overall image as its features of special beauty. As magnificent as some mountain scenery is, it is easy to forget that less distinguished ingredients also contribute to sensory impressions. Landscape design that focuses only on the superlatives thus falls short of its potential.

REFERENCES

Gussow, Alan. 1971. *A Sense of Place: The Artist and the American Land*. San Francisco: Friends of the Earth Library.

Litton, R. Burton, Jr. 1968. Forest landscape description and inventories. U.S.D.A. Forest Service Research Paper PWS-49.

———. 1984. Visual vulnerability of the landscape: Control of visual quality. U.S.D.A. Forest Service Research Paper WO-39.

Lynch, Kevin. 1971. *Site Planning*, 2nd ed. Cambridge, Mass.: MIT Press.

Roberts, David. 1979. Alaska and personal style: Some notes in search of an aesthetic. In *The Mountain Spirit*, ed. Michael Charles Tobias and Harold Drasdo, pp. 63–74. Woodstock, N.Y.: Overlook Press.

Steiner, George. 1979. Cairns. In *The Mountain Spirit*, ed. Michael Charles Tobias and Harold Drasdo, pp. 17–21. Woodstock, N.Y.: Overlook Press.

Twiss, Robert H., and R. B. Litton, Jr. 1965. Resource use in the regional landscape. *Natural Resources Journal* 5, no. 2: 76–81.

PART II

The Mountain Environment: Natural Determinants of Design

In quantitative terms, we know little of ecological stress-tolerance in mountain ecosystems, but in qualitative terms the low stress-tolerance to man in such systems is readily apparent.

—A. Jernelow and R. Rosenberg, "Stress Tolerance of Ecosystems"

Cross-country skier near Crested Butte, Colorado, in a mountain landscape that is a pure expression of climate.

4
ELEVATION AND CLIMATE: DESIGN IMPERATIVES

IMPACTS OF HIGH ALTITUDE

An increase in elevation reduces the amount of oxygen available for respiration and transpiration. At 10,000 feet (3500 m), the air contains only two-thirds the volume of oxygen that it has at sea level. At high altitudes, it is noticeably harder to breathe because there is less air pressure to force available oxygen through the lung walls.

Higher elevation also means longer-lasting snow cover, stronger winds, colder and thinner soils, and more intense ultraviolet rays. Spring comes roughly three days later and winter three days earlier for every 300-foot (100 m) increase in altitude. The growing season may shrink to an average of as few as twenty frost-free days above 9500 feet (2900 m), the elevation of several important Rocky Mountain ski towns. At high altitudes, the incidence of frost is higher, even in summer, and the range of temperature fluctuation during a twenty-four-hour period is greater. The ground freezes deeper and stays frozen longer.

Precipitation increases 2 to 4 inches (5 to 10 cm) for each 300-foot (100 m) increment in elevation, reaching a maximum rate of increase at around 6000 feet (1800 m), when much of the moisture in the air has condensed and fallen. In the Front Range of the Colorado Rockies, precipitation continues to increase up to about timberline at 11,500 feet (3500 m) before it drops off.

At higher elevations, terrain form and aspect make a bigger difference in temperature. Research in Europe (Hess 1968) showed that the difference in daytime temperatures on north- versus south-facing slopes and on convex versus concave slopes (hill crowns versus basins) increases considerably with altitude. The difference in the number of days with heavy frost (temperatures below $-10°$ F, or $-24°$ C) rose by a factor of 6 between test stations at 600 feet (180 m) and 5100 feet (1550 m).

Impacts on Vegetation. The local distribution of plants and animals is significantly affected by the combination of elevation and latitude. Vegetation zones appear as horizontal belts that succeed one another as elevation increases (see Chapter 7). Within these broad altitudinal belts, secondary factors of topography, slope aspect, wind, sunlight, temperature, precipitation, and soil determine the exact upper and lower limits and the composition of local plant communities, which in turn influence the diversity of animal species.

Less than 10 percent of the earth's surface rises above 10,000 feet. Ninety percent of the world's population lives at elevations below 2000 feet (600 m), strong testimony to the restrictive influence of high elevation on community development. At 7000 feet (2135 m) and 36 degrees north latitude, Santa Fe, New Mexico, population 52,300, is the highest city in the United States. Leadville, Colorado, sitting just below timberline at 10,000 feet (3050 m), claims the distinction as the country's highest year-round community (population 3700). In the Swiss Alps (around 47° north latitude), Juf, at almost 7000 feet (2133 m), and St. Moritz, at just under 6000 feet (1825 m), are the highest year-round settlements. In the Nepali Himalayas, small farming villages subsist all year up to about 12,000 to 13,000 feet (3700 to 4000 m), but they are considerably farther south in latitude (27° to 30° north).

Settlement in mountain areas is sparse not only because of altitude, of course. Mountain topography and climate are also limiting factors, but high elevation by itself reduces the capability of land to produce and to support plant, animal, and human populations.

Impacts on Climatic Variables. Elevation has a fundamental impact on oxygen and temperatures. At higher elevations, the air is thinner and the climate is harsher. With increasing elevation, the air becomes colder, and cold air cannot hold as much water vapor. Air pressure, temperature, and absolute humidity all decrease as altitude increases (Figs. 4-1, 4-2).

Every 1000 feet (300 m) of increase in elevation means an average 3- to 5-degree (F) drop in temperature (2 to 3° Celsius). This decrease, called the *lapse rate* (Fig. 4-3), is maintained up to elevations of around 18,000 feet (5500 m). Elevation has a more marked effect on temperatures than latitude. Moving 1000 feet uphill (300 m) yields a decrease in temperature roughly equivalent to moving 300 miles north (500 km) in latitude.

Elevation, together with latitude and slope aspect, influences the amount of solar radiation, the length of a day, and the amount of precipitation. Light intensity at high elevations in the Rocky Mountains on a clear day has been calculated to be 45 percent greater than at sea level, and on a day with scattered clouds, it can be 70 to 90 percent greater (Ronco 1976, p. 17).

In principle, the earth could be a smooth ball with no mountains at all—after all, some of our sister planets have a configuration close to this. . . . But for some reason the earth is a place where being at 10,000 feet is a special experience.

—*James Trefil,* Meditations at 10,000 Feet

Alpine plants tend to grow much more slowly than those at lower elevations, owing to the thin air, low humidity, extreme temperature fluctuations, short growing season, and less fertile soils. New vegetation, particularly trees, can be quite difficult to establish.

Air Pollution. At higher elevations, air density is lower, meaning that the air is less able to absorb emissions. In addition, combustion is less efficient because of the lower oxygen content. The potential for air quality degradation is further compounded by the mountain landform and the air movement patterns which cause temperature inversions over valley floors.

Research by the Colorado Air Pollution Control Division in 1974 showed that the air pollution concentrations generated by fireplaces, auto use, and other residential activities are about ten times as severe in mountain areas above 8000 feet (2440 m) as in the city of Denver, at 5280 feet (1610 m) (Reeser and Kirkpatrick 1975). These studies also found that at 8000 feet autos emit almost two times as much carbon monoxide as they do in Denver (Table 4-1).

Deteriorating air quality has become a major concern in a number of mountain communities, for some of them will be unable to comply with federal air quality standards set by the Environmental Protection Agency. To cope with this problem, several of the larger communities have instituted controls on fireplace installation and usage and have redoubled their efforts to develop effective public transportation systems.

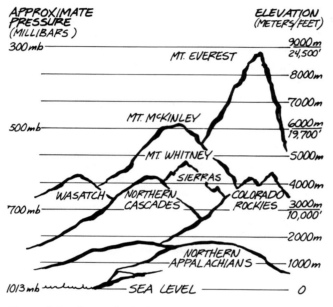

Figure 4-1. *Atmospheric pressure, measured in millibars (mb), decreases as altitude increases.*

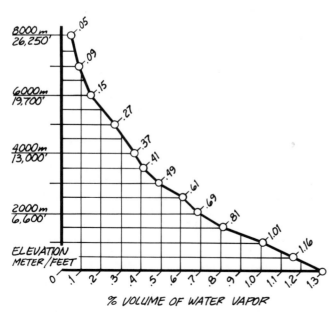

Figure 4-2. *In middle latitudes, the average water-vapor content of air decreases dramatically with increasing elevation. (Based on data from Landsberg 1962, p. 110)*

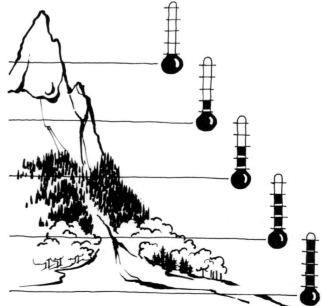

Figure 4-3. *The lapse rate: Average temperatures fall roughly 3° to 5°F for every additional thousand feet of elevation.*

Table 4-1 Predicted Air Pollution Caused by Typical Residential Activities of 30,000 Persons in the Airshed.[a]

Pollutant	Period Average	Concentration[b] at			
		Denver (5280 ft.)	Vail (8170 ft.)	Aspen (7920 ft.)	Federal Standard[c]
Carbon monoxide	8 hrs.	1.6	14.0	10.5	10.0
Hydrocarbons	3 hrs.	97	870	650	160
Particulates	24 hrs.	30	600	600	150
Ozone	1 hr.	44	470	360	160

[a]During inversion periods, assuming current levels of automobile and fireplace use and 1974 automobile emission standards.
[b]In millionths of a gram per cubic meter.
[c]Federal Secondary Air Quality Standard.
Source: Warner K. Reeser, Jr., and Lane W. Kirkpatrick. The air pollution carrying capacities of selected Colorado mountain valley ski communities (Denver: Colorado Department of Health, Air Pollution Control Division, 1975), table 3, p. 8.

Human Stress. For visitors to mountain areas, the net effect of high altitude can be serious biological stress: the stress of exposure to cold and the stress of hypoxia, or the reduction in the amount of oxygen reaching body tissues. In contrast, native highland villagers typically show basic biological adjustments to high-altitude cold and low atmospheric pressure. These adaptations include larger lung capacities, higher ventilation rates (more air moving into and out of the lungs), lower sensitivity to low blood oxygen levels, stockier build, more red blood cells to deliver oxygen, more and bigger capillaries for better blood circulation, elevated basal metabolism rates, and, in women and children, larger proportions of body fat (Weitz 1981).

Lowlanders frequently react to high altitudes with a variety of hypoxia symptoms, including headaches, labored breathing, body fatigue, inability to sleep, loss of appetite, nausea, and fluid in the lungs. In severe cases of altitude sickness, life-threatening pulmonary or cerebral edema can develop. The severity of the reaction does not correlate with the level of physical fitness; however, the less severe symptoms generally retreat over the first week or so as the lowlander's heart, lungs, and circulatory system adjust. Breathing and heart rates increase naturally, as does the number of red blood cells. Still, lowlanders are rarely able to duplicate fully the biological responses of high-altitude natives, particularly if they stay at a high altitude for only a short time.

Implications for Design at High Altitudes.
Elevation is a formidable constraint in the mountain landscape and should be carefully considered when comparing alternative sites. If a high-altitude site has already been chosen, the implications for revegetation and air quality should be taken into account in site planning. The extent of site modification and the level of proposed densities may have to be reconsidered in light of elevation-imposed limitations.

The adverse physiological effects of elevation on human endurance and well-being should be carefully weighed in site planning. The centralized siting of buildings, the control of grade changes, and a compact pedestrian circulation system may be the most appropriate design responses to a high-altitude site. If growth beyond an acceptable walking radius is anticipated, public transportation systems will be necessary to augment pedestrian networks.

In landscape design, observation of species distribution and the site's natural ecology throughout the seasons can indicate the parameters imposed by elevation. The signs may be subtle, but they are convincing evidence that altitude cannot be ignored in design.

MACROCLIMATE: A CONTROLLING VARIABLE

To those who visit the mountains in the summer, the alpine environment hardly seems the hostile force it becomes in the winter. Residents know otherwise. They have learned that to underestimate the effects of high altitude, cold, snow, wind, and sun is to make year-round living in the mountains unnecessarily brutal.

Today, the importance of accommodating local and regional climatic patterns in the design of structures and outdoor spaces is readily acknowledged. In the wake of the soaring energy costs of the 1970s, many local governments made the effort mandatory. Still, in climates of extremes, mistakes are commonplace.

Design shortcomings are the products of both the lack of long-term local experience and a tendency to underestimate Mother Nature's power to cause discomfort. In mountain areas, the problem is often compounded by the desire to create vacation environments in the stereotyped images of other places, even though borrowed forms may not satisfy local climatic requirements. The failure to respect climatic parameters frustrates the enjoyment of a place and mars its regional quality by injecting elements that are functionally inappropriate.

A primary objective in design is to provide environments that make people comfortable. In the mountains, the most elementary way to do this is to minimize their physical exposure. Corollary objectives are to maximize energy efficiency and the durability of structures and materials; to provide public outdoor spaces that can be used year-round; to facilitate safe, efficient circulation in all seasons; and to create an urban landscape that looks attractive and inviting at any time of year. The achievement of any of these objectives requires that climatic patterns, microclimatic conditions, and the special behavior of snow be incorporated into the design process.

General Characteristics of Mountain Climates

Climate is described in terms of average temperatures, precipitation, humidity, wind, and solar radiation. In natural landscapes, it sets the stage for design by controlling vegetation patterns, soil development, hydrology, and the character of surface relief.

Each mountain locale has its own set of climatic characteristics that depend on its elevation, latitude, topography, and position with regard to neighboring landmasses, oceans, and atmospheric high- and low-pressure systems. Temperate-zone mountain regions share certain characteristics that have serious implications for design, the most important of these being the following:

Marked Seasonality. Mountain areas, especially those at high altitudes, are characterized by short, temperate summers lasting from mid-June to late September, even shorter growing seasons, and long, often severe winters from November to April.

If a single season (winter or summer) has traditionally been dominant in the economy of a mountain community, neglect of the off-seasons may be a common design shortcoming. For example, the same community that captivates visitors with flower-bedecked streets in summer can be brought to a standstill by snow and wind if designers fail to plan for winter. Likewise, the same spot that looked charming in the Christmas snow can become a true

affliction for residents in the unpredictable wet weather of spring. Understanding the full year's climatic cycle and enhancing the opportunities to enjoy each season are important to sensitive mountain design, particularly if the intent is to create a community that will be inhabited year-round.

Subfreezing Winters. An extreme winter climate must dominate certain design considerations. Subfreezing temperatures four to six months of the year exact a heavy toll on plants, rock, building materials, and heating bills. Cold stretches human tolerances to the limit. It makes the ground impermeable, impossible to excavate in the deep winter months, and transforms water in the landscape, making it both an aesthetic fairyland and a major hazard.

Diurnal Temperature Fluctuation. At higher altitudes, there is little or nothing in the thin air of the mountain environment to help dampen temperature fluctuations. Rapid and wide swings in mountain temperatures from daytime to nighttime are largely a function of elevation, slope orientation, and the intensity of solar radiation. Above 8000 feet (2440 m) in the middle latitudes, there can be frost on virtually any night, even during the summer. Only a deep snow cover, an important insulator for alpine plants and hibernating mammals, can moderate the extremes.

In an undisturbed and uninhabited environment, temperature fluctuation is not of great consequence, but in any mountain development it can affect human safety, structural stability, and the durability of materials. It causes the continuous expansion and contraction of soils, subsoils, and building materials as they freeze and thaw, as well as the nightly freezing of meltwater on pavements and roads, at building eaves, and in drainage systems.

Semiarid Precipitation Levels and Low Humidity. The two essential elements for precipitation are moist air masses and vertical lifting. As air rises, it expands, cools, and loses its capacity to hold water vapor, a process called *adiabatic cooling.*

The most powerful force causing air to rise is *orographic lifting*, or the forcing of air up and over terrain barriers (Fig. 4-4). Because this lifting produces the highest vertical wind speeds, mountain regions usually receive far heavier snowfalls than flatter areas. And because the prevailing winds in the Northern Hemisphere are from the west, the mountain ranges of the West Coast receive more precipitation than most inland ranges (Fig. 4-5).

Primarily because of orographic lifting, the windward slopes of mountain ranges receive more

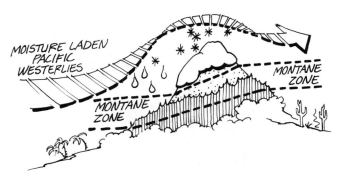

Figure 4-4. *In a process called orographic lifting, mountain barriers force air to rise as it crosses over them. This causes the air to cool and drop its moisture on the windward side.*

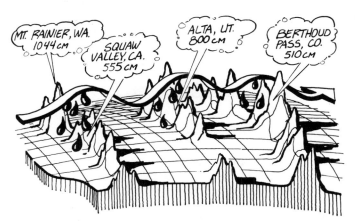

Figure 4-5. *West coast ranges get more precipitation than inland ranges. Along the coast, there is a similar gradient from north to south.*

moisture than intermountain basins and leeward slopes. This rain-shadow effect is compounded by the compression heating of air as it moves back downslope on the lee side. The warmer air enhances the evaporation of water droplets in the air and holds more water vapor.

Many continental mountain regions are semiarid, and half or more of the precipitation they receive falls as snow. Summers in these ranges may be moderately to completely dry, in contrast with the Cascades and the Canadian Coast Ranges, where northwesterly Pacific storms first unload their moisture. Although the Rockies in general follow this dry summer pattern, some parts of the range are exceptions, receiving their highest precipitation levels in spring and early summer.

Afternoon thundershowers, a product of summertime air convection, do occur even in drier mountains. The air over sun-heated ground warms up, evaporates water from vegetation and nearby water bodies, and rises to form cumulus clouds as it cools with elevation. Showers are more frequent at higher elevations, but in the Sierras and much of the Rockies, they are usually of short duration and may make little impression on the predominantly dry summer season. Precipitation that falls as rain on a mountain slope is quickly lost as runoff, whereas snow meltwater may be retained longer, thus providing more useful moisture. However, because water from snowmelt generally runs off before the growing season is in full swing, summer precipitation is still essential to the survival of vegetation.

The low humidity typical of many mountain regions has subtle consequences. Desiccation of plant materials exposed to wind is a constant hazard to revegetation efforts, as is high evaporative stress in plants under intense sunlight. Fire hazard is high in summer and fall. But on the positive side, low humidity has a moderating effect on the perceived discomfort of extreme cold and heat.

Wind. Mountain environments are much windier than flatlands, only partially because of orographic lifting and the daily up- and downslope movements of local air masses. The primary cause is elevation: Higher in the atmosphere, convection is more active, and the friction that retards air movement at lower elevations is diminished. Winds increase steadily in velocity at least up to the troposphere, some 50,000 feet above the ground.

Wind at high elevations has extraordinary power to make cold temperatures seem colder, to dissipate the thermal effectiveness of materials and mechanical systems, to dry and scour; in sum, to exacerbate the extremes of an already severe climate. In mountain design, therefore, localized wind control and shelter must be major concerns.

Snow. Although total precipitation decreases with increasing elevation, snow depths increase. Snow contributes less to total precipitation levels at higher altitudes because it becomes lighter and drier as air masses move upward and inland toward the Rockies. Rocky Mountain powder, "Sierra cement," and "Cascade concrete" did not get their nicknames unjustly.

Given the right combination of climatic factors and slope gradient, snow can paralyze circulation, collapse structures, and bury anything in its path. Because snow is such a dominant factor in mountain environments, a separate section is devoted to it later in this chapter.

Extreme Microclimate Contrasts. The great variation in topography in the mountains amplifies the effect of high elevation and helps create a multitude of individual microclimates within a short distance of one another. Seemingly unimportant physical features can vastly alter snow levels, solar and wind exposure, and species distribution. Contrasts, extremes, and continual change are the norm in the mountain climate, so it is never safe to base design concepts solely on generalizations about macroclimatic patterns.

Regional Variations

Sensitivity to an extreme climate is basic to appropriate design in the mountains. Equally fundamental to regionally inspired design is sensitivity to the important yet sometimes subtle differences in local climatic regimes from one mountain range to another.

Mountains, acting as a barrier, affect the regional climate around them. In turn, mountain climates are controlled by the same global factors that differentiate regional climates from one another: latitude, elevation, the size of the landmass, its proximity to moderating maritime influences, the direction of the prevailing winds, and the location of semipermanent pressure systems. From one mountain range to another, these factors determine rather predictable variations in seasonal and daily temperatures, snowfall levels, and total precipitation.

Regional climatic variations underscore a basic principle: A built form suited to one mountain region is unlikely to be appropriate to another without adjustments for the local climate. Borrowing indigenous forms from other mountain regions without understanding the climatic influences that shaped them is a prescription for inadequate design.

A simple analogy is the stereotypical Swiss chalet: Its overhanging balcony—designed for a meter or so of seasonal snowfall in the Alps—does nothing, however, in the Sierras except trap massive snow piles against the windows during the winter. The resulting claustrophobia may be the least of the problems.

Alps. In the east–west trending Alps, the continental transitional climate of central Europe, with precipitation evenly distributed over the year, keeps the northern side of the range quite moist (Fig. 4-6). In contrast, the south-facing valleys of northern Italy and the Tirol are influenced by the Mediterranean climate: rain mostly in the spring and autumn, warm summers and more temperate winters, and lower annual precipitation levels.

Himalayas. The Himalayas, the earth's tallest mountain range, forms a similar barrier between

Figure 4-6. *Climatic influences in the Alps.*

distinct climatic zones. The imposing east–west trending chain keeps the dry heat and severe cold of the central Asian plateau from penetrating the Indian subcontinent and keeps the tropical monsoons at bay to the south (Fig. 4-7). The northern flanks of the range are largely high-altitude desert, but some of the world's heaviest rainfall (128 in., or 324 cm, annually in Assam) occurs in its southeastern portions (Price 1981, p. 58).

Sierras and Rockies. In the north–south trending ranges of California and the Rockies, conditions vary distinctly from one side to the other because the prevailing winds are from the west. The contrast in annual precipitation between the west and the east sides of the Sierras is considerable (Fig. 4-8).

As moisture-laden Pacific air moves up and over the Sierran barrier, the western side benefits from the 50 inches (125 cm) or more of annual precipitation. At Tamarack, in Alpine County, California, this translates into extraordinary snowfall depths: an average of 37 feet (11.5 m) and an all-time high of 74 feet (22.5 m) in a single winter (Hill 1975, p. 40). In contrast, the average annual precipitation on the eastern flank varies with elevation, from a desertlike 5 inches (12 cm) at the base of the range in the rain shadow to a semiarid 15 to 20 inches (40 to 50 cm) above 5000 feet (1500 m).

In Colorado, this phenomenon causes one of the state's knottiest political problems. At least four-fifths

Figure 4-7. Climatic influences in the Himalayas.

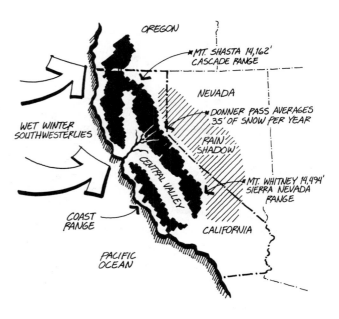

Figure 4-8. Prevailing westerlies load the windward side of the Sierras with snow; the eastern side is in a precipitation shadow.

of all Coloradoans reside on the east side of the Continental Divide, but most of the state's water comes from snowmelt on the western slope and, amid growing controversy, is tunneled under the Divide to provide for the Front Range urban corridor.

In the Sierras, there is also a contrast between the north and south ends of the range. Because there is a gap in the Coast Range at the Golden Gate Bridge, where the Sacramento River enters San Francisco Bay, prevailing winds from the Pacific can head straight for the Sierras west of Lake Tahoe. Here, at Donner Summit, annual snowfall averages around 35 feet (10 m) of wet, heavy snow, representing 86 percent of the year's precipitation (Storer and Usinger 1963, p. 13). Moving south, the figure declines steadily.

Sierran winters are, however, relatively mild. Daytime temperatures in winter can climb to 50 to 60° F (5 to 15° C) with some frequency, and nighttime temperatures are not often below zero (−18° C). The resulting daily melting and refreezing cycle throughout the winter is a much greater problem for property owners there than in the Rockies.

Summers in the Sierras are much drier than those in the Rockies. Less than 3 percent of the average annual precipitation comes in summer, whereas more than half falls as snow in January, February, and March. All but a few tundra snowfields will have melted by midsummer.

In contrast, summer showers, severe afternoon cloudbursts, and flash flooding are more common in

the Rockies above 8000 feet (2500 m). The range also receives a lower average snowfall than the Sierras. With less snow, there is less insulation, and so the ground tends to freeze earlier and deeper and to stay frozen longer. Daily temperatures vary within narrower ranges and seldom exceed freezing during the winter.

The Northwest. The mountains of the Pacific Northwest (the Olympics, the Cascades, and the Coast Range in British Columbia) follow the same general patterns yet are unique in some important respects. As in the other western mountain ranges exposed to the prevailing westerlies, there is a sharp decline in precipitation from the west (coastal) side to the east (interior) side of the ranges. Mean annual precipitation at the southwestern flank of the Olympics, for example, is over 120 inches (300 cm) but falls to just 17 inches (42 cm) or less on the northeast side. Similar gradients in air temperature and precipitation mark the progression from north to south, which in the Cascades is a difference of about 10 degrees of latitude.

The unique factor is the moderating influence of marine air. Because of it, the coastal ranges are warmer in winter and cooler in summer than are inland ranges of comparable elevation and latitude. The range within which daily and seasonal temperatures fluctuate is also narrower because of the moist air.

61

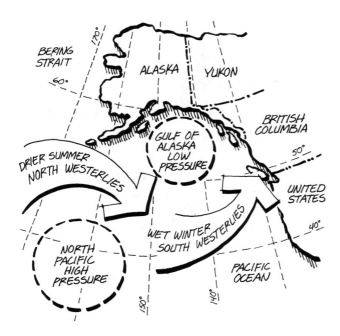

Figure 4-9. *Pacific Northwest seasonal air pressure patterns.*

The singular climate-controlling factor in the northwest ranges is a pair of atmospheric pressure cells over the Pacific (Fig. 4-9). In winter, air masses move in a counterclockwise direction around a low pressure cell over the Gulf of Alaska, bringing moisture-laden, southwesterly storm winds to the ranges. In summer, drier air comes in from the northwest, moving clockwise around a large fair-weather high-pressure system that forms in the North Pacific and displaces the low. Because this air first passes over frigid coastal waters, it cools and forms dense blankets of summer fog when it hits the warmer landmass.

As a result, the number of overcast days is far higher here than in mountains inland or even farther south. Forty percent of the summer days are cloudy in the Washington Cascades, and 84 percent of the winter days are overcast, compared with about 50 percent of winter days in the Cascades of northern California (Whitney 1983, p. 35).

Despite the summer cloud cover, the majority of annual precipitation in these ranges falls as winter snow, a ratio that increases toward the southern end. On the western side, the snow is extremely wet and heavy, which, in view of the rugged topography, gives this area the country's worst record for avalanche accidents. On the eastern side, the snow is drier and lighter, the snowfall levels are lower, and the summers are warmer, clearer, drier, and longer.

The Northeast. The mountains of New England present yet another variation. The ranges here are considerably lower in elevation and gentler in topography than are the western mountains. Mt. Washington in the White Mountains of New Hampshire is the highest peak, rising to just over 6000 feet (1800 m). Consequently, latitude becomes a relatively more important variable. The climate clearly but gradually becomes cooler as one moves northward, with elevation only slightly amplifying the effect.

Proximity to the Atlantic Ocean, the other major controlling factor, makes New England a moist temperate region, with lower average snowfalls than in the inland mountain ranges. Because storms in the Northern Hemisphere move from west to east, however, New England also takes the brunt of frigid arctic air masses moving down from central Canada. Hurricane-force winds from North Atlantic storm systems are common near the mountaintops. Despite their lower elevation, these mountains experience some of the coldest, windiest winter weather in America.

MICROCLIMATE: THE KEY TO COMFORT

Microclimatic variables are among the most important design determinants in mountain development. The intensity of sunlight, ferocity of wind, and extremes of temperature common to mountain areas can preclude a hospitable microclimate in activity areas unless the form and orientation of spaces and the materials of construction have been well chosen. Design decisions on these issues are doubly important, because the way that people perceive the microclimate of a place—whether it is cold or warm, exposed or sheltered—colors the image they retain of its character.

The fundamental concept in microclimatology is the *heat balance:* "the constant interchange between sun, earth and atmosphere, producing small climates that fluctuate markedly on a daily or seasonal cycle" at or near the ground (K. Lynch 1971, p. 65).

The microclimatic elements that are most important to human comfort are radiation, air temperature, air movement, and humidity (Olgyay 1963). In mountain areas, the first three are variables that design can address. There are some predictable relationships between these elements and the physical attributes of a site that can help anticipate microclimatic conditions.

Solar Radiation

At high altitudes, the power of the sun is extraordinary. Indeed, the intense radiation makes

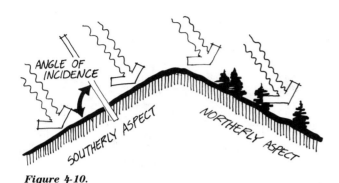

Figure 4-10.

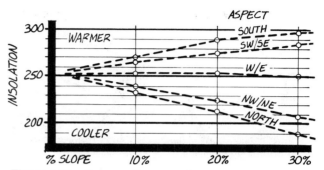

Figure 4-11. *Comparative annual potential solar insolation by slope aspect and gradient. Insolation measured in langleys (×100).*

protected outdoor spaces habitable even in winter, whereas the heat gain inside buildings in south-facing rooms can be excessive when the sun's angle is low. Radiation also causes extreme evaporative stress in newly planted trees and shrubs during wintertime. As well, the sun's intensity accelerates the deterioration, warping, and discoloration of wood and certain other building materials, fading fabric, paint colors, and wood stains both indoors and out. The rates at which deterioration occurs are uneven: Southerly facades and roof pitches are affected to a much greater extent than are other exposures. Radiation levels are intensified by topographical position, slope aspect, and reflective materials.

Glare is a by-product of solar radiation, caused not by an excess of light but by too much contrast between light and dark surfaces in the field of vision, as, for example, the view of a snowy field from inside a dark room. It is more likely to be a problem in the winter.

Microclimatic Effects of Variations in Topography

Topography has perhaps the greatest influence on mountain microclimates, affecting temperatures, air movements, and the amount of snow cover.

The *aspect* of a slope—the compass direction toward which a slope faces—largely determines the amount of solar radiation that reaches it (Fig. 4-10). In the Northern Hemisphere, slopes facing in a southerly direction are warmer than those facing the other way (Fig. 4-11). (In the Southern Hemisphere, these conditions are reversed, with the northern aspects receiving more sun than the south-facing slopes.)

On southern aspects, evaporation rates are higher and soil moisture levels are lower. These slopes accumulate less snow and discharge snowmelt more quickly. Because they are much drier, they may support only grass and shrubs.

Conversely, northern aspects receive less solar radiation, are colder, retain snowpack and moisture

for longer periods, and host denser vegetation (which also increases the wildfire hazard). They have a better revegetation potential but a shorter growing season than warmer aspects.

By the same principle, structures receive substantially different amounts of radiation, depending on their orientation (Fig. 4-12). In the Northern Hemisphere, "south-facing roof surfaces drop their snow or lose it by sublimation more readily than those facing north. Unshielded south-facing windows tend to produce high heat and radiant buildup inside that cannot be overcome by any normal ventilation system" (Mackinlay and Willis, n.d., p. 17).

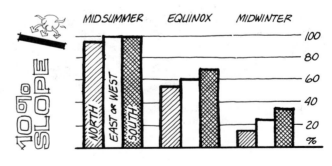

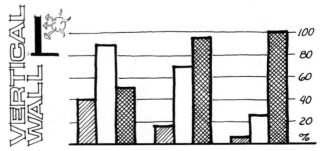

Figure 4-12. *Radiation as a percentage of the possible maximum on a cloudless day at 40° north latitude. Possible maximum for the wall is about half that for the slope. (Data from K. Lynch, 1971, p. 68. Copyright The MIT Press)*

SUMMER **WINTER**

Figure 4-13.

Figure 4-15. Temperature inversions result when a warm air layer traps cold air (and pollutants) in valleys overnight.

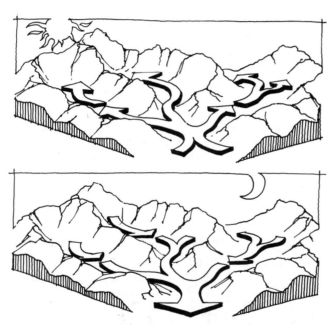

Figure 4-14. Typical valley wind patterns during the day (top) and night (bottom).

Slope gradient compounds this effect. Slopes that are more nearly perpendicular to the sun's incoming rays are warmer than slopes on which the angle of incidence is oblique or acute. The angle changes with the seasons (Fig. 4-13).

Local air movements are products of surface relief interacting with solar radiation (Fig. 4-14). During the daytime, the ground is warmed, and by means of convection, the air in contact with it is warmed as well. This warmed air rises, moving upslope and upvalley generally parallel with the valley axis. After sundown, the soil surface loses its heat through reradiation, and the air in contact with it loses heat through conduction to the soil. The cooled air is denser and flows downslope and downvalley, causing a phenomenon known as *cold air drainage*. At

Beaver Creek near Vail, Colorado, "although these diurnal breezes are light, averaging approximately 2–3 mph. [3–4.5 km/hr.], they are quite consistent, ventilating the valley except for approximately one hour in the morning and one hour in the evening when the winds change directions" (U.S.D.A. Forest Service 1976, p. 29).

Cold air drainage is not an insignificant factor. Some valley floors are measurably colder through the night than the middle slopes above them. In Colorado, the towns of Gunnison (at 7685 ft., or 2340 m) and Fraser (at 8750 ft., or 2670 m), both situated in broad basins, consistently post the lowest nighttime temperatures in the state, even lower than those of nearby ski resorts at higher elevations.

Cold air drainage is also a factor in air quality. In the mountains, the ground surface loses its heat more quickly. Air in contact with the ground is cooled and drains into basins and valleys, setting up temperature inversions (Fig. 4-15). Warm air that retains some of its daytime heat remains suspended over the cooler air, trapping pollutants under it. Because the most intense mountain development commonly takes place in valley bottoms, severe air quality degradation is a serious threat.

In Telluride, Colorado, for example, as in many other mountain valley towns, the air pollution from fireplaces and wood-burning stoves is compounded by temperature inversions on most winter mornings (Fig. 4-16). At Beaver Creek, Colorado, analysis showed that

the critical air drainage period is . . . around fourteen hours a day from evening to early morning. During this time it is expected that pollutants emitted at ground level will not disperse more than 1,000 feet [300 m] above the valley floor, and could possibly be concentrated within the lower 300 feet [90 m], while at the same time be drained out of the valley at a very slow rate. (U.S.D.A. Forest Service 1976, p. 32)

Terrain also contributes to patterns of snow deposition. Local distribution of snow related to

Figure 4-16. *These photos, taken by an automatic camera on the same January day, record a typical inversion pattern in Telluride, Colorado. Photo (bottom), taken at 9:00 A.M., just as the sun crests the ridge, shows cold, smoky air trapped on the valley floor. Photo (top), taken at 2:30 P.M. on the same day, shows that convection currents, fueled by the warming of the side slopes, have broken the inversion and flushed the polluted air from the valley. Photos by Colorado Department of Health, Air Pollution Control Division.*

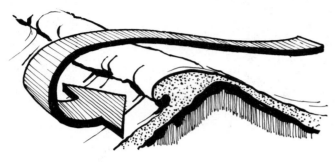

Figure 4-17. *Snow is scoured from the windward sides of ridges, where wind speeds accelerate, and is deposited on the lee side, where velocities are lower.*

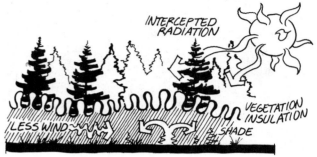

Figure 4-18. *Effects of tree canopy on temperatures.*

small-scale terrain features is just the opposite of the macroclimatic pattern. Continental air masses load the windward sides of mountain ranges as they rise up to cross them, leaving the lee side drier. In contrast, local air movements and storm winds load the lee side with snow (Fig. 4-17). This happens because terrain obstacles exert drag forces that disturb the smooth flow of air close to the surface. The wind in turn exerts a shear stress on the terrain that loosens and erodes snow and minute particles on the windward side.

Airflow meeting a ridge or other obstacle accelerates on the windward side, reaches its maximum velocity at the crest of the ridge, and decelerates as it flows back down the leeward side. Snow is picked up where the wind speed increases and deposited where it decelerates. The sharper the ridge is, the greater the change in wind velocity will be. Doubling the wind speed is estimated to increase the airflow's horizontal transport capacity by a factor of eight (Perla and Martinelli 1976, p. 26).

Microclimatic Effects of Vegetation

Vegetation influences local airflows, temperatures, and the rate of snowmelt. These variables are of considerable importance in design, whether as indications of what to expect on a heavily forested site or what can be done with vegetation to achieve a more favorable microclimate.

In its natural state, forest vegetation reduces wind velocity and solar radiation within the canopy (Fig. 4-18). Low structures and understory plants in a forest thus may receive only 15 to 50 percent of the total incoming solar radiation, depending on the height, density, and foliage character of the trees. Under dense conifers, insolation may be reduced to as little as 1 percent of that in the open (Kittredge 1948, pp. 91–94).

With some exceptions (chaparral, aspen), minimum temperatures under forest cover are higher in both summer and winter than those in the open, as winds are dampened and reradiated energy is retained at night. But in the shade of the forest canopy, maximum air temperatures are lower; temperature ranges are not as wide; soil temperatures are lower; and frost penetrates the ground more deeply (Kittredge 1948, pp. 48–49). On cooler ground, snow is retained longer and does not melt as fast. On slopes, openings in a conifer forest trap cold nighttime air draining downhill (Fig. 4-19), thereby increasing the possibility of frost.

All of these variables need to be considered in site selection, site planning, and building orientation. Mountain buildings and outdoor activity spaces should take advantage of the natural shelter that vegetation provides without sacrificing a beneficial solar orientation.

As a tool for microclimate control, vegetation can be used as a solar filter to reduce glare from snow-covered ground (Fig. 4-20) and as an insulative layer against structures (Fig. 4-21). Selective planting and clearing, when done with regard for the resulting shading, drifting, and wind-scouring patterns, can greatly reduce the problems of pavement icing and the costs of snow removal (see the next section and Chapter 12).

Other typical microclimatic uses of plants, such as channeling airflows through a structure for ventilation or shading the summer sun, are not the central concerns in mountainous regions that they are in areas with much warmer summers. Mountain evenings are cool most of the year, sunny spaces are generally always appreciated, and there is no shortage of natural ventilation. Because the seasonal sun angle is a natural advantage, filtering the sun from south-facing exposures in the summer is a lesser concern than excessive heat gain in the winter. "More solar energy is absorbed through southern windows in the winter, when it is needed, than in the summer when it is not" (Steadman 1975, p. 38).

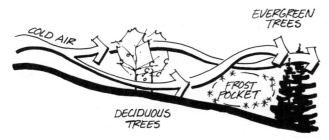

Figure 4-19.

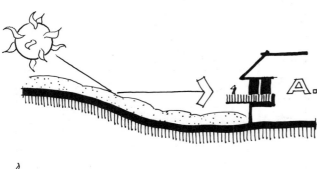

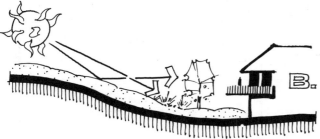

Figure 4-20. *Low sun angles reflected off snow-covered slopes increase the potential for wintertime glare (a), but strategic planting can reduce the problem (b).*

Figure 4-21. *Conifers near structures create a dead-air space that reduces heat loss.*

Wind and Wind Control

Windchill Factor. Wind is most significant in regard to the heat loss it causes. A structure exposed to the full velocity of winter storm winds will have abnormally high heating requirements. For example, when a 12-mile-per-hour (20 km/hr.) wind at 32 degrees F (0° C) is reduced to 3 miles per hour (5 km/hr.) before it strikes a house, fuel consumption may be halved (K. Lynch 1971, p. 67). Reducing a structure's heat load thus is not a function of air temperature but of wind velocity.

A person exposed to winter winds feels what is known as the *windchill factor*, or the reduction of the effective air temperature because of wind (Fig. 4-22). At 10 degrees F (−12° C), a 15-mile-per-hour (25 km/hr.) wind will lower the effective temperature to −20 degrees F (−28° C). When people are damp from precipitation or exertion, the net effect is more severe because they experience evaporative cooling as well.

Windbreaks. Although the flow of large air masses cannot be altered, the velocities of local air movements can be controlled to a certain extent by the arrangement of shelters and windbreaks made of trees, shrubs, earth forms, or structures.

Any barrier diverts air currents upward, creating an area of localized turbulence above and slightly beyond it and an area of relative calm near the ground. Because of this, the greatest protection from a windbreak is in the middle just beyond its leeward side. A rough rule of thumb is that wind velocity can be cut in half inside a distance equal to about ten times the height of the barrier (Fig. 4-23). When the air is compressed—as it passes over a ridge, around the ends of a barrier, through gaps, or under lower tree branches—wind speeds increase over those of the open field.

The amount of turbulence created by a windbreak and its effect on air speeds depend on the initial wind velocity and the height, density, and windward shape of the barrier. Solid barriers are less efficient than partially open ones, which create more turbulence and thus cause a greater decrease in velocity. The more penetrable the windbreak is, the farther beyond it the sheltered zone will extend (Robinette 1977, p. 30). The optimal density for a windbreak is around 50 to 60 percent. Although a barrier of greater density may dampen wind velocity more in the area immediately in its lee, the zone of effective shelter downwind is smaller (Fig. 4-24). The beneficial effects of any windbreak improve as the wind velocities increase.

The effectiveness of trees as windbreaks depends on the foliage density; spacing in the forest; width, height, and length of the forest; and distance from the

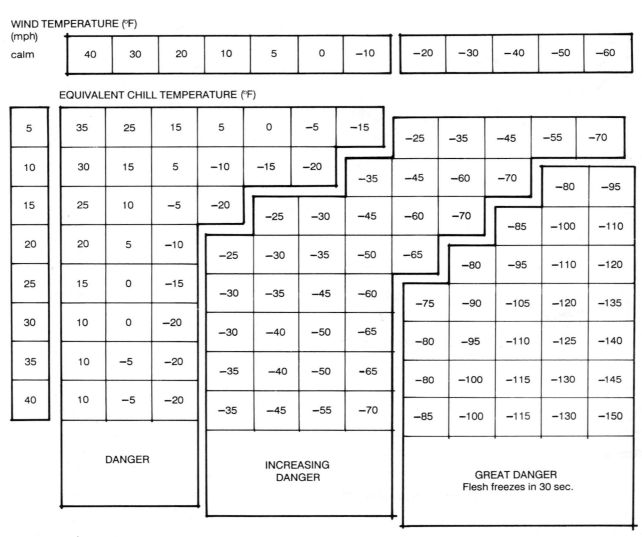

Figure 4-22. *The cooling effect of wind on air temperature is called the windchill factor.*

ground to the lowest branches. The taller the trees, the more rows will be required for effective protection, for older trees grow more open and their lower branches are farther from the ground. The denser the forest, the more effective the windbreak will be. Behind a coniferous forest, wind velocity can be cut to about 20 percent of normal, undisturbed velocity, whereas deciduous trees in winter reduce it only to 50 percent. The most effective planted windbreak in all seasons is one of mixed tree and shrub species and mixed sizes.

Snowdrifting. Every winter, millions of dollars are spent clearing snowdrifts and repairing structural damage caused by imbalanced snow loading on roofs. Much of this expense might be saved if snowdrifting

patterns were projected early in the design process.

Snowdrifts form where airflow obstructions reduce wind velocity. Drifts can be anticipated on the leeward side of structures, roof ridges, walls, fences, vegetation, and prominent landform features (Fig. 4-25). New landforms, buildings, and planting masses will alter windflows on a site, with sometimes unexpected consequences. The key to reducing drifting where it is not wanted is to manage local windflows.

The size of a snowdrift is a function of the general direction and speed of winds during and after snowfall, as well as the size, shape, and density of the obstruction. For example, porous barriers like snow fences lower the wind velocity more and distribute snow more evenly for a greater distance beyond the

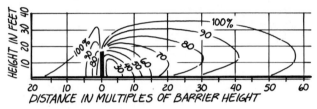

HORIZONTAL PLANE

WIND DIRECTION ⟶

VERTICAL PLANE

Figure 4-23. Rings indicate the reduction in wind velocity around a windbreak, expressed as a percentage of undisturbed air speed.

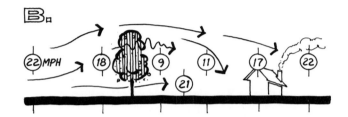

Figure 4-24. Effectiveness of a dense conifer windbreak (a) compared with a deciduous windbreak (b).

Figure 4-25. Heavy snowdrifts around buildings at the base of Mammoth Mountain Ski Area, California, clearly show the direction of prevailing storm winds. Photo by Tom Johnston, Mammoth/June Ski Resort.

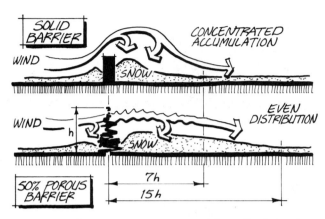

Figure 4-26. *Generalized "snow catch" profiles behind a solid wall and a porous conifer screen, expressed in multiples of barrier height (h).*

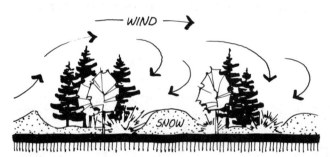

Figure 4-27. *The most effective natural snow fence contains a mixture of plant species.*

Figure 4-28. *The open channel water flume uses water flow to simulate the natural action of wind on snow particles. Photo by Barry Scrimgeour, RWDI, Guelph, Ontario, Canada.*

windbreak than solid walls do (Fig. 4-26). Solid barriers produce drifts on both the windward and leeward sides.

Most of the snow that accumulates in drifts gets there not directly by snowfall, but by the process of *saltation*, in which wind-driven snow particles bounce along the surface in short hops until they arrive at a place of reduced wind velocity. Snow is eroded in any wind over about 8 miles per hour (13 km/hr.). The amount of snow the wind can carry depends on the wind velocity and the height above the ground; 95 percent is carried within 1 foot (30 cm) of the ground (Canadian National Research Council 1964, p. 2). Even the standard 3.5-foot (1 m) slatted snow fence can cause the wind to drop most of its load before it reaches a protected area.

A properly designed natural windbreak is an effective means to reduce snowdrift area as long as it is composed of more than just tall trees. That is, dense thickets of shrubs and ground covers within the windbreak are needed in order to trap more snow within a narrower band on the lee side (Fig. 4-27). Wall placement, roof configuration, structural wind deflectors, and planting can also be designed to

channel airflows so that snow is scoured from areas that must remain clear. The same tools can be used to cause drifts where they are desired for outdoor recreation or snow storage.

Although a perfect simulation of snowdrifting is not possible, the use of models in conjunction with field observations is becoming part of the design process for larger projects in northern climates. Where snowfall is heavy, one of the primary tasks in siting a building is to orient it so that snow will not accumulate against critical areas of the facade. Snow study models, in either wind tunnels or water flumes, can assist in analyzing alternative design concepts. They can simulate many aspects of snow deposition, snowdrifting, and scouring and suggest modifications in site plans and details that can improve snowdrifting patterns.

A wind tunnel is useful in determining wind speed distribution, from which drift patterns can be inferred, but it cannot accurately replicate saltation on such a reduced scale (Irwin and Williams 1983). In a water flume (Fig. 4-28), water flowing around a building model represents the wind, and sand grains represent snow particles. The flume has proved to be a more useful predictive tool than the wind tunnel, because observers can see snowdrift patterns and make simple changes right on the model (Fig. 4-29).

Models have also been used to develop guidelines for roof-mounted solar collectors (Irwin and Williams 1981). Rooftop collectors can generate considerably higher snow loads than those for which a roof was designed, especially if it was originally assumed that the snow on the roof would be scoured away by the wind.

Figure 4-29. (top) Snowdrift study model in the water flume with suggested landscaping in place shows drifting in front of several major entries. (bottom) When the test is run again using a modified landscaping scheme, drifting patterns have changed, and problem areas are left clear. Photos by RWDI, Guelph, Ontario.

Energy Efficiency and Properties of Materials

In a climate in which protection from the cold is essential, the capacity of building materials to store the heat they receive and to release it slowly is an important consideration in microclimate control. In both passive solar applications and the design of outdoor spaces where warmth and rapid snowmelt are sought, these qualities can contribute significantly to human comfort.

If warmth is the object of microclimate control, heat exchange is the process. Heat is transferred by means of radiation, conduction, and convection, but three characteristics of materials—albedo, conductivity, and heat capacity—help determine how efficiently this is done.

Albedo. *Albedo* refers to reflectivity and governs how much heat is absorbed through the surface of a mass. A surface with a high albedo is very reflective and thus absorbs little radiant energy. One with a low albedo absorbs far more energy. Clearly, one would not select a material with a high albedo for a passive solar thermal storage wall or for any surface that would reflect sunlight into active-use areas.

Dark-colored or wet surfaces have lower albedos than light-colored or dry surfaces (Table 4-2). Thus, air in contact with snow, lighter ground, or surfaces with higher albedos is not warmed as much as air near dark soil. Combined with high altitude and intense sunlight, a high albedo can melt snow more

rapidly and cause unbearable glare. It can alter the internal heat balance of any structure receiving reflected radiation through windows. If the exterior materials of a structure have a high albedo, the interior temperatures will be reduced.

Conductivity. *Conductivity* is the ease with which heat (or sound) passes through a material, once it has penetrated its surface. Heat moves rapidly through materials with high conductivity and slowly through those with low conductivity. This principle is the basis for insulation, which requires materials of low conductivity.

Fresh snow, still air, dry sandy soil, and kiln-dried lumber are lower in conductivity (and therefore are better insulators) than wet soil, humus, ice, and granite. The conductivity of natural materials decreases as they dry out and lose density.

When low albedo combines with high conductivity on the ground surface, a milder, more consistent microclimate can be expected, for heat is quickly transferred and stored and then released quickly when the temperature drops. This can be an advantage in mountain structures and public spaces. In contrast, when surface materials are reflective (high albedo) and of low conductivity, they are of little value in heat gain or storage. The microclimate over ground plane materials with these qualities, like snow, tends to be more extreme: hot in the sun and colder at night.

Heat Capacity. The amount of heat that an object can absorb is measured by its *heat capacity*, or the amount of heat that must be transferred to a unit mass of material to raise its temperature by 1 degree. Expressed in another way, it is the amount of heat energy that a unit mass can absorb for each added degree of temperature.

The ability to absorb heat is often expressed in terms of *specific heat*, the ratio of the heat capacity of any mass compared with that of water. This ratio correlates the amount of heat needed to raise the temperature of a unit mass by 1 degree (heat capacity) with the heat needed to raise the temperature of an equal mass of water by 1 degree.[1] Water has a specific heat of one. (For most engineering purposes and most materials, heat capacity may be assumed to be numerically equal to the specific heat.)

Table 4-2 Albedos of Some Common Materials (in order of decreasing reflectivity)

Material	Reflectivity
Mirror	1.0
Aluminum	.85
Fresh snow	.80 to .85
Clouds	.60 to .90
White paint	.71
Old snow	.42 to .70
Wood	.40
Meadow	.30
Cement	.29
Red brick	.27
Aspen forest	.15 to .18
Asphalt	.15
Conifer forest	.12
Water surface	.08
Glass	.03
Matte black	.0

[1]The amount of heat can be measured in either British thermal units (BTUs) or calories. One BTU equals the amount of heat needed to raise the temperature of 1 pound of water by 1 degree Fahrenheit, whereas 1 calorie equals the heat needed to raise 1 gram of water by 1 degree centigrade.

The sound of the freezing of the snow over the land
seemed to roar deep into the earth.
              —*Yasunari Kawabata,* Snow Country

Table 4-3 Specific Heat Ratios of Common Materials

Material	Capacity to Absorb Heat (compared with water)
Brass	.09
Glass	.10
Steel	.11
Rocks, marble	.18 to .20
Cement, concrete	.156 to .20
Aluminum	.21
Clay, brick	.22
Wood	.42 to .6
Moist loam	.42
Organic matter	.45
Cork	.485
Water	1.0

Most natural materials have higher specific heats than do manufactured materials (Table 4-3). Materials with high specific heats, like wood, absorb more heat energy for each degree of increase in temperature than do those, like metal or glass, with low specific heats. Metals and glass feel hotter than wood of the same temperature because they require less heat to reach a high temperature and because, being high in conductivity, they release their heat more rapidly. It is generally true, though not always, that the lower the specific heat, the higher the conductivity of a material will be.

A material's ability to store the heat it absorbs is a function of its specific heat, together with its conductivity and its total mass. That is, a large object with high specific heat whose surface allows heat flow to penetrate (low albedo) can absorb large amounts of heat over a long period of time. Thick paving stones and massive adobe walls, for example, absorb and hold more radiant heat during the day than thin tiles and less substantial walls. Being of low conductivity and larger mass, they absorb heat more slowly, staying cooler during the hottest part of the day and then releasing their stored energy over a longer interval. Such materials are important to thermally efficient design.

SNOW: THE CHIEF PROTAGONIST

Snow is a wily adversary in the alpine environment. It can cause serious hazards and structural problems on any site if its unique properties are not taken into account. Among the characteristics of snow that have implications for design are the following:

Weight. From the time it begins to fall until the time it melts away, snow is constantly changing as a result of gravity, wind, melting, and recrystallization (Fig. 4-30). When it first falls in the deep winter months, snow is loose, very cold, relatively dry, and low in density, weighing as little as 2 or 3 pounds per cubic foot. Almost immediately, though, it begins to transform into coarse grains and to increase in density. By spring, a snowpack 1 to 2 feet deep may weigh around 20 pounds per cubic foot, and a deep pack may tip the scales at up to 60 pounds per cubic

Figures 4-30. *Microscopic photographs of snow particles: (left) delicate crystals of very new snow; (right) older snow particles undergoing melt-freeze metamorphism have become rounded and clumped. Photos by Richard Sommerfeld, U.S.D.A. Forest Service, and Ed LaChapelle.*

foot (Canadian National Research Council 1964, p. 22). Even if the temperature stays below freezing, newly fallen snow, 90 percent of which is entrapped air, will lose 30 percent of this air by bonding of the crystals within the first day or two (Mackinlay and Willis, n.d., p. 2).

Compressive Strength. The strength of snow varies widely according to its density, the degree of bonding between grains, the temperature, the wind velocity, and the past weather. One thing is sure, however: Compacted snow gains in strength. Newly fallen snow may have a compressive strength of only .01 to 1.5 pounds per square inch, whereas late spring snow may support .3 to 300 psi of pressure (Canadian National Research Council, 1964, p. 2). This means that compacted snow can carry foot traffic and, under some conditions, even trucks until it begins to melt.

Instability on Slopes. As new layers of snow are deposited, the upper surface is weathered by radiation, rain, and wind. In contrast, the undersurface is warmed only slightly by ground heat (but a lot if on a warm roof), and the middle is compressed and changed to granules by means of percolation and diffusing water vapor. The result of this series of transformations is a stratified pack of alternating hard and soft layers (Fig. 4-31). The hard layers become impermeable to percolating meltwater, which spreads horizontally and lubricates the attachment between layers (Perla and Martinelli 1976, p. 51). The resulting tendency to shear and slip along these planes can be as dangerous on a high roof as on a known avalanche track.

Snowmelt. A melting snowpack cannot release runoff until it is *primed*, or *ripe*, that is, until its liquid water–holding capacity has been reached. This point is usually between 2 and 8 percent water content by volume (Dunne and Leopold 1978, p. 470), which is normally not reached until the spring, although it can be earlier with unseasonably warm weather. Until the snowpack is ripe, even rain cannot cause runoff; it simply percolates into the pack, often increasing its tendency to slide.

In built-up areas, snowmelt is affected by localized heat sources. It can be accelerated or retarded depending on color, reflectivity, albedo, the specific heat of building and paving materials, exposure to wind and sun, shading by trees or topography, and convection from structures.

Snow Creep. Snow creeps as readily as soil does under the pull of gravity and on any inclined plane. How fast it creeps depends on slope gradient, snow depth, air temperature, the water content of the snow, and the roughness of the ground surface. Snow creep can cause serious structural damage to anything standing upright. It can buckle building walls; displace foundations; break power poles, transmission towers, and guy wires; shear off any protrusions on roofs, including chimneys and vents; and upend shallow-rooted trees (Fig. 4-32). The lateral force of creeping snow can be greatly magnified in regions subject to sudden thaws or winter rains, like the Cascades. Under these conditions, large ice lenses can form within the snowpack and give it the unrelenting power of a glacier (Ellis 1984, p. 102).

Adhesive Tendency. Snow and ice crystals have tremendous adhesive power under the right conditions. Wind-driven, they can adhere to many metals, as well as asphalt, concrete, and stone, causing problems of visibility and mobility. Some of these materials can be coated to resist adhesion, as, for example, on signs, light fixtures, railings, and ramps.

Slickness. The most hazardous characteristic of snow or ice is its low *friction coefficient*, or *drag force*. For example, asphalt and concrete roadways, when dry, exert a drag force on a tire of .55 to 1.0. The coefficient drops a little, to .35, for a tire on sanded ice or snow and still further, to .25, for a tire on crunchy, subzero snow. On wet ice, there is practically no drag at all; the coefficient is .05. The distance required to stop an auto on ice or packed snow is three to ten times greater than that on dry paving, and on glazed ice it may be impossible.

Ice Damming. Another troublesome occurrence related to snow is *ice damming*, the blockage of runoff by an obstruction of ice. It is one of the primary problems with structures in snow country. An ice dam can collapse roof overhangs, force leaks in roofs and sidewalls, and create ice ponds on what would otherwise be a well-drained site.

The most common ice dam is at the building eaves, where meltwater running under the snow on the roof encounters cold air at the edge of the roof and freezes (Fig. 4-33). Melting can be caused by above-freezing daytime temperatures (as in the Sierras) or by interior building heat (Fig. 4-34). Ice dams can be lethal: an ice dam 1 foot thick (.3 m) on a building 40 feet long (12.2 m) weighs over a ton (900 kg).

Ice damming can also occur on decks, outside patios, or any other place where melted snow contacts freezing air. The lower front edge of a plowed snowbank, for example, can function like an ice dam, preventing water from flowing as intended to drains and gutters (see Fig. 12-6). If it occurs along a sidewalk, it can impede pedestrian circulation.

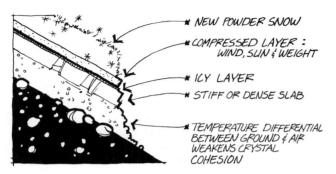

Figure 4-31. *Generalized cross section of layered snowpack.*

Figure 4-32.

Figure 4-33. *The formation of an ice dam at the edge of a roof.*

Figure 4-34. *Lethal ice dam on a poorly insulated building.*

Avalanches. The most devastating and sudden of the hazards of a mountain winter, *avalanches* are a mass of snow, sometimes mixed with rock, ice, soil, and timber, moving rapidly downhill (Fig. 4-35). They may break away in slabs or in a flume of loose powder snow. Although most avalanches occur in areas remote from development, some have done considerable damage to mountain communities.

Avalanche zones are identified in three parts: the *starting zone*, where unstable snow breaks away; the *track*, which is usually the most visible mark on the landscape; and the *runout zone*, where the snow and

Figure 4-35. *Dry powder avalanche above Colorado Highway 110 north of Silverton. Photo by Richard Armstrong.*

hazardous. Avalanches on slopes under 30 degrees are much less common, unless the snow is unusually unstable because of a prolonged warming trend, a heavy snowfall in a short period, or extreme wind conditions (Martinelli 1974, p. 5).

These gradients, however, apply only to the starting zone. The track gradient is not necessarily as steep, with 25 to 35 degrees being common. The runout zone can be gentle or even flat. Indeed, large avalanches have been known to cross a valley floor and run up the other side for some distance.

In addition to the 30- to 45-degree gradient, several other conditions may signal avalanche-prone areas. Avalanches are more likely on lee slopes than on windward slopes because the wind will load more snow there. They are more likely on grass-covered slopes than on brush-covered slopes because grass provides less surface resistance. Likewise, forest cover tends to reduce avalanche danger. Finally, avalanches are more likely on shaded north-facing slopes than on sunny south-facing slopes because the snow stays loose and unstable longer in the shade. Extensive site modification, major grading, or large-scale tree removal can turn a safe area into a hazard zone.

In the identification of potential avalanche paths, some clues are clearly visible. Vertical swaths of grass or aspen through conifer forests usually mark a track. The accumulation of timber and rock debris on lower slopes is indicative of a runout zone, as are fresh scars and broken limbs on standing trees. In the

debris stop (Fig. 4-36). Some experts also include the *airblast zone*, which is the area of damage from the turbulent winds accompanying fast powder avalanches. This zone is usually near the lower track or the runout zone and may extend across the valley.

To estimate accurately the hazard in suspected avalanche areas, one must consider the entire path. The extent of the runout zone, in particular, has occasionally been underestimated, and development has been allowed to proceed in areas mistakenly thought to be safe.

Avalanche danger can generally be assumed for any slope, timbered or not, that has a gradient between 30 and 45 degrees (Fig. 4-37). Anything steeper will rarely accumulate enough snow to be

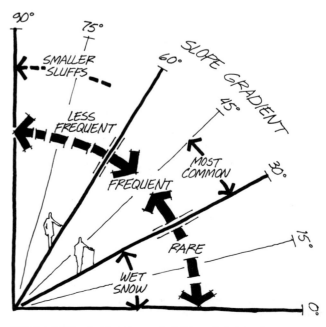

Figure 4-37. *Avalanche probability related to slope gradient.*

Figure 4-36. *Avalanche tracks near Red Mountain Pass (elevation 11,300 ft., 3440 m) above Highway 550 between Ouray and Silverton, Colorado. Photo by Richard Armstrong.*

winter, one can identify fracture lines or faces at the top of the start zone where unstable snow has broken away as a slab. Loose powder avalanches will show as a clean swath through old dirtied snow.

Much of the evidence of avalanche activity is more subtle, however, and requires that a snow specialist survey any mountain site intended for development. In addition to private consultants, help in studying avalanche probabilities for specific areas can be sought from the U.S.D.A. Forest Service's district office, local and state land-planning agencies, state geological surveys, and departments of environmental

sciences, forestry, geography, or geophysical engineering at universities in mountain regions.

Among the various agencies that compile statistical information and issue predictions on avalanche occurrences, the largest are the Colorado Avalanche Information Center in Denver, a quasi-state facility that covers the Central Rockies, and its counterparts in Salt Lake City, covering the Wasatch Range, and in Seattle, covering the Cascades. Smaller centers in Jackson Hole, Sun Valley, Lake Tahoe, Mammoth, and Banff provide avalanche information for more localized areas.

DESIGN GUIDELINES

Site Selection

1. Select a comparatively warm and sunny site, protected from severe wind exposure and cold airflows. Use sun charts and topographical maps to plot seasonal shading patterns, and avoid areas in prolonged winter shade (Fig. 4-38).

2. Keep all structures and primary public spaces out of known or probable avalanche zones. Under most circumstances, mitigating such hazards by engineering structures to withstand the force of an avalanche is the least desirable option and is not recommended.[2]

3. Among prospective sites that suit the development program, select the one lowest in elevation if they are equal in other respects.

4. Avoid narrow, "dead-end" valleys for high-density plans, or reduce densities and auto access to protect air quality.

5. If designing a ski village, choose a site near the ski slopes, but resist the temptation to site the primary high-density village core immediately adjacent to the lifts. A site in perpetual winter shade, jeopardizing both access and pedestrian usage, can never be the best solution.

6. Be aware that at high altitudes the best sites for south-aspect living and solar heating are also the best sites for wildlife in high-stress periods of winter and spring. Thus where a site provides critical winter range and forage, consider other possibilities.

Site Planning and Grading

1. Recognize that responding to the extreme winter climate must be the first priority in mountain design, even though the optimal siting and orientation of buildings for winter may not be the ideal response for summer. To design for winter, the main concerns are orienting to the sun, staying out of areas in perpetual winter shade, reducing exposure to wind, protecting from dangers of avalanche and ice, and facilitating circulation and snow removal.

2. Consider a compact site plan to reduce exposure to the elements, and cluster higher densities in and near the core. Encourage public transportation systems as an alternative to automobiles to link areas beyond walking distance.

3. When designing outdoor spaces and circulation, always consider how the snow will be

Figure 4-38.

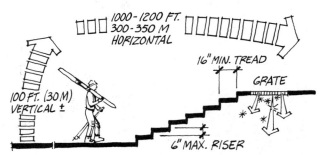

Figure 4-39.

removed, where it can be stored until it melts, and where the meltwater will go. Pile snow where it will melt quickly in the spring, where meltwater runoff can infiltrate the soil, and where the piles will not interfere with circulation or drainage (see Chapter 12).

4. Under high-altitude conditions, control the vertical and horizontal distances that people have to walk outdoors between major destinations (Fig. 4-39). In winter particularly, the acceptable walking range for most people in ski boots is probably not more than 1000 to 1200 feet (300 to 350 m) on the level and around 100 feet (30 m) of vertical change.

5. Plot sun and shadow patterns on proposed streets and building masses in the earliest stages of site planning, and use these diagrams to compare design alternatives. Try to avoid having either side of major pedestrian streets in constant winter shade.

6. Site and design outdoor spaces and pedestrian circulation areas for maximum sun and protection from wind and glare (Fig. 4-40).

[2]See Armstrong and Williams 1986, pp. 162–187, on avalanche hazard zoning, planning, and litigation. See Perla and Martinelli 1976, pp. 149–176, on methods for protecting communities and roads.

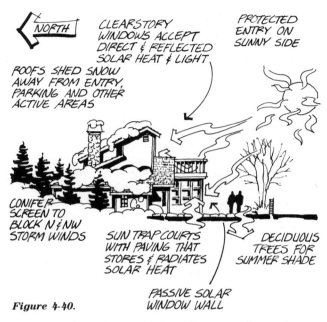

NORTH

CLEARSTORY WINDOWS ACCEPT DIRECT & REFLECTED SOLAR HEAT & LIGHT

PROTECTED ENTRY ON SUNNY SIDE

ROOFS SHED SNOW AWAY FROM ENTRY, PARKING AND OTHER ACTIVE AREAS

CONIFER SCREEN TO BLOCK N & NW STORM WINDS

SUN TRAP COURTS WITH PAVING THAT STORES & RADIATES SOLAR HEAT

DECIDUOUS TREES FOR SUMMER SHADE

PASSIVE SOLAR WINDOW WALL

Figure 4-40.

7. To reduce the wind's heat-draining effect, take advantage of existing forest cover for windbreaks, carefully shape regraded land, use structures and vegetation to block and redirect the wind, and bunker north-facing exposures. Lay out the main circulation to avoid funneling wind down paths and streets. Do not depend on newly planted trees for effective wind screening.

8. Identify areas where snowdrifting and ice accumulation will be heavy after construction. Use windbreaks and manipulate building orientation to control drifting in these areas (Fig. 4-41), or locate building entries, garage entries, and main circulation routes elsewhere.

9. Recognize that drainage systems are one of the toughest site-planning tasks in a mountain community. The culprit is density: the tight arrangement of buildings, walkways, streets, and driveways. The tighter the spaces, the harder it will be to achieve a reliable system. Surface drainage is preferred but is not always possible. Subsurface drain pipes and catch basins tend to freeze and clog up with sediment from sanded and cindered pavements.

In a mountain climate, spring meltwater is slush, not just water. To get slush-laden water to flow, pavements should be canted at a 2 percent minimum, even though this gradient is visible. It is possible to combine flatter grades with heat coils in sand under the pavement or electrical snowmelt systems, but these methods are not durable and require costly maintenance. Cracks in the paving may sever electrical connections, and water can corrode pipes and coils.

Where subsurface drains must be used, drop water quickly below the frost line. Exaggerate the size of drain grates, and make sure they can be removed to permit easy cleaning. Consider running wires down drainpipes and heating the drains to help keep them open. In the grading, provide for overflow surface drainage in case the subsurface system backs up. Do not rely on french drains, for they get covered with snow and freeze up.

In any drainage plan, identify locations for snow storage where it will not block drains and dam meltwater runoff (Fig. 4-42). Take meltwater off paved surfaces as quickly as possible. Do not drain toward the center of a paved space or surround it with walls or curbs, for it will become a skating rink at night if the drains freeze (Fig. 4-43). Crown pavements toward gutters and swales away from pedestrian pathways, entries, and garages.

10. Longitudinal gradients (parallel to the length) of a walk or road should not exceed 5 to 7 percent, less if possible in heavily shaded areas. Use steps to avoid steeper grades on walkways. Give the walks a minimum cross pitch of around 2 percent (¼ in. per ft.) (Fig. 4-44). To minimize icing and accelerate snowmelt, locate important walkways and intersections where they will not be in prolonged shade.

11. For roads outside the core where higher speeds are anticipated, consider superelevating roadway curves to reduce the danger of skidding. Where

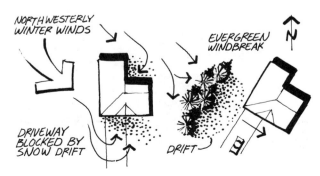

NORTHWESTERLY WINTER WINDS

EVERGREEN WINDBREAK

N

DRIVEWAY BLOCKED BY SNOW DRIFT

DRIFT

Figure 4-41.

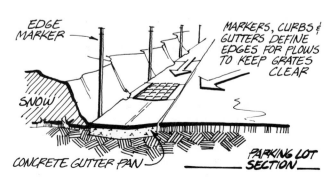

EDGE MARKER

MARKERS, CURBS & GUTTERS DEFINE EDGES FOR PLOWS TO KEEP GRATES CLEAR

SNOW

CONCRETE GUTTER PAN

PARKING LOT SECTION

Figure 4-42.

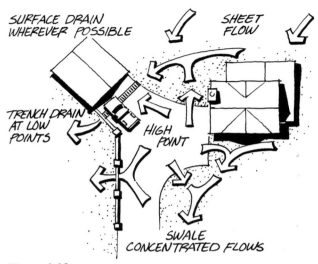

Figure 4-43.

Figure 4-44.

rights-of-way permit, pull drainage ditches away from roadway edges and avoid outward-sloping shoulders, as these can be hazardous in winter.

12. Avoid planting new trees where their shade will cause icing of roadways or where they will be in the way of snow plowing or storage.

Structures and Site Improvements

1. Maximize energy efficiency of structures. Orient and design buildings to capitalize on the available solar radiation for passive and active solar heating in winter. Use materials that absorb heat and re-release it slowly. Use only energy-efficient fireplaces that can recirculate warm air. (Do not make structures airtight, as natural venting is needed for efficient fireplace combustion.)

Insulate structures well. Adding insulation to the roof will keep the exterior surface of the roof colder and retain snow for additional insulation value,

provided the roof pitch is not too steep or the surface too slick. Insulation should have a vapor barrier on the warm side so that moisture cannot permeate the layer and rot wooden structural members.

Restrict window areas and avoid doors on north sides. Windows should be double or triple glazed. Building entries should have vestibules, double doors (or triple sets for heavily used public entries), glazed entry porches, or other weather breaks that will prevent the loss of warm air through the door.

2. Choose a roofing system for structures that discourages ice damming and icicle formation at the eave line. The appropriate roof configuration is not the same for all mountain areas, so ask locals what works. Flat roofs work well in many climates, but the roof drain must be kept warm to keep the system from freezing up.

If the roof is pitched, the recommended slope is 4 in 12 or more (not less than 5 in 12 for shake or shingle roofs). Simple pitched roofs might incorporate a "cold roof" system, which is a double roof with a cold air gap between the outer roof and the insulated inner roof to prevent melting (Fig. 4-45). "Warm roof" systems intentionally use building heat to melt snow and prevent ice buildup. Although there is no consensus on how well either roof works, it is generally agreed that complex roof configurations with lots of valleys and troughs are a sure prescription for leaks.

After exceptionally heavy snowfall, any roof,

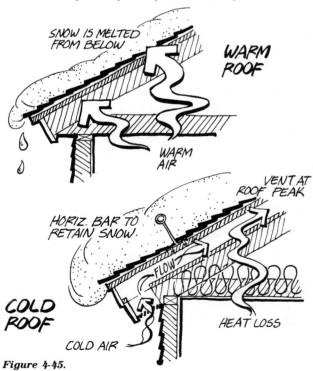

Figure 4-45.

pitched or flat, that retains snow may have to be cleared of snow by hand. On pitched roofs, it is worth including a detail to secure safety cables for maintenance workers.

3. Anticipate how snow will shed from roofs and on what it will land (Fig. 4-46). Roof pitches and overhangs have critical implications for streets, outdoor spaces, and landscaping. As a general rule, roofs should not be inclined toward main pedestrian paths or entries. Because this is not always possible in the urban core of mountain communities, consider protective features such as arcades, loggias, and roof dormers (Fig. 4-47). At the least, extend rooflines over building entries and balconies.

Snow fences on roofs are widely used to retain snow on a pitch that inclines toward a public area. These are reliable only if they are as sturdy as a highway guardrail and about as tall as the maximum seasonal snowpack. If they are placed only at the eaves, they may fail under the tremendous lateral pressure from snow creep and compression of the snowpack. To alleviate the pressure, rails should also be placed near the ridge, which is analogous to the start zone of an avalanche.

4. Incorporate elements into the design of outdoor spaces that will extend their period of use in colder seasons. To trap radiation, this requires, at the least, windscreens and a southerly orientation, out of the shade of buildings. Also helpful are temporary overhead canopies to protect against rain and glare, outdoor radiant heating elements where spaces are already relatively protected, and materials that absorb and hold heat.

5. Select durable paving materials of low porosity and high density. With a 9000 psi rating (compared with 2500 to 3000 psi for concrete), unit pavers on sand or concrete slab have proved to be the most durable in many mountain applications.

Under freeze–thaw conditions, concrete always spalls and cracks. By admitting water, this initiates a spiraling process of disintegration. Spalling occurs wherever water is allowed to stand on the pavement, and so positive drainage is essential. Cracks almost never follow the construction joints. To be effective, troweled joints, normally about ¼ in. deep, need to be roughly one-third the thickness of the slab and then filled with backer rods or asphalt. Some sealers are also helpful in forestalling the inevitable.

Exposed aggregate often spalls down to the level of larger stones, so it is best to keep the aggregate as close to the surface as possible. Troweling concrete to get a smoother surface is not a solution, as it brings water to the surface and reduces the concrete's resistance to air moisture.

6. To reduce icing on bridges, consider a box design with dead-air pockets under the pavement.

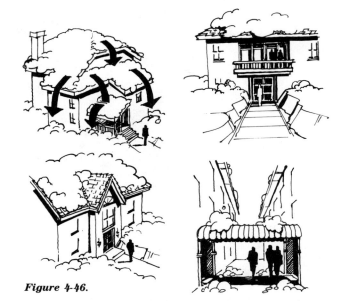

Figure 4-46.

Figure 4-47. Continuous loggias along the street protect pedestrians from rain and snow in Whistler, British Columbia.

7. Recognize that landscape features at ground level that are not visible under the snow will lose any battle with snowplows. Elements that define edges and corners should be exaggerated in scale or mass and made of durable materials, like boulders.

To reduce repair costs, it may be desirable to make some outdoor furnishings and summer signage removable in winter.

8. On slopes, roofs, and in areas of especially heavy snowfall, consider measures to reduce damage from snow creep. To slow its movement, leave natural obstructions, like ledges, stumps, trees, and large boulders, when regrading. To counter the force of snow creep, design heavier, deeper, monolithic foundations and increase the strength of upright elements. To reduce surface friction, try measures

Figure 4-48. *New snow transforms the landscape into an uncommon scene.*

that melt the snow or ease its flow around objects, like heat tapes in rigid conduit or other heat sources on the uphill side of structures; use dark, glossy paints to absorb heat; keep uphill surfaces smooth; use wedge-shaped or rounded forms on uphill sides; and avoid unnecessary protuberances, like vents, chimneys, ladders, brackets, and small corners, on uphill facades.

9. Consider ways to reduce wintertime glare: selection of darker or more textured materials and colors; careful location of light-colored and reflective surfaces with respect to winter sun angles and activity areas inside and out; sizing, positioning, and glazing of windows; and the placement of trees to filter light.

Figure 4-49. *Design guidelines for night lighting at Beaver Creek, Colorado. Beaver Creek Resort Company Design Regulations (1979).*

10. Anticipate the impacts of snow on signage. Essential elements in the signage and information system for the community must be high enough that they can be seen over snowbanks. Wintertime visibility problems suggest increasing the size of key directional signs, lighting them, using materials that resist adhesion, using large cut-out letters, or highlighting the lettering by contrasts in texture or relief. When there is some latitude, locate signs in the sunniest exposures. Important roadway signs should be placed to permit ample time to stop or turn on slick streets.

11. Bury water and sewer lines beneath the frost line.

12. When designing landscape forms, fountains, and pools, consider the potential for added interest when they are transformed by newly fallen snow and ice (Fig. 4-48).

13. In view of the short winter days, take care with night lighting (Fig. 4-49). Lighting that illuminates falling snow is memorable, and warm-colored light is preferable to blue-white light, which makes everything look even colder than it is.

14. Use uncomplicated construction techniques and off-site preassembly of components when possible in order to complete work within the short construction season.

For more guidelines on coping with ice and snow, refer to Chapter 12; on planting, see Chapter 7.

REFERENCES

Armstrong, Betsy, and Knox Williams. 1986. *The Avalanche Book*. Golden, Colo.: Fulcrum.

Beaver Creek Resort Co. 1979. Design regulations— The village. Avon, Colo.

Canadian National Research Council, Subcommittee on Snow and Ice. 1964. Snow removal and ice control. Proceedings of a conference, technical memorandum no . 83, NRC 8146, Ottawa.

Dunne, Thomas, and Luna Leopold. 1978. *Water in Environmental Planning*. San Francisco: Freeman.

Ellis, Jim. 1984. Snow creep. *Ski Area Management*, May, pp. 102ff.

Hess, M. 1968. Method for determining the effect of land forms on mountain climates. *La Météorologie* 5, no. 10/11 (September):75–85.

Hill, Mary. 1975. *Geology of the Sierra Nevada*. Berkeley and Los Angeles: University of California Press.

Irwin, Peter A., and Colin J. Williams. 1981. Prevention of excess snow accumulation due to roof mounted solar collectors. Report for the Ministry of Municipal Affairs and Housing, Toronto.

———. 1983. Application of snow-simulation model tests to planning and design. Proceedings, Eastern Snow Conference, June, Toronto.

Kittredge, Joseph. 1948. *Forest Influences*. New York: McGraw-Hill.

Landsberg, Helmut, 1962. *Physical Climatology*, 2nd ed. DuBois, Pa.: Gray Printing.

Lynch, Kevin, 1971. *Site Planning*, 2nd ed. Cambridge, Mass.: MIT Press.

Mackinlay, Ian, and W. E. Willis. n.d. Snow country design. NEA Grant no. A 70-1-15.

Martinelli, M., Jr. 1974, Snow avalanche sites: Their identification and evaluation. U.S.D.A. Forest Service, Agricultural Information Bulletin no. 360.

Matus, Vladimir. 1988. *Design for Northern Climates*. New York: Van Nostrand Reinhold.

Olgyay, Victor. 1963. *Design with Climate*. Princeton, N.J.: Princeton University Press.

Perla, Ronald I., and M. Martinelli, Jr. 1976. *Avalanche Handbook*. U.S.D.A. Forest Service Agriculture Handbook no. 489, July.

Price, Larry W. 1981. *Mountains and Man*. Berkeley and Los Angeles: University of California Press.

Reeser, Warner K., Jr., and Lane W. Kirkpatrick. 1975. The air pollution carrying capacity of selected Colorado mountain valley ski communities. Denver: Colorado Department of Health, Air Pollution Control Division.

Robinette, Gary O. 1972. *Plants/People/and Environmental Quality*. Washington, D.C.: U.S. Department of the Interior, National Park Service.

———, ed. 1977. *Landscape Planning for Energy Conservation*. Reston, Va.: Environmental Design Press.

Ronco, Frank. 1976. Regeneration of forest lands at high elevations in the Central Rocky Mountains. In *Proceedings: High-Altitude Revegetation Workshop No. 2*, pp. 13–25. Ft. Collins, Colo.: Environmental Resources Center, Information Series no. 21, August.

Steadman, Philip. 1975. *Energy, Environment and Building*. Cambridge, England: Cambridge University Press.

Storer, Tracy I., and Robert L. Usinger. 1963. *Sierra Nevada Natural History*. Berkeley and Los Angeles: University of California Press.

U.S.D.A. Forest Service. 1976. Beaver Creek winter sports site environmental analysis report. Minturn, Colo.: White River National Forest.

Watson, Donald. 1983. *Energy Efficient Building Principles and Practices*. New York: McGraw-Hill.

Weitz, Charles A. 1981. Weathering heights. *Natural History*, November, pp. 72–84.

Whitney, Stephen R. 1983. *A Field Guide to the Cascades and Olympics*. Seattle: The Mountaineers.

84   *Layered rock summits and Tramserku Peak (elevation 21,723 ft., 6623 m), northeastern Nepal.*

5
MOUNTAIN LANDFORM: PROCESSES OF ORIGIN AND CHANGE

In his expedition journal during the geological survey of the Uintas in 1876, John Wesley Powell observed, "Mountains cannot remain long as mountains; they are ephemeral topographic forms. Geologically all existing mountains are recent; the ancient mountains are gone."

In their vast scale and mass, mountains give an impression of permanence. However, like everything in nature, they also change, imperceptibly for the most part, but sometimes in unpredictable and violent fits of housecleaning. Change in the mountains has its own implacable rhythm; nothing can thwart it. Those who build in the mountains can hope only to mitigate its impacts, not to avoid completely the hazards it presents. Discerning the processes and causes of change in the physical landscape is the first step in ensuring that the design product will have a consonant rhythm.

In this process of discernment, flatland design experience usually proves inadequate. Mountain topography, gentle or rugged, poses design constraints that can unnerve the timid, but it also presents distinct design opportunities. Constraints cluster around issues of safety from hazards, availability of land suitable for building, and the costs of coping with these imposed parameters. Their severity is largely a function of topographical character and underlying geology.

The opportunities, on the other hand, are partly a matter of aesthetics: the opportunity to create something with regional character, a product so attuned to its physical setting that the natural origins of the place and the design inspirations of the plan are revealed and intertwined.

MOUNTAIN ORIGINS: GEOMORPHIC CLUES FOR DESIGN

All mountains are not the same. As Kevin Lynch wrote in *Site Planning*, "Every landscape will have its own consistent family of landforms caused by the base material and its stratifications and angle of repose, the history of vulcanism or glaciation, the erosion cycle, the climate, and the vegetative cover" (1971, p. 207). The differences in origin—compounded in recent geological time by local differences in climate, erosion rates, glaciation, or thermal action—create regionally distinct landforms.

Geomorphology is the underpinning of landscape character, the baseline from which the appearance of a place has evolved over the eons. It explains the landforms we see, giving them meaning and value, and helps us differentiate one mountain type from another. It is thus the backdrop for visual imagery in design and the logical point of departure in analyzing the foundation of a mountain site's character.

The evolution of mountain landforms is a process in which all the primeval geomorphic processes—uplifting, folding, faulting, volcanism—and several glacial periods have had a hand. Carefully interpreted, these ancient and continuing events reveal clues to the essence of a landscape, clues that influence design decisions about mass, scale, and spatial relationships, the vocabulary of form, and the palette of building materials in a mountain community's urban landscape. They help us make the built forms of one region different from those of another and thus create human environments well integrated with place.

Plate Tectonics. Geologists have long sought to weave the processes of mountain building into an overall theory of cause and effect that would clarify forces and sequences of events. Until the late 1960s, they assumed that mountains had been uplifted and folded in a rhythmic, evenly spaced series of *orogenies,* or equilibrium-seeking adjustments to the weight of deposits accumulating from erosion. Then the plate tectonics theory burst suddenly upon the scene, rewriting the theoretical score and assembling previously unexplained, random phenomena into a coherent rationale.

Plate tectonics is the story of geological structures: rock types, strata, folds and faults. It explains global landform in terms of *plates,* or segments, of the earth's crust. Most geologists now agree that some twenty plates are constantly shifting position on the earth's surface. Seismological data sketch the boundaries of the plates, at which both earthquakes and volcanoes cluster (Fig. 5-1).

Continents are the high points of plates, and where the plates collide, mountains are pushed up: the Appalachians; the Alps, where the Adriatic Plate is driving Italy into Europe; the Himalayas, where India, on the Australian Plate, is crashing into and under the Tibetan Plateau; the Andes, where the submerged Nazca Plate collides with the South American Plate; and the northwestern Coast Ranges, where the Pacific Plate is diving under the North American Plate, shaving off a berm of jumbled seafloor rocks as it moves downward. The Rockies and the Urals are the world's only mountains not at the edge of colliding plates.

Mountains are to the rest of the body of the earth what violent muscular action is to the body of man.
—*John Ruskin,* Modern Painters

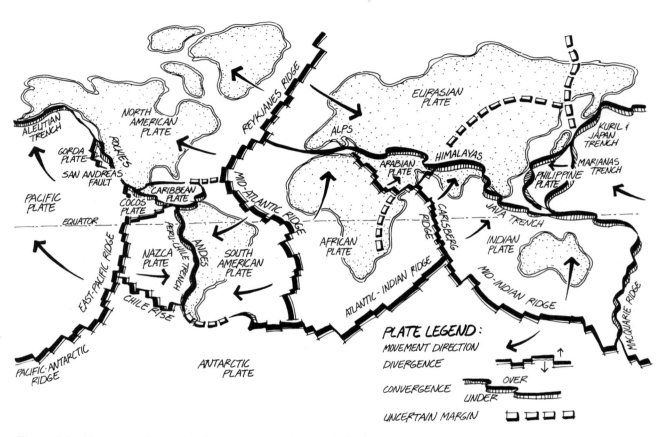

Figure 5-1. *Movement of tectonic plates at the earth's crust is the force that powers mountain building.*

The Sierras are the product of several landmass collisions, each one having added more land to the western edge of California. The eastward movement of the ocean plate that caused these collisions has stopped, and now the plates are sliding past each other along the San Andreas Fault, causing shallow earthquakes along the edges of the rift. The Sierras are a more recent range than the Rockies and consequently pose greater problems of accessibility across the range. There are far fewer communities at high altitudes there than in the Rockies.

The geology of the Rockies, the world's longest mountain chain, is extremely complex. As John McPhee observed, "The Rockies in general will be one of the last places in the world to be deciphered in terms of how many hits created them, and just when, and from where" (1980, p. 199).

The theory of plate tectonics formulates a context in which the processes of uplift, folding, faulting, and volcanism are easier to understand. Plate movement is the motivating force behind the collisions that form mountains; these processes are the means by which the earth's crust responds to the force.

Uplift and Folding. Most of the world's mountain ranges are the product of the forces of compression generated by plates driving into each other. Bent and mashed, squeezed upward, thrust outward and over, folded and warped, the rocks in these ranges reflect the natural tendency of materials to yield to pressure and to seek equilibrium.

Uplift and folding continue even after mountains form, as the earth's crust responds to the changing distribution of material at the surface. While erosion wore down ancestral mountain ranges, sediments accumulated in ancient basins. Downwarping and compression took place under the increasing weight and were balanced by uplift of the eroding landmasses (Fig. 5-2). Folding occurred at the same time: Downwarping caused strong horizontal forces that shoved together the upper portions of the crust, deforming and folding the layers and, by heat and pressure, furthering the metamorphosis of rocks.

Where erosion and deposition are still proceeding actively (in the Alps, Rockies, and Himalayas), warping and folding are still slowly at work, too. In contrast, in very old mountain systems like the

If by some fiat I had to restrict all this writing [about mountain building] to one sentence, this is the one I would choose: The summit of Mt. Everest is marine limestone.
— *John McPhee*, Basin and Range

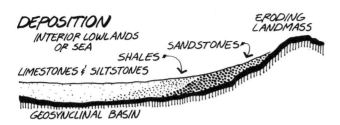

DEPOSITION
INTERIOR LOWLANDS OR SEA
SHALES
LIMESTONES & SILTSTONES
GEOSYNCLINAL BASIN
ERODING LANDMASS
SANDSTONES

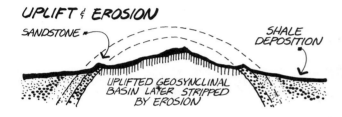

UPLIFT & EROSION
SANDSTONE
SHALE DEPOSITION
UPLIFTED GEOSYNCLINAL BASIN LATER STRIPPED BY EROSION

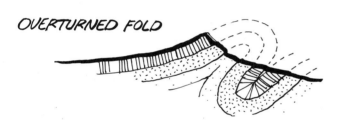

OVERTURNED FOLD

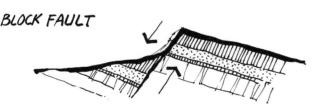

BLOCK FAULT

Figure 5-2.

Appalachians (described as "caterpillar furry and worn-down smooth" by John McPhee), climate has assisted in the evolution of dense vegetation to protect the slopes from erosion, and so these processes are thought to be inactive (Gilluly et al. 1968, p. 131).

Folded ranges have a characteristic regional texture that affects the way that settlement in them organizes itself. Roads often are forced to parallel the ropy trends of folds and ridges. This is the regional pattern, for example, in the Green Mountains of Vermont, the Berkshires of Massachusetts, and in the kindred landscape of Virginia's Blue Ridge. The gentle, even-topped hills of these regions, remnants of long north–south folds in the crust, belie the

difficulty of moving across them. Before the Hoosac Railroad Tunnel in Massachusetts was blasted out in 1874, the unbroken 170-mile length of the Green Mountain–Berkshire ridges was a formidable obstacle to east–west travel. For the same reason, the Blue Ridge Parkway perches on a continuous ridge line in a generally northeast–southwest trend for hundreds of miles. In folded mountain ranges, passes and gaps take on as much landmark prominence as peaks.

Faulting. *Faults* are fracture surfaces along which rocks have been relatively displaced. Mountains that have been formed primarily by faulting are often isolated ranges separated from adjacent valleys and lowlands by normal faults along which there has been great vertical displacement. The presence of fault systems generally indicates the release of pressure when plates are moving apart, an extension of the earth's crust rather than the compression that forced fold mountains.

The Tetons, the Sierras, and the Great Basin ranges between the Sierras and the Rockies are typical fault-block mountains (Fig. 5-3). They are characterized by a steep scarp on one side and a gentle grade to the ridge top on the other. This steep scarp makes for spectacular scenery and is the distinguishing feature that makes the eastern slopes of the Tetons and Sierras and the western side of Utah's Wasatch Range so photogenic. Whereas fold ranges often have similar sedimentational and structural histories for long distances along their trends, fault-block mountains show great variation in their rock types and geological histories (Gilluly et al. 1968, p. 494).

The fault-block ranges of Nevada's Great Basin — the Oquirrhs, the Stansburys, the Rubies, among others — contribute a distinctive landscape texture to an entire region. As described by John McPhee, these ranges are "high, discrete, and austere. . . . [They] come in waves, range after range after north–south range, consistently in rhythm with wide flat valleys: basin, range; basin, range; a mile of height between basin and range" (1980, p. 18).

In the Great Basin, the earth is pulling apart, and the ranges, great broken blocks of crust, are arrayed like stretch marks on the earth. Writes McPhee: "This Nevada terrain is not corrugated, like the folded Appalachians, like a tubal air mattress, like a rippled potato chip. This is not — in that compressive manner — a ridge-and-valley situation. Each range here is like a warship standing on its own. . . ." (1980, p. 45). In mountains like these, there is a sense of isolation and silence, of vastness without enclosure, a different sense of scale and proportion, and a different view relationship with the repeating landscape of plain and peak.

Figure 5-3. *The eastern side of the Tetons, a fault-block range near Jackson Hole, Wyoming.*

Figure 5-4. *Mt. Shasta, a volcanic peak in the Southern Cascades, California.*

Volcanism. Mountains formed by volcanic forces are also related to the movement of plates. Where the seafloor margin of one plate collides with a continental plate, the submerged plate dives under the other, pushing up mountains at the edge of the landmass. It also creates volcanoes all along the seam, where molten material can make its way to the surface. Most of the volcanoes of the world, whether in island arcs along undersea trenches or among chains of mountains, are lined up along these seams. The Andes and Cascades, for instance, are full of volcanoes, some still active. These volcanoes are intruders, independent of the crustal structures underneath them and unrelated to the surrounding rock types.

Symmetrical cone-shaped peaks are characteristic of volcanically derived mountains (Fig. 5-4): Mt. Rainier and Mt. Hood in the Cascades, Mt. Shasta in northern California, and the Spanish Peaks and San Juans of Colorado. Volcanic peaks tend not to be connected in chains.

Molten material sometimes does not reach the surface before it cools and hardens. Under the volcanoes, spreading masses of cooling granitic material form domelike *batholiths,* deep lenses of crystal-filled igneous rock. The Adirondacks of New York and the Black Hills in South Dakota are such dome mountains. In the Sierras, the ancient volcanoes have eroded away, and the subsequent block faulting has exposed the massive granite batholiths, pushing them skyward to 14,000 feet. Batholiths are also exposed in the Pacific Coast mountains and the northern Cascades, and they underlie much of New England, especially New Hampshire ("the Granite State").

The landscape in mountains shaped by volcanic activity differs noticeably from that in both faulted and folded mountain chains. These differences can be subtle and site specific: rock and soil colors, rock forms and textures. Or they can be fundamental expressions of landform and surface relief. As in the fault-block ranges of Nevada, the basic visual relationship between a volcanic peak and the valley bottom is different. The sense of landscape enclosure is diminished. The symmetry of landform and slope and the regional rhythm of terrain suggest that entirely different approaches to site planning and design are needed in mountains of this kind.

Glaciation. Glacial modification of topography, no matter what the terrain's original geomorphic derivation, is one of the more visible of the ancient processes in mountain regions. The four great glacial advances of the Pleistocene Ice Age left a legacy of easily identifiable landforms. High-altitude lakes, ponds, bogs, and wetlands survive in glacially scoured

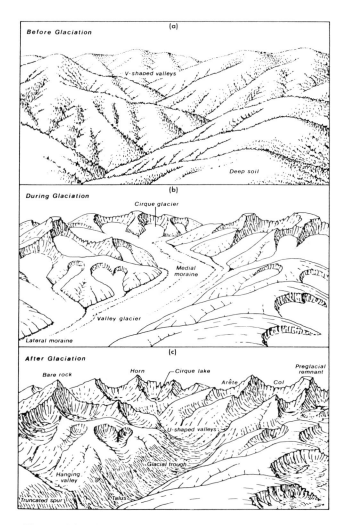

Figure 5-5. *Generalized conception of landform development before, during, and after glaciation. Drawn by Ted M. Oberlander, University of California. Used by permission, University of California Press.*

depressions, trapped behind moraines of unsorted, angular glacial debris that were deposited where the glacial movement halted. Ungraded streams with rapids and waterfalls, born in the ice fields and glaciers of high cirques and horns, tumble down from mountain peaks. Erratic boulders, carried far from their bedrock source, stand out as oddities in unlikely places. Hills, overridden by glaciers, are polished and rounded on their uphill sides, but irregular and jagged downslope. Smooth, broadly curving valleys, their U-shaped profile a trademark of glaciation, have truncated ridges and have left hanging the tributary valleys cut by preglacial streams (Fig. 5-5). Yosemite Valley's towering granite half-domes are the epitome of a glacially derived landscape.

The smaller glacial features are among those most easily destroyed by development in mountain valleys. Wetlands and bogs can be drained. Easily erodible, unconsolidated moraine deposits (called *till*) can be stripped of cover and exposed to the elements. Moraines can be breached and regraded. The continuity of the broad glacial valley floor can easily be interrupted. Without care, therefore, the integrity of the natural landscape and the evidence needed to understand its origins can be lost.

Hybrids. Like most mountain regions, New England's landscape of isolated mountains and gentle, even-topped hills is a product of several geomorphic processes working together. The difference between it and more rugged regions is time. Beginning some 440 million years ago, this northern end of the Appalachian chain, American's most ancient mountain range, was pushed up, folded, and fractured by the force of plate movements. By now, the mountains would have been eroded to a flat plain many times over had there not been subsequent uplifting of the crust as the mountains wasted away.

The ancient plain (*peneplain*) that formed from eroded material is the key to the even skyline of New England's hilltops (Fig. 5-6). The hills are thought to be remnants of the peneplain, sculpted by superimposed streams cutting through the sediments as the plain itself swelled upward (Jorgensen 1977). Almost anything in New England over 200 feet high is a knob or ridge of more resistant bedrock, called a *monadnock*.

The exception to this gentle profile is the irregular skyline of the White Mountain region of New Hampshire. There, intense igneous activity contributed the extensive granite deposits and created the metamorphic rock that makes up the Presidential Range, the highest in New England.

Bedrock is not far down anywhere in New England except Cape Cod. A layer of glacial debris that is nowhere more than about 20 feet thick overlies the entire region. This thin veneer of glacial till is the most pervasive evidence of the effects of glaciation on the New England landscape. The huge ice sheets that covered New England stripped the bedrock of its soil cover and everywhere exposed bedrock ledges. It clogged valleys and streams with the rocky till that makes New England so hard to farm and left behind the many lakes, ponds, swamps, and bogs common to a glacial landscape. The ice did not level the preexisting mountains and hills, but it did give the valleys and notches the characteristic U-shaped glacial profile.

The geomorphic history of the Pacific Northwest is similarly complex. In the northern Cascades and the Coast Ranges of British Columbia, the forces of plate

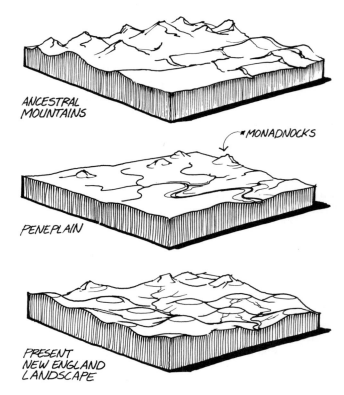

Figure 5-6. *Generalized conception of the evolution of the New England landscape: Ancestral mountains are eroded to a flat peneplain, then uplifted and carved into hills by streams. Adapted from Jorgensen 1977, p. 22.*

movement left ridges of deformed and metamorphosed marine volcanic and sedimentary rocks. Stream-cutting through uplifting terrain, followed by profound glacial sculpting, produced a deeply dissected terrain of fjords and craggy peaks. Even today, over half the area in the United States covered by glaciers is in the northern Cascades (Whitney 1983, p. 20).

In the southern Cascades, from central Washington State to northern California, volcanism, not glaciation, was the dominant force. The dozen or more great volcanoes of the Cascades are the most distinctive (and geologically the youngest) features of this range. Their height and symmetry suggest that they continued to erupt during the Ice Age. Accumulation of volcanic material, not uplift, is primarily responsible for the present elevation of this portion of the range (Whitney 1983, p. 28).

Implications for Design. Geomorphology reveals many things about the mountain landscape that have a direct bearing on design. In practical terms, it can hint at the character of substrata that the designer cannot see. In rugged terrain, it helps predict problems associated with rock structure, shallow

Figure 5-7. *Hemis Gompa in Ladakh, eastern Kashmir, India.*

bedrock, slope instability, groundwater, and revegetation.

In aesthetic terms, geomorphology influences design by explaining the natural fabric of a region—its age, characteristic forms and scenic relationships, relief, texture, and colors. In primitive villages, this sense of having evolved as a literal part of the landscape is one of their most identifiable characteristics (Fig. 5-7).

Designers today can choose to respond to a site's ancient origins on any scale: in site plans and forms that echo the angles and mass of the landform; in spaces whose sense of enclosure or expansiveness matches the ridge and valley rhythm; in views framed to call attention to the evidence of mountain-building processes; and in details that employ local materials and colors. Understanding the evidence of geological time and change transforms generic mountains into differentiated landscapes, opening the way for stronger regional design.

ACTIVE PROCESSES OF LANDSCAPE CHANGE

Constructive forces from within the earth created mountains, but destructive forces from without— weathering, erosion, and mass wasting—are continually at work tearing them down. The particular method by which a given mountain region is worn down and the rate at which this takes place are directly related to the region's original landforms and rock composition, the geomorphic processes that formed it, and the local climate. Individual mountain landforms offer different starting points for the ongoing forces of change. And because water and rock, snow and ice generally follow the paths of least resistance, the active processes of change "tend to reinforce and exaggerate existing slopes and structures" (Price 1981, p. 169). In our short perspective on geological time, these processes are the most visible agents of landscape change, and they influence site planning and design in fundamental ways.

Weathering

Numerous forces cause the weathering of rock, including frost action, differential heat expansion, plant roots, burrowing animals, solvent acids in solution, slope loading by snow, and the sheer weight of weak or saturated materials.

In the mountains, the most common weathering processes are physical rather than chemical. The disintegration of rock (Fig. 5-8) is intensified by the

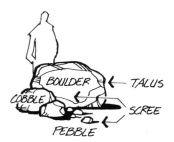

Figure 5-8. *Products of rock disintegration.*

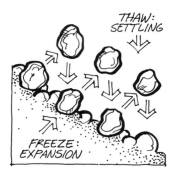

Figure 5-9. *Frost heaving pushes surface particles outward in a line perpendicular to the slope. Because of gravity, the loosened particles slump downhill when the surface thaws.*

mountain climate and the steep slopes, which increase the aggregate weight and downward pressure of the rock mass. As a general rule, the rate of weathering rises with altitude.

Weathering by Frost Action. One of the most powerful factors in the weathering of rock at high altitudes is frost action. The transformation of water into ice encourages flux and instability by causing material to expand and contract, heave and thrust, crack and slump.

Frost heaving is an upward thrust of the ground surface caused by the freezing of moist soil or permeable rock (Fig. 5-9). (Lateral expansion, called *frost thrust*, may also take place under certain conditions.) An extraordinarily powerful process, frost heave requires the presence of water, which expands by more than 9 percent when it freezes and, when frozen, can exert a pressure of 2000 pounds per square inch.

Water that freezes in the joints and bedding or foliation planes of rock formations becomes a wedge causing the rock to separate or shatter from the pressure (Fig. 5-10). The rock's texture and structure partially determine the amount of frost shattering that will occur. The same principle operates on concrete, which deteriorates when water gains a point of entry through its cracks, joints, and pores (Fig. 5-11).

In *Mountains and Man,* geography professor Larry Price observed that "frost processes make a landscape more vulnerable to disturbance, since they are opportunistic and often increase as vegetation is destroyed. Consequently, it may take a very long time for disturbed surfaces to be stabilized by vegetation" (1981, p. 179). Moist zones, such as below cliffs and steep slopes or where snow persists, are the areas of most intense frost weathering. Frost heave also does more damage where soils are clayey and organic and have high moisture retention capacities.

Deep frost penetration of surface layers causes fewer problems in the West Coast ranges than in the Rockies, where there is less snow for insulation and temperatures stay below freezing longer. In the

Figure 5-10. *Weathered boulder.*

Figure 5-11. *Concrete deteriorates rapidly in a mountain climate.*

central and southern Rockies, trenching for water and sewer lines, septic systems, and garbage disposal involves major excavation because the surface freezes to a greater depth, in excess of 6 feet in some areas.

Weathering by Insolation. The repeated heating and cooling of materials is a milder, but equally relentless weathering force. At high altitudes, where atmospheric interference with incoming solar radiation is minimal and heat retentive capacity is low, rapid and wide fluctuations in temperature during the day are possible in any season. The granular disintegration of rocks with large crystals, like granite, and the exfoliation of layered rock formations are common products of the differential heat expansion resulting from these fluctuations. Some architectural materials are equally vulnerable.

Erosion

Erosion is the transport of individual particles of earth by means of water, glaciers, or wind. In the mountains, water, especially in the form of storm runoff, is the erosive agent with which people are most often concerned. In general, the rate of erosion is controlled by the velocity and volume of runoff, combined with the degree of resistance offered by soil or rock. These variables in turn are affected by the density of the vegetative cover and the gradient of the slope.

In high mountain regions, the absence of a protective mantle of dense vegetation or cohesive soils increases the erosion potential. Particularly vulnerable are areas of exposed, highly weathered bedrock, scree slopes and debris fans, and south-facing slopes with lighter vegetation and thinner, rockier soils. Naturally adverse conditions are compounded by disturbances of any inclined surface and by saturation, for which both nature and humans can be blamed.

The velocity and volume of runoff down a given slope vary predictably along its face (Fig. 5-12). Near the crest, both volume and velocity are relatively low. In contrast, at midslope, where the slope gradient is normally steeper, volume is still moderate but velocity is high, causing the most severe surface erosion. It is here that outcrops, barren spots, rills, gullies, and the heads of alluvial fans are visible. The gentle inclination at the base of the slope slows velocity and causes deposition (Marsh 1978, p. 59).

It is easy to underestimate the potential for erosion. An environmental study in the foothills west of Denver, for example, found that "slopes over 12 percent reflect a critical point in runoff generation and erosion potential" (McLaughlin and Bevis 1975, p. 35). A 12 percent slope is deceptively shallow; it is a gradient of just over 6 degrees, or only slightly steeper than 10 to 1.

Underscoring the same point, an architectural study of housing on hillsides cautions:

Figure 5-12. *Rates of erosion vary down the face of a slope.*

Slopes as shallow as 1 in 50 [2 percent] can be eroded by run-off storm water. However, it is not necessarily the gradient alone that determines erosion. Long slopes of moderate steepness may suffer more erosion than steep but very short slopes. It is more difficult to control a large volume of water over a great length than to control the movement of less water over a short distance, even if the flow is more rapid. (Abbott and Pollit 1981, p. 213)

Field-observable details of topographical conditions are important site planning clues. Understanding what influences the propensity for erosion helps anticipate points where difficulties may be expected.

Erosion by Snowmelt Runoff. Although relatively little research has been done on snowmelt runoff as an agent of erosion, it is an exceptionally powerful force, accounting for most of the total annual erosion in many mountain drainages. In a draft water quality report, the town of Vail, Colorado, estimated that about 80 percent of its annual erosion occurs during snowmelt in late spring.

Snowmelt in temperate-zone mountains starts around May, with higher elevations (subalpine and alpine zones), more northerly latitudes, and north aspects lagging behind lower (montane) elevations, southern latitudes, and south aspects. The rate of snowmelt is a function of temperature and hours of exposure to sunlight.

The process of snowmelt erosion is believed to be similar to that of rainfall erosion, without the erosive

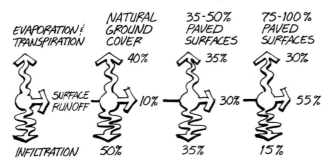

Figure 5-13. *In urbanizing areas, surface runoff typically increases, and infiltration decreases.*

impact of falling raindrops. It is probably a slower process than rainfall erosion, and the quantity of overland flow is smaller, perhaps even half the volume. One reason for this is the snowpack itself, which tends to retain water as it melts and thus to delay the passage of water through the pack. Another reason is that a thick snow cover insulates the ground, preventing it from freezing deeply and allowing it to absorb some of the meltwater as the snow thaws.

Some circumstances, however, can increase the erosive power of spring snowmelt. If fall rains and hard freezes arrive before the first major snowstorm, it is likely that the ground will freeze more deeply. The spring ground thaw will take longer, and the absorption of snowmelt runoff will be impeded. Also, unseasonably warm spring weather or spring rains can cause sudden and premature ripening of the snowpack, so that the still frozen ground is unable to absorb any of the snowmelt runoff.

Snowmelt erosion has tremendous downstream consequences. It was estimated in the Vail study that up to 100 percent of eroded material is transported out of a drainage area, largely because the sustained overland flow during snowmelt promotes the transport of sediment once it is suspended.

For the contractor, snowmelt erosion is an important consideration in scheduling site work. To reduce springtime erosion potential, regraded slopes should be stabilized and replanted before the onset of winter.

Design Implications of Erosion. The urbanization of any natural area inevitably brings with it an increase in impervious surfaces, which in turn increases runoff (Fig. 5-13). The unwanted consequences include erosion of topsoil, increased flood volume and more frequent flash floods, sedimentation of stream courses, lower dry weather stream flows, and the consequent disruption of riparian ecosystems. The visual quality of land and water probably deteriorates as well.

In mountains, several factors give erosion control added urgency. First, because most mountain communities take their water supply from nearby streams, suspended sediment poses serious problems for water treatment facilities. Second, the loss of topsoil at high elevations makes the task of revegetation even trickier than it already is. When topsoil and vegetation are disturbed, the subsoils thus exposed are far less fertile, less cohesive, and more susceptible to erosion, water absorption, and mass movement. Scars in such materials, especially on steeper slopes, take great time and effort to repair, if indeed it is possible at all.

Mass Wasting and Slope Instability

Any weathered and loosened material on an inclined surface is exposed to the downward pull of gravity. The resulting downslope movement of materials is a process called *mass wasting,* which refers to movement without a specific transporting medium (such as water, wind, or ice). Whereas erosion works particle by particle, mass wasting can move whole mountainsides at one time. It is the dominant agent of transport at high altitudes and is responsible for many of the characteristic features, and hazards, of high mountain landscapes.

The forms of mass wasting (Table 5-1) are categorized by the type of movement (falls, topples, slides, spreads, and flows) and by the kind of material involved (bedrock, debris, or earth). It is not unusual to see instances in which more than one kind of motion occurs; in fact, almost all large-scale slope instability problems involve a complex of failure types and causes. The terms used to distinguish among the types of slope movement do not suggest correct design responses in specific instances, but they do ensure that everyone involved is speaking the same language.

Types of mass movement are distinguished from one another not only by the speed of movement but also by whether the moving material remains in contact with the ground from which it separated and whether it moves parallel to the surface of separation (Fig. 5-14). For example, when *falls* detach from a steep slope or cliff, the displaced mass typically moves outward and down in a free fall. There is little or no shear displacement. *Topples,* which have been recently designated as a separate type of movement, tilt forward in a rotating movement around a pivot point beneath the moving mass. *Spreads* are complex failures that extend laterally when materials liquefy or become plastic and flow. Most of the spreading failures in the western mountains are associated with seismic events.

Flows are movements that resemble the behavior of

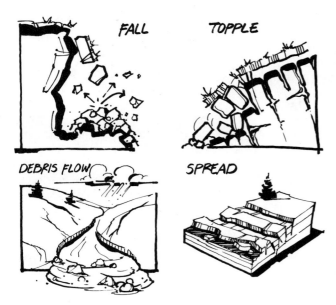

Figure 5-14.

viscous fluids. They can take place in bedrock or in unconsolidated earth and debris, and they can be fast or slow, wet or dry. The most common types of flows are *debris flows* (also called *mud flows*), typically very rapid events that are triggered in preexisting drainageways by unusually heavy rainfall or snowmelt runoff.

In mountainous areas, debris flows are among the most destructive forms of mass wasting (Fig. 5-15). They are "favored by the presence of soil on steep mountain slopes from which the vegetative cover has been removed . . . but the absence of vegetation is not a prerequisite. Once in motion, a small stream of water heavily laden with soil has transporting power that is disproportionate to its size . . . " (Schuster and Krizek 1978, p. 18).

Creep is a term often used interchangeably with flow, but technically it is a distinct type of movement in which almost imperceptible deformation in soil or rock continues indefinitely under constant stress. Creep can occur in conjunction with many types of topples, slides, spreads, and flows.

Although the word *landslide* is often used generically to refer to all types of slope movement, the term *slide* correctly describes only those events in which shear failure and displacement occur along a definable rupture surface. Of the five types of slope movement, only slides are susceptible to a quantitative stability analysis of potential rupture surfaces. Slide planes can be roughly predicted using circular-arc or sliding-wedge formulas, slope inclinometers, and computer analysis of the slope's structural components.

Slides (Fig. 5-16) are classified as either *rotational* or *translational,* a distinction that is useful in the analysis of stability and the design of control methods. The most common rotational slides are *slumps,* which

Table 5-1 Forms of Mass Movement

Type and Speed of Movement	Type of Material		
	Bedrock	**Debris[a]**	**Earth[a]**
Falls (extremely rapid)	Rockfall	Debris fall	Earth fall, soil fall
Topples (extremely rapid)	Rock topple	Debris topple	Earth topple, soil topple
Translational Slides (very slow to rapid)	Rock slide, rock block slide	Debris slide	Earth block slide, mudslide, soil slip
Rotational Slides (extremely slow to moderate)	Bedrock slump	Debris slump	Earth slump, soil slump
Spreads	Bedrock, lateral spread		Earth lateral spread (very rapid)
Flows (extremely slow to extremely rapid)	Gravitational sagging (Sackung)	Debris flow (mudflow)	Wet sand/silt flow
		Debris avalanche, solifluction, blockstream	Dry sand flow, earth flow, loess flow
	Rock creep	Talus creep	Soil creep
Complex	Rockfall/debris flow rock slide/rockfall	Slump/debris flow	Slump/earth flow

[a]In engineering geology, both debris and earth are referred to as engineering soils and include all unconsolidated material above bedrock. Debris is coarser than earth.

Figure 5-15. *Damage from a debris flow in Glenwood Springs, Colorado. Photo by the Colorado Geological Survey.*

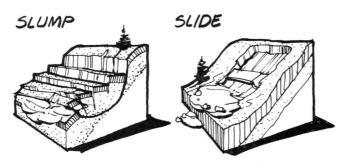

Figure 5-16.

rotate on an axis parallel to the slope. The rupture surface is typically concave and spoon shaped, and the scarp at its head may be almost vertical. At the top of the slump, strata will appear to have tilted backward, and at the toe, some of the displaced material will bulge out over the original ground surface. When the backward tilting traps water at the head of a slump, it can become a self-perpetuating area of instability. In the absence of ponding, the rotary movement of a slump may restore equilibrium in the unstable mass if the curving rupture surface dips into the hill at the foot of the slide. Because slumps occur most frequently in fairly homogeneous materials, their incidence in constructed fill slopes is high relative to other types of slope failure.

Translational slides are the classic landslides, in which a moving mass of rock or earth slides downslope along a more or less straight failure plane and comes to rest on the original ground surface below. These slides are most commonly a result of structurally weak joints or planes in the rock or weak bonds between rock and the overlying mantle of soil and debris. A translational slide may remain unstable indefinitely if the surface on which the moving material comes to rest is sufficiently inclined and as long as the driving force of its weight is greater than the opposing forces of friction and cohesion.

Causes of Slope Movement. The stability of a slope is influenced by the innate strength of its constituent elements and by their behavior under stress and strain. Cohesion (a material strength independent of external pressures on the slope) and the friction between particles are the forces that resist slope movement. These forces are a function of weight and mass.

Friction is greatly influenced by water content and, to a slight extent, by the angle of repose of the slope's constituent material. The angle of repose—the maximum gradient at which a particular material can be inclined before failure occurs—is not particularly relevant, however, unless the material on a slope is homogeneous and completely unconsolidated, like loosely dumped sand or gravel.[1] Any consolidated rock

[1]The approximate angle of repose for saturated clay is 5–20 degrees; compacted and well-drained clay: 45 to 80 degrees; wet sand: 17 to 22 degrees; dry sand: 33 to 38 degrees; compacted sand: 35 to 50 degrees; and well-drained loam, boulders, or cobbles: 35 to 40 degrees.

or clay is at some other state of stress unrelated to this friction angle. If the stress is sufficient to break all cohesive bonds, then the angle of repose will come into play, but by then the distinction will hardly matter. Much more predictive than the angle of repose is the correlation between failure modes and slope gradient (Fig. 5-17).

The cohesion and strength of materials alone do not determine stability. Rather, the tendency of a slope to slide is a function of the *balance* between *resisting forces* (friction and cohesion) and *driving forces* (mass and weight). Anything that upsets this balance — by adding weight, which increases shear stress, or by decreasing friction or cohesion, which reduces shear strength — can trigger slope failure (Fig. 5-18).

Drainage and its effect on subsurface moisture are closely related to the stability of a slope. *Water is the single most prominent culprit in slope failure.* This is not because it lubricates but because it reduces friction among particles. When a slope becomes saturated, the water has nowhere to drain. As a result, pore pressure increases, making particles buoyant and decreasing intergranular pressure. The net effect is to diminish or remove the resistance of materials to the pull of gravity.

Destabilizing changes in water content within a slope can result from natural causes, such as rainstorms and snowmelt, and from a number of development-related actions, such as stream diversion, impounded drainage, and irrigation. Disturbance to

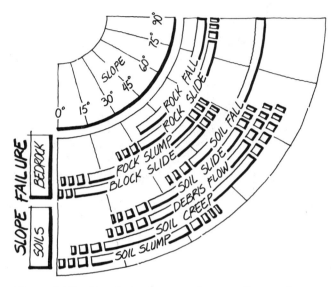

Figure 5-17. *Correlation between slope gradient and types of slope failure. After Campbell 1980, Figs. 5 and 6.*

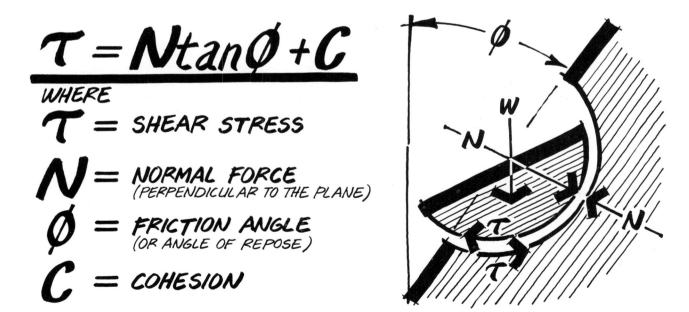

Figure 5-18. *The basic equation in soil and rock mechanics shows the relationship of forces acting to stabilize or destabilize a slope.*

Shear stress (τ) is the result of forces applied to a plane that affect the tendency of contiguous materials to slide relative to one another along their point of contact.

N and O represent the friction component that, when combined with cohesion, resists movement. Cohesion is a strength independent of pressure or load on the plane.

In this section, the opposing forces of weight (W), which is always exerted straight downward, and normal force (N) interact to influence shear stress along a potential slide plane.

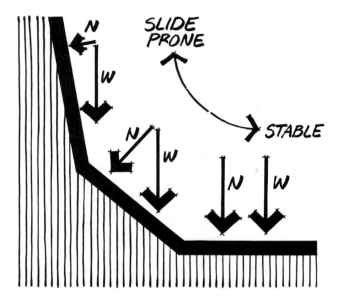

Figure 5-19. *Weight (W) and normal force (N) are equal on a flat site, but weight is a stronger force on a slope.*

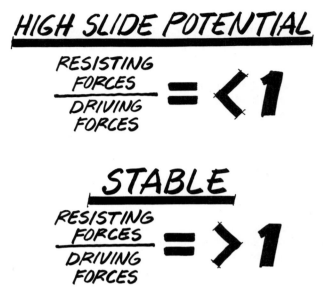

Figure 5-20.

the overburden or vegetation on a slope can alter natural drainage patterns and lead to chronic problems of slope instability.

In bedrock, jointing patterns are, after water, the next most powerful factor governing slope failure. It is not intact rock that fails. Regardless of the strength of the rock itself, discontinuities and weak bedding planes within it determine, like weak links in a chain, potential points of failure in rock slopes. Because in most instances, joints also determine drainage patterns, their significance in slope stability is compounded. Whereas soil slope stability is largely a two-dimensional question, jointing patterns transform the analysis of rock slope stability into a three-dimensional problem.

A host of factors characteristic of high mountain environments encourages the tendency of surface materials to move downhill. Primary among these are steep slopes and highly variable local relief. Weight, which is mass under the influence of gravity, is always a purely vertical force (*W*), and its downward pressure increases with slope gradient. Most of the shear tension on a slope is near the top of a hill, generally the area of maximum grade, and most of the support is at the toe (Fig. 5-19). The pressure of weight acting perpendicularly across a slope (*N*, or *normal force*), which helps hold materials in place, is least effective where the gradient is steepest.

Also impairing the stability of mountain slopes are less abundant vegetation, constant freezing and thawing of pore water, and springtime saturation by snowmelt. With their high permeability, the rocky, thin, uncohesive soils of many mountain regions,

though reasonably stable when dry, are particularly prone to debris flow because they can quickly absorb large quantities of water.

What prompts a mountain slope to fail after decades of stability? Many factors, some gradual and some not, can upset the natural equilibrium of a slope. Stream erosion, glaciers, previous slides, faulting, or development activity may remove lateral slope support. Stream undercutting, rock weathering, mining, regrading at the toe of a slope, or the tensile failure of inherently weak materials may remove the slope's underlying support. Snow and avalanches, talus accumulation, new buildings, railroad lines, fill, or water seepage may overload (surcharge) the slope. Frost action or swelling clay soils may cause excessive lateral pressure. Seismic events can be the sudden catalyst for any of these. In most cases of slope failure, however, there is not a single cause. More typically, the apparent triggering cause is part of a sequence of largely imperceptible changes wrought by climate and water over a long period of time.

Predicting Slope Instability. The relationship between resisting and driving forces is often expressed in terms of a slope's *factor of safety*, a predictive ratio that yields a rough approximation of slope stability (Fig. 5-20). Theoretically, when the ratio is lower than one, meaning that the forces favoring instability exceed those resisting it, slides may be anticipated. Unfortunately, the ratio is unrealistic for natural landscapes. Mountain slopes are full of cracks, seams, holes, and other surprises, making it difficult to achieve as high a level of confidence in quantitative analysis as is possible in a controlled environment, such as on constructed fill slopes.

Because the factor of safety ratio does not make allowances for variability in contributing factors, the recent trend in quantitative prediction has been toward probability analysis, which can more effectively incorporate the unknowns on a slope. Among the difficulties with this approach, however, is integrating the element of time. A 50- to 100-year timeframe is important when analyzing slopes that have never failed; statistically, many decades of data are needed to predict the near-term probability of failure events with any confidence. Because it is rarely possible to find records dating back far enough, engineers generally must resort to analyzing sites in similar environments where slope failures have already taken place. With time and effort, the forces that produced a past landslide can be determined, yielding a better understanding of the present status of nearby slopes similar in terrain and geology.

Symptoms and Responses. The evaluation of slope stability is an essential first step in any mountain project involving site selection, site planning, road layout, grading, and the siting and engineering of structures. Unwise decisions in any of these tasks can raise the potential for slope movement.

Stability investigations of a site typically start with a review of topographical maps, engineering reports on soils and geological conditions, and aerial photographs. Landforms that as a class have proved more susceptible to slope movement are identified, and the influence of climate, hydrology, and human factors is assessed.

Next, a preliminary field reconnaissance is undertaken to verify conclusions about the terrain developed from this review and to survey evidence of previous slope movement. Subsequent in-depth field investigation diagnoses the causes of past slides and provides essential input for design to avoid, mitigate, or control potential hazards.[2]

Red flags often associated with unstable slopes include the following symptoms (Table 5–2): steep gradients; cliffs, scarps, subsidence, or surface cracks; concentrations of fractures or faults; hummocky topography or unnatural bulges at the toe of a slope; accumulation of rock debris in valleys and drainage ditches at the base of a slope; seepage zones and areas

[2]See Shuster and Krizek 1978, pp. 34–80, "Recognition and Identification," and pp. 81–111, "Field Investigation." See also U.S. Department of Transportation, Federal Highway Administration, 1986, "Guidelines for Slope Maintenance and Slide Restoration," for a summary of preslide symptoms to look for in the field.

where soils on slopes are wet and muddy; areas where drainage concentrates or that are being undercut by streams; changes in drainage or channel alignment; springs that are new, discolored, or changed in volume; areas where soils are distinctly darker or vegetation is unseasonably green (indicating higher moisture levels); and tilted trees, posts, fences, or walls.

There are a number of things that one should *not* do where these symptoms exist. Under no circumstances should a questionable slope be loaded with fill, undercut, or overexcavated when removing debris at the toe. Bulges should not be cut or regraded, as they may be supporting unstable earth above; instead, ramps should be built over them if necessary. Cracks in the soil provide a clear demarcation of disturbed areas to be avoided and should not be obliterated. Natural drainageways should never be blocked with retaining structures or fill, and runoff should not be directed toward the problem area. Vegetation should not be removed.

Constructive actions can also be taken. As a basic precaution, record and monitor the symptoms, amount of slope movement, and changes in water levels. Repair surface and subsurface drainage problems, and redirect runoff away from the problem area. Protect eroded areas and reestablish vegetation. Reroute circulation if it seems to be aggravating the problem. Consider retention structures (Fig. 5-21), piles, anchors, rock buttresses, and counterweight fills; removal of unstable rock; sealants to close cracks in pavement that admit water; and systems to protect roads and structures from rockfall (berms, ditches, fences, slope drapes, bolting). Above all, seek professional advice to decide the best course of action.

Appropriate design solutions begin by recognizing that a problem exists. Most landslides or potential failures can be predicted if proper investigations are performed in time. The cost of preventing landslides is usually less than the cost of correcting them.

Natural Hazards and Land-Use Control

The mountains have rules. They are harsh rules, but they are there, and if you keep to them, you are safe.
—Walter Bonatti, mountaineer

In the mountains of Europe and Japan, valleys are more densely populated than they are in the United States, and so the human impacts of farming and timber removal are more pronounced. There, alarm is growing and land-use control is becoming more restrictive as landslides and avalanches occur with greater frequency. In the most rugged mountains of the United States, such extensive development has not yet occurred, but pressures on the environment

Table 5-2 Factors Indicating Potential Slope Instability

Factor	Indicators	Degree of Hazard			
		Low	Moderately Low	Moderately High	High
Landform	slope gradient	0–10° (5:1)	10–18° (3:1)	20–22° (2:1)	25–45° (1.5+:1)
	slope length, valley depth	small	moderate	long, deep	very long, large
	cliffs, escarpments, lobes	absent	—	—	present
	slope aspect	northerly	east, northeast	west, southwest	south
Natural History	active or inactive faults	absent	few	some	many
	evidence of previous slides	absent	few	some	many
	tremors felt	never	seldom	some	many
Bedrock	exposed rock faces	absent	partial	—	full
	direction of joints or strata	right angle to slope	—	—	parallel to slope
	density of joints	low	moderate	high	very high
	amount of dip in bedding planes	horizontal	slight tilt	moderate tilt	near vertical
	strong beds over weak beds	absent	—	—	present
	degree of weathering	none	small	moderate	extensive
	compressive strength	very low	low	moderate	high
	coherence	high	moderate	low	very low
	slope loading by rock debris	absent	—	—	extensive
	expansive minerals in rock	absent	negligible	some	extensive
Soil	location	valley floor	gentle slopes	moderate slopes	steep slopes
	angle of rest	low	moderate	steep	very steep
	depth	thin	moderate	thick	very thick
	degree of consolidation	high	moderate	—	uncohesive
	organic content	peaty	loam	hydrophobic clays	inorganic, sandy, rocky
	soil moisture level	low	moderate	high	waterlogged
	saturated soil over frozen subsoils	absent	—	—	present
	tendency to expand when wet or frozen	none	low	moderate	high
Hydrology	stream gradient	gentle	moderate	steep	very steep
	standing water	absent	localized	slowly draining	rapidly draining
	concentrated groundwater seepage	absent	—	—	very apparent
	pore water pressure	low	moderate	high	very high
	slope/bank undercutting	none	moderate	high	very severe
	evidence of surface erosion by water	none	—	—	extensive gullies

Adapted from William M. Marsh, *Environmental Analysis* (New York: McGraw-Hill, 1978), p. 246. Used with permission.

Table 5-2 *(continued)*

| Factor | Indicators | Degree of Hazard | | | |
		Low	Moderately Low	Moderately High	High
Climate	general character	humid	temperate	semiarid	arid
	heavy cloudbursts	never	rare	sometimes	often
	percentage of precipitation as snow	none	low	average	over 60 percent
	winter days with temperature above freezing	very few	some	—	most; frequent freeze–thaw
	snow loading	wind stripped	average depth	—	very deep snow
Vegetation	degree of cover	dense	moderate	light to moderate	sparse, barren
	type of cover	healthy forest	deep-rooted shrubs, declining forest	shallow-rooted shrubs	annuals and perennials
Previous Disturbances	fills	well compacted	—	—	uncompacted
	cuts	shallow cuts, gentle side slopes	—	—	steep side slopes, deep cuts
	drainage diversion across hillside	absent	—	—	present
	structures and roads on upper slopes	none	few	some	major
	reservoirs	absent	—	—	large, deep
	removal of native vegetation	none	some; quickly revegetated	some; not revegetated	wildfires, extensive stripping
	underground mining	none	some	considerable	extensive

are increasing. Here, lacking the lessons that come from generations of living on the land, concern is rising that the relationship between development and natural disasters is poorly understood.

In 1974, Colorado became the first American state to require hazard mapping by each county. Legislation defined a hazard as "a phenomenon that is so adverse to past, current and foreseeable construction as to constitute a significant hazard to public health and safety, or to property" (Colorado House Bill no. 1041).[3] Other states have since followed suit with hazard regulations of their own.

Natural hazards are usually mapped by type and ranked by degree (Fig. 5-22). Lines on a map marking the boundaries of hazard areas are often only transition zones, not distinct lines of demarcation. For a better perspective on mitigation, identified hazards should be interpreted not as discrete phenomena but as part of a local context and the expression of active processes.

The criteria for ranking the degree of hazard vary somewhat from place to place, but the initial breakdown is generally made according to the severity of the consequences. This means that the areas of highest risk are those where catastrophic

[3]See Rogers et al. 1974, for details on Colorado House Bill no. 1041, as well as definitions of specific geological hazards, criteria for their recognition, consequences of improper actions, and methods of hazard mitigation.

TIMBER

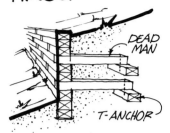

DEAD MAN

T-ANCHOR

CONCRETE

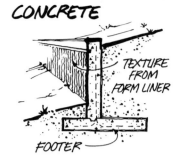

TEXTURE FROM FORM LINER

FOOTER

COBBLE

DRY LAID STONE

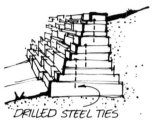

DRILLED STEEL TIES

MODULAR CONCRETE

BUTTRESS

STONE OR BRICK ON CONCRETE BLOCK

TERRACED

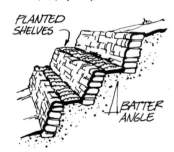

PLANTED SHELVES

BATTER ANGLE

GABION

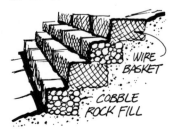

WIRE BASKET

COBBLE ROCK FILL

SCREEN and BOLTS

BOLTS INTO BEDROCK

Figure 5-21. *Slope retention methods.*

economic loss or loss of life is possible and where the costs of mitigation are unjustifiable given the risks. In the context of landslide hazards, high risk is a matter of speed more than volume of material. For example, a rapidly moving landslide increases the risk of catastrophic loss because it curtails the warning and response time. Areas susceptible to rockfalls, rockslides, debris flows, and all active avalanche areas

usually fall into the category of highest risk because they can occur with little or no warning and with lethal effect (Figs. 5-23, 5-24).

Areas of moderate hazard are those where there is risk of significant economic loss and/or major disruption of activity. These include active, recently active, or potential landslide areas (unless they are also active avalanche runout zones, in which case

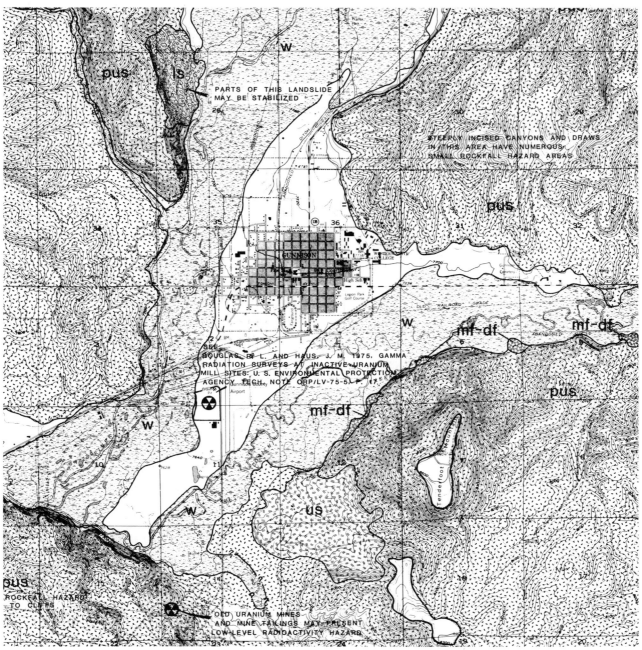

Figure 5-22. *Hazard map for part of Gunnison Quadrangle, Colorado.* ls *means evidence of landslide;* us, *unstable;* pus, *potentially unstable. Colorado Geological Survey.*

Figure 5-23. *High-hazard area east of Vail, Colorado.*

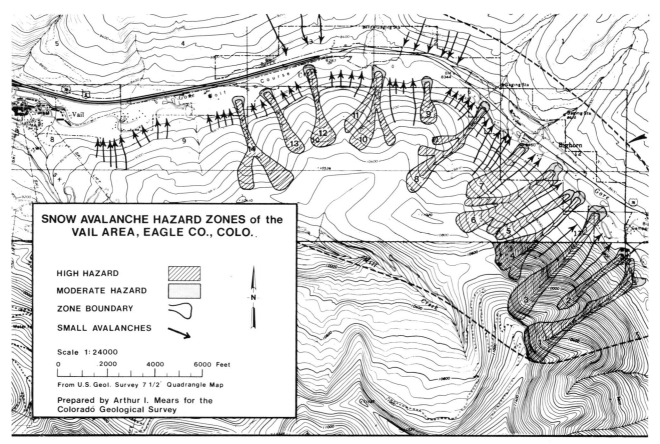

SNOW AVALANCHE HAZARD ZONES of the
VAIL AREA, EAGLE CO., COLO.

HIGH HAZARD

MODERATE HAZARD

ZONE BOUNDARY

SMALL AVALANCHES

Scale 1:24000

0   2000   4000   6000 Feet

From U.S. Geol. Survey 7 1/2´ Quadrangle Map

Prepared by Arthur I. Mears for the
Colorado Geological Survey

Figure 5-24. *The avalanche hazard map for the same area. Map prepared by Arthur I. Mears for the Colorado Geological Survey.*

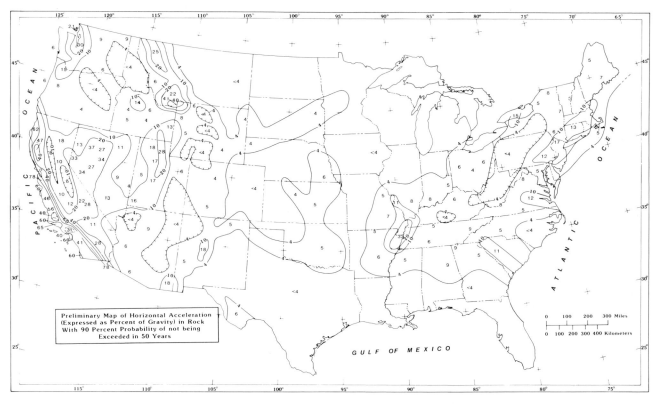

Figure 5-25. *Seismic hazard map used to develop earthquake-resistant design provisions for building codes. The map, contoured in percentages of the acceleration of gravity, projects expected maximum horizontal ground motion at any place in a 50-year period. As a very general guide, contour values above 10 correlate with moderate damage to one- and two-story masonry buildings. Where values are above 20, significant damage can be expected. Prepared by S. T. Algermissen, U.S. Geological Survey.*

they are more hazardous), physiographic floodplain zones, and areas with thick soils that show evidence of instability.

> *Areas deemed moderately hazardous are considered to be in a delicate state of balance that could be upset by improper use. Development [there] should pay particular attention to the design and location of structures, excavation, and deforestation, so as to minimize physical disturbance. . . . Development of landslide areas should avoid any change in the local stability factor, from irrigation and drainage, excavation and construction. (Ives and Bovis 1978, p. 209)*

Where these conditions overlap with zones that could become avalanche prone, care should be taken to preserve the forest, as it has a stabilizing influence on the snowpack.

The low risk category includes hazards that can cause minor economic loss or disruption of functions, hazards that would not prevent development but would increase the costs of mitigation and control. Such areas include inactive slides, zones showing

evidence of creep, areas with expansive soils or substrata, mine tailings, and areas subject to subsidence, swampiness, or a high water table. In these cases, development constraints pertain mainly to access, road and foundation maintenance, drainage problems, and accelerated erosion.

Hazard maps may not be detailed enough in resolution to be reliable guides in siting permanent improvements. They may also fail to note the effects of any recent development in the vicinity. It is important to recognize that an area considered hazard free on a map may not remain so after terrain is modified or forest is removed. Also, potentially unstable slopes may become more susceptible to failure after forest fires, major storms, or floods. To assess the impacts of recent and proposed changes on a specific site, developers should consider engaging a geotechnical specialist for field investigations in the early stages of any project.

Most mountain areas are also subject to seismic hazards. The degree of seismic risk has been assessed on a general scale (Fig. 5-25) but should be refined by on-site geological analysis for site-specific planning, engineering, and design in earthquake-prone areas. Large portions of the Sierras and Rockies and most of Alaska are in seismic zones of the highest hazard.

The severity of seismic hazard depends on the intensity of an earthquake and the way the ground behaves during the event. The ground can break along fault lines, move and shake, settle differentially, subside, crack, lurch, or liquefy. Still, the biggest risk associated with earthquakes in mountain areas is slope failure: Strong ground motion dislodges materials that are already loose, unconsolidated, or destabilized because of human activities. Hazards are compounded where large rockfalls or landslides can fall into water bodies, causing dam failure or flooding of the shoreline. Hazard mapping that identifies those areas most susceptible to landslides will give a reasonable idea of the degree of risk in the event of an earthquake, but fault zones, saturated granular subsurface deposits, and unstable ground conditions should also be identified for a more complete picture.

Although the need for public protection is clear, natural hazard mapping and evaluation in the mountains is not easy. It is difficult for specialists to anticipate the conditions that will trigger an event, to predict the intervals at which it might be expected to occur, or to evaluate the severity of a potential hazard. It is time-consuming and expensive to determine these conditions on a scale that is useful to site planners. And even after potential hazards are identified, it is difficult for those affected to agree on how to respond, especially when uses exist that predate the mapping or when land values may be seriously impaired by hazard designations. Still, the effort to identify hazards and assess the degree of risk remains crucial to appropriate mountain design.

THE ROLE OF MOUNTAIN STREAMS

The behavior of water in mountain drainages is not unlike that of streams in other natural environments. However, alpine streams do have some unique characteristics: They have bigger, steeper watersheds than streams in other terrain, and their peak annual discharge happens all at once, with the spring snowmelt.

The typical mountain stream is a high-gradient gravel-bed river that originates in a high alpine basin. The effect of steep slopes and high relief is clear in the mountain stream's irregular and concave profile. In glaciated mountain watersheds, the stream profile often transitions abruptly from oversteep gradients in the upper watershed to valley flats with gradients as low as 1 or 1.5 percent.

In its upper reaches, a mountain stream is characteristically steep but carries a relatively small discharge because its drainage area is small. Because it is less powerful in the higher reaches, it can move little of the larger material that falls into it. Evidence of this is found in particle-size distribution and the characteristic clearness of the water, even at bankfull flow (Price 1981, p. 213). In mountain streams, most of the material being transported occurs as bedload bouncing along the bottom, not as suspended sediment. As the stream descends, the volume of water and bedload typically increases, and more bedload material can be moved until the channel levels out on the valley floor.

Mountain streams are the surface expression of groundwater; direct precipitation is not their primary source. They are fed mainly by water from melting snowfields and glaciers, and as a result, the volume of water they carry shows wide seasonal and even daily fluctuations (Fig. 5-26). Affected by temperatures and the rate of snowmelt, mountain streams typically rise in the late afternoon and discharge their peak seasonal flows in late June and early July, when the snowmelt at their headwaters is heaviest.

Streams as Agents of Landscape Change

A stream's erosive force, or *stream power,* is a function of the unit weight of its water, the amount of discharge, and the slope gradient. Streams erode not only by abrasion of the bed and banks but also by chemicals in solution and by physical weathering of channel material during periods of low discharge. In the mountains, most stream-bank erosion is triggered by freeze–thaw conditions, not the high water of spring snowmelt, when the banks are typically still frozen.

Erosion rates in mountain watersheds are among the highest on earth (Price 1981, p. 212). It is not as a destructional force, however, that streams play their most important role, but as an agent of transport. In the span of geological time, nature's conveyor belts have carried out huge amounts of debris.

A stream is thought to be in equilibrium when it removes all the material that is supplied to it. Its capacity to transport material is a function of the rate of supply and the range of stream power. Other factors include the width, depth, and nature of the channel (that is, its hydraulic geometry at various flows), the channel pattern (straight, meandering, braided), the gradient, the bed's roughness and resistance to flow, and the amount and character of the load being transported.

It is during the rise and fall of the snowmelt hydrograph, perhaps 30 to 40 days a year, that mountain streams are most effective in moving sediment. In effect, with rare exceptions, they are

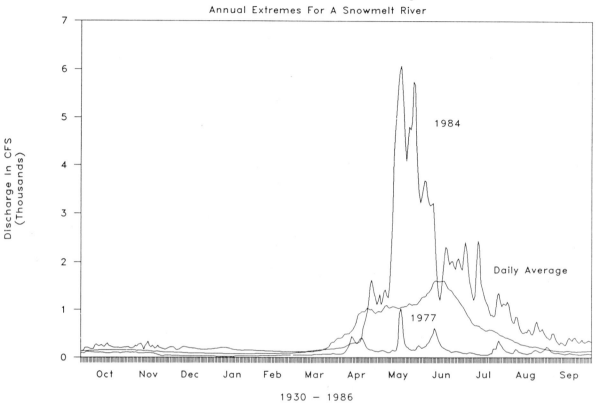

Figure 5-26. *Hydrograph of an undammed mountain stream shows the extreme seasonal effect of snowmelt. Daily flows are plotted for a year of maximum discharge (1984), one of minimum discharge (1977), and an average for the 56 years of data.*

impotent the rest of the year. If a watershed has not been affected by human activity, its streams are most likely starved of sediment and rarely move their beds. In an undisturbed watershed, most of the mineral material that is transported out every year comes out in solution, not in suspension or as bedload (Cleaves et al. 1970).

Impacts. Although they may still look natural, most of the rivers in habitable valleys of the mountain West have been severely affected, first by settlers who burned off the natural riparian vegetation to clear grazing land, then by mining, and now by second-home development.

It is vegetation that holds streams together, and when it is removed, they quickly fall apart. More vulnerable to erosion, denuded stream banks cause sediment loads to increase and the level of local streambeds to rise. Because the channel cross section must carry the same volume of water, the river compensates for the shallower bed by moving its

banks outward and, in the process, pulling even more sediment into the stream. With an oversupply of sediment for the stream's natural regime, bars clog the channel, width to depth ratios continue to increase, and braiding tends to develop. This change in channel character also provokes adverse changes in the fish population. Ultimately, the river seems to roam at will back and forth across the valley floor in a broad, gravel-filled swath.

Restoration. Very few artificial structures placed in a river are effective in stabilizing it. Most of the time, water responds by going around them or taking them out during high water. In trying to improve a stream reach, many people focus only on water velocity, assuming that bank erosion can be prevented by protective riprap on the outside edge of river bends. But in fact, during high water, turbulence in three dimensions is more important than downstream velocity. Most bank erosion occurs at the toe of the bank, and large, angular riprap can actually increase

107

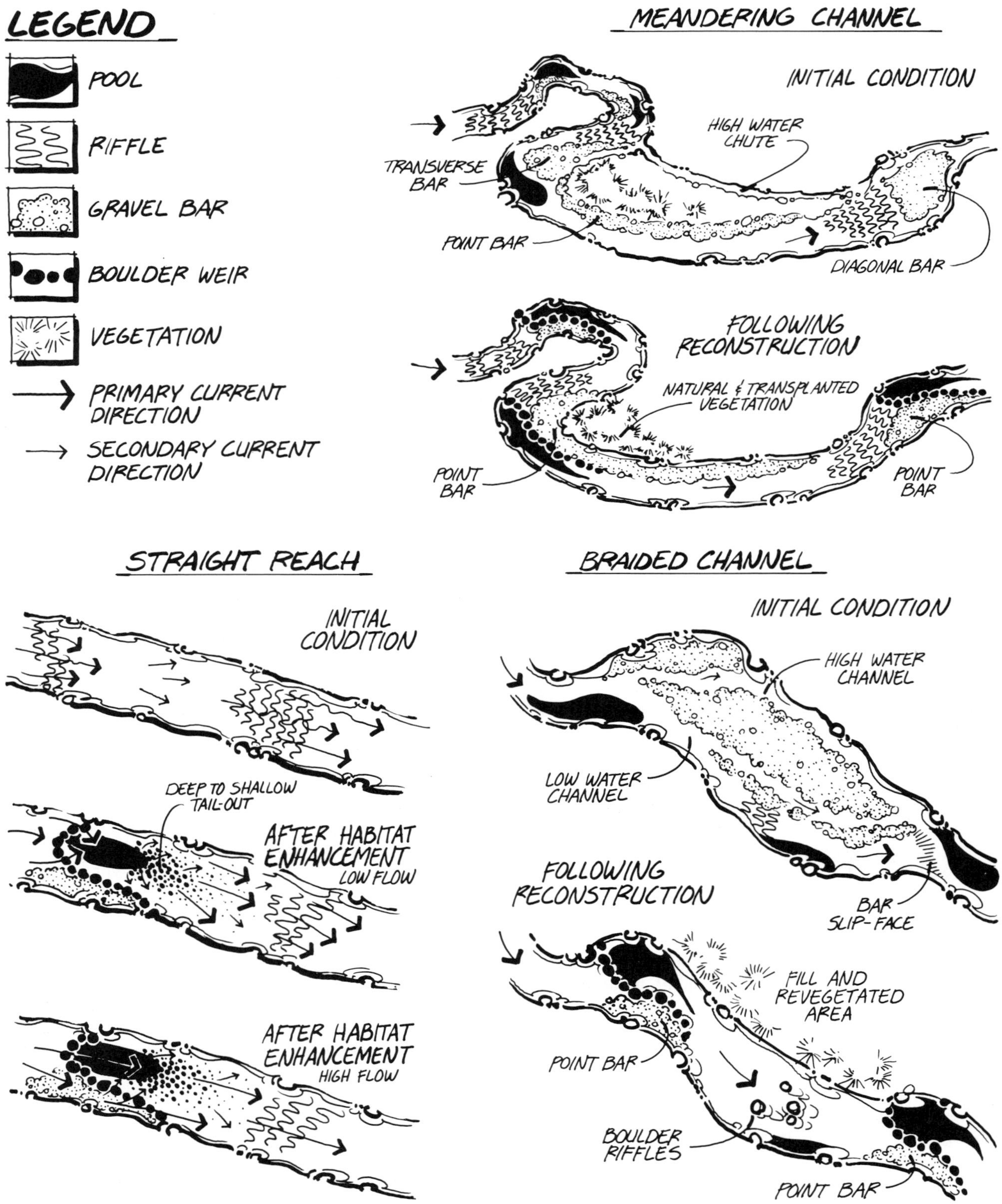

LEGEND

- POOL
- RIFFLE
- GRAVEL BAR
- BOULDER WEIR
- VEGETATION
- → PRIMARY CURRENT DIRECTION
- → SECONDARY CURRENT DIRECTION

MEANDERING CHANNEL

INITIAL CONDITION

HIGH WATER CHUTE

TRANSVERSE BAR

POINT BAR

DIAGONAL BAR

FOLLOWING RECONSTRUCTION

NATURAL & TRANSPLANTED VEGETATION

POINT BAR

POINT BAR

STRAIGHT REACH

INITIAL CONDITION

DEEP TO SHALLOW TAIL-OUT

AFTER HABITAT ENHANCEMENT LOW FLOW

AFTER HABITAT ENHANCEMENT HIGH FLOW

BRAIDED CHANNEL

INITIAL CONDITION

HIGH WATER CHANNEL

LOW WATER CHANNEL

BAR SLIP-FACE

FOLLOWING RECONSTRUCTION

FILL AND REVEGETATED AREA

POINT BAR

BOULDER RIFFLES

POINT BAR

Figure 5-27. Techniques for restoration of gravel-bed streams.

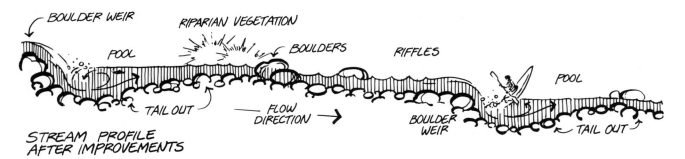

Figure 5-28.

turbulence there, which may eventually undermine the structure. Far better for bank stabilization are willows, as a first choice, or rounded river rock with biodegradable geotex fabric and gravel filling the spaces between rocks.

The effective restoration of a natural stream involves more than hardening its banks against erosion. It also means inducing compatible bedforms that accelerate the stream's natural healing processes. This strategy requires an understanding of the existing patterns in the channel: how much water and material are moving and how the channel is changing.

Trends in a stream channel can be discerned from a number of visual cues. The presence of extensive willow cover is indicative of stable banks. The shape, location, and extent of gravel bars hint at the channel's state of equilibrium. Both the bars and the particle-size distribution in the bed reveal what size material is moving and whether certain reaches are starved of sediment. The roughness and resistance of the bed surface also relate to the amount of material in transport. High water marks, such as scour marks on trees or lichen limits on banks, show where bankfull levels are. Moss limits and mineral deposits on boulders generally indicate the average low water mark.

These observations, along with cross-section measurements and discharge modeling, give some idea of seasonal flows and the stream's transport power. They also suggest how the river will adjust to future changes in channel width, depth, and gradient.

In one approach to channel stabilization (O'Brien 1988), gravel bars are the pivotal elements. As storage depots for bedload sediments, bars tend to form where stream flows diverge. There are different types of bars, representing an evolutionary spectrum toward increasingly stable bar forms. Diagonal bars which are attached to both banks are the most resistant to flow and seem to be the most stable form. In this approach, stream banks in a given reach are stabilized by reinforcing the downstream edge (the slip-face) of a diagonal bar with large rock material

that the stream cannot move. Properly located at the natural break from riffle to pool, the slip-face will force the river to expend its erosive energy within the water flow itself and on the point bar and keep it away from the banks. If the banks are protected in this way, vegetation will recover and the river will heal itself.

Figure 5-27 illustrates this approach in the reconstruction of three types of stream channels. The braided and meandering channels before rehabilitation were broad and filled with gravel bars that dissected the stream flow. In each case, reconstruction narrowed the channel, consolidated bars, stabilized slip-faces with boulder weirs, deepened and enlarged the pools, and revegetated the banks with willows. Pools are located below the stabilized slip-face, where the turbulence created by the shearing motion of the water over the boulder weir naturally scours the bottom and keeps the pools from filling in.

In the straight reach, the stream profile was altered to improve its value as a fishery (Fig. 5-28). In its initial state, the stream's continuous riffles were too shallow and the water too fast to provide good cover for adult trout, and so bars, weirs, pools, and transitions (tail-outs) were constructed.

In these examples, the weirs are placed diagonally to the flow to distribute the stream's power over a greater area. Their height is extremely important. It should not be higher than the natural grade of the channel bed. If it is (as drop structures usually are, for example), it will cause water to back up behind it, where increased deposition will raise the bed elevation, possibly leading to the structure's failure. The most important consideration in designing the weir is the channel cross section, which must remain adequate for projected flood volumes.

Rivers respond to anything that happens to them. They can be restored, their channels can be stabilized, and their biological productivity can be improved (Fig. 5-29). But to be successful, one must work within the river's preexisting trends and constraints.

Figure 5-29. *Stream section before improvement, all riffles, is poor fish habitat (top). Reconstructed (bottom), excess gravel in the bed has been excavated to build a new point bar and deepen the channel. Boulders reinforce the bar's slip-face. Photos by Robert O'Brien, Inter-Fluve Inc., Bozeman, Montana.*

Alluvial Landforms in Mountains

Alluvial transport and deposition lead to the
development of characteristic landforms that,
although not unique to mountains, have important
implications for siting and design in the mountain
environment (Fig. 5-30).

Floodplains. Because of periodic flows and because
bedrock channels typically carry a stream's peak
discharge without overflowing, floodplains tend not to
form in the higher reaches of mountain streams
(Leopold 1974, p. 92). Flat valley floors may
occasionally resemble floodplains, but these are more
often formed by other processes such as landslides,
avalanches, or moraine dams (Price 1981, p. 213).

At lower elevations where stream flow is sustained
all year long, floodplains may form by means of
deposition associated with lateral movement of the
stream channel. Floodplains in larger rivers are wider,
rates of downcutting the channel are slower, and the
material of the valley walls is less able to withstand
erosive forces.

For purposes of hazard mapping, mountain
floodplains have been defined as those portions of a
river valley that "undergo frequent erosional and
depositional changes and where the threat of
inundation supercedes all other geomorphic hazards"
(Ives and Bovis 1987, p. 202). The maps that use this
definition may not cover all of the 100-year
floodplain. Instead, they generally approximate
floodplain limits by interpreting landform and
vegetation, rather than by a detailed hydraulic
analysis of discharge data.

Even conventional hydraulic analysis may not
accurately determine floodplain limits. Because of
debris loads, mountain creeks often do not behave as
normal streams do during flooding (Jochim 1986,
p. 30). Therefore, to construct a more realistic picture
of the actual flood hazard, one should supplement the
analysis with photos of past floods, aerial photo
interpretation, and interviews with long-time residents
(Fig. 5-31).

There is widespread recognition of the hazards
associated with building in floodplains. But where
there is no floodplain and the stream channel appears
adequate to carry flood flows, safety still cannot be
assumed for development on the valley floor. What is
not widely recognized is the much greater potential
for spectacular discharge events in high-relief
topography. Because mountains cannot store much
summer precipitation, thunderstorm rainfall surges
quickly through the watershed and can set off flash
floods, debris flows, and other landslide events.

It is astounding how much pressure can be exerted
to build right at the stream's edge. In Colorado's Big

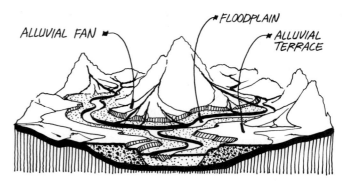

Figure 5-30.

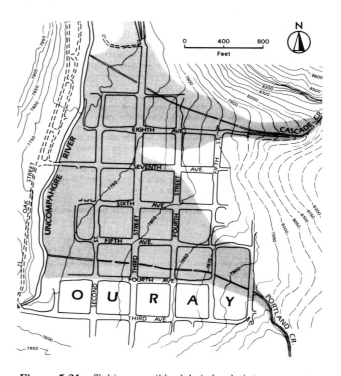

Figure 5-31. *Taking possible debris loads into account, a
map of the high flood hazard area of Ouray, Colorado,
suggests a greater area is actually at risk. Jochim 1986,
Colorado Geological Survey.*

Thompson Canyon, for example, there was an effort
following the devastating flash flood of 1976 to
prevent reconstruction of buildings on the river. But
the prohibition was never legislated because of the
vehement public outcry against it in a county whose
livelihood is based almost exclusively on summer
tourism.

Alluvial Terraces and Fans. A floodplain that has
been abandoned because of a change in climate or a
tectonic uplift becomes an *alluvial terrace*. If its
elevation, gradient, or volume of flow is changed, a

111

stream will erode down through the old floodplain, leaving it as a pair of remnant terraces on either side of the valley.

Alluvial fans are conical landforms made of unconsolidated alluvial debris that is deposited where streams come out of steeply sloping terrain onto valley floors. With the reduced slope gradient, velocity drops and the stream can no longer carry the heavier debris. "Each stream valley opening onto the lowlands may have its own alluvial fan, and adjacent fans may eventually coalesce to form a relatively large apron of debris at the base of the mountain front" (Price 1981, p. 218). Alluvial fans are good indicators of the amount of erosion and mass wasting taking place upstream. Mountains that are no longer being uplifted as they erode will eventually be buried by these floods of rock debris.

Alluvial fans have been attractive for both agriculture and development because of their relatively smooth surface, flatter gradients, and productive soils. They often contain excellent aquifers and are good sources of groundwater. With increasing pressure for land in some mountain areas, housing is spreading beyond the valley edges and up the fans, sometimes even into canyon mouths. But as Professor Price asserted, "This is foolhardy." Alluvial fans are visible evidence of the power of runoff, and so development sited on or below fans runs a high risk of recurring damage (Fig. 5-32).

> *Debris fans are of particular interest to the planner since often they provide the only apparently suitable construction sites within otherwise steep, unstable terrain. Unless they bear recent signs of debris flows, or flood scars, the intrinsically hazardous nature of the site may escape the nonspecialist. . . . Also, many debris fans are avalanche runout areas. (Ives and Bovis 1978, p. 197)*

Alluvial terraces, on the other hand, usually have fewer drawbacks. As noted in Chapter 2, it has been the traditional practice in the Alps to locate villages on terraces, some of which, owing to several hundred years of logging on the slopes above, have become dangerously vulnerable to avalanches.

In the development of an alluvial terrace, among the most important site planning issues are the estimation of flood and avalanche hazard; the sizing of development in proportion to the land available; the preservation of forests above the site, as well as riparian and agriculturally productive land below; and sensitivity in siting, scaling, and massing the development.

Understanding streams and the landforms they produce is an integral part of designing in the mountains. Their constraints refer to the natural hazards associated with them and the potential for

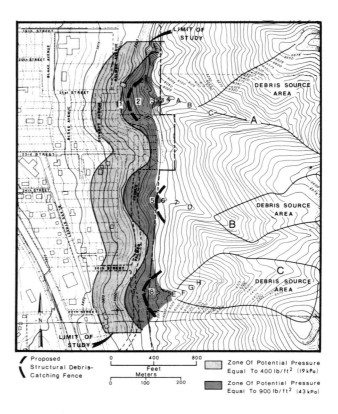

Figure 5-32. *Map of debris-flow drainage basins shows significant risk in residential neighborhoods of Glenwood Springs, Colorado. Mears 1977, Colorado Geological Survey.*

damage to valuable ecosystems. Water diversion, destruction of streamside vegetation, disturbance of the soil mantle, tainting of the water supply, and increased runoff and erosion are likely by-products of insensitive design near streams.

The advantages offered by streams in their natural form are their biological diversity and aesthetic and sensory qualities. In addition to vital habitat, streams will provide focal points, meditative spaces, edges, linkages, and natural flood protection if communities treat them as the important resources they are.

SLOPE: DESIGN ASSET OR DEVELOPMENT HAZARD?

Mountainous regions are composed of limitless variations on three themes: valley, peak, and slope. Slopes are the diagonals, the connective elements between peaks and valleys. They largely determine accessibility, visibility, and landscape character. Slopes consume more area than peaks or valleys.

The greatest challenge of a sloping site is the necessity to design in a diagonal plane. Partly because this compounds the constraints and costs of mountain building, developers tend to avoid slopes, opting instead for less complicated valley bottom sites.

In the mountains, however, flatter sites are always in short supply. Pressures are multiplying to preserve these more open expanses as scenic or agricultural resources. The dwindling supply of accessible, relatively flat land for building in the mountains makes it reasonable to weigh more seriously the utilization of slopes, even for projects of concentrated densities.

Throughout history, small-scale village clusters on sloping sites have been familiar images of traditional mountain development. The concept of constructing larger, higher-density buildings on slopes usually surfaces in a more urban context and is often categorized as futuristic (that is, impractical). Paolo Soleri's Arcosanti and Moshe Safdie's Habitats are such examples: massive design schemes in which stepbacks and terracing of upper stories mimic hilly topography in order to break up apparent building mass.

It is the scale of such schemes as much as their modernistic architectural style that makes them seem so inappropriate in the less populated mountain context. But this obscures their ability to teach ways of coping more efficiently with a sloping site. They illustrate technical advances in construction that make it increasingly feasible to consider larger structures and mixed-use complexes oriented to the diagonal plane.

Constraints and Land-Use Parameters Determined by Slope

Hazards.   Our modern bias against density on slopes is not so surprising in view of the well-established relationships among slope gradient, environmental hazards, and costs of building. Slope undeniably presents problems.

Although there is no exact "threshold" gradient above which all potential hazards become intolerable, increasing gradients do correspond to increasing difficulties. As slope increases, so does the potential for mass wasting, erosion, avalanche, and wildfire. The velocity and erosive power of runoff increase with slope, and accessibility and revegetation become more problematic. Landslides are most severe at gradients of 25 to 45 percent (1.5:1 to 1:1), and avalanches are most common at 30 to 45 percent. Wildfire hazard becomes critical at 30 percent or more because the forest canopy preheats downslope. These broad correlations between slope gradient and environmental hazards point to practical limitations on the development potential of slopes.

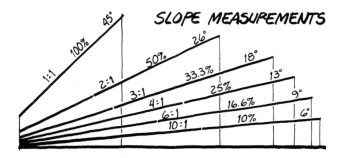

Land-Use Guidelines.   Some general conclusions can be made regarding development suitability based on slope and the soil and water conditions that tend to characterize certain gradients (Fig. 5-33). Typical parameters for arranging specific land uses, such as those suggested by the American Society of Landscape Architects (1978, p. 29), are understandably biased in favor of flat or near-flat land for housing and higher-intensity uses (Fig. 5-34).

According to these standards, slopes over 4 to 1 (25 percent) have limited functional use. On slopes over 2 to 1 (50 percent), the costs of development are generally thought to outweigh the benefits. Experience indicates that a slope over 1 to 1, natural or not, will require stabilization if there are to be any uses nearby. Boulder County in Colorado considers 30 percent the outside limit for subdivision development, and in Jefferson County west of Denver, the only land uses permitted on slopes over 30 percent are 5-acre subdivision lots.

Circulation Guidelines.   There are also standard parameters for circulation on slopes. Slopes over 10 percent are considered moderately steep for pedestrian circulation, and urban pathways in the fall line (perpendicular to the contours, or straight up the hill) are not appropriate. Even on a hiking trail, a sustained 10 to 15 percent grade is quite a workout for most people. For bicyclists, grades up to 5 percent are sustainable, but over 10 percent, many people have to walk their bikes.

Maximum gradient standards for automobile circulation are extremely difficult to accommodate in mountainous terrain without considerable disturbance (Fig. 5-35). The maximum grade for safe vehicular circulation is in the range of 7 to 8 percent. On slopes of 8 to 15 percent, roads built to the standards of most counties can no longer negotiate the fall line and must begin traversing the face of the slope. On slopes of 15 to 30 percent, extensive cut and fill is necessary for roads and structures, and sideslope erosion can be severe.

Because the effects of slope aspect are more prominent in the natural vegetation at steeper gradients, revegetation of regraded road banks often

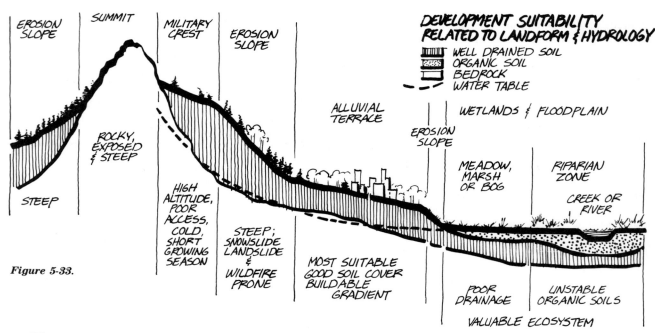

DEVELOPMENT SUITABILITY RELATED TO LANDFORM & HYDROLOGY
WELL DRAINED SOIL
ORGANIC SOIL
BEDROCK
WATER TABLE

Figure 5-33.

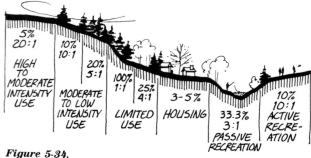

Figure 5-34.

proves to be more difficult. On slopes over 20 percent, most of the right-of-way is consumed by the drainage ditch alongside the roadway. Private property easements are required to provide adequate shoulders, and cut and fill slopes along the road grade can no longer be contained within the normal county right-of-way. In its landscape management handbook on roads, the Forest Service cautions that in many mountainous situations, a roadside fill slope of 1.5 to 1 or 2 to 1 will not catch natural grade until it reaches the bottom of the canyon (Fig. 5-36).

Costs and Opportunities of Building on Slopes

Although such standards are valid, they do not respond in a particularly helpful way to the limited range of choices or the costs and trade-offs faced by those building in the mountains. For mountain residents, practical limitations on available valley land may force consideration of sloping sites for building, although the same gradients would not be attractive in gentler geographies. From an aesthetic and ecological standpoint, the use of sloping sites may sometimes be preferable to site plans that consume the only open areas in the mountain landscape.

Sloping sites inevitably require more costly infrastructure and engineering solutions than would be true in "normal" flatland situations, but little research has been done to quantify the relationship of unit building costs to increases in slope gradient. In his article "Resort Construction Will Cost You," architect Sherwood Stockwell briefly noted the increased costs of building on hillsides:

For a hillside with a slope of 10 percent, a 60-foot-long unit must have a foundation six feet higher on the downhill end than on the uphill end. Moreover, the foundations must be stepped to offer adequate bearing. The net increase in area for this particular wall will be nearly 100 percent. It is possible to design the unit layout so that the floor levels step with the hill, but this may result in more complicated utility runs and adds to the cost of connecting stairs at $1,500–2,000 a run. (1983, pp. 12–13)

Other cost increases that can be attributed to sloping sites include foundations, because building codes in high-frost areas typically require them to be deeper than foundations in frost-free locations;

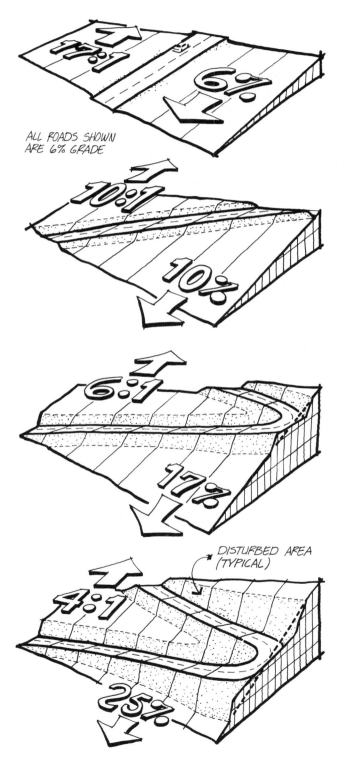

Figure 5-35. *Implications of slope gradient for the construction of a roadway with a consistent 6 percent grade.*

ALL ROADS SHOWN ARE 6% GRADE

DISTURBED AREA (TYPICAL)

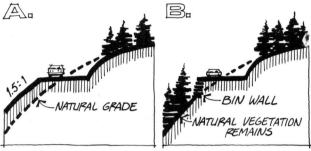

Figure 5-36.

foundation excavation, because site access is typically limited and boulders will probably be encountered under the topsoil; additional drainage measures, such as perforated perimeter drains and waterproofing of foundation walls to protect against groundwater seepage from hydrostatic pressure above the structure; deeper burial of utility lines; and outside stairs, ramps, retaining walls, and other slope stabilization measures.

The costs of building and maintaining roads also go up exponentially with increasing gradient. On steeper roads, the subgrade and surface asphalt must be double thick to resist the greater shear force of vehicles stopping on a downhill grade. In winter, icy inclined roads require more sand and cinders.

Given the problems and costs related to slope gradient, one might be inclined to share the general feeling that slopes are best avoided. This may not, however, do justice to the natural ecology of a mountain site or take advantage of its aesthetic potential.

One advantage of slope in the physical arrangement of a community is its potential as a "democratizing" factor in the distribution of intangible amenities. Clustered and stacked residential buildings on a slope, for example, can expose many more people to highly desired values, such as sunlight, private outdoor space, and views, than can buildings of equal density and height on a flat site (Fig. 5-37). Hillside developments on southerly slope aspects receive more solar radiation and stay warmer than those on the valley floor. South-facing slopes also provide an ideal way to protect against northerly storm winds and nighttime cold air drainage (Fig. 5-38).

The impact of slope gradient on the layout of circulation systems is usually viewed as negative. Yet there is an opportunity here to design separated circulation networks for cars and pedestrians, to restrict auto circulation in certain zones, and to create an experience of discovery for those on foot (Fig. 5-39).

Slopes also provide a design opportunity to manipulate and reduce the apparent bulk of larger

115

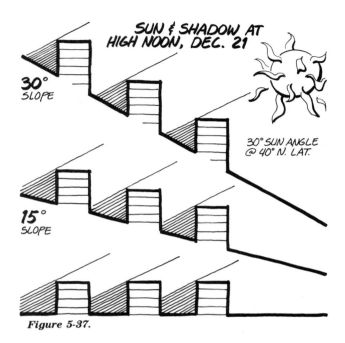

Figure 5-37.

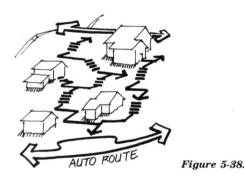

Figure 5-38.

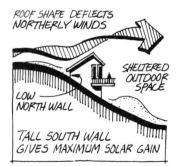

ROOF SHAPE DEFLECTS NORTHERLY WINDS

SHELTERED OUTDOOR SPACE

LOW NORTH WALL

TALL SOUTH WALL GIVES MAXIMUM SOLAR GAIN

Figure 5-39.

building masses. A structure will look smaller if it is terraced up a slope than if it is stacked vertically. The diagonal orientation breaks up the mass, reduces the perceived scale, and reveals the underlying terrain inclination (Fig. 5-40).

Figure 5-40. *Breaking up building masses on a slope.*

Because a sloping site is more visible from afar than a flat site is, building on a slope means dangers to visual quality as well as place-making opportunities. The scale, form, siting, and detailing of structures (especially rooflines), as well as the response to natural vegetation patterns, are essential to the ease with which a development fits on a slope. The retention of pockets of natural landscape and a sensitive layout of roads help integrate structures into the setting and make them less obtrusive.

Highly visible development on mountainsides need not be an unwelcome intrusion. To the contrary, vernacular hillslope architecture offers evidence that it can be appealing. Successful siting on slopes can be achieved with the right combination of density, scale, topographic sensitivity, and budget.

DESIGN GUIDELINES

Site Selection

1. Match the development program to the available land. Consider the minimum and maximum slope gradients that can work for each type of land use in the development program. Then compare the amount of land needed for the program with the amount of usable land on each alternative site at various gradients. Select the site that best matches the program with the land, remembering the visual opportunities of building on slopes and the scenic value of meadowland left open.

2. Respect relationships between topography and climate. Look for a site with warmer slope aspects, understanding that these areas are drier and so will limit new landscaping. If possible, avoid narrow, shaded valley bottoms, north-facing slopes, and lateral valleys aligned with prevailing storm winds.

3. Avoid sites that show evidence of slope instability, landslides, avalanches, or other high-risk natural hazards.

4. Avoid sites within the physiographic floodplain, on important groundwater recharge areas, or where the groundwater table is near the surface.

5. Seek a site that is distinguished by special vantage points, views, natural landmarks and water features, a sheltering sense of enclosure, and topographically defined boundaries.

Site Planning

1. Focus on the circulation plan as the first order of business in organizing a mountain site plan. Lay out a circulation network that works with the topography, achieves sensible slope gradients (8 percent maximum for paths, roads, and driveways; 6 percent or less in north-facing or shady areas), and adheres to accepted standards for minimum turning radii. If it is not possible to accommodate the traffic projected in the design program under any reasonable site plan alternative, then reconsider decisions made in selecting the site, choosing transportation methods, or allocating densities.

2. Avoid long street and pathway segments perpendicular to the contours on a slope, as they will channel torrential runoff in heavy rain. Size stormwater drains to handle major rainstorms (50- or 100-year events). On footpaths, use a cross pitch, water bars, and rock-lined swales to do the same.

3. Consider the disabled in the layout of uses and linkages. To date, few mountain projects have attempted to respond to the needs of the disabled, for whom circulation in sloping terrain can be a major obstacle. As programs for the disabled expand into winter sports, this is an oversight that should be reversed. For projects constructed with federal funding, accessibility is mandated by law.[4] Despite the inadequacy of uniform standards for handicapped access in extreme climates, many unnecessary obstacles can be avoided by thoughtful site planning of urban pathways, ramps, parking areas, building entries, and trails.

In planning handicapped-accessible circulation systems, attention should focus on gradients (in developed areas, not in excess of 5 percent, with flat

[4]The Architectural Barriers Act of 1968, Public Law 90–480 (as amended through 1978), 42 U.S.C. 4151 et seq., was passed to ensure that buildings constructed with federal funds are accessible to the handicapped. The Rehabilitation Act of 1973 (as amended in 1978), Title V, Section 504, prohibits discrimination on the basis of handicap in all federally funded programs or activities.

In accordance with the Architectural Barriers Act, Uniform Federal Accessibility Standards (UFAS) were published in 1984 (*Federal Register*, 49 FR 31528, August 7, 1984) and subsequently reprinted as a booklet (U.S. Government Printing Office: 1985–494–187).

areas every 100 feet, or 30 meters), cross slopes (no more than 2 percent, or 1 to 50), and pathway widths (minimum 6 feet, or 2 meters, for two-way movement) (Fig. 5-41 and Table 5-3). Because of the extreme winter climate, consider putting important entries, linkages, grade changes, and passenger unloading areas under roof. (Regarding outdoor facilities for the disabled, see Site Improvements and Structures, guideline 6.)

4. Envision the site plan in all three dimensions. Pay attention to the way that the massing fits the terrain and buildings meet the ground, especially on slopes. Use models, simulations, and sketches to see the effect of various siting alternatives on the ground form, on outdoor spaces adjacent to structures, and on views of and from the site (see Chapter 9, Distant Views: Massing, Textures, and Fit, for examples).

5. Preserve important sight lines, views, overlooks, and landmark natural features, and orient activity areas to these features to reinforce the public's perception of the place's character. Make sure that long-term control of visually important areas and view corridors is retained in the public interest.

6. Preserve natural stream courses, lakes, and ponds, using them as edges, trail corridors, and destinations.

7. If any local landforms are particularly expressive of mountain-building processes in the vicinity, use them as form-giving clues or focal interpretive references in a community site plan. Preserve and feature geomorphic evidence; link it with view corridors and the circulation network to give the fullest experience of the site's natural history.

8. Take advantage of opportunities to use contrasts in the natural setting. Mountain landforms are full of drama: places where views are unexpectedly revealed, cliff meets valley floor, rock meets water, forest meets meadow, or the ground falls steeply away. Buildings or spaces for people interjected at these points may be more memorable.

Grading, Land Shaping, and Slope Retention

1. Minimize the modification of natural terrain. In the difficult mountain environment, the best way to avoid long-term problems with slope stability and revegetation is to leave the natural landscape alone whenever possible. The foot and crest of any slope are especially sensitive to disturbance.

2. As a general rule, avoid disturbing natural slopes steeper than 2 to 1. Although exceptions are necessary on some mountain sites, the decision to disturb steeper slopes must be based solely on local soil types and site-specific geological and hydrological conditions, not on the demands of the design program. On all slopes where the consequences of slope failure would be significant, qualified geotechnical professionals must be engaged early in the process to assist in slope analysis and site planning.

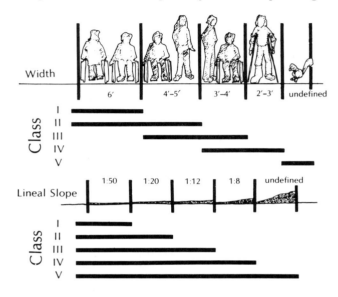

Figure 5-41. *Width and gradient guidelines for trails that can accommodate the disabled. U.S. Department of the Interior, Heritage Conservation and Recreation Service, 1980.*

3. Reduce the amount of grading on slopes. If a sloping site has been chosen for building, a number of strategies can be tried to minimize grading (Fig. 5-42): Concentrate the site plan to pull in the limits of sitework. Test various alternatives for siting roads and buildings in order to find the one that requires the least cut and fill. Experiment with grade adjustments and various types of slope retention methods.

Don't feel obliged to bring cars right to the front door; keep driveways and surface or covered parking some distance uphill or downhill on flatter ground and provide less intrusive pathways from there to the structures.

Reduce the amount of land required for a given floor area by trying multistoried buildings, split levels, and floor elevations that step in increments up the slope. Provide elevators and buildings entries at several different levels. Reject any plan that calls for a large flat building pad on a slope. Consider orienting buildings perpendicular to the contours and stepping them down the hill if that would require less grading to facilitate driveway access and positive drainage around the structure. Consider other foundation solutions: pole foundations, cantilevers, or foundations that daylight on the downhill side (Fig. 5-43).

For roads and pathways, use retaining structures to regain natural grade more quickly, and use bridges rather than fill over creeks and gullies.

Table 5-3 Planning Guidelines for Accessible Trails

| Features | Class of Trail | | | | |
	I	**II**	**III**	**IV**	**V**
Length	100 to 150 ft.	.25 to 1 mi.	1 to 3 mi.	3 to 10 mi.	over 10 mi.
Rest Stops	100 to 150 ft.	200 to 300 ft.	500 to 600 ft.	every mile	none needed
Width	1-way: 4 ft. 2-way: 6 ft.	3 to 4 ft. 4 to 5 ft.	3 to 4 ft.	2 to 3 ft.	undefined
Shoulder	1.5 ft. grass, slight slope toward trail	1 ft.	1 ft., no abrupt drops	½ ft.	undefined
Slope	1 to 50	1 to 20; 5-ft. level space every 100 ft.	1 to 12; 5-ft. level space every 30 ft.	1 to 8; level spaces where possible	natural (steps OK)
Cross Slope	none	1 to 50	1 to 25	1 to 20	undefined
Surface	concrete, asphalt	asphalt, wood planks, very fine crushed rock	firm, well-compacted surface	woodchips, coarse gravel	sand, rock
Edge	curbs, with 3-ft. rails where necessary	gradual ramps, with safety rails at cross slope	compacted earth level with trail	natural	nothing

Source: U.S. Department of the Interior, Heritage Conservation and Recreation Service, A guide to designing accessible outdoor recreation facilities (Ann Arbor, Mich.: Lake Central Office, 1980), p. 24, based on standards developed by the Minnesota Department of Natural Resources.

DISCOURAGED   ENCOURAGED

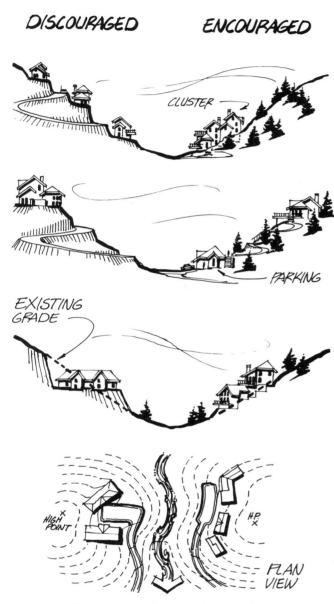

Figure 5-42. *Ways to reduce grading on a slope.*

Figure 5-43. *Varying foundation design to reduce grading.*

As a last resort, if all proposed grading schemes seem awkward or excessive or if the budget won't support these more expensive measures, go back to the beginning. Review the way that development parcels have been defined; perhaps the property lines are making things unnecessarily complicated. Redrawing boundaries, consolidating parcels, or organizing cooperative development approaches might reduce pressures to put improvements where they don't fit the slope.

4. Restore disturbed terrain to a natural appearance (Fig. 5-44). Create forms consistent with the character of the local surface relief; leave manicured berms in the suburbs. Blend cut and fill limits into the existing contours and slope gradients of the undisturbed landscape. Avoid straight planes in cut and fill banks, as the sharp angles they make at the top and bottom of slopes are not stable. It looks more natural to warp the slopes and round off the transitions. Lay back the sides of draws on cut slopes, and restore natural drainage channels and swales.

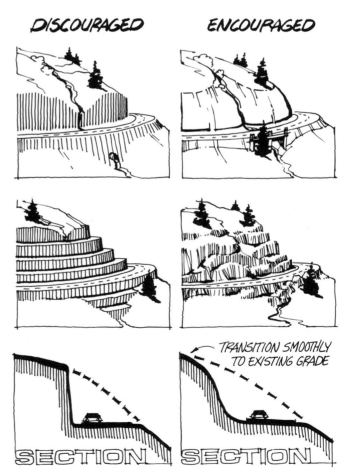

Figure 5-44. *Restoring landform to a natural appearance.*

119

Enhance landscape diversity by varying slope angles, creating false draws and ridges, and adding terraced pockets for new vegetation. Use treewells and binwalls to preserve as many mature trees as possible.

5. To reduce the risk of slope failure in restored terrain, grade new fill slopes no steeper than 2 to 1, and preferably around 3 to 1 for easier revegetation. Gradients on cut slopes can usually be a little steeper than those on fill slopes, but in both cases, the appropriate gradient must be derived from the specific rock and soil conditions in the area. General standards are not adequate guides.

6. Pay attention to the ground under a fill slope, for foundation preparation is the single most important factor in fill slope stability. The most sensitive point is along the plane of contact between fill and subgrade. Steps should be taken to key the fill into the slope, as by benching the underlying ground surface (Fig. 5-45).

7. Test the fill slope for adequate compaction. Even after the fill is compacted, there will still be a skin of looser soils on the slope that cannot be as well compacted. This layer should not be thicker than 12 to 18 inches (.3 to .5 m), or it may slip. If it is too deep, the slope should be overgraded and the skin trimmed back to get a good, firm surface.

8. Remember that although revegetation reduces erosion, it does not protect against slope failure. In fact, the need to water new vegetation may seriously conflict with the measures necessary to retain slope stability, especially on fill. Select dryland species for slope revegetation, and control irrigation to avoid destabilizing slopes or reactivating ancient slides.

9. If fill slopes steeper than 2 to 1 are required to rejoin existing grades, consider instead the use of terracing, retaining walls or other engineered support structures, and bedrock anchors for building foundations (Fig. 5-21). Although each site is different, a number of helpful publications address the technical aspects of designing adequate retention systems.[5] On sensitive slopes, enlist professional engineering assistance.

Minimize the visual impacts of slope stabilization measures. Engineered slopes almost always look engineered, and in a natural setting, they can be offensive (Fig. 5-46). If engineered slope retention devices cannot be avoided, they should be designed with respect for the landscape's aesthetic qualities, and they should make purposeful transitions from the retained slope back into the natural environment (Fig. 5-47).

[5]See Schuster and Krizek 1978, pp. 172–192, design and construction of soil slopes, and pp. 193–228, engineering of rock slopes; Abbott and Pollit 1981, pp. 245–256, geotechnics, and pp. 257–281, substructural case studies.

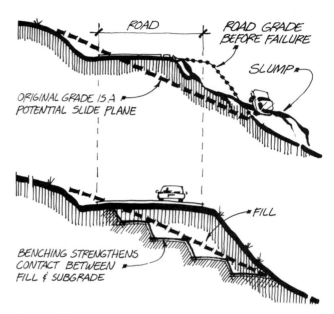

Figure 5-45. *Preparing the foundation for a stable fill slope.*

Figure 5-46. *Brutal slope treatment.*

Figure 5-47. *More attractive ways to retain a slope: (top) parabolic interlocking panels in reddish-tan precast concrete along Interstate 70 over Vail Pass, Colorado; (bottom) terraced timber walls and boulders from on-site excavations, Beaver Creek, Colorado.*

Options for making engineered features less intrusive include integrating retention features into the foundations of structures and the enclosing edges of public spaces; warping, curving, or otherwise varying wall planes across the slope; terracing and stepping back walls to reduce their scale and make room for planting; tinting or texturing concrete to match rock and soil on the site; incorporating rock masonry or natural rock outcrops; and screening with vegetation at the toe.

10. Orient cut-slope planes so that they work with existing jointing and bedding planes in the rock (Fig. 5-48). This may significantly reduce cut volumes and blasting costs. If slopes are cut without an understanding of the underlying rock structure, they can increase the potential for rock slope failure.

11. Use blasting techniques that fracture rock along existing joints and planes, giving the fracture plane a form and texture compatible with the rock's inherent structure. Accent existing ledges, natural rock outcrops, and boulders. For example, when Interstate 70 over Vail Pass, Colorado was constructed, "rock cuts were designed to produce a staggered bench effect which would reflect natural terrain and accent natural fracture lines in the rock. . . . Where slope stability was not a factor, 'wild cat' blasting techniques allowed natural rock fractures to be exposed . . ." (Colorado Dept. of Highways, n.d., p. 18).

12. Minimize the use of large earth-moving equipment in areas of particularly difficult access or gradient. For large projects, the use of helicopters to deliver and place some building components may be feasible.

13. If slope instability is not a risk, shape the ground plane and roughen the surface to trap and store meltwater in order to increase the soil moisture available to vegetation (also see guideline 8).

14. Grade to ensure drainage away from all structures, especially those cut into hillsides. Use drainage swales and perforated foundation drains to collect and carry runoff and subsurface water away from buildings on slopes.

15. Naturalize affected stream reaches to stabilize banks and improve fish and wildlife habitat (Figs. 5-27, 5-28, 5-29).

16. When developing the grading plan, consider the psychological messages associated with different landforms and angles of slope. The steeper the slope, the stronger the sense of spatial separation between the slope and the flatter ground. Activities sited within depressions and enclosing forms will seem more secluded, private, protected, and perhaps claustrophobic, whereas those on rising landforms will feel exposed, expansive, and dramatic. Designs that provide enclosure on one side and vistas on the other give the best of both. Curving and asymmetrical

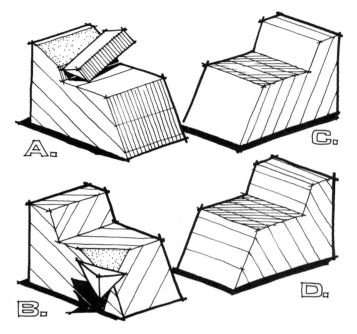

Figure 5-48. *Cut slopes oriented to the joints and bedding planes in rock (C, D) are more stable than those cut at other angles (A, B).*

forms seem more natural, tranquil, and harmonious than straight lines and planes, axial plans, or symmetrical forms. This does not mean that the latter are inappropriate but only that the designer understand the contrast they represent and use them accordingly.

Refer to Chapters 4 and 6 for related guidelines on drainage and erosion control.

Site Improvements and Structures

1. Pay attention to the transition in scale from mountain landforms to human activity places: Balance height-to-space relationships in building clusters, clarify hard and soft spatial edges to provide at least a partial sense of enclosure, frame views from protected vantage points, and inject design elements in controlled gradations of scale from background to foreground. The sense of shelter and proper human scale, psychologically important to a wilderness refuge, is vital to comfortable mountain spaces.

2. Design built forms that are consistent with the area's geomorphic origin. For example, use rooflines and building massing to echo the angles and shapes repeated in the natural landscape (Fig. 5-49); break up the building mass to conform to the slope; use indigenous materials and compatible colors; and mimic natural textures.

Figure 5-49. *Condominiums at Keystone Resort, Colorado, echo the angle of the slope behind. Backen Arrigoni & Ross, San Francisco, architecture; Berridge Associates Inc., San Francisco, landscape architecture.*

3. Use water features as a connective theme in the urban design of a community. Relate the form of new water features to natural stream processes and edge conditions. Take advantage of cut slopes and changes in grade to let water fall and make noise.

4. Avoid awkward changes of grade within major public open spaces; instead, take advantage of grade changes to separate and define activity areas.

5. Locate building entries where outside slopes meeting the building are gentle enough to facilitate auto and pedestrian access.

6. Review designs for structures and outdoor facilities to ensure that disabled persons can use them. Consider wheelchair dimensions and maneuvering requirements (Fig. 5-50), as well as the special needs of those who are less mobile, elderly, and/or vision or hearing impaired. Incorporate these in the detailing of the outdoor circulation system, especially pathway edges and surface materials, step risers and treads, ramp gradients, pavement grates, handrail grips and heights, and signage.

Consider these people's needs, too, in the design of outdoor activity areas (Fig. 5-51). Provide shade and rest areas at short intervals along trails, leaving room for wheelchairs and strollers near outdoor benches. Include benches with backrests and tables on flat ground with clearance and overhangs for wheelchairs. Add wheelstops on inclined surfaces, accessible drinking fountains and barbecue grills, and vantage points where handrails won't block the view for a seated person. Distinguish some activity areas by color and textural clues in pavements and furnishings. Ensure access in some manner to special recreational opportunities like lakeshores and streams, fishing spots, nature walks, chairlifts and gondolas, picnic areas, amphitheaters, and playgrounds.[6]

[6]See U.S. Dept. of Interior, Heritage Conservation and Recreation Service 1980; U.S. Dept. of Interior, National Park Service 1985; and Nordhaus et al. 1984, for guidance in designing accessible outdoor recreation facilities.

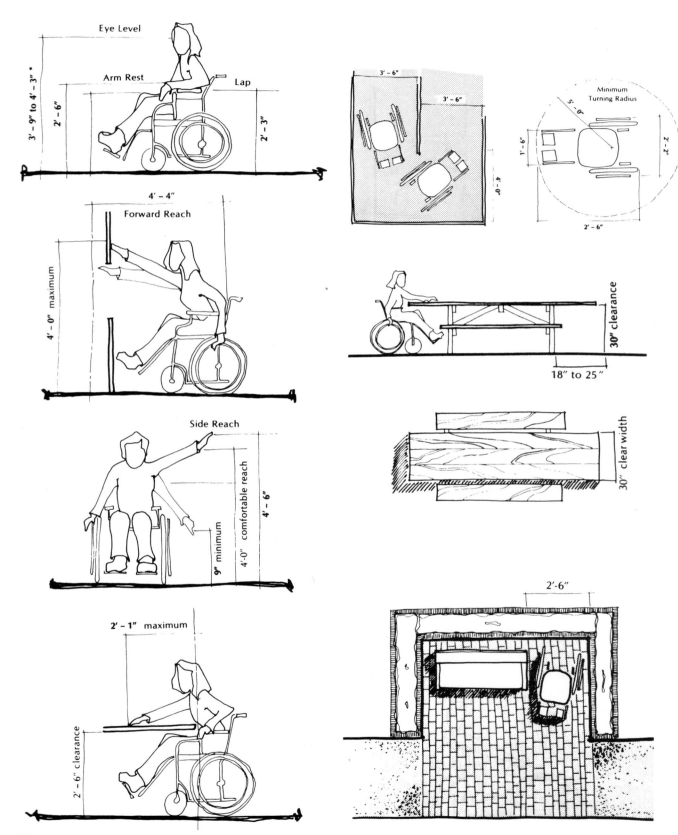

Figure 5-50. *Dimensions needed to maneuver in a wheelchair. U.S. Department of the Interior, Heritage Conservation and Recreation Service, 1980.*

Figure 5-51. *Outdoor amenities designed to accommodate the disabled. U.S. Department of the Interior, Heritage Conservation and Recreation Service, 1980.*

REFERENCES

American Society of Landscape Architects. 1978. Creating land for tomorrow. Landscape Architecture Technical Information Series 1 (no. 3).

Abbott, Derek, and Kimball Pollit. 1981. *Hill Housing.* New York: Watson-Guptill.

Campbell, Russell H. 1980. Landslide maps showing field classification, Point Dume Quadrangle, California. U.S. Department of the Interior Geological Survey, Miscellaneous Field Studies Map no. MF-1167.

Cleaves, E.T., A.E. Godfrey, and O. P. Bricker. 1970. Geochemical balance of a small watershed and its geomorphic implications. *Bulletin of the Geological Society of America,* 81:3015–3032.

Colorado Department of Highways. I-70 in a mountain environment. Report no. FHWA-TS-78-208.

Gilluly, James, A. L. Waters, and A. O. Woodford. 1968. *Principles of Geology,* 3rd ed. San Francisco: Freeman.

Ives, Jack D., and Michael J. Bovis. 1978. Natural hazard maps for land-use planning. San Juan Mountains, Colorado. *Arctic and Alpine Research* 10, no. 2: 185–212.

Jochim, Candace L. 1986. Debris flow hazard in the immediate vicinity of Ouray, Colorado. Denver: Colorado Geological Survey, Department of Natural Resources.

Jorgensen, Neil. 1977. *A Guide to New England's Landscape.* Chester, Conn.: Globe Pequot Press.

Leopold, Luna B. 1974. *Water, a Primer.* San Francisco: Freeman.

Lynch, Kevin. 1971. *Site Planning,* 2nd ed. Cambridge, Mass.: MIT Press.

Marsh, William M. 1978. *Environmental Analysis for Land Use and Site Planning.* New York: McGraw-Hill.

McLaughlin, William, and Frederick Bevis. 1975. Indian Hills environmental inventory—A citizen's tool for planning. Ft. Collins: Colorado State University Press.

McPhee, John. 1980. *Basin and Range.* New York: Farrar Strauss Giroux.

Mears, Arthur I. 1977. Debris-flow hazard analysis and mitigation: An example from Glenwood Springs Colorado. Colorado Geological Survey Information Series 8.

Nordhaus, Richard S., Min Kantrowitz, and William J. Siembieda. 1984. Accessible fishing: A planning handbook. Santa Fe: New Mexico Natural Resources Department.

O'Brien, Robert. 1988. Rehabilitation techniques for gravel-bed channels. Manuscript.

Price, Larry W. 1981. *Mountains and Man.* Berkeley and Los Angeles: University of California Press.

Rogers, William P., et al. 1974. Guidelines and criteria for identification and land-use controls of geologic hazard and mineral resource areas. Colorado Geological Survey, Department of Natural Resources, Special Pub. No. 6.

Schuster, Robert L., and Raymond J. Krizek, eds. 1978. *Landslides—Analysis and Control.* Washington, D.C.: National Academy of Sciences, Transportation Research Board Special Report no. 176.

Stockwell, Sherwood. 1983. Resort construction will cost you. *Urban Land,* October, pp. 12–15.

U.S.D.A. Forest Service. 1973–. *National Forest Landscape Management Handbooks.* (See bibliography for list of volumes.)

U.S.D.A. Soil Conservation Service. n.d. A guide for erosion and sediment control in urbanizing areas of Colorado (interim version). Denver.

U.S. Department of the Interior, Heritage Conservation and Recreation Service. 1980. A guide to designing accessible outdoor recreation facilities. Ann Arbor, Mich.: Lake Central Regional Office.

U.S. Department of the Interior, National Park Service. 1985. Some important items to consider when providing handicap accessible facilities. Denver Service Center.

U.S. Department of Transportation, Federal Highway Administration. 1986. Guidelines for slope maintenance and slide restoration. Report no. FHWA-TS-85-231.

Vail, Colorado. n.d. Draft report on water quality.

Whitney, Stephen R. 1983. *A Field Guide to the Cascades and Olympics.* Seattle: The Mountaineers.

Coast Range, California, landscape is overlain with the Soil Conservation Service's land capability classes. Classes I through IV soils are considered suitable for cultivation, but classes V through VIII are not. Photo by the Soil Conservation Service.

6

MOUNTAIN SOILS: A PROFILE OF EXTREMES

Soil is the weathered layer of the earth's crust in which plant roots, living organisms, and the products of their decay are intermingled. As a growth medium for plants, soil both influences and is influenced by the biotic environment. Its character is the net result of the action of climate and organisms, especially vegetation, on the soil's parent material.

The Soil Profile. Soil is formed by plant growth, by the introduction and decomposition of organic matter, and by leaching. Water moving downward through the pores in the soil carries with it chemicals in solution and very fine particles, such as clay, in suspension. Without the influence of additive processes, leaching increases the percentage of sandy material in the surface soil layer and, depending on the rate of organic decay, reduces the nutrients there. At the same time, it increases the content of clays and nutrients in the lower layers.

Individual soils reflect a chronology of development related to time, temperatures and precipitation, length of the growing season, vegetation types, rate of organic decay, topography, groundwater, and parent material. The history of a site is also a factor, for past and present land uses, fires, floods, and excessive erosion help determine the soil's character as well.

The soil body consists of layers, or *horizons,* of variable thicknesses in which mineral and organic elements are combined in varying proportions. Although some geological deposits and depositional layering look similar to soils, they are not the same; soils differ from parent materials in important physical, chemical, and mineralogical properties and in the presence of organic components.

A *soil profile* is the vertical arrangement of all the soil horizons down to the parent material (Fig. 6-1). The "master" horizons are designated O, A, E, B, C, and R. Not all of them are present in every soil. These horizons may be further broken down into subhorizons according to their mineral and clay content. The soil profile can be used as a qualitative measure of the amount of change that has taken place in the parent material.

The *O horizon* is a layer of fresh and decaying plant matter on the surface of a mineral soil. Under it (if it is present), is the *A horizon,* a surface layer of mineral material mixed with humified organic matter. The *E horizon,* if present, is an eluviated (leached) layer characterized by a lack of clays and soluble minerals and a concentration of sand and silt particles.

Underneath the surface layer(s) is the *B horizon,*

Figure 6-1. *Soil test pit shows the depth in inches of the horizons in the Earcree gravelly sandy loam, Front Range, Colorado. On 9 to 15 percent slopes and with an aspen overstory, the relatively dark, cold soil is a mollisol (great group: cryoboroll). Photo by the Soil Conservation Service.*

which exhibits a variety of characteristics related to the parent material but in which decomposition has left little or no evidence of the original rock structure. In this horizon, there may be an accumulation of clays, mineral compounds, and resistant materials left after the soluble constituents have been removed by weathering and leaching.

The *C horizon* consists of slightly weathered subsurface materials, excluding bedrock. It may contain a concentration of mineral oxides, silica, carbonates, and more soluble salts. In desert environments, there may also be a *K horizon,* impregnated with carbonate and laminated or cemented. Beneath these is the *R horizon* of unweathered bedrock.

Figure 6-2. *The Troutdale–Rogert–Kittredge complex of loams in the Front Range, Colorado, shows a fairly typical mountain soil profile. These shallow, residual mollisols (cryoborolls) are nowhere deeper than 20 inches (.5 m) to bedrock. Photo by the Soil Conservation Service.*

Common Traits of Mountain Soils. Profiles of mountain soils reflect the extreme diversity of mountain environments. Soil types occur in an intricate, geographically discontinuous mosaic. Soils at higher altitudes vary widely in depth, rockiness, water-holding capacity, susceptibility to erosion, and fertility.

Still, many mountain soils have common traits: Except in drainages, they are often shallow; though some soils have a high clay content, many lack finer-textured particles; and they are typically deficient in nitrogen and phosphorus, relatively low in organic matter, excessively acidic or alkaline, and inadequate in soil moisture (Nishimura 1974, p. 5). In general, the steep slopes, rapid downslope drainage, and cold temperatures of the higher mountains contribute to soils that have higher percentages of undecomposed organic material and that are less well developed, colder, and stonier (Fig. 6-2).

FACTORS IN SOIL CHARACTER

The Mountain Climate. Of all the factors influencing the nature of a soil, climate is perhaps the dominant one, for it determines the soil's organic content. Humus will accumulate if vegetative productivity, which requires moisture, is greater than decay. Low temperatures and decreasing moisture at higher elevations restrict the biological activity of both animals and plants. There are fewer organisms in the soil, less organic matter is produced, and what material does accumulate decomposes more slowly (Price 1981, p. 235). In colder, semiarid mountain climates, physical weathering thus becomes relatively more important than biological weathering is to the process of soil formation.

In contrast, the wet climate of the Pacific Northwest has produced some of the least fertile mountain soils in the country, its lush forests notwithstanding. In areas of constant fog, effective precipitation levels are so high that virtually all soluble nutrients are leached out of the surface layers.

In the Appalachian mountains, the humid and relatively warmer climate supports the growth of hardwoods and oaks and encourages a much higher rate of biotic decay. This, in combination with the igneous geology of the parent rocks, causes the soils to be very acidic, a problem rarely encountered in the semiarid West.

Given the climate and altitude, a mountain soil takes considerably more time to form than those in wetter places and lower elevations. A study in the subalpine zone of the Colorado Rockies estimated that it takes some 2750 years for a soil with distinct horizons and a stable pH to form, and much longer for complete development (Retzer 1974, p. 784). In warmer, more humid climates, a few centuries might be sufficient. Clearly, it is not a resource we can afford to take lightly.

Parent Materials and the Factor of Time. The mineral composition, fertility, texture, and moisture-holding capacity of an alpine soil, like those of any other soil, are largely derived from the parent material. Parent materials vary in their response to the forces of weathering. Softer sedimentary rocks break down more readily and tend to form finer-textured, nonacidic soils. Basalt and volcanically derived bedrocks also break down relatively quickly.

Hard, crystalline rocks, however, are more typical of mountain environments because of the pressure and heat associated with mountain-building processes. Granite, the spine of many mountain ranges, is generally slow to decompose (unless it contains unusually expansive mineral particles) and yields a coarse-textured soil. Because granitic rocks are generally rich in minerals containing iron, potassium, and magnesium, water leaching downward through weathered material of this type may carry large amounts of dissolved mineral matter and clay, so that marked horizons will eventually result.

Once weathered, rock particles may remain in place over bedrock to form a *residual* soil, or they may be moved by wind, water, or glacial erosion to form a deposited, or *transported,* soil (Fig. 6-3). *Alluvium* (material transported by water), *colluvium* (material at the foot of a slope that was moved downhill by the force of gravity), and *loess* (windblown silt, often from glacial till) form the basis for most transported soils. Soils generally form more quickly on unconsolidated deposits than on bedrock. In mountains, because of the high surface relief, transported soils are the more frequently encountered of the two types.

The landscape's geomorphic origins sometimes provide useful clues to identifying parent materials. Certain peak and valley landforms characteristic of volcanic or alluvial processes, for example, may be reflected in the composition and color of soils in the vicinity.

The influence of the parent material is more apparent in young soils and diminishes with time (Price 1981, p. 240). Because mountains, especially glaciated ranges, are geologically younger landscapes than lowlands, parent rocks play a disproportionately greater role in the mineral composition, pH, and texture of an alpine soil.

Parent material is the primary factor in soil texture, which is classified according to the relative percentages of sand, silt, and clay in the soil (Fig. 6-4). *Loams* are soils having roughly equal amounts of sand and silt and about half that proportion of clay.

Alpine soils are most commonly loams and sandy loams (Nishimura 1974, p. 5). Sandy loams, being coarse, rocky, and often shallow, are typically well drained. Derived from igneous or metamorphic rocks, they show higher acidity and low fertility, making them harder to revegetate.

Mountain loams may be either well drained or poorly drained. Well-drained loams and silt loams generally develop in fine-textured parent materials such as weathered limestone, shale, or wind-blown loess. These soils are relatively deeper and darker in color, productive, and easier to revegetate, unless they are compacted. Poorly drained loams are usually found in drainageways and have formed over alluvium, colluvium, or glacial materials. They are productive, too, but they often signal a high water table and potentially unstable soil.

Topography. Even when the parent material is the same, soils in topographically different positions

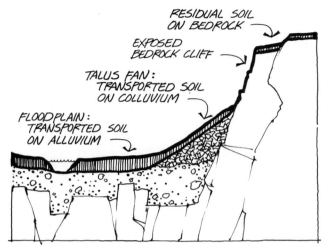

Figure 6-3.

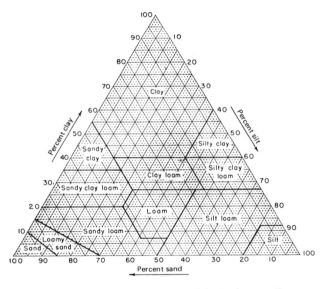

Figure 6-4. *The U.S. Department of Agriculture soil texture classification chart. Particles from 2.0 mm to 0.05 mm in diameter are sand; from 0.05 to 0.002 mm, silt; smaller than 0.002, clay.*

develop differently. The infiltration rate of water into a soil, the velocity of runoff on its surface, and the degree of soil moisture retention all are affected by variations in slope gradient, aspect, and topographic shading.

Pronounced changes in slope gradient often suggest a change in the intensity of erosion by runoff or a change from erosion to deposition as the predominant process shaping the land. These changes correspond to variations in the soil's texture, composition, and depth. On slopes, the soil formation process may be

129

Figure 6-5. *This edge between aspen forest and grassland in Summit County, Colorado, is marked by a change in soils. The Youga loams in the foreground have properties slightly different from those of the Anvik loams under the aspen, though both series are mollisols (cryoborolls). Photo by the Soil Conservation Service.*

constantly interrupted, as ongoing erosion and mass wasting continually expose new rock surfaces, where the process must start anew.

Position on the slope is also a factor. On hilltops, erosion and wind desiccation may be more severe, and there is little chance for water to percolate into the developing soil. Price described the influence of slope:

> Soils on elevated and steeper slopes are generally well-drained, and surface water is quickly lost as runoff. On lower slopes and in valleys, soils are moister because of the greater precipitation collection area above them, a higher water table, and more persistent shade climates (the sun is blocked by surrounding slopes). (1981, p. 239).

On some higher slopes, average soil temperatures may actually be warmer than they are at lower elevations because there is more sun, less duff to shade the ground, and more snow to insulate it in winter.

The best soil moisture conditions in mountain regions occur in bottomlands, not on ridges or slopes. (The exception is in the arid and semiarid intermountain basins in the West, where soils on the basin floor are often saline or alkaline and only a few plant species can adapt.) In rolling terrain, soils on north- or east-facing slopes retain more moisture than those facing south or west. Despite the semiarid climate of most higher-altitude mountain regions, soils high in organic content can be found where the

terrain allows moisture to collect and where overgrazing has not occurred.

Mountain Vegetation. Soil and the vegetation it supports interact in a delicate process. The kind of organic matter added to the soil makes one soil distinct from another even when the parent rock, topography, and time are the same. On large scales, soil types are mapped on aerial photos simply by differentiating vegetative ecosystems.

Though not always the case, the edge between grasslands and forest is typically one of the sharpest and most predictable soil boundaries in the mountain environment (Fig. 6-5). Soils supporting grasses and perennials generally have thicker, more highly organic A horizons than soils under shrubs or conifers, and similarly, soils under deciduous trees differ from those under evergreens (Fig. 6-6). Evergreen needles, rich in silica and slow to decompose, add less organic material and make the soil more acidic.

Soils under aspen or hardwood forests and those associated with riparian ecosystems are generally more productive than those under coniferous forests (that is, they produce more organic material by weight, or *biomass*). In the western mountains, aspen contribute to soils that are porous, loamy, and moist; they are typically deeper and less rocky than soils occupied by conifers (D. Lynch 1974, p. 25). U.S. Forest Service research has shown that where aspen have been removed, the soil's organic content has declined (Tew 1968). In the study's test plots, removal of aspen resulted in a decrease in the soil's moisture-holding capacity. Such a decline slows the cycling of mineral nutrients and over time can reduce soil productivity. Cohesiveness and soil porosity also drop, thereby increasing the potential for slope instability.

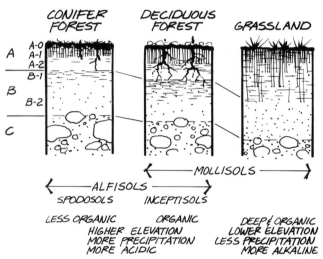

Figure 6-6. *Soils and soil characteristics under forests, compared with those under grasslands.*

COMMON MOUNTAIN SOIL TYPES

In 1960, in an effort to remedy imprecision in the system then being used to describe soils, the U.S.D.A. Soil Conservation Service introduced a new system of soil classification called the *7th approximation.* Amended several times since then and finally published in 1975 as *Soil Taxonomy,* this system assembles unnerving strings of Latin, Greek, and invented syllables to describe in detail the characteristics of a soil.

The 7th approximation system organizes soils into ten soil orders differentiated from one another by quantifiable characteristics of the horizons in their soil profiles. Classifications are based exclusively on a soil's morphology (form and structure) rather than on its origin or association with certain ecosystems. To categorize a soil, the system considers the soil's formative processes, its relative wetness or dryness, its mineralogy and age, its texture and temperature, and the amount of organic matter it contains. These are called the soil's *diagnostic properties.*

Orders are further divided into suborders, great groups, subgroups, families, and series (Table 6-1).

Suborder names always have two syllables, the first suggesting the soil's dominant diagnostic properties, such as moisture or temperature regime, and the second repeating the formative syllable from the name of the order. Great group names combine the suborder name with a prefix that again flags the soil's diagnostic properties (Table 6-2).

A typical Soil Conservation Service soil survey focuses on the *soil series,* which groups together soil profiles that are somewhat similar in thickness, arrangement, and properties of the soil horizons. Soil series are named for local places or features and are subdivided into *soil types* mainly by differences in texture.

Soil types are further subdivided into *soil phases,* the mapping units used in detailed soil surveys. On soil maps, phases are differentiated by slope gradient, physiographic position, thickness of the soil profile or horizons, and the amount of erosion, stoniness, and salinity.

Table 6-1 Categories in the Seventh Approximation System of Soil Classification

Category	Example
Order (10)	Alfisol
Suborder (47)	Boralf
Great Group	Cryoboralf
Subgroup	Typic Cryoboralf
Family	Fine-loamy, mixed, Typic Cryoboralf
Series	Frisco, Peeler
Soil Type[a]	sandy loam
Soil Phase[a]	6 to 25 percent slope

[a]These two categories are used in soil surveys but are not part of the soil taxonomy system.

Table 6-2 Common Diagnostic Syllables in Mountain Soil Names

alb-	light colored
aqu-	prolonged wetness
arg-	argillic horizon (accumulated clays)
arid-	dry
bor-	associated with cool environments
cryo-	associated with frigid environments
ferr-	high iron content
fluv-	floodplain soils
ochr-	light in color and low in organic matter
orth-	common, normal
torr-	hot and dry
ust-	limited moisture (intermediate moisture regime between *arid-* and *xer-*)
xer-	cool, moist winters; warm, dry summers
umbr-	dark

Of the ten orders, seven are represented in temperate-zone mountains (Table 6-3). Of those, only three (inceptisols, alfisols, and mollisols) are common throughout most mountain areas.

Entisols. (The formative syllable, *ent-,* is an invented one meaning "recent"; *sol* means "ground" or "soil.") Entisols are very young mineral soils, the youngest of the ten orders. They show little evidence of distinct soil horizons and usually have a pale (ochric) surface layer. The thinnest entisols overlie bare rock on exposed, actively eroding ridges and slopes. Slightly deeper entisols are found over unconsolidated rocky material on moraines, talus slopes, fans, and floodplains, where continual deposits of new alluvium or colluvium prevent the

Table 6-3 Soil Orders Found in Temperate Mountain Regions

Entisols	Rocky ridges, talus slopes, floodplains
Inceptisols	Tundra grasslands, alpine meadows, glacial till
Alfisols	Coniferous forests
Mollisols	Montane grasslands, deciduous forests
Aridisols	Dry intermountain basins
Spodosols	Coniferous forests in areas with more precipitation in winter (xeric)
Histosols	Bogs and depressions

Figure 6-7. *Parklike stands of lodgepole pine grow on the Scout–Upson association of loamy soils in Grand County, Colorado. The Scout soils are cold, light-colored inceptisols (cryochrepts), and the Upson soils are typical coarse-loamy entisols (cryorthents). Photo by the Soil Conservation Service.*

development of soil horizons. In general, entisols are uncohesive, rocky, fairly dry, and highly erodible and support sparse vegetative cover (Fig. 6-7).

Inceptisols. (The formative syllable is *ept-,* derived from the Latin *inceptum,* meaning "beginning.") Inceptisols are developing soils. They have a better-defined A horizon than entisols but a less well defined B horizon than most other soil orders.

Inceptisols are typified by tundra soils above timberline, soils underlying alpine meadows and turf grasses, and soils on glacial till. They tend to be coarse, gravelly, and slightly acidic. One to 3 feet deep (30 to 80 cm), they suffer from nutrient depletion in the surface horizon because of continual leaching. They generally support a tight mat of herbs and grasses, without which they would rapidly erode (Fig. 6-8). Some inceptisols support forest cover, like lodgepole pine, that is tolerant of lower moisture and nutrient levels.

Inceptisols range from very poorly drained to well drained. The soils under turf are more often on upper slopes and exposed areas, dry in summer, and better draining. The meadow soils, more common in valleys and lower slopes, are moist nearly all the time and are less well drained.

Alfisols. (*Alf-* is a meaningless syllable identifying an order of soils that in the mountains are found primarily under spruce–fir forests) (Fig. 6-9). The central distinguishing features of alfisols are a light-colored (ochric) surface layer and the presence of an argillic horizon (an illuviated layer in which clays have accumulated) beneath a layer that has been leached of clay particles (eluviated).

Mollisols. (The formative syllable, *oll-,* is derived from the Latin *mollis,* meaning "soft.") Mollisols are the dark-colored soils of the steppes. Common in the European mountains, they are relatively deep, good soils with distinct horizons. They have A horizons high in organic matter content, a neutral to slightly alkaline pH, and a great number of the negatively charged ions (bases) that soil particles need to hold and make nutrients available to plants.[1] Mollisols are deeper, somewhat drier, and less leached than inceptisols. In the Rockies and Sierras, mollisols typically underlie subalpine and alpine grasslands or aspen forests. They often support highly productive range and big game habitat (Fig. 6-10).

[1]This is known as the *base-exchange capacity.* The higher it is, the better able the nutrients in solution are to adhere to the surface of soil particles. Clays have the highest base-exchange capacity, silts half as high as clays, and sand one-tenth to one-fifth as high.

Figure 6-8. *At timberline (11,500 ft., 3500 m) in Summit County, Colorado, the Grenadier gravelly loam in the foreground is an inceptisol (cryochrept), and the grassy alpine slopes in the background are underlain with cold, clayey mollisols (cryoborolls). Photo by the Soil Conservation Service.*

Figure 6-9. *Homesites in a subdivision along the Blue River, Summit County, Colorado, sit on mollisols (cryoborolls and cryaquolls) of the Handran series. Forested slopes in the middle distance are cold, fine-textured, clayey alfisols (cryoboralfs) of the Muggins series. Photo by the Soil Conservation Service.*

Figure 6-10. *The highly productive Mord loams under this subalpine range in Grand County, Colorado, are fine-textured, clayey mollisols (cryoborolls). They support occasional patches of aspen and provide important summer habitat for big game. Photo by the Soil Conservation Service.*

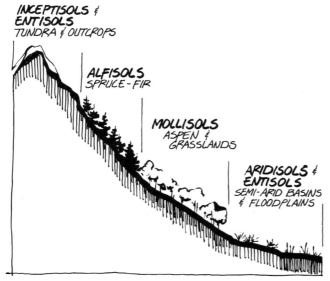

Figure 6-11.

These four soil orders form a rough spectrum of soil development. Under grasses, mountain soils in areas of less favorable climate or topography tend to be inceptisols, changing to mollisols over time or where conditions are better. Similarly, soils under trees change from entisols to inceptisols to alfisols, a sequence that also corresponds to the influence of time and a more favorable climate or surface relief.

There is also a discernible sequence related to elevation: Inceptisols tend to occur at the higher altitudes, changing to alfisols under conifer forests below timberline and then to mollisols under aspen and lower grasslands (Fig. 6-11). Entisols, occurring wherever soil formation processes have been interrupted, do not fit this sequence, nor do the other three soil orders represented in mountain regions. Aridisols and spodosols are more the result of climatic factors, and a glaciated topography plays a primary role in the formation of histosols.

Aridisols. (The formative syllable is *id-*, from the Latin *aridus*, meaning "dry.") Found in virtually all intermountain basins, aridisols are typical of very dry regions, where low precipitation and high evaporation contribute to high concentrations of carbonates, salts, or silicas in the lower soil horizons. Usually very light colored, aridisols are often accompanied by a hardpan K horizon (Fig. 6-12).

In these environments, mountains are like oases. Reversing the more typical relationship of altitude and moisture, mountains in arid regions provide (up to a certain point) greater moisture with increasing altitude, despite the lower temperatures (Price 1981, p. 246). Above the basin floor, forests begin; soils change to other types and become deeper; and both species and biomass increase (Fig. 6-13).

Figure 6-12. *Profile shows the stoniness and light color of the shallow Dahlquist series, an aridisol in Grand County, Colorado. Photo by the Soil Conservation Service.*

Figure 6-13. *A characteristic western mountain landscape in winter. The Forelle loam in the foreground is irrigated for hay, and the steep Dahlquist–Stunner loams in the background provide good winter range for big game. Both are cold, somewhat organic, clayey aridisols. Photo by the Soil Conservation Service.*

Spodosols. (The formative syllable, *od-,* comes from the Greek *spodos,* meaning "wood ash.") Spodosols exhibit distinct horizons and are moderately deep, well drained, and acidic. What sets them apart is their characteristic grayish white, highly leached A horizon and, beneath it, a spodic horizon where organic carbon and iron have accumulated. Spodosols can form over many parent materials, although granitic rocks are the most common.

Spodosols are typical of northerly regions where temperatures are cool, wintertime precipitation is heavy, and the predominant vegetation is coniferous forest. Because decomposition under these circumstances is very slow, it takes a long time for organic matter to be integrated into the soil. A layer of evergreen needles and humus accumulates on the surface, and water moving through it becomes charged with a dilute solution of humic acid. Percolating through the A horizon, the mildly acidic solution dissolves the mineral oxides and leaves the quartz, which is sterile. The oxides, as well as clays and bases, accumulate in the B horizon.

Spodosols are common throughout the Pacific Northwest and the mountains of northern New England, where they form over granitic glacial till. They are not characteristic of the hardwood forests of New England and the Cascades. Except for oaks, leaf detritus is not as acidic as conifer needles, and because hardwoods have deeper roots, air and organic matter can penetrate the soil more deeply.

Histosols. (The root comes from the Greek *histos,* meaning "tissue.") Histosols are peat and bog soils. They are poorly draining and waterlogged, with highly organic surface horizons and partially decomposed plants covering the soil surface. They are generally acidic, although there are exceptions. They occur in depressions into which water seeps or accumulates and are always anaerobic for most of the growing season. Although they can be found in most mountain regions, they are not common in America outside the glaciated areas of New England.

SOIL PROPERTIES RELEVANT TO DESIGN

Soil analysis helps define the extent of landscape change that designers can expect to attain. Success in restoring a disturbed mountain landscape is heavily dependent on the nature of its soils and substrata, for these, along with slope gradient, strongly influence the potential for slope instability and control the moisture available for plants. The descriptive classifications of formal soil surveys call attention to site conditions critical to intelligent site planning, such as drainage and runoff patterns, hazardous and erosion-prone zones, and areas where soils can safely support construction and revegetation.

Soil properties that relate to engineering and construction can be roughly identified in the field by simple tests for pH, plasticity, texture, and depth. More accurate quantitative analysis must be done in a laboratory from soil-boring samples. For engineering purposes, the qualities of the topsoil are disregarded. Among the soil properties that have the greatest bearing on mountain design options are the following:

Bearing Capacity and Stability Under Structures and Paving. Bearing capacity and stability are largely a function of a soil's tendency to swell when wet. The greater the tendency, the harder it will be to achieve adequate soil compaction. Shrink–swell potential is related to a soil's plasticity and liquid-holding limit. Soils and subsoils that are high in silt, though stable when dry, swell when saturated and heave when frozen. Clays are less affected by frost but also swell and slip when wet. Organic soils and peats are too compressible. They subside under loads and must be avoided or removed. Gravelly and sandy soils provide good structural foundations because they are well draining and high in bearing strength.

Building and road foundations over less stable soils must go deep enough to reach strong bearing layers or bedrock. Foundations on fill, except well-compacted sands and gravels, are not reliable.

Figure 6-14. *Fill slope failure southwest of Morrison, Colorado, spring 1970. Floodwaters at the toe caused the newly constructed roadside slopes to slough and cave in. Photo by the Soil Conservation Service.*

Soils that are difficult to compact or that have a tendency toward frost heaving can ruin the best-laid plans for paving. Expansion or subsidence of soils and subsoils can cause cracks that, once opened, get worse as water enters, freezes, and expands. Paving materials must be strong, dense, unitized, or elastic to cope with expansive soils.

Stability on Slopes. The saturation of soils is a primary cause of slope failure and mudslides. Thin, unconsolidated soils and thicker, clayey soils, expanding and increasing in weight when wet, respond more readily to the pull of gravity. On slopes over 10 percent, wetted subsoil clays swell and become impervious and may cause overlying permeable soils to slip. Many mountain subsoils prove difficult to compact adequately on reconstructed slopes, with the result that fill slopes are particularly prone to slippage (Fig. 6-14).

A number of reference works on site planning offer broad parameters for soil stability. They note that undisturbed soils are less likely to slip on slopes with gradients of up to 10 degrees or over 45 degrees (where there isn't much soil anyway) and that soil slippage is most common on slopes of 2-to-1 to 1-to-1 gradients (25° to 45°). However, because slope gradient is not the only controlling variable, these guidelines are too general to be of any real value on specific sites. One must also take into account the soil type and depth, vegetative cover, and physical mechanisms of slope movement, such as water or seismic events. (See Chapter 5, Mass Wasting and Slope Instability.)

Susceptibility to Erosion. Silty soils are extremely vulnerable to erosion, as are shallow horizons of unconsolidated soil and rock debris, which often cannot support a vegetative cover adequate to bind them. Once disturbed, these soils can be very difficult to protect even when severe slope gradient is not an aggravating factor.

Moisture and Drainage. A soil's porosity and permeability—its capacity to hold and transmit water—have implications for slope stability, foundation and roadway design, and septic fields. Sands and gravels, especially those having less than 10 percent silt or clay (called *clean*), typically drain well and are the only soils suitable for engineering purposes in their natural state. Clays usually drain very poorly.

Drainage is also a determining factor in plant growth. Inadequate soil porosity, extreme porosity, low percolation rates, and soils saturated by high groundwater are evidenced by the growth of specially adapted plant species and signal potential problems for the development of a site. Sandy soils cannot hold water well, as they drain and dry out too quickly.

Forest soils store as much as fifty times more soil moisture than urbanized land does (Untermann 1978, p. 171). When development replaces forested areas, it can change natural drainage and moisture regimes in ways that sooner or later prove devastating to existing soils and vegetation. Soils dry out because clearing allows more direct sunlight to reach the ground; thus their organic content and moisture-holding capacity are gradually reduced. New impervious surfaces increase runoff, drainage velocity, and erosion. With proper design, these impacts can be avoided or greatly reduced.

Quality as a Plant Growth Medium. Soil quality is a function of topography, climate, parent material, organisms, and time. The interaction of these five variables influences a soil's ability to support vegetation by controlling the soil's moisture regime, humus content, relative acidity, presence of available nutrients (especially potassium, phosphorus, and nitrogen), and depth.

Organic topsoils are typically the most productive soils as long as they are well drained, fertile, and not too acidic. A good topsoil will have approximately 7 percent minimum available soil moisture capacity (by weight), 3 to 20 percent organic matter, and 30 to 35 percent maximum clay content (Nishimura 1974, p. 7).

Before completing planting plans, it is advisable to make simple field tests for soil acidity and the presence of nutrients, as deficiencies that affect fertility can sometimes be remedied with preparatory and ongoing soil amendments.

Mountain subsoils are rarely suitable as a plant growth medium, as they are inherently low in plant nutrients, especially nitrogen, and usually have less than 1 percent organic matter. Exposed subsoils at high altitudes may also be highly acidic and toxic to plants. It is important, then, to distinguish between topsoil and subsoils in cut and fill calculations. It is also a good practice to stockpile topsoil at the site when grading and excavation begin. It may even be

advisable to amend the subsoil to improve long-term revegetation potential.

If more topsoil is required than is available on the site or nearby, sources of material should be identified before the plan is completed. If the topsoil must be imported, it may mean significant extra costs, which could influence the planned extent of the site work.

Revegetation Potential. Successful revegetation requires soils that are not prone to slippage and soils that provide what plants need for growth. If soils are less fertile, thin, rocky, cold, or lacking in moisture, the revegetation of disturbances will be problematic, lengthy, and expensive at best. The seed bank already resident in local soils is also critical to revegetation, an advantage that is often overlooked when on-site soils are replaced.

Soil Color. The mountain substrata and many of the mountain soils, except for the peats and grassland soils (histosols and mollisols), tend to be light in color. When exposed, they contrast starkly with the darker tones of the coniferous forest.

Marked differences in color between soils and their surroundings should dictate to some degree the particular method of treating cut slopes and other scars on the landscape. To mask exposed soils successfully, revegetation, mulching and erosion control, and the blending of existing and new soil materials are essential. Because it is often so difficult to conceal cuts, the amount of regrading and the extent to which subsoils would be exposed should be considered in evaluating site plan alternatives.

Soil Depth and Deposition Patterns. Mountain soil layers can hold many unwanted surprises. Irregular terrain and more violent processes of geological change in the mountains contribute to unpredictable soil deposition and layering patterns (Fig. 6-15). The thickness of an individual horizon in a soil profile can change within very short distances and must be checked by test pits at numerous intervals. Interspersed within the layers can be boulders of any size, as well as ledges and bedrock, all of which add greatly to the costs of excavation.

Red Flags. In summary, certain soil conditions hint at problems that ought to bring the mountain site planner back to the site for a closer look: the presence of peat or other highly organic soils; loose silty soils; clayey soils that are relatively more plastic, especially those on slopes; fine water-bearing sands or hydric soils (soils periodically deficient in oxygen) that indicate a high water table; evidence of soil slumps, mudslides, or subsidence; and rock outcrops or bedrock close to the surface.

Figure 6-15. *Soil profile of the Troutdale–Rogert–Kittredge complex in the Front Range near Golden, Colorado, shows the great variation in soil depth and subsurface conditions that can exist within small areas. Here, gneiss and schist have been intruded by lighter-colored pegmatite dikes. Photo by the Soil Conservation Service.*

DESIGN GUIDELINES

Site Planning

1. Avoid site plans that would destroy prime areas of fertile soils. Such soils are scarce in the mountains and should remain to support healthy zones of native vegetation in and around a community.

2. Use soil maps and surveys as prime indicators of development suitability, and arrange uses and densities on the site according to the limitations flagged by soil analysis.

Grading, Drainage, and Erosion Control

1. In regrading, restore drainage patterns as nearly as possible to their preexisting natural conditions. Quantify projected surface runoff volumes after

development, and provide for these flows in hard and soft landscape features integral to the design of outdoor spaces.

2. Keep flow volume low by providing multiple channels to drain large areas; do not funnel all runoff into a single channel. Pick up drainage at frequent intervals, as the areas where runoff concentrates cause serious erosion problems.

3. Keep runoff velocities low by lining drainage ditches with rocks or other rough-textured materials and by constructing barriers that interrupt runoff flows down long or steep slopes.

4. Because culverts generally cause flow velocities to increase, line both ends with rock to dissipate the erosive force of the water (Fig. 6-16). Use willows or other erosion protection devices where needed to stabilize banks.

5. Protect regraded slopes against oversaturation,

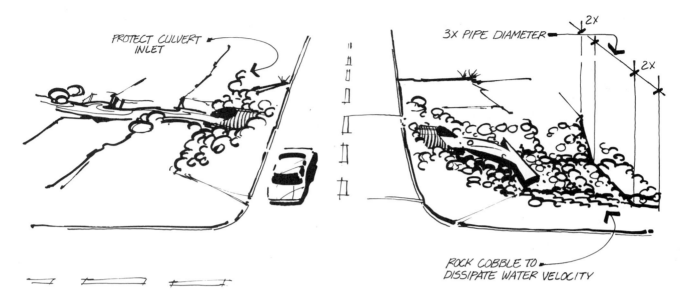

PROTECT CULVERT INLET

3X PIPE DIAMETER

2X

2X

ROCK COBBLE TO DISSIPATE WATER VELOCITY

Figure 6-16.

slippage, and erosion. Avoid excessive slope gradients, compact adequately, and control the amount of water flowing across the slope. Use interceptor ditches at the top of the slope to divert surface runoff. Terraces with additional drainage ditches may be needed at intermediate levels across the face of a long slope (Fig. 6-17). Ditches should be lined with a resistant surface and should be more closely spaced on fill slopes than on cut slopes.

6. Do not use frozen, mucky, or easily compressible materials for fill slopes or for fill under structures and paved surfaces. Proper moisture content is essential to adequate compaction.

7. Minimize the extent of impervious surfaces added to the site in roofs and paving, because the runoff from these sources flows at a higher velocity and greatly increases the potential for erosion and sedimentation. Direct the runoff from roofs and paving into french drains, infiltration trenches, and dry wells so that as much of it as possible can be absorbed into the ground. (Note that in areas of prolonged and deep ground freezing, these devices may be ineffective during snowmelt periods.)

8. Stockpile mountain topsoil on-site and protect the stockpile against erosion. Keep topsoils separate from excavated subsoils. Also stockpile native turfgrass sod, small trees, shrubs, and boulders that could be used in the finished landscaping. Replace stockpiled turf level with or slightly lower than the general ground surface, as fill above this level may dry out and break up, preventing reestablishment of the turf.

9. Use low-contrast mulch and dark topsoil over lighter subsoils to reduce the visual contrast of exposed cut slopes. Minimize slope cutting where soils are very light in color and where other factors, like slope gradient, make it impossible to conceal the cut.

10. Use standard erosion control methods during construction to protect water quality, control drainage, and reduce soil erosion (Fig. 6-18). Such temporary measures as detention ponds and diversion channels reduce the velocity of runoff and trap sediments before they can enter natural watercourses. Sediment traps, small dams, or barriers of straw bales should be located wherever grade changes will slow the velocity of runoff. Clear streams flowing onto the site from above should be intercepted and temporarily diverted or channeled through the construction area to prevent discharge of sediments into them.

Before construction starts, prepare an erosion control plan that locates ponds, channels, and barriers and monitors the results. Review it with construction supervisors and local officials.

11. Consider hand clearing steeper slopes to retain ground cover that could protect the soil from erosion.

12. Do not leave soils on regraded areas exposed any longer than absolutely necessary. Immediately replant and reseed, in phases if necessary on larger jobs, and cover the soil surface with an erosion control mulch or fabric. Without fail, do this before winter snows arrive, for spring snowmelt is highly erosive.

13. On larger projects, consider adding to construction specifications a limitation on the regraded area that can be exposed at one time before it is revegetated.

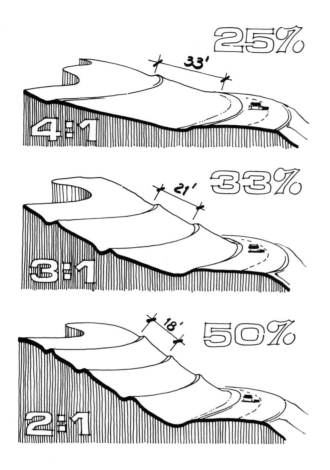

14. Implant boulders and other protrusions on newly graded slopes where soil (or snow) creep threatens to tip trees or sever irrigation and utility lines.

See Chapter 5 for related guidelines on slope stability and Appendix C for a summary of common erosion control methods and costs.

Site Improvements

1. Avoid large expanses of concrete slab, asphalt, or grouted paving materials over soils that cannot be compacted adequately or that are prone to frost heaving. Use more dividers and joints in paving over expansive materials and in areas of extreme temperature fluctuation. (See Chapter 4, [Guidelines for] Structures and Site Improvements, for more on concrete paving.)
2. Plan for a community sewage treatment facility; avoid septic tank systems where soils are not amenable, where seepage may induce slope instability, or where high densities are planned.

Figure 6-17. *Recommended intervals between drainage interceptor ditches on regraded slopes.*

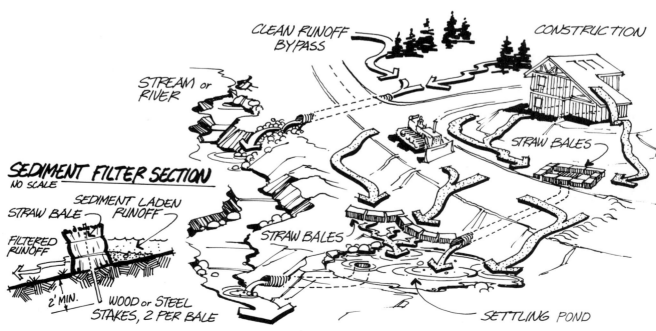

140   *Figure 6-18.* *Temporary erosion control measures.*

REFERENCES

Jenny, Hans. 1941. *Factors of Soil Formation.* New York: McGraw-Hill.

Lynch, Dennis L. 1974. An ecosystem guide for mountain land planning. Ft. Collins: Colorado State Forest Service and Colorado State University.

Nishimura, John Y. 1974. Soils and soil problems at high altitudes. In *Proceedings of a Workshop on Revegetation of High-Altitude Disturbed Lands,* pp. 5–9. Ft. Collins: Colorado Water Resources Research Institute, Information Series No. 10.

Price, Larry W. 1981. *Mountains and Man,* chap. 7, Mountain soils, pp. 233–254. Berkeley and Los Angeles: University of California Press.

Retzer, J. L. 1974. Alpine soils. In *Arctic and Alpine Environments,* ed. J. D. Ives and R. G. Barry, pp. 771–804. London: Methuen.

Soil Survey Staff. 1987. *Keys to Soil Taxonomy.* Ithaca, N.Y.: SMSS Technical Monograph no. 6.

Tahoe Regional Planning Agency. 1978. *Lake Tahoe Basin Water Quality Management Plan.* Vol. 2: Handbook of best management practices for control of erosion and surface runoff. Zephyr Cove, Nev.

———. 1982. How to protect your property from erosion: A guide for homebuilders in the Lake Tahoe Basin. Zephyr Cove, Nev.

Tew, Ronald K. 1968. Properties of soil under aspen and herb–shrub cover. Ogden, Utah: Intermountain Forest and Range Experiment Station Research Note INT-78.

U.S.D.A. Soil Conservation Service. 1975. *Soil Taxonomy.* Agriculture Handbook no. 436.

Untermann, Richard K. 1978. *Principles and Practices of Grading, Drainage and Road Alignment: An Ecological Approach.* Reston, Va.: Reston Publishing.

7
VEGETATION: THE SYMPTOMATIC ELEMENT

In mountainous regions, climate and topography pose such stringent constraints that they often dominate the design response, and the living elements of the landscape receive far less attention. We know much more about how plants and animals relate to their environment than we use in design. As we are painfully learning, however, the environment is an integrated system: Living organisms and their physical setting each influence the characteristics of the other, and the health of both is essential to the survival of the whole. Trade-offs compelled by chosen courses of action, as well as the design opportunities inherent in the landscape, become clearer when these ecological relationships are better understood.

DISTRIBUTION PATTERNS IN MOUNTAIN VEGETATION

Vegetation is a bellwether. The growth, reproduction, and distribution of plant life are controlled not only by the genetic characteristics of species but also by physical and chemical factors in the environment. Because it represents the integration of environmental factors, vegetation reveals clues to localized environmental conditions and is an important tool in site analysis. And because it is so intimately bound up with the visual character of a landscape, it is an essential material in the design palette.

On land, the most important regulatory factors in the growth of vegetation are light, temperature, and precipitation. In the mountains, terrain greatly affects all of these. Patterns in the distribution of mountain plants are microcosmic reflections of variations in elevation, landform and slope aspect, soil and bedrock geology, moisture and exposure to wind.

Certain factors common to mountain environments are particularly limiting to plants. The mountain climate demands adaptations to heavy frost and deep snow cover, extreme temperature variability, desiccating winter winds, and, in many ranges, low summer soil moisture. Higher elevations and middle to northerly latitudes constrain growth with shorter days and growing seasons, reduced average temperatures and moisture levels, and increased intensity of solar radiation. Topography moderates or exaggerates these conditions according to local variations in slope

aspect, gradient, and landform, factors that equally affect the process of soil formation.

Plant distribution and soil characteristics are a chicken-and-egg combination. Soil types and plants each affect the traits and limit the boundaries of the other. Their mutual relationship is clearly mirrored in the vegetative mosaic of the mountain landscape. Changes in soil types are not the only cause of this mosaic, however, as both soils and vegetation are projections of elevation, climate, topography, underlying geology, and time, working in unison.

Because of the great diversity in physical conditions that these five factors combine to produce, the distribution of plant communities in the mountains is extremely complex. There are very few ecological principles on which to base generalizations. Some patterns do exist, however, that help clarify the survival parameters for vegetation on a given mountain site.

Altitudinal Zonation

The difference between a mountain and a hill is that as one ascends a mountain, things change. Climate changes. Forest species change. Inhabitants change. The look of the landscape changes.

In the mountains, these changes proceed in a vertical sequence in which major plant communities appear as irregular bands, often with very narrow zones of transition (ecotones) between them. Vegetational banding is largely a result of changes in climate. It reflects a set of biological responses to increasing altitude, which causes progressively wetter and cooler conditions. Bands at higher elevations are generally marked by a decrease in the number of species, as well as "smaller and less elaborate plants with slower growth rates, decreased productivity, . . . and less interspecies competition" (Price 1981, p. 258).

Life Zones. Vegetational bands occur within a general pattern of life zones. Each is distinguished from the others by climatic conditions and, reflecting climate, by climax ecosystems that are associated with particular sets of dominant plant species.[1] Up to four life zones are represented in temperate mountains (Fig. 7-1), fewer in the southern Rockies and the Appalachians.

Starting at the summits, the *alpine zone,* a treeless

143

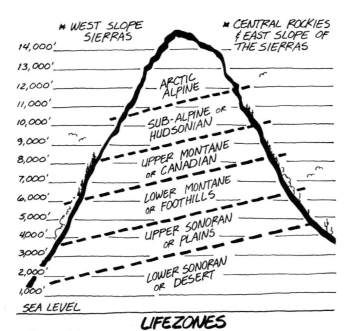

Figure 7-1.

area of tundra, spreads across the highest elevations above timberline. Below this, the *subalpine zone* of high forest begins, first in glades of stunted and wind-deformed trees around timberline and then lower in closer-knit stands. On the lower slopes, in the *upper montane zone,* these species give way to other forest trees. Below this is a transition zone of varied species called the *lower montane zone.*[2] In the central mountains of the United States, forests composed of other species adapted to warmer, drier conditions sometimes extend into this zone, but more commonly, there is a lower timberline where forests are replaced by plains grassland or desert vegetation. (This is not true of New England and the Pacific Northwest, however, where the greater moisture at these lower elevations supports still other forest species.)

[1]The *ecosystem* is the basic functional unit in ecology and includes both organisms and the abiotic environment (climate, inorganic substances, organic compounds) with which they interact. A *community* includes all the populations of individual species that occupy a given area. It functions as a unit and is the living part of the ecosystem.

Dominant species are those that, by virtue of their numbers, size, production, or other activities, largely control the energy flow and strongly affect the environment of all other species in an ecosystem. *Indicator species* are those that have a narrower niche (more restrictive parameters for survival) than dominants and whose presence is evidence of the physical conditions with which they are particularly associated (see Odum 1971).

The upper and lower elevational limits of a life zone are not constant but become gradually lower moving northward through a range. A move to the north of 600 miles (965 km) roughly approximates an increase of 1000 feet in elevation (305 m) in its effect on the altitudinal ranges of plant communities. The upper timberline is the most visible manifestation of this pattern: It is lower by approximately 360 feet (110 m) with every extra degree of northerly latitude (Fig. 7-2).

The ecotones between life zones are rarely abrupt or distinct. Instead, the transition between two adjacent life zones hosts a mixture of species reflecting a gradation of physical factors from one habitat to the other. Only the upper timberline, the ecotone between the alpine and the subalpine zones, is a relatively sharp boundary.

Vertical Banding. The vertical segregation of tree species is the visible expression of mountain elevation (Fig. 7-3). In the central and southern Rockies, for example, ponderosa pine (*Pinus ponderosa,* also known as yellow pine in the Sierras), pinyon pine (*P. edulis*), and various native junipers (for example, *Juniperus scopulorum* in the Rockies, *J. osteosperma* and *J. monosperma* in Utah and the Southwest, and *J. occidentalis* in the Great Basin and Sierras) favor the lower, drier zones. Lodgepole pine (*P. contorta latifolia*) sticks to the higher, warmer sites. Engelmann spruce (*Picea engelmannii*) and subalpine fir (*Abies lasiocarpa*) take the coolest, wettest, highest sites. Quaking aspen (*Populus tremuloides*) is an important species at higher elevations, but it grows best on lower sunny and moist sites also occupied by Douglas fir (*Pseudotsuga menziesii*).

Certain forest species do not conform to this pattern of vertical zonation. Both the bristlecone pine (*Pinus aristata*) and limber pine (*P. flexilis*), for example, are found from the lower montane zone to timberline, and both favor rocky, wind-exposed sites. Limber pine (Fig. 7-4) is more often found at the lower limits of the subalpine zone, and bristlecone pine at the higher limits (Ronco 1976, p. 14).

[2]The terms *mountain, alpine,* and *montane* are often used interchangeably, but they are not the same. *Mountain* is the broadest of the three, applying generally to elevated terrain characterized by steepness of slope, high relief, and great environmental contrast within a short vertical distance. *Alpine* refers specifically to the highest elevations, a cold, windy, rocky zone above continuous forests where tundra vegetation exists in what is basically an arctic climate. *Montane* is used inclusively to refer to the other three mountain life zones (subalpine and upper and lower montane), where the climate is more temperate but the terrain is still mountainous.

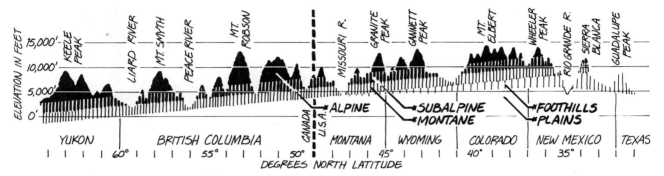

Figure 7-2. *North–south section through the Rocky Mountains showing relationship between life zones and latitude. Based on a drawing by Ray Radebaugh in Williams 1986, p. 17.*

Regional Variations in Dominant Forest Species

The extensive forests in mountain ranges are largely a result of higher available moisture, compared with that of the adjacent plains and intermountain basins, where precipitation is lower and higher average temperatures increase the evapotranspiration rate. Forest communities of evergreen conifers dominate the mountains of the Northern Hemisphere because they have adapted more successfully than most deciduous species to a wide range of marginal habitats. They are well suited to cold temperatures and short growing seasons and require fewer nutrients from the soil. Their tapered form and narrow crown expose a minimum of surface to wind and sun. Their

needles lose less moisture through transpiration than broad leaves do and are ready to begin photosynthesis earlier in the spring (Price 1981, p. 260).

The Inland Mountains. Due to the lack of moisture, typical forest communities of the central Rockies and the Great Basin ranges are among the least diverse in America's mountain regions. With exception of the mixed conifer forests of northern Arizona and New Mexico, many forests here are almost pure stands of a

Figure 7-3. *Vertical zonation of forest species.*

Figure 7-4. *Limber pine* (Pinus flexilis) *in its characteristic gnarled form near timberline.*

145

Figure 7-5. *The spruce–fir community forms a somewhat diverse and often dense forest on moist, protected sites. Individually, the Englemann spruce is spiky, stiff, tall, and narrow, with many branchlets hanging down from the main limbs, which reach to the ground.*

single dominant conifer, like lodgepole pine or subalpine fir. Aspen in pure stands are the only widespread deciduous forests, although paper birch and cottonwood occur intermittently where moisture levels permit. Usually occurring where moisture

Figure 7-6. *Hardwood forest in the White Mountains of New Hampshire.*

conditions are more favorable, the Douglas fir and Engelmann spruce communities show slightly more species diversity (Fig. 7-5).

The West Coast. In contrast, many coniferous species appear in the Sierras that are not found in the inland ranges: sugar pine (*Pinus lambertiana*), Jeffrey pine (*P. jeffreyi*), whitebark pine (*P. albicaulis*), red fir (*Abies magnifica*), incense cedar (*Calocedrus decurrens*), mountain hemlock (*Tsuga mertensiana*), and the redwoods (*Sequoia gigantea* and *S. sempervirens*) (Fig. 7-6).

Some of these species are found farther north in the ranges of the Pacific Northwest, but many are replaced by a variety of other conifers adapted to coastal conditions of higher precipitation: Sitka spruce (*Picea sitchensis*), western red cedar (*Thuja plicata*), western white pine (*Pinus monticola*, also known as silver pine), and silver fir (*Abies amabilis*). At lower elevations in these coastal ranges, there are also some native deciduous forest trees: alders, cottonwoods, big leaf maple (*Acer macrophyllum*), and paper and water birch (*Betula papyrifera* and *B. occidentalis*) in wetter areas; madrone (*Arbutus menziesii*), Pacific dogwood (*Cornus nuttallii*), black

Figure 7-7. *The coast redwood* (Sequoia sempervirens)*, pictured here, is native to the Coast Range of northern California, and the giant sequoia (S.* giganteum*) is indigenous to elevations above 4000 ft. (1220 m) in the Sierra Nevada. The coastal species grows faster and is taller at maturity, but the Sierran species lives as much as a thousand years longer.*

oak in the southern Cascades (*Quercus kelloggii*); and white oak (*Q. garryana*) north to British Columbia.

The East. In the eastern mountains of America, lower average elevations mean that vertical stratification, though still evident, does not exhibit as many zones. Very few summits in New England (and none in the southern Appalachians) are high enough to have a treeless alpine zone (Fig. 7-7).

The other basic difference from the western mountains is fewer conifers. The boreal (northern) forest conifers—spruce and balsam fir (*Abies balsamea*)—are largely restricted to the coolest, wettest areas of Vermont, New Hampshire, and Maine, although some local species of fir can be found in the southern Appalachians.

Except in some parts of northern New England, deciduous forest trees predominate. Most of these are second-generation hardwoods: beech (*Fagus sylvatica*), sugar maple (*Acer saccharum*), and birch are the dominant species, joined variously by red oak (*Quercus rubra*), ash (*Fraxinus* sp.), hemlock (*Tsuga* sp.), and white pine. Farther south, oak and hickory (*Carya* sp.) take over. These forests regenerate easily; since the decline of farming in the mid-nineteenth century, they have been filling in abandoned fields at a rapid rate.

Patterns Related to Microclimate

Within the same life zone in the same mountain range, a mosaic of microclimatic and physiographic conditions causes considerable variation in plant communities. Site-specific variations are determined by the tolerances of individual species to small differences in such factors as ultraviolet and visible solar radiation; soil and air temperatures; snow distribution and length of the snow-free period (growing season); wind speeds; the steepness of the slope; the chemical composition of bedrock; and soil characteristics, including pH, moisture, and susceptibility to frost action and needle ice (Billings

147

1978, p. 2). Local plant distribution is also affected by the competition among species and by periodic disturbances such as fire and insects.

These localized differences occur all over every mountain, giving rise to the vegetative patchiness so often apparent at higher elevations. It is evident even at a very fine scale: Snowdrifts forming in the lee of rock outcrops or shrubs and small depressions that catch blowing snow afford wintertime protection and additional springtime moisture (Fig. 7-8). These small

places often encourage the growth of different species.

Many shrubs and herbaceous plants are more sensitive to microclimatic conditions than to elevation. Some plant communities, such as those found in bogs, riparian areas, mountain grasslands, shrublands, and meadows, cut across elevational zones and can be found wherever their moisture, sun, and soil prerequisites are met. The removal of forest cover or the interruption of normal drainage patterns can change conditions on the ground, triggering corresponding adjustments in the mixture of species.

Slope Aspect and Exposure. Because of its influence on microclimate, slope aspect is perhaps the most powerful local variable in plant growth and distribution. Plants are extremely sensitive to differences in the level and intensity of sunlight. North-facing slopes in the middle latitudes never receive a full measure of radiation, whereas south-facing slopes get maximum sun in the coldest part of the year, when the low sun angle is nearly perpendicular to the slope. On a broad scale, one general result is that the elevation limits of life zones are slightly lower on north-facing slopes than on southern aspects, but aspect is a factor on much smaller scales as well.

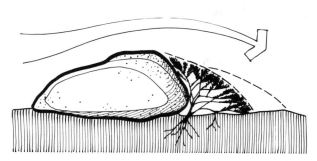

Figure 7-8. *A plant becomes established in the lee of a boulder and may later expand into the protected area in its own lee. Adapted from Zwinger and Willard 1972, p. 59.*

Figure 7-9. *Stark evidence of the influence of sun exposure: Slopes facing north are forested in conifers, whereas those facing south support only rocky, thin soils and dryland grasses. Photo in Colorado Front Range, by the Soil Conservation Service.*

At the same elevation on adjacent slopes with different exposures, there may be significant changes in the plant species present (Fig. 7-9). Plants on north-facing slopes are species adapted to lower average temperatures, more frost, longer periods of snow cover, and more saturated soil. Plants on south-facing slopes are better adapted to the drier conditions, more frequent freeze–thaw cycles, and higher evaporative stress that results from intense winter sun.

The two sides of a Rocky Mountain canyon provide a good illustration. The lichens and mosses growing on the south-facing wall are the same as those in high deserts all over the world. And those on the north-facing wall across the canyon are the same as the subarctic plants found in the Gulf of Alaska.

In the quest for more sun and the maximum growing season, newcomers to the mountains often assume that the best microclimate for plants near a structure will be on its southern and western sides. But in fact, these exposures are high-stress environments because of intense sun, drying winds, and re-reflected heat, especially in winter. The east side of a building is more amenable in two respects: It typically gets more summer sun, as thunderstorms frequently block the western sun in the afternoons, and it is protected from winter storms and drying chinook winds.

The exposure of a new plant to sun and heat may be the single most important factor in its prospects for survival. In selecting plants for landscaping, therefore, it is important that all the survival parameters of individual species—their growth requirements for water, air, sun, and room to grow—be carefully matched with conditions on the site. Mountain plants exist within very narrow tolerances and generally respond negatively to changes in their regime.

Plant Succession

At any point in time, the composition of a plant community is a reflection of its history, always changing and maturing. This change over time—a somewhat predictable process if disturbances do not intrude—is called *succession*. The physical environment controls the pattern and rate of change but is at the same time modified by the plant and animal communities that inhabit it. A *climax community* is theoretically the final one in the maturation process: stable, self-perpetuating, and in equilibrium with its physical habitat.

Climate and competition among species generally play the controlling role in succession (Price 1981, p. 258). Yet it is difficult to project successional change, and the criteria by which climax vegetation types can be identified as such do not always inspire consensus. What makes plant succession relevant to mountain site planning is the response of climax communities to disturbance and the consequent impact on revegetation potential.

Successional change is site specific. Under natural conditions, seedlings of shade-tolerant trees establish themselves under shade-intolerant species or in the protection of stumps and rocks. Shrubs frequently act as a transitional nurse crop for climax species that, once matured, can reproduce by seed in their own shade. Thus a climax forest will contain trees in all stages of development. If disturbances—fire, landslide, disease, logging, development—alter the sun–shade balance, climax species may be unable to reproduce.

Lodgepole pine and aspen, for example, neither of which are climax types, are usually the first species to regenerate on disturbed slopes (Fig. 7-10)—lodgepole because its cones persist and fire causes them to spew seeds prolifically, and aspen because it sprouts from the roots. Both require full sun. Neither can regenerate by seed in the shade of its own canopy. Limber and bristlecone pines are also sun-loving pioneer forest species.

In contrast, spruce–fir stands are stable climax communities, perpetuating themselves by reproducing in their own shade. If their seed stock is present during a disturbance, they can take over the pioneer aspen or lodgepole forest in thirty to fifty years (Ronco 1976, p. 14) (Fig. 7-11). But if they are not on the site before it burns or is cleared, the natural establishment of a spruce–fir community can take centuries. Spruce and fir cannot regenerate from seed in full sun. *Solarization,* or injury from high-intensity sunlight, causes a reduction in the rate of photosynthesis that can kill seedlings.

Aspen is a transitional subclimax species. As a general rule, the presence of aspen in areas where conifers are normally the climax forest type is evidence of a recent disturbance. Without continued interruption of the successional pattern, scenic areas now cloaked in aspen cannot be counted on to remain that way indefinitely.

Likewise, the existence of open meadows within forests is often a sign that poor drainage, excess snow accumulation, or fire has prevented normal successional change. In time, unless the area remains too wet, the meadow will eventually be overtaken by evergreens (Fig. 7-12).

Disturbances can alter not only solar radiation levels but also other factors that influence successional change. They can cause gradual changes in soil characteristics, including nutrient and moisture levels, pH, compaction, and erosion. They can redirect drainage flows. They can cause the elimination of

Figure 7-10. *Aspen* (Populus tremuloides) *regenerating a slope after a conifer forest was clearcut, Escudilla Mountain, Arizona. Photo by David J. Cooper.*

Figure 7-11. *Blue spruce saplings* (Picea pungens) *have become established in the shade of an aspen grove at 9000 ft. (2740 m) in the Booth Creek drainage near Vail, Colorado. (Aspen trunks are bent because of the pressure from snow creep.)*

some associated species and introduce others, including invasive weeds and exotics. Any of these changes can inhibit the reestablishment of climax species (Billings 1978, p. 12).

Design Implications. The principles of mountain plant distribution suggest several lessons for site planning and design. Perhaps the most important, as demonstrated by the banded vegetation mosaic and the process of succession, is that the parameters for the establishment and growth of native species are precise. New plants must be selected from a palette of native species adapted to specific microclimatic conditions in the planting area.

The presence of a species on a site before a disturbance does not ensure that revegetation with that species is possible. That is, a disturbed site may no longer meet the survival requirements of the species that were originally present.

Conditions on a site after development may call for the planting of subclimax native species not previously on the site to function as nurse crops for less-tolerant climax species. Aspen, some pines, willows, and other mountain shrubs are ideal for this purpose. As in the reconstruction of mountain streams, the strategy in landscaping a newly developed site should be to identify the indigenous vegetation trends and work with them to accelerate natural processes. In both cases, the effort is best

Figure 7-12. *Meadow in the Hunter Creek Valley near Aspen, Colorado, is too wet for forest species.*

viewed as a long-term process of landscape restoration that demands continuing involvement. Landscaping a mountain site is an evolutionary process, not a one-month construction contract.

The lesson of change over time is also a consideration in site plans organized around focal vegetation features, like a grove of mature aspen or a meadow. These plans risk losing their focal point after some period of time, either because of induced changes or simply the natural course of plant aging and succession. Valuable features may require continued intervention to survive.

Given the narrow growth tolerances of mountain plants, landscape designers in this environment must proceed with an orientation different from that of designers in more urban areas. *In the mountains, the key word in landscape design is siting, not planting.* The sensitive siting of all improvements allows the retention of more of the existing vegetation. This is essential because remedial landscaping may never repair the damage caused by poor siting.

Vegetation analysis is essential to intelligent site planning. An inventory of plant communities on a mountain site can reveal many conditions that should affect the decision-making process: soil qualities, moisture levels, and geological characteristics; limiting factors that influence sensitivity to disturbance; and evidence of existing or potential natural hazards. Reading these signals gives clues to the health, value,

and fragility of the ecosystems that will be affected.

An example of some of the site planning clues that are signaled by the presence of certain plant communities on a mountain site is given in Appendix B.

THE UNIQUE ADAPTATIONS OF ALPINE PERENNIALS

Forests—where the majority of mountain development has taken place—cover a far greater area than those ecosystems in which alpine perennials are dominant: mountain meadows and grasslands, bogs, and, in particular, the tundra, where development constraints are virtually irrelevant. Except for ski lifts and warming huts, nothing is likely to be developed there.

It may seem digressive, then, to consider why alpine perennials are uniquely suited to an environment of extremes. Their peculiar adaptations are instructive, however, if only to underscore the message of the previous section. Their special traits reemphasize the narrow parameters that one must respect in selecting and substituting plant materials on mountain sites. And they begin to explain why so many introduced plants fail to thrive and so many mountain planting plans are never fully realized.

In part because perennials are more primitive on the evolutionary scale, they are better able than more

151

complex species to cope with adverse growing conditions. Perennials are more common in the mountains than annuals because the environment is too harsh to permit the completion of a full life cycle—from germination through pollination and seed maturity—in one growing season. In the tundra of the alpine zone, only 1 to 2 percent of the flora are annuals (Price 1981, p. 294). Among the adaptations that perennials have made to survive the stresses of the alpine environment are the following (Billings 1978):

Biomass Distribution.   Most mountain perennials have much more living tissue below ground than above. This is particularly true of tundra species, which may have two to six times more biomass in their root system than in their leaves (Price 1981, p. 296). (This is not true of dwarf shrub species.) Little or nothing of the plant remains exposed above ground during the winter. A large root system can also reach and store more moisture during the semiarid summers.

The leaf tissue above ground during the short growing season is arranged to make the most of adverse conditions. The typical rosette pattern of many perennials (Fig. 7-13) exposes a maximum of leaf surface to light. These rosettes sometimes clump together to form a mounded cushion that traps wind-blown debris and dead leaves, gradually raising the soil level under it.

Figure 7-14.   *Snow buttercups* (Ranunculus adoneus) *breaking through a melting tundra snowbank. Photo by David J. Cooper.*

Dormancy.   Mountain plants have a longer period of dormancy, up to nine or ten months at higher elevations. Dormancy means the hardening of tissue and is essential to plant survival through the winter, especially in cold, snow-free areas. The onset of dormancy is very early, near the end of summer. It is brought on by cues to which a species automatically responds, usually low temperatures, drought, and the shortening of the day (photoperiod).

Early Growth.   Perennial species break dormancy rapidly after snowmelt, in late May or early June. Photosynthesis and respiration rates are unusually high at this time, and the vegetative regrowth of shoots is very rapid. The perennating bud is usually close to the ground surface, where it is better protected (Fig. 7-14).

Rapid Adjustments.   At least some alpine species are able quickly to adjust their photosynthesis and respiration rates in response to sudden changes in temperature.

Low-temperature Functioning.   Alpine plants are able to convert starches into sucrose at lower temperatures than low-elevation plants and to move these compounds in plant fluids to storage organs at the same low temperatures. Photosynthates are stored not only in current growth and reproductive organs but also in roots, rhizomes (fleshy underground stems, as in iris), and evergreen leaves, thereby enabling the plant's early growth the following year.

Figure 7-13.   *The typical rosette pattern of an alpine perennial.*

Figure 7-15.   *Meandering stream and wetland at 11,000 ft. (3350 m), Cross Creek, Colorado Rockies. Photo by David J. Cooper.*

Drought Tolerance.   Alpine plants are more tolerant of late-season drought stress, although researchers do not fully understand how this works.

Reproduction.   Most alpine species flower from buds formed the year before, thereby enabling them to bloom soon after breaking out of dormancy. The seeds of seed-producing species are ripe by middle to late summer, depending on the weather and the presence of pollinators, the scarcity of which can be a major problem in the higher zones. The seeds do not germinate, however, until at least the following year. Many species that produce seeds also reproduce by means of rhizomes, stolons (runners, as in strawberries), or bulbs, as seedling establishment is only occasionally successful and seedling growth is extremely slow.

These are not the only adaptations; many more are unique to individual species. The important point is that alpine perennials are beautifully adapted for survival under extreme temperatures, heavy snow, intense sun, and exposure to wind. They are a potentially valuable landscape material for which there are few equivalent substitutes. With increasing experimentation in the cultivation of alpine perennials at elevations below their usual range, and with steady progress in commercial propagation, they may become a mainstay of finely scaled landscape design in the mountains.

WETLANDS: A CRUCIAL ECOSYSTEM

The term *wetland* is generally applied to landscape features such as very shallow lakes and ponds, marshes, bogs, swamps, wet meadows, sloughs, riparian areas, and lowlands intermittently covered with water (Figs. 7-15, 7-16). The most widely accepted legal definition is that contained in the Clean Water Act of 1972, which describes wetlands as "those areas that are inundated or saturated by surface or groundwater at a frequency and duration sufficient to support, and that under normal circumstances do support, a prevalence of vegetation typically adapted for life in saturated soil conditions."

Because there is so much variation in wetland types, the U.S. Fish and Wildlife Service has provided a more precise definition:

Wetlands are transitional between terrestrial and aquatic systems where the water table is usually at or near the surface, or the land is covered by shallow water. For purposes of this classification, wetlands must have one or more of the following three attributes: (1) at least periodically, the land supports predominantly hydrophytes [plants growing in water, on saturated soil, or in anaerobic conditions]; (2) the substrate is predominantly undrained hydric soil [soil that is undrained or deficient in oxygen]; (3) the substrate is nonsoil and is saturated with water or covered by shallow water at some time during the growing season of each year. (Cowardin et al. 1979, p. 3)

153

Figure 7-16. *Development at the edge of a wetland area at 9100 feet (2775 m), Summit County, Colorado.*

Consistent with the Fish and Wildlife Service's definition, the factors used to determine wetland boundaries are the hydrology of the site, its soils, and its vegetation. Of these three, vegetation is often considered the primary indicator of wetland status, although the U.S. Army Corps of Engineers follows a "multiparameter" approach in which positive evidence in all three categories must be present. This may seem straightforward, but wetland boundaries are not always clear-cut, and differing opinions may be expected in specific cases.

Mountain Wetlands. Mountain wetlands are an extremely varied group, reflecting equal diversity in subsurface hydrology, geology, watershed topography, soils, and microclimate that is typical of mountains. They are found at all elevations, in all mountain life zones, and in an enormous range of conditions.

As a group, wetlands in mountain valleys are distinct from those in intermountain basins because of significant differences in topography, geomorphology, weather, and the soil types that

result. But even where these factors are roughly equal, their precise characteristics differ according to altitude and distance from stream headwaters.

A study of Rocky Mountain wetlands noted the relationship between geology and wetland types:

> *In subalpine regions where soils are thin, collected surface water is rare and the water table essentially nonexistent. Seepage slopes are common. . . . Glacial valleys characterized by glacial and alluvial accumulation often have a shallow depth to water table. High groundwater tables have also been observed in intermountain basins where sediments are porous, gradients low, and internal drainage frequent. (Windell et al. 1986, p. 64)*

The water that supports mountain wetlands may be associated with periodic overbank flooding, river meander patterns, water impounded by glacial landforms or landslides, a high water table maintained by snowmelt and summer storms, impermeable substrates, or some combination of these. On the basis of differences in hydrology, the same Rocky Mountain study divided wetlands into four general categories, distinctions that are equally useful beyond the Rockies. It identified (1) plant communities located in permanent shallow standing waters, (2) communities with seasonal or permanent high water tables but without permanent standing water (an extremely diverse group), (3) communities located in running water, and (4) communities adjacent to running waters (riparian areas).

Riparian Wetlands. Riparian areas (Fig. 7-17) are generally defined as those fed directly by stream systems. Although most streamside areas are considered riparian, some are not, and not all riparian areas are wetlands.

Riparian wetlands are defined as ecosystems having a high water table because of their proximity to an aquatic ecosystem or subsurface water (American Fisheries Society 1980). "Aridity, topographic relief, and presence of depositional soils most strongly influence the extent of high water tables and associated riparian ecosystems. . . . [They] are most commonly recognized by bottomland, floodplain and streambank vegetation in the West" (Windell et al. 1986, p. 3).

Riparian ecosystems, wetlands or not, are valuable because they are high in species diversity, species density, and productivity. In the mountain context, because they occur in terrain that elsewhere is much drier, they are prime wildlife habitat areas and represent a crucial zone of interaction between aquatic and terrestrial ecosystems.

Section 404 Permit Requirements

Wetlands serve valuable ecological functions. They act as groundwater recharge areas, as filters to reduce sedimentation and protect water quality, and as water storage reservoirs that trap and delay snowmelt runoff and attenuate flood peaks. They also moderate temperature fluctuations, reduce stream bank erosion, promote nutrient cycling, and provide food and refuge for waterfowl and other wildlife.

Because of the ecological value of wetlands and because they were being destroyed at an alarming rate, the Federal Water Pollution Control Act of 1977 brought them under the purview of the federal government. Section 404 of the act instituted a program requiring permits for any discharges of dredged or fill materials into waters of the United States, including wetlands. The U.S. Army Corps of Engineers was designated to oversee the permitting process, although both it and the Environmental Protection Agency (EPA) are responsible for enforcing the law. In addition, the U.S. Fish and Wildlife Service was made responsible for reviewing proposed activities that may affect fish and wildlife resources.

The effect of the act is to require a 404 permit whenever an activity or development may destroy or in any way affect a wetland. An applicant may be considered for a "nationwide general" permit if the impacts of proposed activities are deemed minor (that is, where the area that may be affected is less than 1 acre) or for an "individual" permit in cases involving

Figure 7-17. *Dense vegetation in the riparian zone along Gore Creek, Vail, Colorado.*

major impacts in larger wetlands and streams.

Until recently, the Corps of Engineers concentrated its attention on (1) lakes and surrounding wetlands with a total area of 10 or more acres and (2) streams and adjacent wetlands with an average annual flow of 5 cubic feet per second (cfs) or higher. Generally, only activities in wetlands of this size were required to go through the lengthier application process for an individual permit; activities in wetlands smaller than 10 acres or streams flowing lower than 5 cfs were approved under the nationwide general permit.

These parameters have been superseded, however, by revised guidelines on size. Since a change in regulations in October 1984, resulting from a lawsuit, the Corps is now required to review impacts on any "environmentally sensitive" wetlands, regardless of size. Activities in isolated wetlands under 1 acre in size are still generally given a nationwide general permit, and those affecting wetlands over 10 acres in area still require individual permits. For proposed activities in wetlands between 1 and 10 acres in size, the Corps has discretionary authority to require individual rather than nationwide permits. Development affecting streams with flows under 5 cfs is now considered under the procedure for individual permits (Fig. 7-18). These changes effectively establish federal jurisdiction over most proposed mountain valley developments.

A 404 permit requires applicants to describe in detail the type, condition, and boundaries of the existing wetland; to specify how they propose to change them and how much area will be affected; to assess the positive and negative impacts of the development on the wetland; and to offer a detailed plan for avoiding, minimizing, or compensating for all negative consequences. Wetland impacts in mountain areas are most commonly associated with the construction of roads, recreational facilities, and reservoirs.

Compliance Guidelines. Section 404 gives the Corps of Engineers the authority to decide whether to approve or deny permit applications, based on a public interest review and on compliance with the EPA's 404 (b)(1) guidelines governing impacts on waters of the United States. The act also directs the EPA to review all applications for compliance with the same guidelines and to submit agency comments and recommendations to the Corps of Engineers. If the EPA disagrees with the Corps's decision to approve an application, it may request a review of the matter at a higher level in the Corps. If that does not resolve the disagreement, the EPA has the power under Section 404 (c) to veto the Corps's approval, a power it has exercised in a few landmark cases. In addition

Figure 7-18. *Meandering stream with an intermittent flow of around 5 cfs. Snowmass–Maroon Bells Wilderness, Colorado. Development affecting streams of this size is subject to 404 permit requirements.*

to the EPA, other federal and state agencies, as well as any interested parties, may review applications during a 30-day comment period.

In formulating its decision, the Corps of Engineers is obliged to balance the public benefits of a development against its negative impacts. The factors to be balanced in this public interest review process include "conservation, economics, aesthetics, general environmental concerns, historic values, fish and wildlife values, flood damage prevention, land use, navigation, recreation, water supply, water quality, energy needs, safety, food production, and in general, the needs and welfare of the people." The decision process must also address the need for the development, the extent to which the development is truly "water dependent," the availability of alternative sites or methods, the nature of the impacts (positive, negative, temporary, permanent), the cumulative effects of the proposed and other developments in the area, the ecological importance of the wetland to the regional environment, and the views of state, local, and regional officials.

The EPA's charge focuses more narrowly on the protection of "the chemical, physical, and biological integrity of waters of the United States." The agency's evaluation is based solely on the 404 (b)(1) guidelines, which specify substantive criteria for assessing the acceptability of proposed wetland impacts of dredging or filling. The guidelines detail four conditions that applicants must meet in order to be judged in compliance[3] and the factual basis on which the severity of impacts will be projected. Subsections describe the chemical, physical, and biological components of specific aquatic ecosystems and how discharge activities can be expected to affect them. The guidelines also outline testing procedures and actions that can be taken to prevent or minimize adverse impacts.

Impact Mitigation.   The EPA's policy on the mitigation of impacts is basic to its evaluation of compliance. Mitigation is defined as a range of actions including (1) avoiding the impact altogether by staying out of wetlands on-site or by choosing an alternative site, (2) minimizing the impacts by reducing the magnitude or extent of the action, (3) repairing or restoring the impacted area or reducing the impact over time by preservation and maintenance ("on-site compensation"), and (4) replacing lost wetlands with substitute resources ("off-site compensation").

These four steps are viewed as a sequence; applicants must show that they have attempted the highest level of mitigation (avoidance) before resorting to the techniques in each subsequent step. If the loss of a wetland can be avoided, then no lesser mitigation techniques may be used to compensate for its loss. Understood in this context, the EPA's mitigation policies do not consider the creation of new wetlands or the enhancement of existing areas to be in compliance with the guidelines unless it is clear that no "practicable alternative" exists and the adverse impacts cannot be avoided. The burden of proof is on the applicant.

When adverse impacts cannot be avoided or minimized, compensatory mitigation techniques can

[3]These four conditions specify that no discharge of dredged or fill material will be permitted (1) if there is a practicable alternative; (2) if it violates state water quality standards or toxic effluent standards, jeopardizes endangered or threatened species, or adversely affects designated marine sanctuaries; (3) if it causes or contributes to significant degradation of U.S. waters; and (4) unless appropriate and practicable steps have been taken to minimize potential adverse impacts.

be proposed. The EPA favors mitigation plans based on restoring previously abused or destroyed wetlands.

Mitigation plans based instead on creating new wetlands to replace what the project will destroy are viewed with less enthusiasm. Ecological know-how lags behind earth-moving technology, and the best efforts of engineers and plant ecologists have not always produced manufactured wetlands as expected. Results have been disappointing on sites without the high water table to be self-maintaining or where on-going maintenance will be required to sustain the new wetland. Thus, permits for such plans frequently do not receive the EPA's endorsement.

When the applicant proposes to create new wetlands, the EPA looks for "functional equivalency" between the lost and the added wetlands. The agency expects new wetlands to match those destroyed, not simply acre for acre, but also type for type so that the ecological values provided by the lost wetlands will be regained. If the new wetlands are not in an area physiographically similar to the old one, they may not function in the same way ecologically and would therefore not be in compliance. Thus, when montane wetlands adjacent to streams are destroyed, the best way to achieve replacement wetlands of equivalent value is to seek out other streamside sites.

Even when impacts are minimal, the EPA typically recommends that standard mitigation steps be added as conditions of a permit: a permanent 25-foot buffer zone along the wetland edge; measures to control soil erosion, sedimentation, and stormwater runoff; no discharge of dredge or fill material into water on the site and measures to protect water quality; protective fencing around the wetlands to be preserved; restrictive covenants in deeds to retain the preserved wetlands in perpetuity; and flood protection measures. Optional measures include improving the stream as a fish habitat and stabilizing stream banks.

Attitudes toward wetlands are changing. Scientific understanding of wetland ecosystems is improving, more clearly revealing the environmental costs incurred when they are lost. Areas once viewed only as complications for construction are now more frequently considered significant to a place's ecological and visual quality. In a number of recently completed developments, both in the mountains and elsewhere, positive correlations are being confirmed between public enthusiasm for a project and preservation of wetlands and riparian areas. The rigors of the 404 permitting process can be most constructively approached with this in mind.

East Fork Ski Area: A Wetlands Case Study.   An innovative twist in the approach to mitigating wetland impacts has been approved on the East Fork of southwestern Colorado's San Juan River.

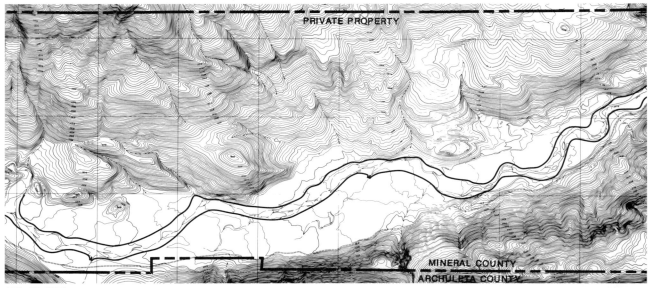

FLOOD PLAIN

EAST FORK
MINERAL AND ARCHULETA
COUNTIES, COLORADO

EAST FORK JOINT VENTURE
OLD ORCHARD ROAD, SKOKIE, IL.

WINSTON ASSOCIATES
PLANNING AND LANDSCAPE ARCHITECTURE
BOULDER, COLORADO

Wright Water Engineers Inc.
Glenwood Springs, CO

JUNE 1986

ESTIMATED 100 YEAR
FLOOD PLAIN

NOTES:

1) SHALLOW SHEET FLOW LIKELY TO EXTEND OUTSIDE OF MAPPED FLOOD PLAIN.
2) A MAJOR RUNOFF EVENT MAY CHANGE THE MAIN COURSE OF THE CHANNEL AND ALTER THE FLOOD PLAIN.
3) FLOOD PLAIN LIMITS APPROXIMATED BY HEC II CALCULATION.
4) BASED ON 2 FOOT, 1975 TOPOGRAPHY.

Figure 7-19.

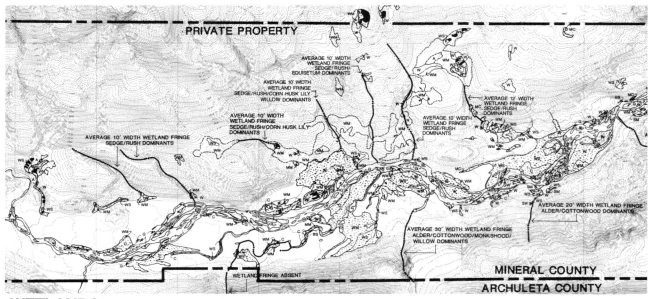

WETLANDS

EAST FORK
MINERAL AND ARCHULETA
COUNTIES, COLORADO

EAST FORK JOINT VENTURE
OLD ORCHARD ROAD, SKOKIE, IL.

WINSTON ASSOCIATES
PLANNING AND LANDSCAPE ARCHITECTURE
BOULDER, COLORADO

Aquatic and Wetland Consultants
Boulder, CO

NOVEMBER 1985

REVISED
JAN. 28, 1986
FEBRUARY 17, 1986
SEPT. 4, 1986
JAN. 12, 1987

Figure 7-20.

LEGEND

⬭ FIELD VERIFIED WETLANDS	C	COTTONWOOD	21.5
	DC	DRY CONIFER	2.0
⬭ POSSIBLE WETLANDS	G	GRAVEL BAR	45.6
	MC	MOIST CONIFER	4.5
A ASPEN 7.3 ACRES	MM	MOUNTAIN MEADOW	29.6
BS BLUE SPRUCE 4.8			

SM	SEDGE MEADOW	1.0
WM	WET MEADOW	178.1
WS	WET SEDGE	51.6
W	WILLOW	63.2
	TOTAL	409.2 ACRES

Developers have proposed building a major downhill ski area on National Forest and private land, with a four-season resort at its base. Earlier, in its land and

Figures 7-19 through 7-21. *Wetland mapping from the 1987 environmental impact statement for the proposed East Fork ski area, San Juan National Forest, Colorado (U.S.D.A. Forest Service 1987). Developer, East Fork Joint Venture, Skokie, Illinois. Lead consultant, Winston Associates, Boulder, Colorado, planning, urban design, landscape architecture; floodplain mapping, Wright Water Engineers Inc., Glenwood Springs, Colorado; wetlands inventory, Aquatic and Wetland Consultants, Boulder. See also Figs. 8-8 through 8-12.*

resource management plan for the forest, the Forest Service had noted the need for more winter recreation facilities and agreed in 1985 to study the ski area permit application.

The site planning was driven by natural factors. The watershed has soft, volcanic, easily erodible bedrock and oversteepened sideslopes showing evidence of past slippage. The toes of slopes are unstable, and slope instability increases with steeper gradients. Of necessity, development had to be restricted to the valley floor, where it would inevitably affect wetlands on the site (Figs. 7-19, 7-20, 7-21).

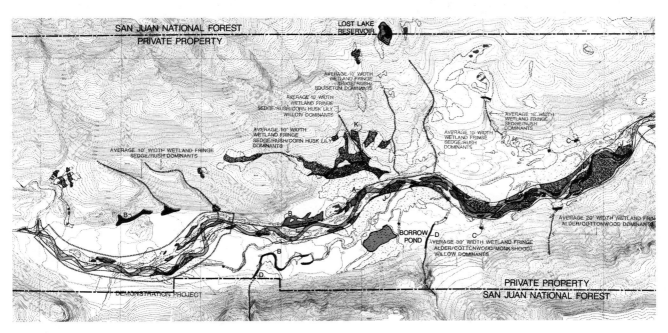

IMPACTED WETLANDS

EAST FORK
MINERAL AND ARCHULETA
COUNTIES, COLORADO

EAST FORK JOINT VENTURE
OLD ORCHARD ROAD, SKOKIE, IL

WINSTON ASSOCIATES
PLANNING AND LANDSCAPE ARCHITECTURE
BOULDER COLORADO

Aquatic and Wetland Consultants
Boulder, CO   MAY 1987

LEGEND

≈ PROPOSED ACTIVE CHANNEL

PROPOSED FLOOD PLAIN

FIELD VERIFIED WETLANDS

PHOTO IDENTIFIED (UNVERIFIED) WETLANDS

HIGH QUALITY WETLANDS: Well established, highly functional quality wetlands underlain by organic soils.

LOW QUALITY WETLANDS: Sparsely vegetated wetlands that have colonized since the 250 year flood; rooted primarily in gravel/cobble/sand substrate; have low functionality due to position within active channel and non-organic soils.

DIRECT IMPACTS: the dredging/filling of ACOE verified wetlands impacts resulting in long term elimination of wetlands

INDIRECT IMPACTS: do not result in elimination of ACOE verified wetlands

Positive -
(due to river renovation only)
1. stabilization of existing high quality wetlands to protect from erosion
2. inter-connecting the separate, existing, high quality wetlands into a continuous system

Negative -
(mountain development, adjacent base area development)
1. modification but not removal of high quality wetlands
2. development adjacent to high quality wetlands which affects wildlife, urban runoff etc.

Note: See Mitigation Section (Appendix A) for a complete discussion of wetland mitigation. Total acres of high quality wetlands to be created is 41.23 AC.

DIRECT IMPACT TO HIGH QUALITY WETLANDS

INDIRECT IMPACTS TO HIGH QUALITY WETLANDS

DIRECT IMPACTS TO LOW QUALITY WETLANDS

Figure 7-21.

Figure 7-22. *An aerial view of the braided channel of the San Juan River's East Fork before redevelopment. Photo by Winston Associates.*

Deforestation and grazing in the watershed had caused severe bank erosion, and as a consequence, the riverbed had grown into a broad, braided channel that consumed much of the valley floor (Fig. 7-22). The resulting sedimentation was identified as a major problem for municipal water supplies downstream, where much of the sediment was carried.

A plan was developed to reconstruct almost a mile of the stream, confining it in a new meandering channel of the same capacity with stabilized banks, thereby reducing the river's projected sediment load by close to half its present levels. Existing wetlands were protected from further erosion, and new wetlands were developed, using the unchanged 500-year floodplain terrace as a defined perimeter that future development will not breach. The Corps of Engineers approved the 404 permit as a demonstration project to save and restore land, reduce sediment deposition, retain wetland quality, and improve fish habitat. Work on the channel was completed in late 1986 (Fig. 7-23).

Figure 7-23. *In reconstruction, a meandering channel was excavated to confine the East Fork, stabilize its banks, and stop the loss of wetland vegetation on alluvial terraces that were being eroded. Photo by Winston Associates.*

PRESERVATION AND REVEGETATION

Because revegetation is so difficult in semiarid and high-altitude environments, there is a marked advantage in preserving as much of the existing native plant cover as possible. The ecological benefits of existing vegetation are significant. The thicker the vegetative cover, the lower the debris load in mountain streams will be. Vegetation protects water quality by reducing soil erosion and filtering out sediments. It safeguards soil moisture and productivity, and it moderates temperature fluctuations at ground level. Established forest cover helps retain slope and soil stability, and it reduces avalanche and landslide hazards.

Saving Vegetation

Maintaining the existing regime is the necessary prerequisite for retaining vegetation on a site. Around those plants that will remain after development, there should be no measurable change in drainage conditions, wind exposure, soil fertility, soil compaction, grade at ground level, amount of sunlight, or root space.

Trees. Retaining forest cover within a development is not simply a matter of flagging trunks; a more active role is required. The trees to be saved should be healthy, not near the end of their normal life span, and protected from changes in their water regimen. When thinning or clearing, foresters try not to leave trees, especially mature ones, standing alone where they will be exposed to more sun and wind than they can withstand. Under such stress, they are more vulnerable to insects, disease, and wind throw.

A general rule for protecting the trees to be retained has been to keep foundation excavations, utility trenches, and paving out of the area inside the drip line, an imaginary circle projected downward from the longest branches to the ground. The drip line is not an entirely reliable guide, however, for it assumes that roots are evenly distributed. For some forest species, however, this is not the case, even in uniformly developed soils. In the rocky soils of mountain areas, it is impossible to know where the root system goes. A better policy, therefore, is to allow a generous buffer around trees to be retained and to fertilize well beyond the drip line.

Changing the air and water regimen around an established tree can kill it. Excavation can damage the roots, and filling and compaction around the trunk can reduce the amount of air that reaches the roots. Changing the gradient can greatly affect

the natural flow of surface and subsurface water on which the tree depends. For these reasons, grades within the drip line should be altered as little as possible.

Increasing soil moisture can also be destructive to a tree. Understory plants that need more frequent watering should not be planted under forest trees. "Post-construction watering of forest trees has never been a good substitute for precipitation falling during the winter period and, in fact, should be avoided" (University of California 1984, p. 7).

Conditions for Successful Revegetation

Every undertaking requires some revegetation. Its chances of success depend on the selection of suitable areas for revegetation, proper preparation of the site, identification of appropriate plant materials, and careful installation and long-term maintenance. No matter how successful, however, revegetation cannot stabilize overly steep or long slopes or slopes with drainage or seepage problems. It cannot prevent landslides, but it can hold soil in place. It is an integral part of competent sitework, but it is not a panacea for all potential problems.

Before disturbing a site, its rehabilitation potential should be evaluated so that the intensity and cost of revegetation methods can be estimated and areas with poor potential avoided. In this process, topographical maps, soil surveys, and vegetation inventories are essential.

Obstacles to the successful revegetation of a mountain site are plentiful indeed. Primary among them are the short growing season, the extremely slow growth rate of transplanted or seeded native shrubs and trees, and the spotty commercial availability of species native to a site. Excavation and construction can compound the problem by so disrupting the natural hydrologic regime and altering the soils that restoring original vegetation is no longer possible.

Preparing the Site. Inadequate site preparation has been the most common problem hindering revegetation (Nishimura 1974, p. 5). Plants need stable, noneroding slopes to survive. Not surprisingly, they establish themselves more easily on fill. And because fill slopes are more susceptible to failure, it is important that they be carefully graded, using stable material and incorporating necessary slope drainage measures.

To establish native grasses on large areas, gradients of no more than 1.5 to 1 are recommended for south-facing slopes; 2 to 1 is preferable for colder aspects, where cover takes longer to become established. The Forest Service has been able to reseed grasses on slopes as steep as 1.5 to 1, but only in small areas with much success. For high-activity areas where bluegrass is the best alternative, 4 to 1 is the generally accepted maximum for easy mowing, but in the mountains, that guideline has necessarily been exceeded. For ground covers, slopes over 3 to 1 complicate maintenance and increase the probability of erosion during irrigation (Fig. 7-24).

A 6- to 8-inch (15 to 20 cm) layer of fertilized topsoil is recommended. In the Forest Service's recommendations for revegetating ski slopes, 4 to 6 inches (10 to 15 cm) of topsoil on steeper slopes is thought to be more practical, as topsoil more than 6 inches deep on slopes is liable to slump. Conversely, topsoil less than 2 inches deep is of little benefit unless the area is fairly flat and the subsoil has enough fine particles. The subsoil should be tilled or loosened so that the topsoil can bond and will be less likely to slip. The top 18 inches (45 cm) should be aerated to enable plant roots to penetrate and to improve the water-holding capacity of the surface layers.

It is not realistic to plant trees and shrubs in semiarid mountain regions without some kind of irrigation. To assist, regraded landforms can be shaped to trap and store precipitation, provided that care is taken not to saturate any potentially unstable slopes. Contour furrowing and roughening of the surface also help retain runoff.

Rates and types of fertilizers vary according to soil factors. Because most subsoils are deficient in nitrogen, it will probably have to be applied yearly. And because nitrogen is water soluble, it can be broadcast. Fall is the best time, just before the snows come. A late summer application is not a good idea, as it promotes late season growth and makes plants more vulnerable to winterkill. Phosphorus may also be advisable, but it does not leach and so should be tilled into the soil before planting.

Selecting Plants. Choosing inappropriate plant materials is the other most common shortcoming. The best way to select plants and to place them where they will grow best is to observe the conditions in which native species are growing on or near the site. Some natives can be successfully planted above or below their usual elevation zone if their requirements for moisture, nutrients, and sun or shade are met, but most species have extremely narrow tolerances.

The chances of reestablishing trees and shrubs on a given site are better when the plant propagation material (seed, transplants, cuttings) is collected from areas having soil and climatic conditions similar to those of the planting site (Ronco 1976, p. 19). From the plant communities already growing on a site, select species from early successional stages that

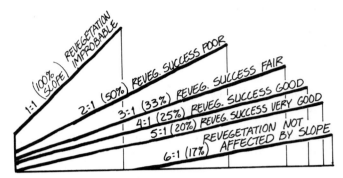

Figure 7-24. *Prospects for revegetation related to slope gradient.*

appear most effective in reducing erosion and providing habitat and forage. Seek the advice of local nurseries early in the landscape design process to identify commercially available natives and suitable substitutes.

Trees and shrubs should be planted after the ground thaws, around early June, so that the root system has the full growing season to get established. Bare-root planting is possible only when plants are dormant. Containerized nursery stock, even in native species, may be more vigorous and shapely than field-dug specimens. Trees that have become root bound in small containers should be avoided, as the roots will spiral and eventually strangle the plant.

Long-term efforts to reestablish forest cover have often been disappointing. Where trees were sparse before development, forestation even with forest species native to the region may prove impossible. In Elkhorn at Sun Valley, Idaho, for instance, only four trees were native to the area (aspen, cottonwood, Engelmann spruce, Rocky Mountain Douglas fir). None grew in abundance, and neither of the conifers was commercially available at the time the development began. Substitution of similar, but nonnative species of pine and fir was the only alternative, and even this approach was only marginally satisfactory. Shrubs, grasses, and perennials were much more successful.

In unforested areas like Elkhorn or Copper Mountain, Colorado (see Chapter 9), crucial factors in the attempt to establish trees are shading, moisture, and control of competition from other plants. However, horticultural experience in creating favorable site conditions is not well advanced, particularly at high altitudes. If the lack of trees has been due to factors such as high groundwater or severe exposure, these inhibiting conditions will be virtually impossible to reverse. The outlook for success on an unforested site will be better if there is evidence that it once was forested (that is, that a forest was burned or cleared). Then, using sun-tolerant tree and shrub species, revegetation can jump-start the natural process of forest succession.

Ninety percent of plant losses are in winter. Even if a plant makes it through the first winter, there is no assurance that it will survive the following one. Winterkill, a result of intense solar radiation combined with cold or frozen soil, is a major hazard. In these conditions, plants transpire but cannot rehydrate. Another wintertime killer is the reflection of radiation off the snow onto the underside of needles. With the short growing season, conifers never recover the needles they lose in this way over the winter.

Seeding. At higher altitudes, seeding is generally less effective than preserving and replacing native turf sod. However, seed may often be the only affordable alternative for revegetating larger areas. Germination rates are affected by aspect, slope position, altitude, shading, snow collection patterns, and the depth, texture, and fertility of the soil (Berg 1974, p. 31). Consequently, the seed should be a diverse mixture tailor-made for specific site conditions.

If an extensive revegetation area is involved and there is adequate time, possible seed mixes, application rates, and soil amendments should be tested in situations close to actual conditions. On drier south and west slope aspects, as much as 50 to 100 percent more pounds of seed per acre may be required. Keep in mind that "actual conditions" may change dramatically after the subsoils and topsoil are stripped, stockpiled, mixed, and replaced.

Because most native seeds are quite small, they must not be covered too deeply. The best results have been achieved when seed is drilled or broadcast first and covered lightly with soil, and then mulch is applied last in a separate operation. When mulch and seed are applied together, it is more difficult to make sure that the seed is in contact with the soil and, in semiarid regions, to keep the seed from drying out (Cook et al. 1974, p. 7). Mulches shorten the time it takes to establish new vegetation because they reduce evaporation and erosion by wind and water. Long-fiber mulches, well anchored, are the most effective. On steeper slopes, hydromulches, tackifiers, or netting are needed to hold down the mulch. (See Appendix C for a comparative analysis of common erosion control methods for seeded slopes.)

The timing of seeding is critical to its success. Seeding should be done immediately after the topsoil is applied, in order to minimize erosion and weeds, and it is best to do it just before the season of greatest precipitation. In areas where most of the precipitation falls as snow, sowing in the fall is recommended, although this requires extra care with erosion control through the winter. At lower elevations, spring is usually also a safe time, after the

soil has thawed and the snow has melted. This has an advantage over fall plantings in that "the site will be subjected to fewer erosive events such as high winds, rain and snowstorms prior to seed germination. It is important . . . not [to] be tied to inflexible seeding dates. Soil and weather conditions and not just the time of year should dictate the proper course of action" (Theisen 1986, p. 17).

AESTHETIC CONSIDERATIONS

As one of the materials at a designer's disposal, plants have many aesthetic uses in addition to their functional utility in erosion and microclimate control. Plants are used in landscape design as edges, textures, and screens; for directional control, linkage, spatial definition and articulation; and as character-givers, softeners, unifiers, symbols, and ornaments. There are many good reference works on landscape design that discuss the aesthetic functions of plants.[4] Although most of these uses are relevant to a mountain setting, the severity and visual dominance of the natural environment suggest that some are more appropriate than others.

The central constraint on landscape design in the mountains (the Northeast and the Pacific Northwest excepted) is the limited plant palette. Because most mountain plants have narrower growth requirements, there are simply not as many native varieties from which to choose. It is therefore harder to accomplish certain spatial objectives, like formal colonnades, umbrellalike canopies, and uniform blankets of coarser textures, that are commonplace in less severe climates.

The maturation of a designed landscape in the mountains takes longer than in less severe climates, as new plants have far slower growth rates and higher mortality rates. Consequently, land-shaping and structural elements are relatively more important in defining outdoor spaces. Moreover, the task of reconstructing a mountain landscape is sufficiently difficult that one is forced to take it on in smaller bites and to confine intensive landscaping to smaller areas. In regard to design opportunities, the aesthetic qualities of the mountain landscape encourage the following uses of plants.

Plants as Interpreters of Local Ecosystems. One of the best ways to educate people about the mountain environment is to bring it closer to hand. This can be done by retaining existing vegetation

[4]See the Bibliography for references on planting design and books listing native mountain plants.

The tall trees,
Growing up together by the small village,
A landmark.

—*Haiku poet Shiki (1869–1902)*

where possible and adding newly planted areas that are reminiscent of the mountains, like aspen groves, riparian margins, and alpine rock gardens. (See Chapter 9, Natural Landscape Themes and Linkages.)

Plants as Habitat.   Wildlife is an important part of the mountain environment. Many plants can make an area more attractive to birds, fish, and small mammals, by providing cover and food. Riparian plants and berry-producing native shrubs are particularly enticing.

Plants as Linkage.   Natural riparian corridors, forest remnants, and other greenbelt connections provide functional and visual links. They are the most reliable way to unite a built place with its natural setting.

Plants as Pathfinders.   Plants that stand out because of their character, color, or massing can be used to mark directions and points of entry. They are like gateways and rock cairns along a trail.

Plants as Scale Modulators.   Trees and shrubs are among the most effective ways to make transitions in scale from foreground elements to the backdrop of peaks and broad vistas.

Plants as Comfort in the Wilderness.   Sometimes elements of urbanity and refinement are a welcome contrast with the apparent wildness and disorder of the natural landscape. Within well-defined spaces, a valid use of plants is to create an oasis of controlled formality.

Plants as Spatial Articulators.   Many mountain plants can be used to define outdoor edges (walls), but few can achieve a canopy (ceiling) effect in a reasonable period of time. Shrubs are perhaps the most versatile plants, offering great variety in edge character and height. Conifers and aspen also make good edges and can be layered with shrubs to vary the character and density of the edge and help modulate the scale. For screening and privacy, shrubs offer fullness at eye level and a speedier growth rate than trees. On slopes, their visual effect as a divider of space is enhanced. Native vines, in conjunction with skeletal outdoor structures, are an underutilized resource.

When designing edges, it is important to think about snow, for it tends to accumulate here, by either wind or snowplow. Planted edges thus should be designed to accommodate predictable patterns of snow deposition and snow removal.

Plants as Landmarks.   Among the most noteworthy natural landmarks are specimen forest trees, mature groves, and riparian areas that have been retained and protected on the site. In most cases, these plants become cultural symbols of a place's character and history.

Figure 7-25.   *The open, parklike composition of a ponderosa pine/prairie ecotone near Boulder, Colorado. Photo by David J. Cooper.*

It is difficult for newly planted vegetation to serve as a landmark, although masses of flowering perennials and annuals have attained this character-giving stature in some mountain towns.

Plants as View Frames. Mountain trees and shrubs can be used to hide, reveal, and frame views in a sequence that entices and stimulates. In mountain scenery, the frame is often essential to focusing attention on a special view.

Plants as Sensory Stimuli. Mountain plants, well selected, bring color, sound, smell, and motion. In a western mountain landscape of conifer forests, deciduous trees and shrubs are reminders of seasonality and oases of bright green. In an eastern landscape of hardwoods, conifers and meadow clearings are equally prized for their sensory contrast.

Plant Communities as Models for Planting Design. Each plant community has its own visual and ecological patterns. If native plants are combined in ways that contradict the patterns in which they naturally occur, the built environment may not feel in harmony with the site.

Visualize, for example, a ponderosa pine forest (Fig. 7-25). Preferring drier country, ponderosas respond to the competition for moisture by spacing themselves in parklike open stands. They form scattered forests spreading down the lower flanks of mountains and mingling at the lower tree line with sage and prairie or desert vegetation. Stimulated by this openness, the understory is a rich, multitextured blanket of shrubs, perennials, and grasses, uniting the composition and adding variety to the foreground view. This ecosystem thus lends itself to specimen plantings and intensive ground plane development.

In contrast, a lodgepole pine forest is dense and uniform in pattern and line (Fig. 7-26). As a pioneer species, the slow-growing, slender lodgepoles often grow in nearly pure stands. They are small compared with most other pines and disappointing as a specimen. A lodgepole forest is more interesting when it shares an edge with clearings, water, and other vegetation types. Landscape design compatible with this ecosystem focuses on the forest edges, uses selective clearing to improve spatial quality within the forest, and leaves the shaded ground plane free of visual interruptions.

Aspens have a loose, open habit of growth and fine-textured leaves that communicate energy when a breeze is blowing (Fig. 7-27). Spreading by means of suckers, aspens occur naturally in dense clumps, preferring wetter sites in full sun. Their distinctive gray-white bark and golden fall color contrast vividly with dark conifer backdrops. Aspens' ability to

Figure 7-26. *The uniformly textured fabric of a lodgepole pine forest.*

transmit light and movement makes them an important part of the design palette in an environment in which variety in trees is almost nil.

The choice and placement of plant materials, the purposes for which they are selected and combined, and the reshaping of the landforms on which they are arranged are important design decisions in the mountain landscape. The choices made can either reinforce the bonds between people and place or emphasize their differences.

165

Figure 7-27. *Best known for fall color and leaves that are always in motion, aspen are equally distinguished in winter, when their catkins and white bark stand out against the dark forest backdrop.*

DESIGN GUIDELINES

Site Selection

1. Avoid sites where the prospects for revegetation are poor. In particular, avoid sites on steep or potentially unstable slopes.

2. Use vegetation communities to help identify land suitable for building and land that is unstable or too wet.

3. Look for sites offering diversity in plant species, as this may make it easier to repair disturbances.

Site Planning and Grading

1. Retain as much existing vegetation as possible. Concentrate disturbances in ecosystems more tolerant of changes in their ecological regimes.

Minimize disturbances where vegetation is vital to wildlife or to aesthetic values, and clearly define the limits of grading.

2. Discourage development in wetlands. Engage professional ecologists to map and evaluate existing wetlands on a site. Seek consensus on a site plan that to the greatest extent possible avoids construction in wetlands.

3. Identify the probable constraints to revegetation and the restoration methods required by alternative site plans, and then estimate costs before selecting the preferred alternative.

4. Bring open space with natural vegetation into the heart of a community. This requires that the site plan be open enough to let the natural landscape penetrate. Overly dense or overly dispersed site plans risk obliterating the natural landscape. Study ecosystems on the site—their processes, forms, and interrelationships—to create new landscapes inspired by the natural place.

5. Use existing and added vegetation to reinforce edges and transitions from the natural to the urban landscape and from public to private spaces.

6. To reduce the visual impacts of development, site structures at forest edges rather than in meadows and clearings.

7. Avoid stream diversions that will have serious downstream consequences for vegetation, fish, and wildlife.

8. Minimize changes to the natural hydrological regime of existing vegetation; consider the possible damage to vegetation from changes in runoff patterns upstream and upslope. Duplicate natural runoff patterns wherever possible. It is ecologically preferable to slow runoff so that it can be absorbed by the soil than to direct it to constructed drainage systems. Direct the runoff from slopes and roofs to vegetated areas that can use and retain water.

9. Distribute open areas for snow storage alongside roads and pathways; these areas should not be planted with trees or shrubs.

10. Before cutting trees, remember that at high altitudes, large trees take half-centuries or more to mature. One cannot assume that a new tree can be planted where an old one was chopped down or died. Without expensive excavation, it may not be possible to dig out the old root system, and in a semiarid climate, it may not rot in our lifetime.

11. When trees must be removed to carve out activity areas, roads, and view lines, get a forester's help in thinning and culling so that the forest retained will be healthy. Glade the timber to create natural openings. Pay attention to the edges of the cleared area; irregular or feathered edges may be less noticeable (Fig. 7-28).

12. Keep changes in grade well away from trees to

be retained. Use treewells where necessary to maintain natural grade around the tree trunk (Fig. 7-29). Avoid cut slopes or excavation for trenches and foundations in the general vicinity of the drip line. Finally, consider adding a penalty clause for tree damage to the contractor's specifications.

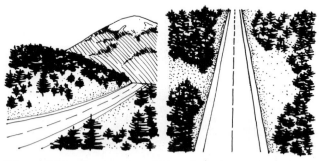

Figure 7-28. *Feathered and irregular edges make forest cuts less noticeable.*

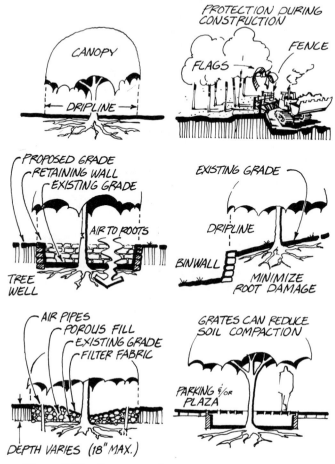

Figure 7-29. *Tree protection measures.*

Planting

1. Provide optimal conditions for the establishment of new vegetation: Prepare the site adequately (topsoil, fertilizer, mulch, water, erosion control), and select plant materials and seed appropriate to the conditions. Schedule planting according to local climatic patterns.

2. Use native plants. Mowed lawns, fenced yards, and most nonnative ornamentals obscure the natural landscape in mountain settings, look out of place, and create an ongoing maintenance burden. Developments should stipulate a native plant list that meets the needs of privacy and usable outdoor space. The landscaping of public spaces can provide a model.

3. Restrict planting on slopes to dryland species. Closely regulate the timing and rate of irrigation to avoid water-induced slope failure.

4. Don't expect revegetation miracles where soils are thin, rocky, dry, or on steep slopes. When areas like this must be disturbed, budget for intensive remedies. Major tree and shrub plantings on elevations exposed to severe wind may be a waste of money.

5. Don't envision new forests where no trees occur in the natural landscape; there are usually good reasons for their absence (like aridity or high groundwater) that no amount of time or money can effectively overcome on a large scale.

6. If the natural site won't support trees, depend on shrub masses for effect; shrubs offer as much versatility in form and function as the landscape designer is likely to find among native plants. Secure nursery sources as far ahead as possible, preferably one growing season before intended installation dates. Use transplanted shrubs from elsewhere on the site. When there is a choice, select early successional (subclimax) species for the best survival rates.

7. Consider the aesthetic impacts on spatial perception of tree clearing and planting. Concentrate new trees where they will have the greatest effect on the definition of outdoor space.

8. Consider the scale of the natural landscape. In this context, finely detailed planting efforts have negligible visual effect except in small, well-defined spaces. Rely on perennials wherever the scale favors smaller plantings. For larger areas, a combination of native trees, shrubs, native grasses, and wildflowers appears more natural.

9. Get horticultural assistance in selecting a native grass seed mixture suited for local conditions. Buy only seed produced locally or under environmental conditions similar to those of your site. On slopes, use species that form thick root mats.

10. For ground covers other than grasses, select carpetlike growth forms that spread by runners rather than cushion forms that have a single taproot. In most mountain regions, the fastest-spreading ground covers are deciduous, not evergreen.[5]

11. Never dig up alpine plants to transplant elsewhere. The hole you leave will take decades to recover, and the tundra needs the reproductive stock. Besides, there is no assurance that the plant you take will transplant successfully. Instead, rely on commercial propagators or use their expertise to gather your own seeds.

12. Design protected niches for new trees and plants—pockets among rocks or terraces undulating across slopes—so that they can benefit from natural drainage and moisture retention patterns (Fig. 7-30). Place rocks to direct runoff to plant roots and to create wind shelter for understory plants.

13. Anticipate where snow will shed, drift, or be shoveled up in piles; do not plant species in those areas unless they can tolerate the snow load. The best way to figure out which ones can is to look around; except for perennials and willows, the options are limited. Protect planting areas from snowplow damage. Near plowed areas, use only minor plantings and keep the gradients on berms very gentle.

14. Consider using for irrigation the sediment-laden water from detention ponds.

15. Mulch with rock, wood chips, or bark to retain soil moisture and discourage weeds. Black plastic does not work as a weed barrier. Rather, it simply collects weed seeds that germinate on top of it and keeps moisture from infiltrating.

16. Avoid putting plants (except annuals) in planters. All mountain plants need full ground insulation to survive the winter. If you must try it, construct planters with liners that have a high R value, and cover them over the winter with a plastic-covered styrofoam blanket.

17. Encourage owners to provide for long-term landscape maintenance by budgeting for labor and materials in their financial projections. If the long-term budget does not appear sufficient to maintain the level of landscaping proposed, reassess design intentions for a better match between maintenance requirements and the financial resources to support them.

For intensive planting schemes, advocate phased installation over several years, revegetating in the interim with native grasses. This permits owners to assess the amount of maintenance required and to make adjustments in later phases.

[5]Among the best are three from the strawberry family: wild strawberry (*Fragaria americana*), mock strawberry (*Duchesnea indica*), and spring cinquefoil (*Potentilla verna*). Also fast spreaders are creeping buttercup (*Ranunculus repens*), snow-in-summer (*Cerastium tomentosum*), and ground ivy (*Glechoma hederacea*), the last considered a weed in some places.

Figure 7-30.

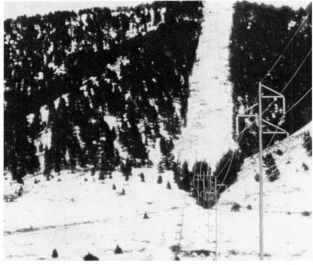

Figure 7-31. *Visual simulation is a regular part of the planning process for major projects. In the bottom picture, a transmission line and cleared right-of-way were painted in by hand to show local residents and agencies the visual effects of one proposed alignment alternative. Simulation by Stephen R. J. Sheppard, Dames & Moore, San Francisco. Courtesy of Montana Power Company.*

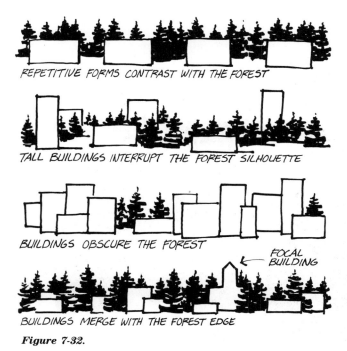

REPETITIVE FORMS CONTRAST WITH THE FOREST

TALL BUILDINGS INTERRUPT THE FOREST SILHOUETTE

BUILDINGS OBSCURE THE FOREST

FOCAL
BUILDING

BUILDINGS MERGE WITH THE FOREST EDGE

Figure 7-32.

18. Deciduous trees should be pruned every year to minimize breakage under heavy snow.

Site Improvements and Structures

1. Use computer models and visual simulation to evaluate the impacts of forest clearing caused by various configurations of building massing and height. Consider the alternatives from a variety of vantage points. Use the same process for roads, transmission lines, or any other project that requires forest clearing (Fig. 7-31).

2. Keep most rooflines below the forest canopy. As landmarks, public buildings can exceed the height of the canopy, but do not let density and scale overcome the forest edge (Fig. 7-32).

3. To soften the presence of buildings in the landscape, choose colors compatible with the seasonal shades of the surrounding vegetation.

REFERENCES

American Fisheries Society, Western Division, 1980. Position paper on management and protection of Western riparian stream ecosystems. Bethesda, Md.

Berg, W. A. 1974. Grasses and legumes for revegetation of disturbed subalpine areas. In *Proceedings of a Workshop on Revegetation of High-Altitude Disturbed Lands*. Ft. Collins: Colorado State University, Information Series no. 10, pp. 31–35.

Billings, W. D. 1978. Aspects of the ecology of alpine and subalpine plants. In *Proceedings: High-Altitude Revegetation Workshop No. 3*. Ft. Collins, Colo.: Environmental Resources Center, Information Series no. 28, pp. 1–17.

Cook, C. Wayne, Robert M. Hyde, and Phillip L. Sims. 1974. Revegetation guidelines for surface mined areas. Ft. Collins: Colorado State University, Range Science Department, Science Series no. 16.

Cowardin, Lewis, et al. 1979. *Classification of Wetlands and Deep-Water Habitats of the U.S.* U.S. Fish and Wildlife Service, Biological Services Program, Report no. FWS/OBS-77/31.

Davis, J. Gary, and Sarah Fowler. 1985. A wetlands assessment and mitigation pre-proposal handbook for Colorado. Boulder, Colo.: Aquatic and Wetlands Consultants.

Litton, R. Burton, Jr. 1973. Esthetic resources of the lodgepole pine forest. Berkeley, Calif.: Pacific Southwest Forest and Range Experiment Station, U.S.D.A. Forest Service.

Nishimura, John Y. 1974. Soils and soil problems at high altitudes. In *Proceedings of a Workshop on High-Altitude Disturbed Lands*. Ft. Collins: Colorado Water Resources Research Institute, Information Series no. 10, pp. 5–9.

Odum, Eugene P. 1971. *Fundamentals of Ecology*, 3rd ed. Philadelphia: Saunders.

Price, Larry W. 1981. *Mountains and Man*. Berkeley and Los Angeles: University of California Press.

Ronco, Frank. 1976. Regeneration of forest lands at high elevations in the Central Rocky Mountains. In *Proceedings: High-Altitude Revegetation Workshop No. 2*. Ft. Collins, Colo.: Environmental Resources Center, Information Series no. 21, pp. 13–25.

Theisen, Marc. 1986. Practical approaches for cost effective erosion control. *Colorado Green* (Spring): 16–21.

U.S.D.A. Forest Service. 1987. East Fork Ski Area draft environmental impact statement. Durango, Colo.: San Juan National Forest, Pagosa Ranger District.

University of California, Division of Agriculture and Natural Resources, Cooperative Extension. 1984. Protecting trees when building on forest land. Leaflet no. 21348.

Williams, Jean, ed. 1986. *Rocky Mountain Alpines*. Portland, Or.: Timber Press.

Windell, J. T., et al. 1986. *An Ecological Characterization of Rocky Mountain Montane and Subalpine Wetlands*. Ft. Collins, Colo.: U.S. Fish and Wildlife Service, Biological Report no. 86 (11).

Zwinger, Ann H., and Beatrice E. Willard, 1972. *Land Above the Trees*. New York: Harper & Row.

8

THE DESIGN PROCESS: USING NATURAL FACTORS AS A FRAMEWORK

If you wish to know the road up the mountain,
You must ask the man who goes back and forth on it.
  —*Zen verse, unknown author*

Both the creative act of designing and the process of design are colored by the designer's values, sensitivity, ethics, and personal history. They are also influenced by time and the speed of change, the scale and complexity of the task, and the available technology. In design fields like architecture and landscape architecture, whose products are public concerns, the process itself becomes a determinant of the product's quality.

This is no less true for the design of human environments in rural areas than for design in cities. In both, the same design objective prevails: to ensure that new development reinforces the quality of community life and at the same time respects what is special about the landscape. In the mountains, because the natural landscape dominates the physical context for development, sensitive design requires an understanding of the environment, its ecology and functions, its dynamics and rhythms, and its value as part of a larger natural fabric.

When designing in a difficult natural environment like the mountains, it is tempting to underrate the physical constraints. Today, although environmental information is almost always invoked to justify design choices, seldom are the real restrictions on a given site fully respected in the final development. It has been too easy to compromise basic ecological principles, to think of environmental parameters only as a basis for mitigation and not as grounds for respect and restraint.

Information alone does not guarantee sensitive design. Another important variable is process: what site-specific information is generated and how it is interpreted, how and when it is introduced in the evolution of a design project, and how decision makers respond to what it reveals. Process is both a sequence and a method, asking the right questions at the right time, asking the sources best equipped to answer, and then devising design solutions that reflect a site's capacity to support development.

A CHECKLIST FOR NATURAL FACTORS RESEARCH

Gathering information is an ongoing task, for at each step in the design process, plans and designs may be altered by what was discovered during the preceding step. The more the designer knows about the environment, the better able he or she will be to differentiate among landscapes of the same generic type and to plan land uses according to a particular site's ecology.

It is important to maintain a fairly broad perspective throughout the investigation, focusing neither too quickly nor too narrowly on the site itself to the exclusion of its regional and neighborhood context. Both regional and site-specific data on natural factors are needed for clues to development programming, site planning, and design form. These data also establish a baseline against which the effects of development can be projected and later monitored.

Topography

Those elements of a site's topography with which the designer should be familiar are slope, aspect, elevation, surface relief, and landform, but from a regional perspective, watersheds and landscape units are also important. The best sources of information on these elements are topographical maps, aerial photos in stereo pairs, and on-site surveys. Maps and aerial photos are available for many mountain sites from the U.S. Geological Survey, the U.S. Forest Service, or those state departments responsible for natural resources. If maps with topographical contours are not available, they can be produced from professional aerial photo surveys (for large areas) or by on-site surveyors (for small sites). The series of maps in Figs. 8-1 through 8-4 illustrates how siting decisions in a Canadian project evolved in response to the topographical character of the site.

The topographical analyses that you will need are the following:

1. Slope gradient analysis. A slope gradient analysis determines the development suitability of land, its visual vulnerability, physical hazards, potential for revegetation, and the difficulty of repairing disturbances. The gradients on land above or below a site may be as pertinent as those on the site itself because of their relationship to drainage, natural hazards, and access.

After the gradient categories are mapped, it is helpful to return to the site and compare the map with one's first visual impressions. People with less experience in dealing with mountain terrain often underestimate slope gradient in the field and

Figures 8-1 through 8-4. *Environmental inventory maps from the master-planning process for Blackcomb near Whistler, British Columbia. Slope gradient (Fig. 8-1), along with bedrock and floodplain limits (Fig. 8-2), shows up as a primary constraint on the environmental summary map (Fig. 8-3). These factors largely determined the siting of the new base village (Fig. 8-4). Developer, Intrawest, Vancouver, B.C. Design Workshop Inc., Aspen, planning and landscape architecture.*

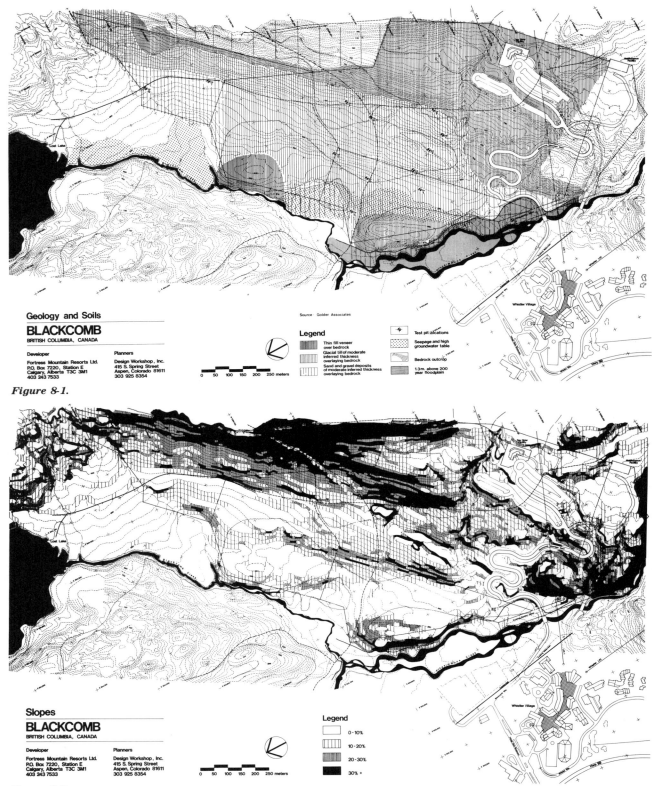

Geology and Soils

BLACKCOMB

BRITISH COLUMBIA, CANADA

Developer
Fortress Mountain Resorts Ltd.
P.O. Box 7220, Station E
Calgary, Alberta T3C 3M1
403 243 7533

Planners
Design Workshop, Inc.
415 S. Spring Street
Aspen, Colorado 81611
303 925 8354

Source: Golder Associates

Legend

- Thin fill veneer over bedrock
- Glacial till of moderate inferred thickness overlaying bedrock
- Sand and gravel deposits of moderate inferred thickness overlaying bedrock
- Test pit locations
- Seepage and high groundwater table
- Bedrock outcrop
- 1.3 m. above 200 year floodplain

0   50   100   150   200   250 meters

Figure 8-1.

Slopes

BLACKCOMB

BRITISH COLUMBIA, CANADA

Developer
Fortress Mountain Resorts Ltd.
P.O. Box 7220, Station E
Calgary, Alberta T3C 3M1
403 243 7533

Planners
Design Workshop, Inc.
415 S. Spring Street
Aspen, Colorado 81611
303 925 8354

Legend

- 0 - 10%
- 10 - 20%
- 20 - 30%
- 30% +

0   50   100   150   200   250 meters

Figure 8-2.

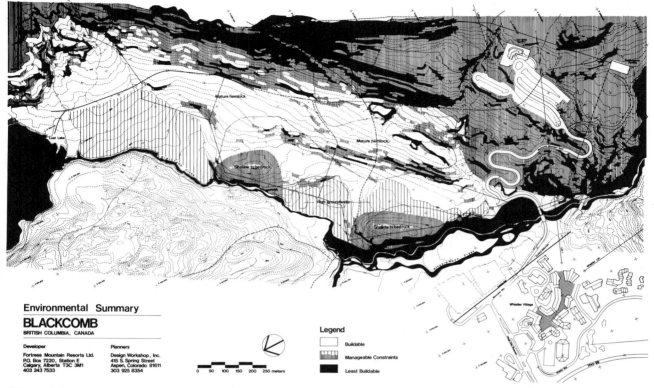

Environmental Summary

BLACKCOMB

BRITISH COLUMBIA, CANADA

Developer

Fortress Mountain Resorts Ltd.
P.O. Box 7220, Station E
Calgary, Alberta T3C 3M1
403 243 7533

Planners

Design Workshop, Inc.
415 S. Spring Street
Aspen, Colorado 81611
303 925 8354

Legend

☐ Buildable

▥ Manageable Constraints

■ Least Buildable

0   50   100   150   200   250 meters

Figure 8-3.

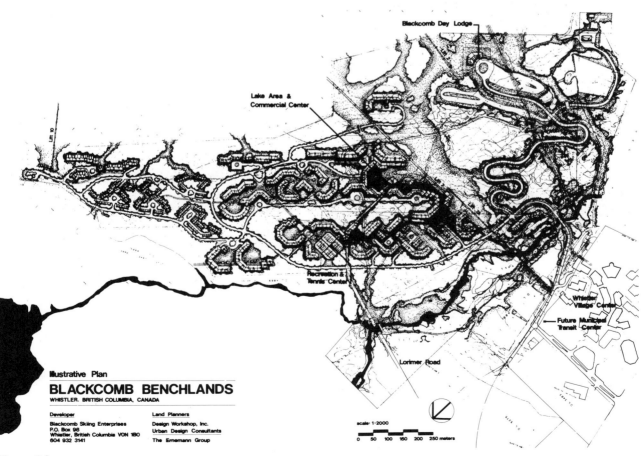

Illustrative Plan

BLACKCOMB BENCHLANDS

WHISTLER, BRITISH COLUMBIA, CANADA

Developer

Blackcomb Skiing Enterprises
P.O. Box 98
Whistler, British Columbia VON 1B0
604 932 3141

Land Planners

Design Workshop, Inc.
Urban Design Consultants

The Ernemann Group

scale 1:2000

0   50   100   150   200   250 meters

Figure 8-4.

consequently design site plan layouts for which the actual gradients may be too steep.

2. Slope aspect map. A slope aspect map, useful in siting decisions, shows how the site is oriented to the sun—where it is warmest and driest and where it is coolest and wettest. Because it depicts light and solar radiation, it anticipates patterns in vegetation and soil character and is essential to the siting of comfortable human environments.

3. Delineation of natural landscape units and viewsheds. Landscape units establish logical boundaries for a development or a community site; identify natural edges, views, and connective elements between it and its neighbors that can be reinforced through site planning; and clarify topographically imposed constraints on access and circulation.

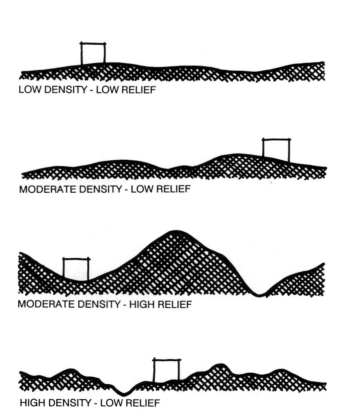

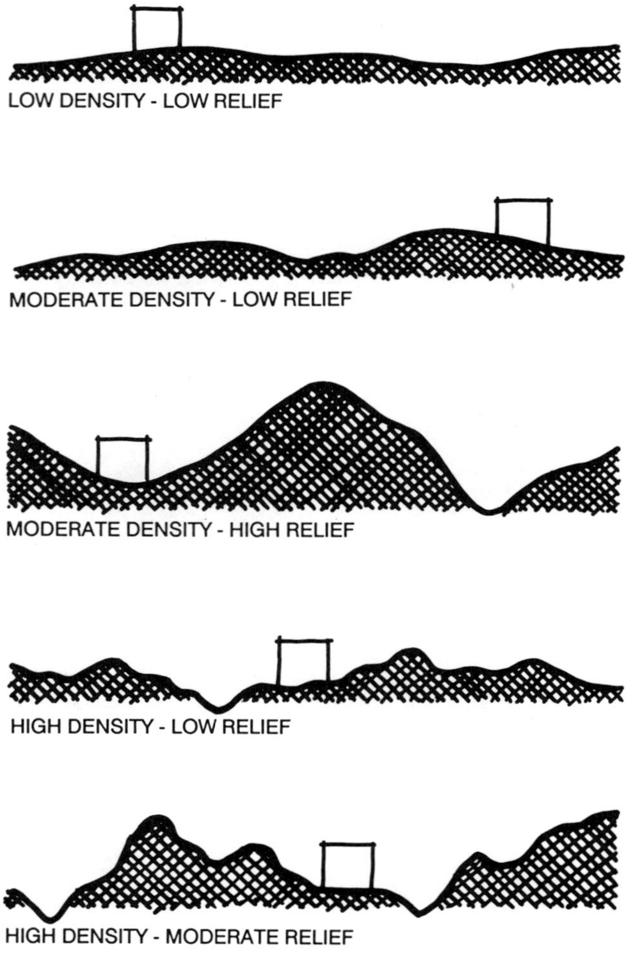

LOW DENSITY - LOW RELIEF

MODERATE DENSITY - LOW RELIEF

MODERATE DENSITY - HIGH RELIEF

HIGH DENSITY - LOW RELIEF

HIGH DENSITY - MODERATE RELIEF

4. Analysis of surface relief (Fig. 8-5). A measure of the terrain's ruggedness, surface relief is another regional factor determining visual vulnerability, ease of access, physical unity, and circulation patterns. The products of a terrain analysis may be both verbal and graphic, representing in plan and profile the landform patterns characteristic of the region. Descriptors of surface relief include typical landform shapes, number of peaks, average horizontal distances between summits or ridges, differences in height between peaks and valleys, and percentages of surface area covered by different slope gradient categories. The objective of this analysis is not only a better understanding of the physical constraints posed by the terrain but also a greater sensitivity to local landscape character.

5. Visual quality analysis (Fig. 8-6). A visual quality analysis is a way of graphically summing up observations and impressions of a place's aesthetic character. It identifies important natural features, views, view corridors and barriers, distinctive surface patterns of vegetation and rock, and sensory qualities or aesthetic deficiencies of a site and its surroundings. The purpose is to ensure that the important qualities of a site are respected in design and preserved in development.

A visual quality analysis evaluates a landscape on the basis of certain qualitative factors and measures its visibility and visual vulnerability to disturbance. It is an exercise that has been refined by the Forest Service in its visual management system, which measures visual quality on forest lands (Fig. 8-7). This system is described in a set of U.S.D.A. Forest Service landscape management handbooks.

A visual analysis may include survey techniques to reveal public attitudes toward certain features and trademark characteristics of the existing local landscape. Because public consensus on visual quality helps determine a place's future character, how visual quality objectives are derived and communicated to those who have an interest in the area is often as important as the analysis itself. Communication methods range from maps and diagrams to photographic, video, and computer-aided simulations (see Fig. 7-31). In scenic areas, it has proved difficult to maintain visual quality without a consensus among residents on the objectives they wish to pursue.

Figure 8-6. Facing page. *Part of the master-planning process for the Sugarbush Valley in Vermont was an inventory of the area's visual character, including the identification of visually sensitive slopes, important buffers, views, and landmarks. Developer, Sugarbush Resort. Design Workshop Inc., Aspen, Colorado, planning and landscape architecture.*

Figure 8-5. *Descriptors of surface relief.*

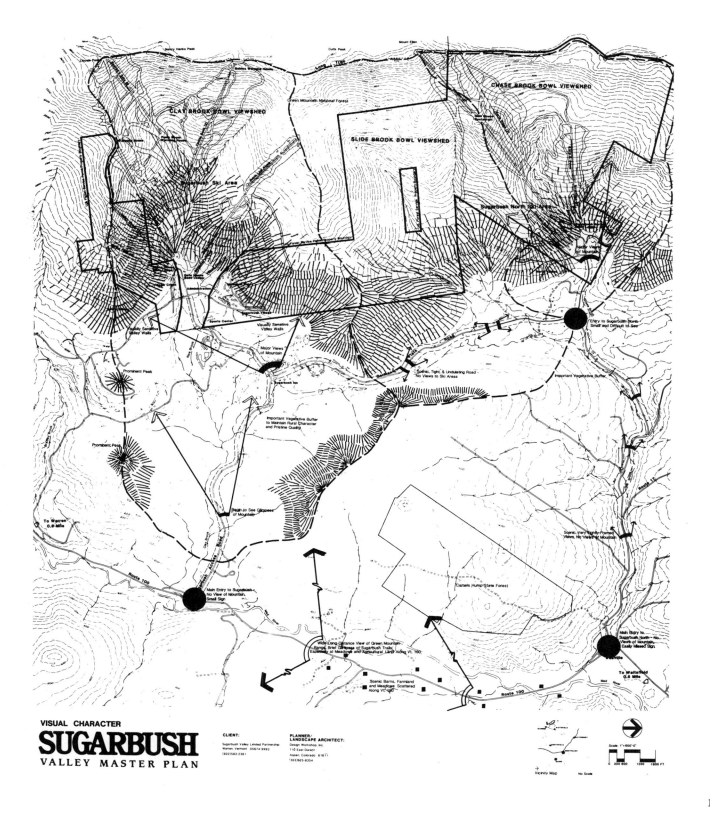

VISUAL CHARACTER

SUGARBUSH
VALLEY MASTER PLAN

CLIENT:
Sugarbush Valley Limited Partnership
Warren, Vermont 05674-9993
(802)583-2381

PLANNER/
LANDSCAPE ARCHITECT:
Design Workshop, Inc.
710 East Durant
Aspen, Colorado 81611
(303)925-8354

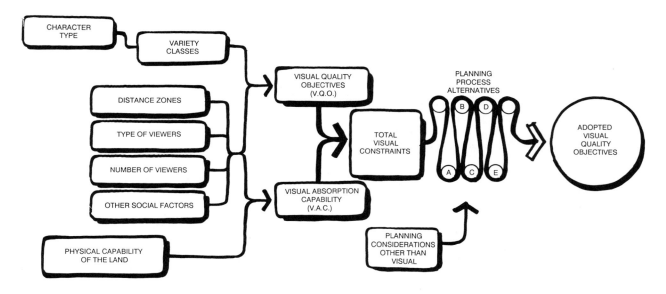

Figure 8-7. *The U.S.D.A. Forest Service's visual management system. The process measures visual quality on the basis of the physical attributes of a landscape, people's sensitivity to changes in it, and its ability to accept alteration without losing its inherent visual character.*

Geology and Soils

Geological information is generally available from the U.S. Geological Survey or from state and county natural resources agencies. However, it is often mapped on very large scales and may have to be interpolated by geologists for smaller areas. Figs. 8-8 through 8-12 illustrate the influence of geological factors in the evolution of a development plan for a site in southern Colorado.

Soil surveys are available from the Soil Conservation Service (U.S. Department of Agriculture) for areas that have been farmed, which means that information on mountain soils may be incomplete for many sites. Other possible sources of information are local county extension agents or colleges with natural resources departments. The U.S. Forest Service district ranger may also be helpful in alpine areas. On-site soils tests are necessary to back up large-scale interpolations with more reliable site-specific information.

The geological information you will need is the following:

1. Geomorphic origin and underlying geology (Figs. 8-8, 8-10). Interpretive geological maps of a particular site and its vicinity may explain rock derivation and character, stability, durability, and depth to bedrock. These factors, both on the site and near it, highlight possible constraints to development and also explain how the particular regional landscape evolved.

2. Geological hazards (Fig. 8-11). Geological hazards maps locate areas in the vicinity and on-site

where there is evidence of seismic hazard, unstable faults, subsidence, swelling, excessive erosion, slope failure, and slides or where the potential for these is

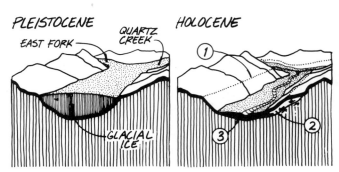

Figure 8-8. *Diagrams of the geomorphology of East Fork Valley, Colorado, helped planners understand development constraints on the site. (1) Pleistocene glaciers scoured out a typical U-shaped valley and then retreated, leaving overly steep lower slopes. (2) Without the supporting glacial ice, landslides developed along the bedding planes that dip into the valley. (3) Since the glacial retreat, landslide material has been filling and leveling the old valley floor. Developer, East Fork Joint Venture, Skokie, Illinois. Winston Associates, Boulder, Colorado, planning and landscape architecture.*

Figures 8-9 through 8-12. *Maps from the 1987 environmental impact statement for the proposed East Fork ski area, San Juan National Forest, Colorado (U.S.D.A. Forest Service 1987). Unstable side slopes restrict development to the valley floor (Fig. 8-12). Developer, East Fork Joint Venture, Skokie, Illinois. Lead consultant, Winston Associates, Boulder, Colorado, planning, urban design, and landscape architecture; geological hazard mapping, GeoWest–Colorado Springs, Inc.; soils mapping, James P. Walsh & Assoc. Inc., Boulder. See also Figs. 7-19 through 7-21.*

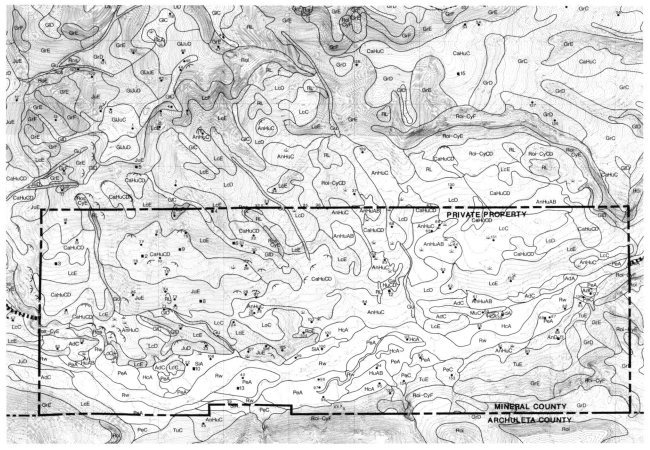

SOILS

EAST FORK
MINERAL AND ARCHULETA
COUNTIES, COLORADO

EAST FORK JOINT VENTURE
OLD ORCHARD ROAD, SKOKIE, IL

WINSTON ASSOCIATES
PLANNING AND LANDSCAPE ARCHITECTURE
BOULDER, COLORADO

James P. Walsh & Assoc., Inc.
Boulder, CO

NOVEMBER 1985
REVISIONS
FEB 28, 1986
MARCH 12, 1986
MAY 14, 1986

⌐ **SOIL SLUMP**

x x x **BOULDERY AREA**

↙ **WET AREAS LESS
THAN 3 ACRES**

56
• **SOIL SAMPLE**

■11 **TYPICAL PEDON LOCATION**

LEGEND

AdA	ADEL LOAM, 0 TO 4 PERCENT SLOPES	
AdC	ADEL LOAM, 9 TO 19 PERCENT SLOPES	
AnD	ANIMAS SANDY LOAM, 20 TO 29 PERCENT SLOPES	
AnHuAB	ANIMAS-HUNCHBACK COMPLEX, 0 TO 8 PERCENT SLOPES	
AnHuC	ANIMAS-HUNCHBACK COMPLEX, 9 TO 19 PERCENT SLOPES	
CaHuC	CASTELLIA-HUNCHBACK COMPLEX, 20 TO 29 PERCENT SLOPES	
CaHuCD	CASTELLIA-HUNCHBACK COMPLEX, 9 TO 29 PERCENT SLOPES	
GlC	GRALIC GRAVELLY SANDY LOAM, 9 TO 19 PERCENT SLOPES	
GlD	GRALIC GRAVELLY SANDY LOAM, 20 TO 29 PERCENT SLOPES	
GlJuC	GRALIC-JUDY COMPLEX, 9 TO 19 PERCENT SLOPES	
GlJuD	GRALIC-JUDY COMPLEX, 20 TO 29 PERCENT SLOPES	
GrC	GRANADIER GRAVELLY LOAM, 9 TO 19 PERCENT SLOPES	
GrD	GRENADIER GRAVELLY LOAM, 20 TO 29 PERCENT SLOPES	

GrE	GRENADIER STONY LOAM, 30 TO 60 PERCENT SLOPES
GrF	GRENADIER STONY LOAM, 60 PERCENT SLOPES
Gu	GULLIED LAND
HcA	HISTIC CRYAQUEPTS, 0 TO 4 PERCENT SLOPES
HuAB	HUNCHBACK LOAM, 0 TO 8 PERCENT SLOPES
JuD	JUDY SILT LOAM, 20 TO 29 PERCENT SLOPES
JuE	JUDY SILT LOAM, 30 TO 60 PERCENT SLOPES
LcC	LEIGHCAN SANDY LOAM, 9 TO 19 PERCENT SLOPES
LcD	LEIGHCAN SANDY LOAM, 20 TO 29 PERCENT SLOPES
LcE	LEIGHCAN SANDY LOAM, 30 TO 60 PERCENT SLOPES
LcF	LEIGHCAN SANDY LOAM, 60 PERCENT SLOPES
LlD	LEAL COBBLY LOAM, 20 TO 29 PERCENT SLOPES
LlE	LEAL COBBLY LOAM, 30 TO 60 PERCENT SLOPES
MuC	MUGGINS COBBLY LOAM, 9 TO 19 PERCENT SLOPES

PeA	PESCAR SANDY LOAM, 0 TO 4 PERCENT SLOPES
PeC	PESCAR BOULDERY LOAM, 9 TO 19 PERCENT SLOPES
RL	ROCKLAND, 9 TO 59 PERCENT SLOPES
RoE	ROGERT GRAVELLY LOAM, 30 TO 60 PERCENT SLOPES
Roi	IGNEOUS ROCK OUTCROPS, 30 TO 60 PERCENT SLOPES
Roi-CyCD	IGNEOUS ROCK OUTCROP-CRYORTHENTS COMPLEX, 9 TO 29 PERCENT SLOPES
Roi-CyE	IGNEOUS ROCK OUTCROP-CRYORTHENTS COMPLEX, 30 TO 59 PERCENT SLOPES
Roi-CyF	IGNEOUS ROCK OUTCROPS-CRYORTHENTS COMPLEX, 60 PERCENT SLOPES
Ros-CyE	SEDIMENTARY ROCK OUTCROPS-CRYORTHENTS, 30 TO 59 PERCENT SLOPES
Rw	RIVERWASH, 0 TO 8 PERCENT SLOPES
SiA	SILAS LOAM, 0 TO 4 PERCENT SLOPES
TuC	TYPIC USTORTHENTS, 9 TO 19 PERCENT SLOPES
TuE	TYPIC USTORTHENTS, 30 TO 60 PERCENT SLOPES

Figure 8-9.

177

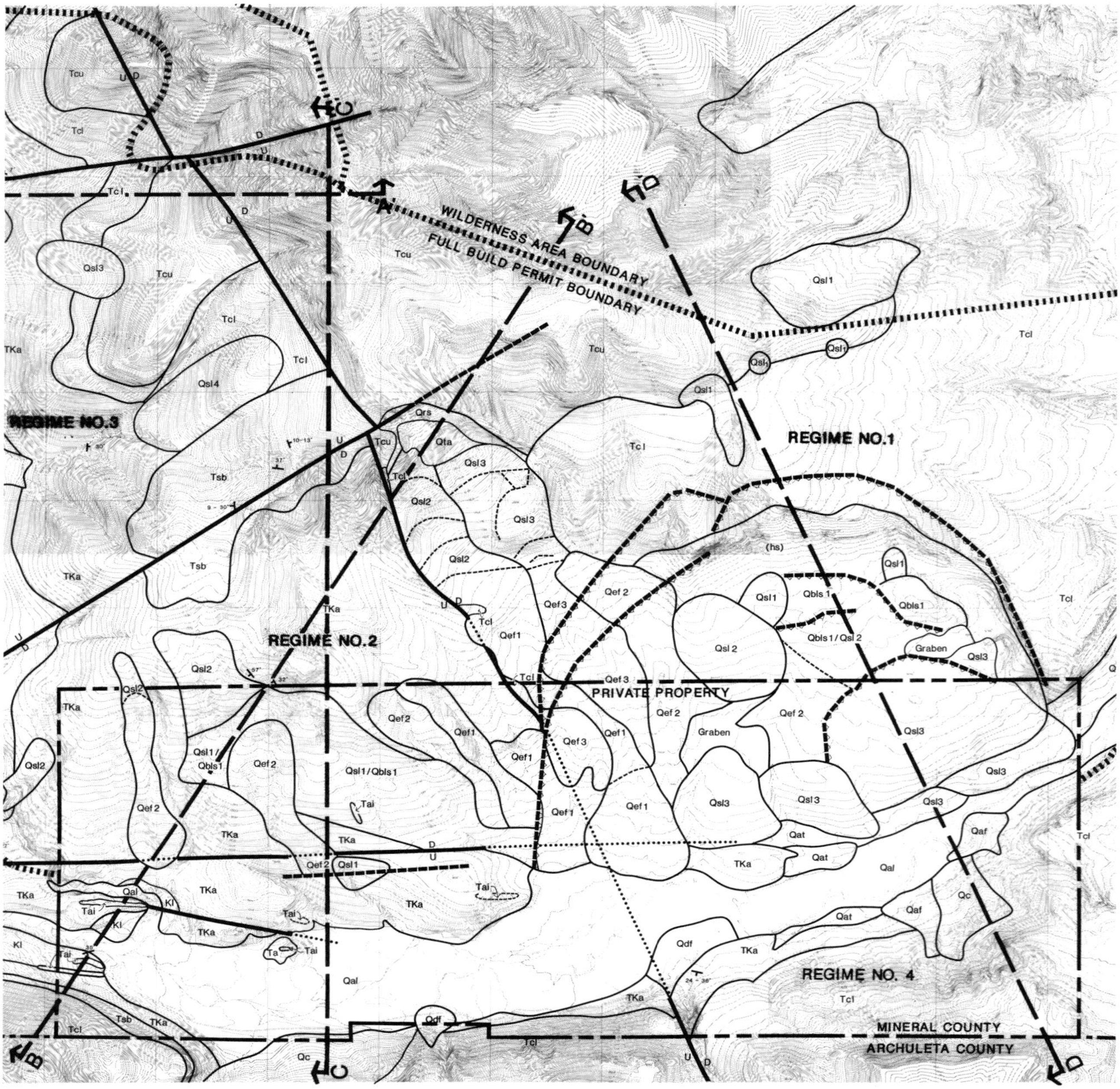

GEOLOGY

EAST FORK

MINERAL AND ARCHULETA
COUNTIES, COLORADO

EAST FORK JOINT VENTURE
OLD ORCHARD ROAD, SKOKIE, IL

WINSTON ASSOCIATES
PLANNING AND LANDSCAPE ARCHITECTURE
BOULDER, COLORADO

SCALE 1" 500'
0 250 500 1000

Rocky Mt. Geotechnical Inc.
Colorado Springs, CO

NOVEMBER 1985
REVISIONS:
JAN. 29, 1986
MARCH 10, 1986

LEGEND

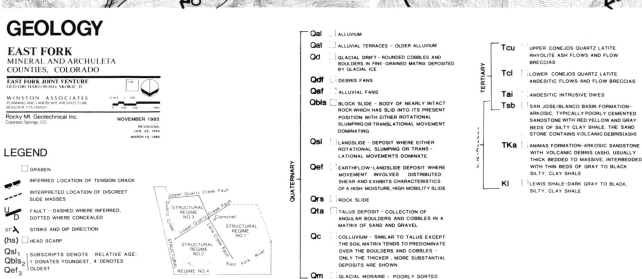

- GRABEN
- INFERRED LOCATION OF TENSION CRACK
- INTERPRETED LOCATION OF DISCREET SLIDE MASSES
- U/D FAULT - DASHED WHERE INFERRED, DOTTED WHERE CONCEALED
- 37° STRIKE AND DIP DIRECTION
- (hs) HEAD SCARP
- Qsl_1, $Qbls_2$, Qef_3 SUBSCRIPTS DENOTE RELATIVE AGE: 1 DONATES YOUNGEST, 4 DENOTES OLDEST

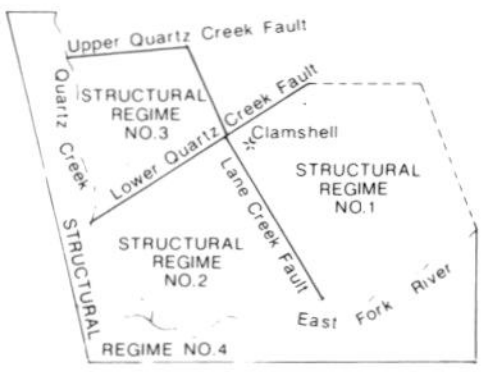

QUATERNARY

- **Qal** ALLUVIUM
- **Qat** ALLUVIAL TERRACES - OLDER ALLUVIUM
- **Qd** GLACIAL DRIFT - ROUNDED COBBLES AND BOULDERS IN FINE-GRAINED MATRIX DEPOSITED BY GLACIAL ICE
- **Qdf** DEBRIS FANS
- **Qaf** ALLUVIAL FANS
- **Qbls** BLOCK SLIDE - BODY OF NEARLY INTACT ROCK WHICH HAS SLID INTO ITS PRESENT POSITION WITH EITHER ROTATIONAL SLUMPING OR TRANSLATIONAL MOVEMENT DOMINATING
- **Qsl** LANDSLIDE - DEPOSIT WHERE EITHER ROTATIONAL SLUMPING OR TRANSLATIONAL MOVEMENTS DOMINATE
- **Qef** EARTHFLOW-LANDSLIDE DEPOSIT WHERE MOVEMENT INVOLVES DISTRIBUTED SHEAR AND EXHIBITS CHARACTERISTICS OF A HIGH MOISTURE, HIGH MOBILITY SLIDE
- **Qrs** ROCK SLIDE
- **Qta** TALUS DEPOSIT - COLLECTION OF ANGULAR BOULDERS AND COBBLES IN A MATRIX OF SAND AND GRAVEL
- **Qc** COLLUVIUM - SIMILAR TO TALUS EXCEPT THE SOIL MATRIX TENDS TO PREDOMINATE OVER THE BOULDERS AND COBBLES - ONLY THE THICKER, MORE SUBSTANTIAL DEPOSITS ARE SHOWN
- **Qm** GLACIAL MORAINE - POORLY SORTED GRAVEL, COBBLES AND BOULDERS IN A SILTY TO CLAYEY SAND MATRIX

TERTIARY

- **Tcu** UPPER CONEJOS QUARTZ LATITE RHYOLITE ASH FLOWS AND FLOW BRECCIAS
- **Tcl** LOWER CONEJOS QUARTZ LATITE ANDESITIC FLOWS AND FLOW BRECCIAS
- **Tai** ANDESITIC INTRUSIVE DIKES
- **Tsb** SAN JOSE/BLANCO BASIN FORMATION-ARKOSIC, TYPICALLY POORLY CEMENTED SANDSTONE WITH RED, YELLOW AND GRAY BEDS OF SILTY CLAY SHALE. THE SAND STONE CONTAINS VOLCANIC DEBRIS(ASH)
- **TKa** ANIMAS FORMATION-ARKOSIC SANDSTONE WITH VOLCANIC DEBRIS (ASH), USUALLY THICK BEDDED TO MASSIVE, INTERBEDDED WITH THIN BEDS OF GRAY TO BLACK SILTY, CLAY SHALE
- **Kl** LEWIS SHALE-DARK GRAY TO BLACK, SILTY, CLAY SHALE

Figure 8-10.

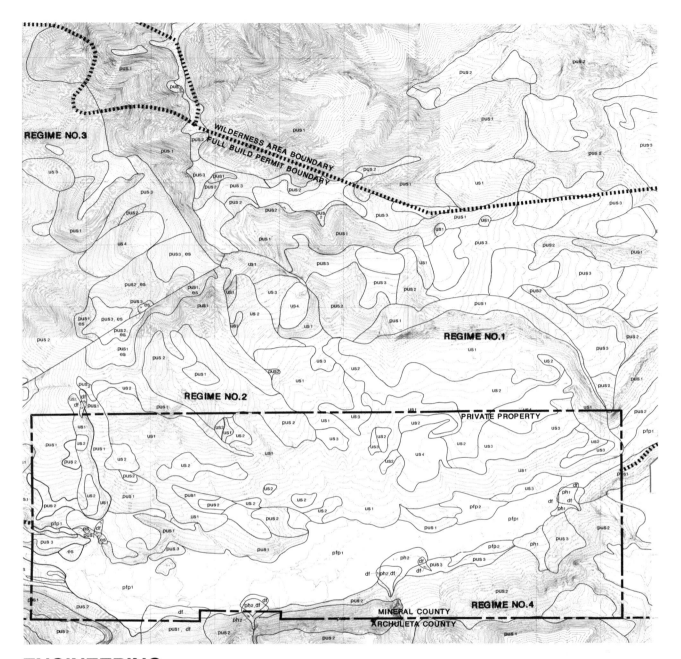

ENGINEERING GEOLOGY

EAST FORK
MINERAL AND ARCHULETA
COUNTIES, COLORADO

EAST FORK JOINT VENTURE
OLD ORCHARD ROAD, SKOKIE, IL

WINSTON ASSOCIATES
PLANNING AND LANDSCAPE ARCHITECTURE
BOULDER COLORADO

Rocky Mt. Geotechnical Inc.
Colorado Springs CO

NOVEMBER 1985
REVISIONS
JAN. 29, 1986
MARCH 10, 1986

LEGEND

us 1 UNSTABLE SLOPE
    2
    3
    4

pus 1 POTENTIALLY UNSTABLE SLOPE
    2
    3

pfp 1 PHYSIOGRAPHIC FLOODPLAIN AREA
    2

ph 1 POTENTIAL HYDROCOMPACTION AREA
    2

es   EXPANSIVE (SWELLING) SOIL OR ROCK

df   DEBRIS FLOW

NOTE: THE NUMERICAL SUBSCRIPT IDENTIFIES
      THE RELATIVE DEGREE OF HAZARD
      WITH SLOPES HAVING A SUBSCRIPT
      OF 1 HAVING THE HIGHEST RISK
      AND THOSE WITH A SUBSCRIPT OF
      4 THE LOWEST RISK

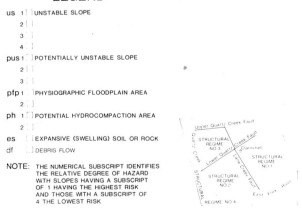

Figure 8-11.

179

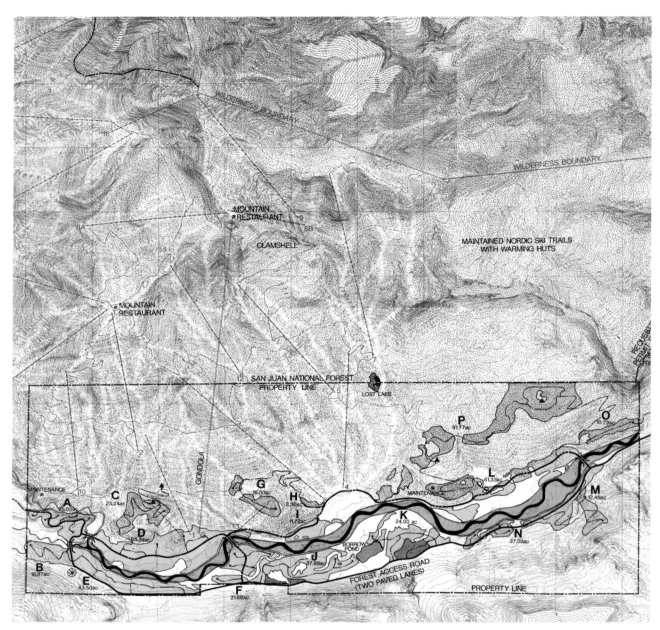

FULL BUILD ALTERNATIVE

EAST FORK
MINERAL AND ARCHULETA
COUNTIES, COLORADO

EAST FORK JOINT VENTURE
OLD ORCHARD ROAD, SKOKIE, IL

WINSTON ASSOCIATES

MOUNTAIN PLAN
Mountain Research Assoc.
Denver CO

JANUARY
REVISIONS:
JAN 1987
JULY 1987

DEVELOPMENT ACREAGES

FULL BUILD ALTERNATIVE (13500 SAOT)

POD	ACREAGE	UNITS/ACRE	UNITS
A	25.00	2.00	50
B	16.87	3.00	51
C	23.24	4.00	93
D	85.34	11.00	939
E	43.50	6.00	261
F	21.88	7.00	153
G	16.00	4.00	64
H	2.30	2.00	5
I	11.72	4.00	47
J	37.88	6.50	246
K	24.00	6.70	161
L	61.33	4.00	245
M	12.45	2.00	25
N	37.00	4.00	148
O	10.73	8.00	86
P	81.77	1.00	82
Q	6.71	0.00	0
TOTAL	517.72	4.70	2655

*(ADDITIONAL GOLF COURSE ACREAGE IS INCLUDED WITH DEVELOPMENT PODS)

DEVELOPMENT SUMMARY

PRIVATE LAND	2780 acres	100.0%
RESIDENTIAL	433	15.0%
RESIDENTIAL/COMMERCIAL	85	3.0%
ROAD R.O.W.	49	1.6%
PARKING	13	0.4%
OPEN SPACE	2217	80.0%
* Golf Course	35	1.5%
Proposed Floodplain	91	4.0%
Ski Runs, Lifts & Mountain Access Roads	457	20.5%
Undeveloped Open Space	1634	74.0%
PUBLIC LAND	4662 acres	100.0%
TOTAL DISTURBED ACRES	994	21.0%
UNDISTURBED ACRES	3668	79.0%
(Including Nordic Use Area)		

LEGEND

- DEVELOPMENT PODS
- GOLF COURSE
- PROPOSED ACTIVE CHANNEL*
- PROPOSED FLOOD PLAIN *
- ACCESS ROAD
- SECONDARY ROAD
- COLLECTOR ROAD
- MAJOR TRAFFIC BRIDGE
- PUBLIC PARKING
- WATER TANK LOCATION
- COGENERATION PLANT

*Refer to Fluvial Hydrology illustrations

Figure 8-12.

suspected. Possible hazards in the entire region must be identified if the risks on a particular site are to be accurately assessed.

3. Soil classification map and analysis (Fig. 8-9). Each soil type present on those portions of a site that may be developed should be analyzed for its engineering qualities and limitations for construction, ability to support plant growth, stability on slopes, erosion potential, and drainage characteristics.

4. Areas of previous fill on a site, if any, should be identified.

Climate

Regional data can be obtained from the National Climate Data Center and from some libraries. For some mountain sites, there may also be a cooperative weather station (part of the Cooperative Observer Network) nearby.

Unless there is a weather-recording station in the immediate vicinity, data on local microclimates may have to be gathered on-site. Difficult access to undeveloped mountain sites in winter makes automatic monitoring equipment the most effective, though the most expensive, way to do this.[1]

The data you will need on climate are the following:

1. Temperatures: seasonal fluctuations, average highs and lows; average number of cloudy days and potential for use of solar energy; and statistical probabilities of frost outside winter months.

2. Sun angles: the azimuth of the sun, winter and summer, for the latitude of the site (Fig. 8-13). From these, seasonal shadow patterns and solar radiation levels related to topographical variations can be projected. See Appendix D for assistance in plotting topographical shadows.

3. Precipitation: seasonal levels and patterns of occurrence; storm frequencies; 50- and 100-year storm levels; percentage of annual precipitation that falls as snow; and humidity.

4. Wind: the directions of prevailing and storm winds by season (Fig. 8-14); average velocities, also by season; topographical features that produce localized increases in wind velocity or that offer

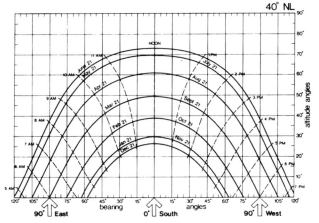

Figure 8-13. *Sun chart for 40° north latitude. Beaver Creek Resort Company, Design Regulations (1979).*

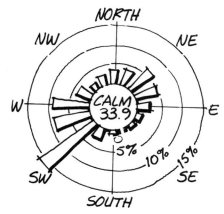

Figure 8-14. *Wind rose for the site of the proposed East Fork ski area, Colorado.*

natural shelter from extreme winds (Figs. 8-15, 8-16); and the potential for using the wind to generate energy.

5. Snow: average depth and density of the snowpack at various elevations, snowpack water content and weight, typical patterns of snow accumulation through the winter, and chronology of major storms.

6. Avalanche hazard: maps of probable avalanche paths (Fig. 8-17) assembled from slope gradient maps (Fig. 8-18), aerial photos of vegetation, and field observation by specialists; and records of past avalanches on and near the site, as well as on access corridors leading to the site.

7. Microclimate: local breezes and diurnal air movements; areas subject to cold air drainage and temperature inversions; wind deflection patterns and their effect on snow drifting, snow accumulation, and avalanche risk; and local sun–shade effects of topography and vegetation on slope and valley temperatures, summer and winter.

[1]In January 1987, Copper Mountain, Colorado, became the first ski area in the country to install computerized remote weather-sensing devices. Three mountaintop stations record air temperature, wind velocity, and direction. The data are logged and transferred by modem to the computer at Copper's ski patrol headquarters, where an hourly report gives the one-hour average wind direction, peak gusts, and high and low temperatures. Two of the remote stations also make sonar readings of the settled snowpack depth. For more information, contact the director of the Copper Mountain Ski Patrol, P.O. Box 3001, Copper Mountain, Colo. 80443.

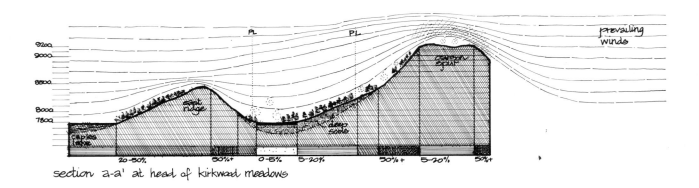

section a-a' at head of kirkwood meadows

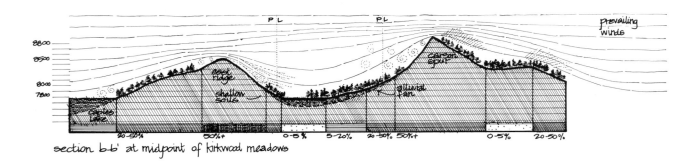

section b-b' at midpoint of kirkwood meadows

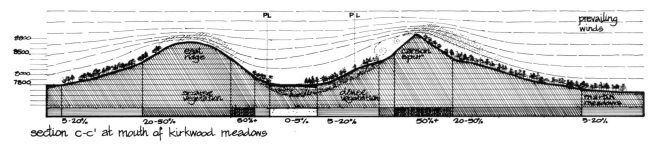

section c-c' at mouth of kirkwood meadows

Figure 8-15.

Figures 8-15 through 8-18. *Diagrams of wind patterns (Figs. 8-15, 8-16), avalanche hazard (Fig. 8-17), and landform (Fig. 8-18) from the early planning stages of the ski village at Kirkwood, California. Developer, Kirkwood Associates, Inc. Berridge Associates Inc., San Francisco, land planning and landscape architecture.*

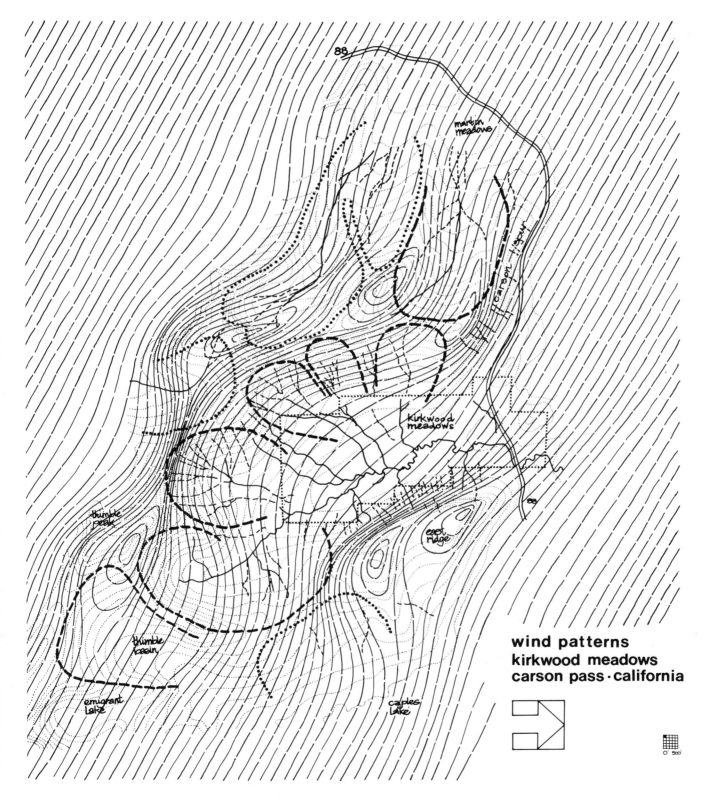

wind patterns
kirkwood meadows
carson pass · california

Figure 8-16.

183

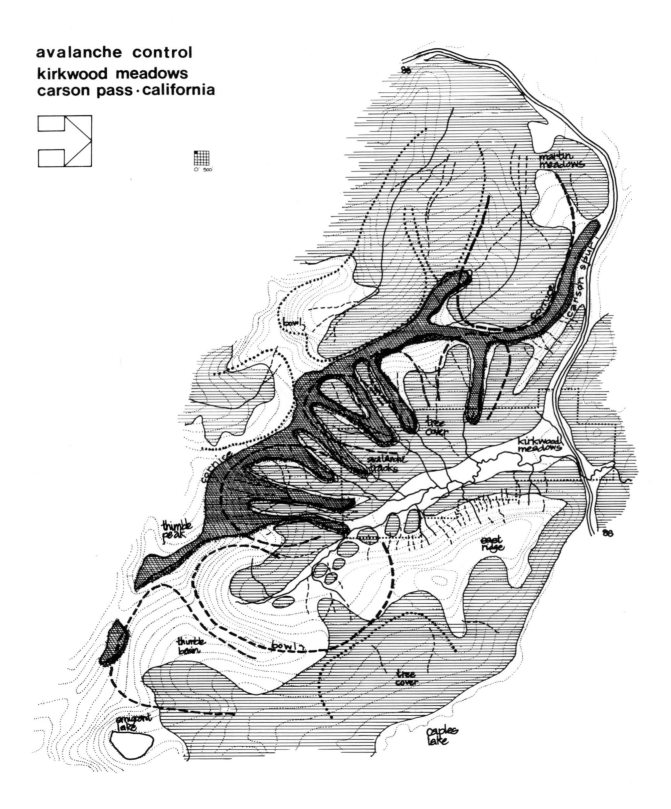

avalanche control
kirkwood meadows
carson pass · california

Figure 8-17.

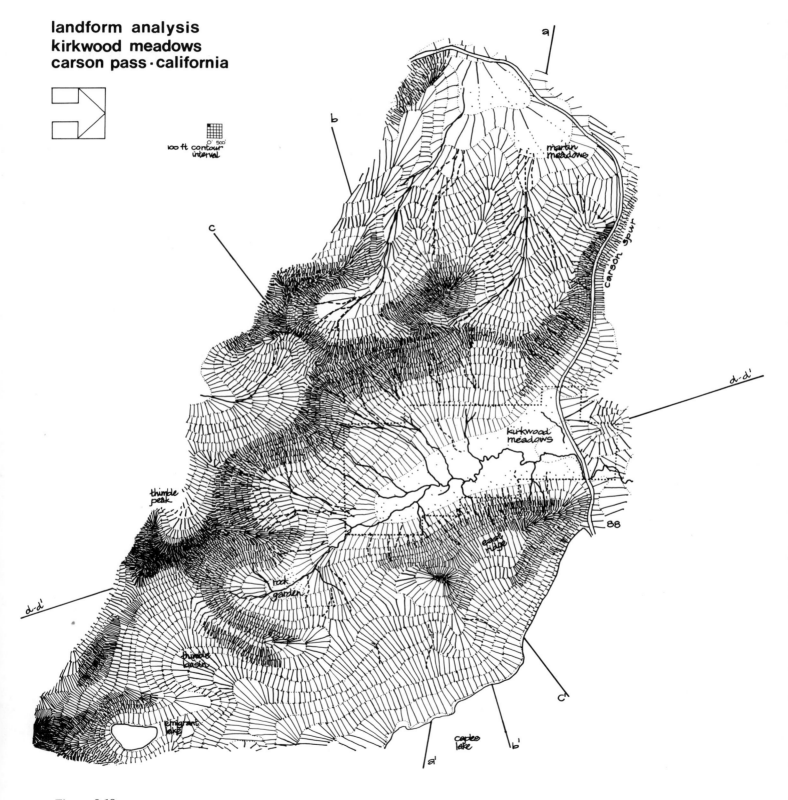

landform analysis
kirkwood meadows
carson pass · california

100 ft contour interval

0   500

Figure 8-18.

Water

Water flows on a site are affected by its topography and the configuration of the watershed, by the condition of the vegetation and soils on and above the site, and by precipitation levels. Data on all of these are needed in order to interpret hydrological patterns correctly and to assess their implications for design. For a particular site, the most important indicators are precipitation, runoff volumes, and stream-flow volumes. For these data, the historical context is significant, as the longer the statistical record, the more reliable the projection will be.

The best source of hydrological data is the U.S. Geological Survey (USGS). Its water data volumes for daily and peak stream flows at every gauging station are available from any library that is a federal depository or from its district offices. Additional data can often be obtained from the local water utility, which may have its own gauging stations, and from the state engineer's office or the state's department of natural resources or environmental affairs. (Department names vary by state.) For computer users, complete daily and peak flow records for every USGS gauging station are marketed on compact digital disk, along with software programs for convenient formatting and analysis of the data.

In lieu of stream-flow data, engineers can convert precipitation records into estimates of runoff volume per unit drainage area. The U.S. Forest Service may be needed to estimate the amount of precipitation retained in forested areas above the site.

What you need to know about water on a site is the following:

1. Watersheds and on-site drainage patterns (Fig. 8-19). Size and nature of the watershed; peak and seasonal runoff volumes; channel capacities and seasonal fluctuations in stream-flow volume; normal (predevelopment) stream sediment loads, especially in times of storm and snowmelt; and undrained or poorly drained areas and natural obstructions to runoff.

Watersheds define where precipitation and snowmelt drain and how much runoff can be anticipated at a given place. The study of drainage patterns thus needs to consider the entire watershed.

Designers should relate development concept alternatives to their hydrological impacts, including on-site impacts on runoff and erosion potential, possible damage to drainage from activities above the site, downstream implications of development on the site, and aggregate impacts of development throughout the vicinity.

2. Surface water features: size, character, source, and accessibility; volume and purity of water; visual quality and vulnerability; wintertime character;

recreational potential; and importance for fish and wildlife habitat.

3. Floodplain limits and flood hazard areas. The topography of a valley floor often gives a rough indication of the extent of a floodplain, but more precise limits must be mapped by a hydrological engineer based on stream-channel cross sections and statistical prediction of water volume in major flood events. Flood hazards cannot be accurately assessed from on-site data alone, for the risk of flooding on an individual site is affected by development in the watershed as a whole.

4. Groundwater: seasonal fluctuations in the depth to the water table, purity of groundwater, recharge areas, and springs.

5. Water supply and water rights. Water law in the western United States is a complicated system in which the ownership of water (as well as mineral) rights is separated from the title to land. It is markedly different from the system followed in the East.

The "riparian code" from English common law is the basis for water law in the eastern United States. This code permitted those living along a stream to use its water for "natural" purposes (drinking, cooking, washing) but required a special permit for streamside industrial uses (milling, mining, manufacturing). In either case, the user had to return the water to the stream, without changing it in quantity or quality.

When the Mormons settled the arid country of Utah and Nevada, it was clear that this doctrine would have prevented irrigation because it would have been impossible to return an equal flow to the stream. Therefore they worked out a new code called *prior appropriation,* according to which irrigation was considered a "natural" use; water could be used without returning an equal amount; persons other than those living by the stream could use its water; and water use was based on the order in which users legally secured their water rights.

In 1866, these principles were written into federal law, and all of the semiarid western states eventually adopted them. More recently, several of these states have modified their codes by recognizing the doctrine of "reasonable beneficial use," according to which users are obligated to show that they are using their water for beneficial uses in order to retain their rights to it (Merk 1978, p. 338).

In most western states, water rights are adjudicated each year, and the appropriation date is important, for older, more senior rights have priority over those more recently appropriated. Many western streams are overadjudicated, meaning that more rights have been conveyed on paper than the average volume in the stream can supply. It is only because many owners of water rights do not use what they have

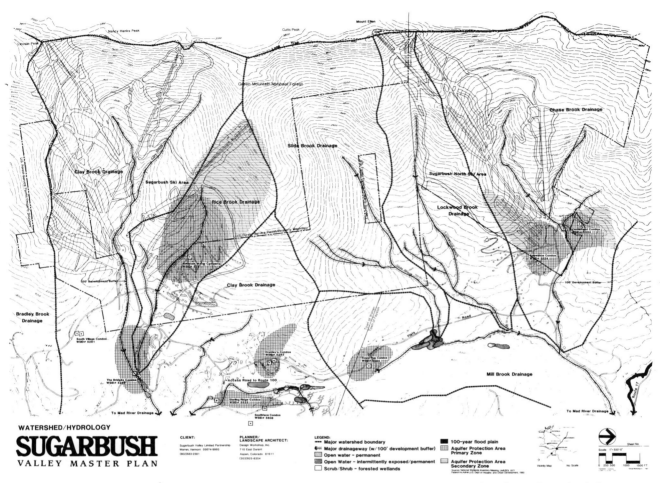

WATERSHED/HYDROLOGY

SUGARBUSH
VALLEY MASTER PLAN

Figure 8-19. *Map of important hydrological features in the Sugarbush Valley, Vermont. Developer, Sugarbush Resort. Design Workshop, Inc., Aspen, Colorado, planning and landscape architecture.*

title to that junior rights holders are not routinely shut out.

Underground water is often regarded legally in the same manner as stream flow if it is tributary to a stream (that is, if it affects the rate or direction of flow of a stream). It is hard to prove otherwise, and so ownership of water in underground aquifers must be resolved on a site-by-site basis.

Rights to use stream water do not convey the right to drill wells or divert water into storage reservoirs; well permits and storage rights must be separately acquired. Permission of the water court must also be obtained in order to alter drainage patterns, to relocate the point of diversion of stream water, or to change the type or place of use.

The services of a local water resources attorney should be retained to verify the seniority and quality of a property owner's water rights and to assess whether these are adequate for the level of development proposed. If the landowner does not also have title to water rights and the property is not part of a municipal water district, the state water

authorities should be consulted about the prospects for obtaining a well permit.

Vegetation

Information on native plant communities is not always available for mountain regions on a useful scale. In the West, where so much mountain land is owned by the federal government, the district ranger's office of the U.S. Forest Service is a good place to begin the search for information. For some areas, the Forest Service has mapped and analyzed vegetation on a large scale using aerial photo interpretation. State departments of natural resources, county planning agencies and extension agents, local colleges and universities, and published natural history field guides may also be helpful. In most cases, however, field surveys will be necessary to obtain material specific to a site.

The following is what you need to know about vegetation.

1. Important plant communities: their location on the site, extent, composition, health, approximate stage of succession, and relative stability; their requirements for growth; and their sensitivity to change. Site planners usually need to augment available vegetation maps with on-site field surveys in order to map the plant communities on their site. Rare or endangered species must be identified.

2. Wetland areas: their boundaries and species composition. Where development will affect wetlands, the Corps of Engineers and the Environmental Protection Agency must be consulted and a 404 permit must be obtained (see Chapter 7, Section 404 Permit Requirements). Specialists in soils and aquatic ecology may be needed to map wetland limits more precisely than can be done through aerial photo interpretation and to analyze the ecosystem's functional value.

3. Condition of the forest cover: its density, height, health, stage of maturity, and visual character; virgin timber or landmark specimens to be preserved; and the possible impacts of forest clearing.

4. Length of the growing season: expressed as the average number of frost-free days per year.

5. Revegetation potential and constraints: analysis and map identifying troublesome areas, and later, as site plan concepts are developed, a map of the extent of disturbance, a plan specifying revegetation methods, and an estimate of long-term revegetation costs and practical limitations.

6. Wildfire hazard.

7. Lists of native plants recommended for use in the vicinity and commercially available. These lists can generally be obtained from the Forest Service, local nurseries, county or municipal planning agencies, and subdivisions or resorts that have published landscape design guidelines. There are also software programs and computerized plant information networks that provide lists of native plants sorted according to site conditions and plant characteristics, although not all of the listed species are commercially available.

Wildlife

The increasingly intense development in some mountain areas has brought with it the danger of intolerable levels of stress on fish and wildlife. All sites, but especially those where large developments are contemplated, should be examined for the quality of wildlife habitat, range, and forage they offer. Wildlife species that use the site either year-round or seasonally (particularly rare or endangered species) should be identified and their survival requirements understood. The probable changes in their range or habitat because of proposed development must be assessed. Special attention should be given to wildlife needs during crucial winter months when animals are already under significant biological stress. The analysis of wildlife patterns cannot be arbitrarily

Figure 8-20. *Wolf Creek Valley, Colorado. Photo by Design Workshop, Inc.*

limited to the area within the boundaries of a site; seasonal migratory regimens and the aggregate impacts of development throughout a region demand a broader view.

Composite Constraints and Development Suitability Maps

Investigation into each of the preceding factors will reveal conditions that impose development constraints of varying severity. Few of these factors alone, however, can be sufficient guidance for informed land-use decisions; rather, their sum is far more indicative of development suitability.

A composite map of constraints and opportunities is an effective and graphic method of compiling and communicating scientific evidence. *It may well be the most important document to come from the analysis of natural factors*. It reveals where limitations are compounded by the presence of other negative factors, and conversely, it shows the relative concurrence (or absence) of positive factors. The locations where the majority of positive (or negative) factors coincide, one may assume, are the most (or least) suitable for the land uses under consideration. In this form, overlay maps also provide a baseline against which the costs and benefits of various proposals can be tested, as they can demonstrate the

extent to which a plan would enhance or diminish the land's identified values.

Figs. 8-21, 8-22, and 8-23 show a series of composite constraints maps for a mountain site in southern Colorado, shown in the photo in Fig. 8-20, and illustrate how the constraints shaped development concepts (Fig. 8-24).

Other Data

Depending on a project's scale, several other areas of research unrelated to natural factors may be pertinent to the design process:

1. Regulations governing development permits and the public review process vary from place to place. At the outset of any project of consequence, legal requirements and the timetable they will impose should be reviewed with local authorities. It may also be instructive to investigate the history of governmental decisions made on similar development applications proposed in the vicinity.

2. Economic variables are needed to give an indication of regional economic health. Useful data include such statistics as household income, unemployment rates, sales tax revenues, real estate transfers, construction permits, property tax assessments, income and growth figures for primary

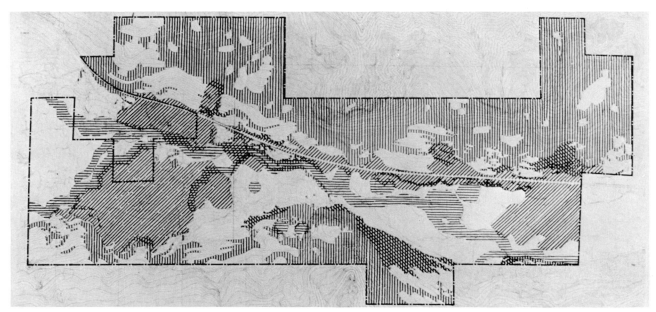

Figure 8-21. *Environmental sensitivity map. Vertical lines indicate slopes steeper than 25%; horizontal lines are zones within 100 feet of surface water; diagnosis lines show visually sensitive areas and highly erodible soils.*

Figures 8-21 through 8-23. *A sequence of constraints maps for Wolf Creek Valley, Colorado, (Fig. 8-20) where a new ski resort has been proposed. The degree of environmental sensitivity (Fig. 8-21) and the severity of constraints (Fig. 8-22) are reflected in a composite map of development suitability (Fig. 8-23) and in the conceptual development program (Fig. 8-24). Darkest areas are those with the most severe limitations on development. Developer, West Fork Investment Co., Pagosa Springs, Colorado. Design Workshop, Inc., Aspen, planning and landscape architecture.*

Figure 8-22. *Aggregate constrains map. More severe constraints, like slopes, are represented by thicker lines.*

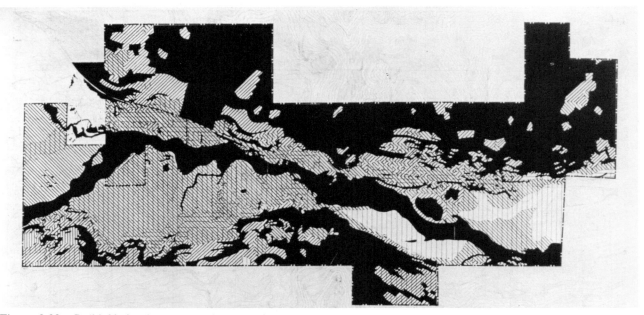

Figure 8-23. *Buildable land summary. Aggregated constraints make black areas unbuildable.*

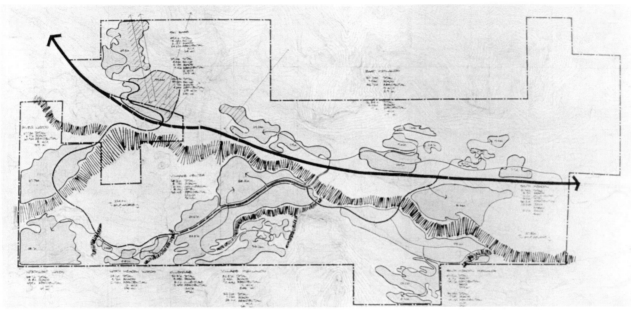

Figure 8-24. *A conceptual development scheme baised on constraints maps outlines buildable parcels, basic circulation, uses and densities.*

local industries, bankruptcies, and public funds spent on transportation, schools, and other municipal services in the area. It is also helpful to study similar factors for important target markets.

3. Traffic counts showing the use of local highways and airports should be commissioned if none is available, as projected traffic congestion often emerges as a major constraint in larger projects.

4. The availability of local labor with needed construction and management skills should be assessed, as this will have a bearing on project costs.

STEPS IN THE DESIGN PROCESS

The design process is a problem-solving pathway leading from larger and more general contexts to those that are smaller and more refined (Fig. 8-25). At each step in the process, information is interpreted, goals are formulated, conditions inventoried in increasing detail, alternatives proposed and evaluated, and decisions made that define the parameters for the next level of detail. In virtually any location, the design process encompasses a number of fairly standard steps. In the mountains, what sets these steps apart from the process in urban locations is that natural factors play a more central role as design determinants.

Definition of Needs and Statement of Intent. The client's needs shape the design project. The only

effective way to launch a process that will yield a built environment appropriate to the mountains is to begin with a clear statement of development needs, desires, preferences, and essential time frames. The users' needs, often different from the client's, must also be taken into account.

Needs translate directly into project goals. A statement of intent should articulate the client's goals, including visions of the place's character, desired standards for design quality, and social objectives. Developers should expect to adhere to these commitments.

This first step, the statement of needs and goals, is sometimes thought to be independent of environmental issues or site-specific physical conditions, but this is not the case. Goals must be consistent with the setting, its natural processes, and its physical capacities to support development. Respect for place must be part of the project from its inception.

Program Formulation. Reflecting identified needs and goals, the design program should itemize the plan's social, physical, and economic elements, such as intended uses and activities; number of people likely to be accommodated in the place and their demographic characteristics; the space, facilities, services, circulation systems, and economic infrastructure needed to support them; and the investment required over the term of development. The program should include a statement of desired

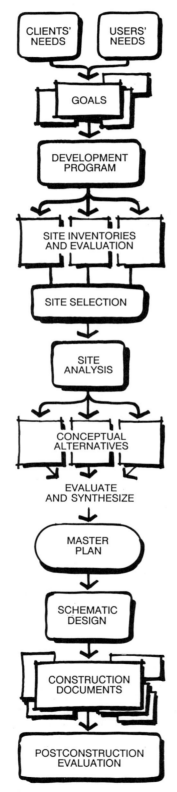

aesthetic quality and should demonstrate an understanding of the opportunities and constraints of the site, as well as the realities of the market and the client's budget.

Site Reconnaissance and Identification of Alternative Sites. At this stage of the design process, a wide-ranging search is launched for sites that are compatible with key elements of the design program. To identify sites worthy of further consideration, the assets and limitations of each site are compared with one another and with development priorities. The goal is to gain a general sense of a site's development potential and the probable densities it can sustain. The level of development that a particular site can support is then compared with the design program and its stated environmental ethic.

To furnish a basis for evaluation, design-influencing data for each site are gathered. These data should include accessibility, slope gradients and solar aspects, soils and vegetation, water availability and rights, wetlands, floodplains, and major geological hazards. With the help of hydrologists, meteorologists, soil scientists, geologists, avalanche experts, ecologists, foresters, and wildlife specialists, natural factors data are collected for at least one full cycle of seasons. Natural hazards are then mapped, and the severity of risk is roughly assessed.

Land capability or development suitability mapping is part of the site reconnaissance task. Overlay maps of natural constraints and opportunities must be made before environmentally sensitive site plans can be realized. By acknowledging the real obstacles to development, these maps may also take on the force of a legal document, governing how the development of the site will be allowed to proceed.

Using conclusions derived from the composite constraints map, one can roughly quantify the amount of land suitable for the various land uses being considered on the sites and translate it into graphic expressions of alternative densities, building heights, and massing that could satisfy the program. This will reveal both whether a site contains adequate space for the intended uses and the approximate extent to which the site would have to be disturbed to make the uses fit.

When analyzing a site's environmental constraints and development potential, one must take into account the site's "area of influence": the regional fabric of which it is a part and the neighboring areas that would be affected by its development. Environmental and cultural conditions beyond the site often impinge on its development potential, and rarely can the impacts of substantial change on a site be confined within its boundaries.

Coincident with the environmental reconnaissance,

Figure 8-25. *Steps in the design process.*

surveyors may be needed to make accurate boundary and topographic maps. Civil engineers should be engaged to determine the feasibility of bringing roads and utilities to the site. Historians may be enlisted to find out about the site's cultural traditions, historic events, and human settlement patterns. Archaeologists may be called in to survey the site for evidence of prehistoric or Native American cultures. Regulatory requirements and legal issues of ownership, water rights, environmental protection, and land-use control must be reviewed. Finally, public opinion and methods for soliciting public involvement should be appraised early in the process.

The sites should also be surveyed for their scenic quality and visual vulnerability to change. The aesthetic opportunities in the form and character of the landscape—views and landmarks, water features and vegetation, topographical form and natural boundaries, colors and textures—should be inventoried and mapped, for these elements may prove vital to the developed site's image. Special natural features that may be too valuable or fragile to tolerate the intrusions of development should also be noted. Likewise, characteristics of a site that detract from its visual quality should be identified and the difficulty of repair assessed.

On any natural site, whether completely wild, rural, or in transition, the site analysis will be superficial if it has not been derived from firsthand, personal knowledge of the place. It is important, therefore, to spend time on the site, to walk around, and to observe its daily and seasonal rhythms as if one were going to live on it. This cannot be done in a matter of hours or even days; it demands repeated trips over a period of months to sense the feel and the dynamics of the site in all seasons. In addition, site visits should not be confined to days when weather and field conditions are favorable; visits during adverse conditions and right after storms may be more instructive in highlighting hazards, potential problems, microclimatic variations, and ephemeral qualities. Without the experience of extended on-site observation, it is virtually impossible to retain the integrity or express the true character of a mountain site, to reap the fullest sensory benefit from its most valuable natural features, or to respond in the most effective way to its climatic extremes.

The end product of this reconnaissance is the selection of the one site that best satisfies the design program's goals. If a site is already owned and site selection is not an issue, then this analysis is likely to be the first step in formulating a design program. In either case, the natural characteristics of the environment play a controlling role in determining the most appropriate uses of the site and how intensively it can be developed.

Detailed Site Inventory and Analysis. The detailed site inventory and site analysis consist of tasks that must precede site planning and conceptual design, tasks that relate primarily to construction engineering and hazard mitigation on the chosen site. Among these, for example, are soil borings, laboratory analyses of soil and rock samples, quantitative slope stability analyses, detailed hydrological studies and groundwater surveys, more precise identification of floodplain limits, and more detailed field mapping of wetlands. The object is to define as exactly as possible all factors that pertain to site layout, structural systems, and human safety.

Conceptual Site Planning and Design. In mountain settings, the central issues in site planning are the facilitation of movement and retention of landscape quality. The challenge is to match densities, uses, road networks, and structures to the terrain and to relate design concepts to the natural landscape. These issues are the motivating force in all decisions relating to the key components of a site plan: circulation systems and parking, access routes and arrival points, the physical arrangement of and functional linkages among activities, and the sequencing of sensory experiences.

Good conceptual site plans evolve from conclusions made evident by development suitability maps and detailed site analysis. However, even though site constraints will have become relatively clear by this point, the best solutions may not be so apparent, and the creative process can rarely be expected to follow a straight line from analysis to concept proposal. Rather, plan elements are generally conceived in a looping trail of learning, testing, rejection, and revision.

Because it is unlikely that the first concept proposed will be the only or the best answer, anyone planning a project should be prepared to experiment with a number of alternative site plan concepts. These alternatives can then be compared according to how well they satisfy the development program, including its statement of desired character, how closely they conform to the budget, and to what extent they respect the parameters imposed by the site. Criteria for comparing various approaches to density and layout include the extent of site disturbance required, the severity of regional and on-site environmental and visual impacts, and the relative costs of construction.

When generating alternatives, historical and contemporary development prototypes can be a source of inspiration. Insights into probable costs, suitable construction technologies and materials, effective marketing programs, and avoidable development pitfalls can be gained by visiting other projects similar in scale, geography, or land use in

193

order to discern their achievements and deficiencies.

On larger projects, the broader context should also have been considered by this time. Economic variables and regional scenarios for growth and their possible effects on the project should be studied. Legal requirements governing the site's development should be reviewed with federal and state agencies and local regulatory bodies, with which regular contact should be maintained throughout the process to avoid surprises later. Possible effects on public opinion of alternative approaches to development should be discussed and efforts made to keep the public (including opponents) informed. Reflecting assessments of public response and economic conditions, basic work on marketing programs may start here, with special attention to the sales implications of different approaches to development.

Concept alternatives should be sufficiently detailed that the costs of each can be roughly estimated, including the engineering of roads, utilities, and impact or hazard mitigation measures. Building heights and massing must be studied to organize densities, and aesthetic intent must be translated into preliminary choices of forms, materials, and acceptable levels of workmanship. If these questions have not been resolved, alternative design concepts will be difficult to compare and evaluate or to price reliably.

As costs are refined, project planners must begin to consider alternatives for financing and phasing the development. Municipal bonds, industrial revenue bonds, private investment, and lending institutions all should be explored as possible financing sources. The influence of financing institutions on a project's timing, final shape, and quality is usually underestimated, and so the developer should have adequate lead time to secure funding from those sources most supportive of the goals for the project.

Master Plan. One concept is chosen as the best of the suggested alternatives, and from this concept a master plan is then refined. The master plan is a public record of proposed densities and land uses, shown graphically as they will be distributed on the site. Although the master plan is often thought of as a single illustrative site plan drawing, it generally includes architectural studies as well, to show how the structures will relate to the landscape. The master plan will be most effective if it also communicates the concept through narrative, additional drawings, or other visual media.

In many states, the submission of a master plan to regulatory authorities triggers the formal environmental impact review. Clearly, however, important environmental issues play a decisive role in the final selection of a design concept and must have

been identified long before this point so that the master plan can incorporate the appropriate responses.

If the site plan includes areas with a significant danger of flooding, wetlands destruction, slope instability, or avalanche, mitigation measures must be developed in conjunction with the site planning and should be submitted as part of the master plan. In the case of avalanche hazards, a control plan should be completed to make sure that the risks can be held within tolerable levels (Armstrong and Williams 1986, Perla and Martinelli 1976).

In addition, the master plan should reflect the suggestions of the public works staff to satisfy snow removal and maintenance concerns, as well as those of local fire protection officials to ensure adherence to fire codes and adequate access for emergency vehicles.

For communities and larger development projects, this is also the time to consider how design intentions and standards of quality will be maintained over the longer term. Graphic design guidelines and development standards have been helpful in many instances in encouraging consistent quality. In community development, planners should consider how to use public-sector improvements to set up a framework and a model for subsequent private development.

Gaining approval of a master plan often depends on communication with officials and interested segments of the general public. Few major projects have been successful without community participation and visibility. Thus an effort to communicate purpose and plans and to involve the public in testing their validity should be viewed as a indispensable part of the design process.

The series of site plan drawings for Kirkwood, California, Figs. 8-27 through 8-31, illustrates how basic concepts for the organization of development on the site (pictured in Fig. 8-26) evolved into a finished master plan.

Schematic Design. Increasing levels of detail are addressed as the design process moves toward resolving unanswered questions. Design concepts are fleshed out and refined. Engineering of roads and utilities continues. Questions of character and style are decided in regard to siting, scale, building mass, architectural forms, and materials. Visual and functional linkages and microclimatic effects are tested. Environmental impacts are quantified and mitigation plans are completed. Costs are constantly revised, and plans for marketing, construction and development phasing, and financing are detailed. Attempts are made to conclude negotiations with investors, lenders, and underwriters. The regulatory review continues.

Figure 8-26. *Aerial view looking southeast, Kirkwood, California, before development. Photo courtesy Kirkwood Associates, Inc.*

Final Design and Concept Implementation. The production of drawings and documents for construction forces the final resolution of questions relating to technical and structural issues, architectural and plant materials, grading, drainage, and design details. In the mountains, design detailing and timing become critical variables because of the extreme climate and the short construction season. Construction specifications must include temporary measures to protect the site's natural processes until the site work can be completed. Regulatory, marketing, legal, and financial issues should be resolved before construction begins.

Postconstruction Evaluation. The project is finished, but how well does it work? From the perspective of the regulatory agencies, the objective of postconstruction evaluation is public protection: ensuring that what was built is what was promised and evaluating the success and the impacts of development they have approved. This should be, but rarely is, a formal process supported by staff and budget.

From a developer's standpoint, the purpose of a postconstruction evaluation is to learn from mistakes. Among those working in the mountains, there could be more pooling of experience in design and detailing. Until there is more information correlating conditions in the mountain environment with concepts and techniques for building there, the danger is that many new projects will start almost from scratch.

There are many opportunities for joint efforts to

195

Figure 8-27 through 8-31 *The evolution of a design concept for Kirkwood, California: early diagrams of functional relationships between ski slopes and the base village (Fig. 8-27), 1971 schematic plan for the resort (Fig. 8-28), 1972 diagrammatic site plan (Fig. 8-29) and illustrative site plan (Fig. 8-30) for the village core, by Berridge Associates Inc., San Francisco, planning and landscape architecture. Updated master plan, 1981 (Fig. 8-31), by Terry R. Barnhart, Gage Davis Associates, Boulder, Colorado, planning and landscape architecture. Although densities have been rearranged over the years, the underlying concept limiting development to the edges of the meadow has remained. Developer, Kirkwood Associates, Inc.*

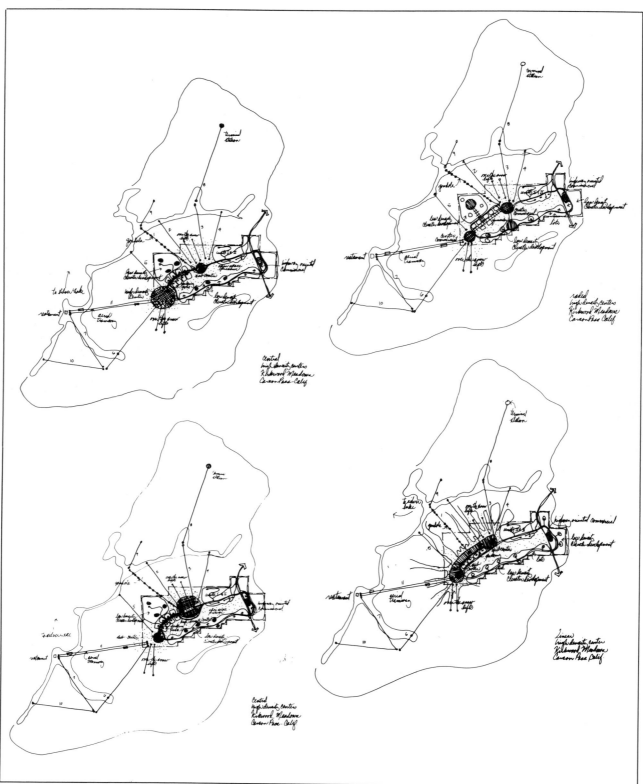

Figure 8-27.

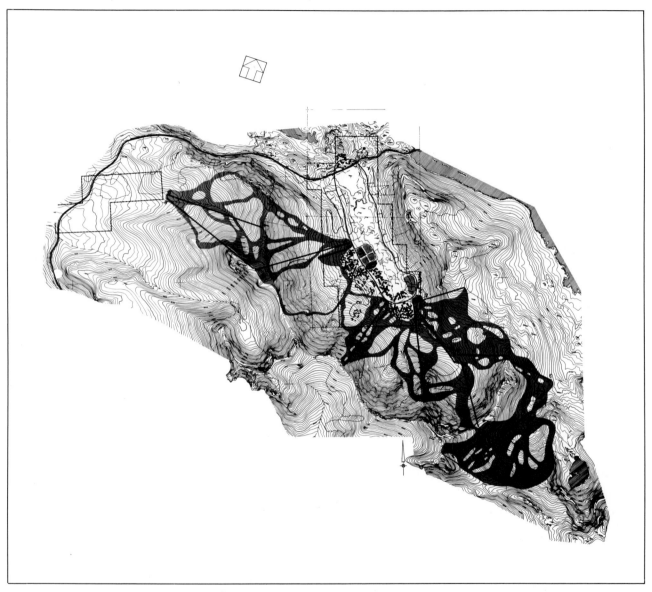

Figure 8-28.

understand the densities that different mountain ecosystems can tolerate; the kinds of mitigation measures that most effectively reduce natural hazards; and the kinds of transportation systems, building materials, insulation techniques, and roofing configurations that work best with the mountain climate and terrain. There is room for more debate about the styles of architecture best suited to the landscape and for greater commitment to standards of quality and durability.

Long-term Maintenance Plans. A developed landscape, like a natural one, is dynamic, not static,

and so the initial design objectives can gradually be lost as a built landscape matures or deteriorates. To guard against this, long-term maintenance responsibilities should be clarified before a project is built, and adequate funds should be set aside for care and replacement as needed. Procedures for snow removal and emergency access, drawn up before the designs were completed, should be periodically reviewed so that original design intentions are not compromised over time and so that adjustments can be made for problems not anticipated in the original site plan.

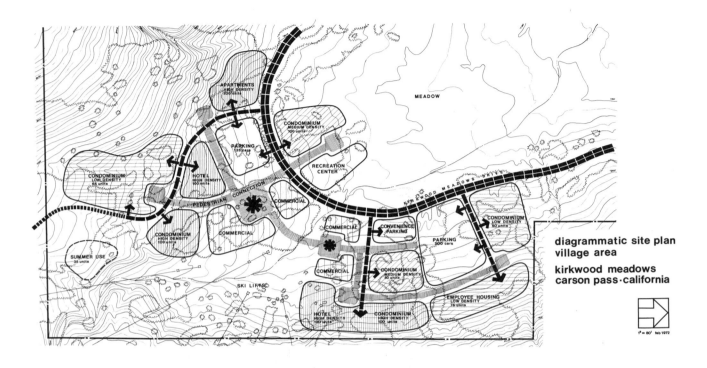

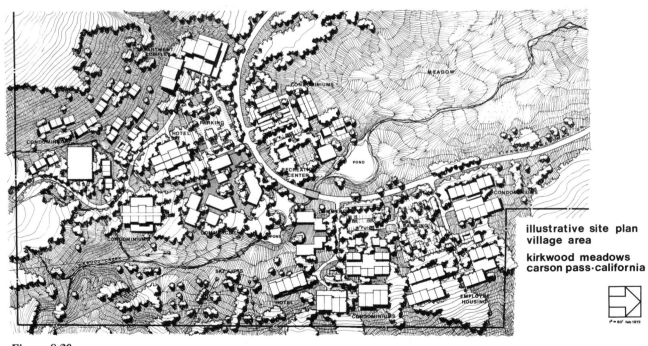

Figure 8-30.

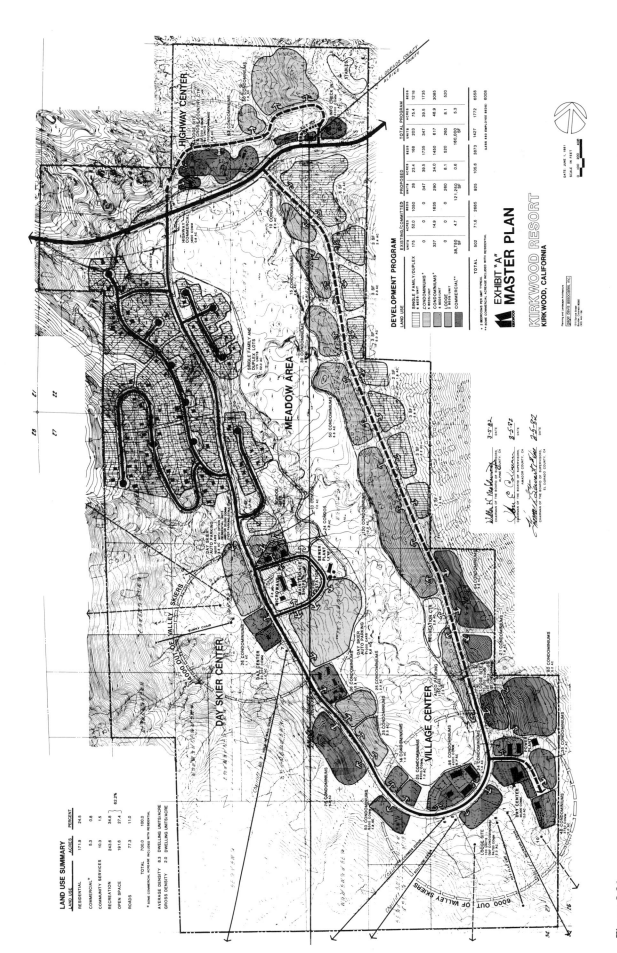

Figure 8-31.

199

REFERENCES

Armstrong, Betsy, and Knox Williams. 1986. *The Avalanche Book*. Golden, Colo.: Fulcrum.

Marsh, William M. 1978. *Environmental Analysis for Land Use and Site Planning*. New York: McGraw-Hill.

McHarg, Ian. 1969. *Design with Nature*. Garden City, N.Y.: Doubleday.

Merk, Frederick. 1978. *History of the Westward Movement*. New York: Knopf.

Perla, Ronald I., and M. Martinelli, Jr. 1976. *Avalanche Handbook*. U.S.D.A. Forest Service Agriculture Handbook no. 489.

U.S.D.A. Forest Service. 1973. *National Forest Landscape Management Handbook,* vol. 1, no. 434.

———. 1974. *The Visual Management System,* vol. 2, ch. 1, no. 462.

———. 1987. East Fork Ski Area draft environmental impact statement. Durango, Colo.: San Juan National Forest.

PART III

Applications:
Design Tasks and Prototypes

Forces generate form. In the case of simple natural systems, this is literally true; in the case of man-made systems it is a metaphor. The forces which are not provided for do not disappear.

—Christopher Alexander

9
DERIVING COMMUNITY FORM FROM LANDSCAPE

There are various ways of painting landscapes . . . also different ways of looking at landscapes. If we approach them with the heart of forests and streams, their value is high; but if we approach them with the eyes of pride and extravagance, their value is low. . . .
— *Kuo Hsi, Chinese painter and theorist (active ca. 1050–1090)*

Form is a composition of masses and edges. In the context of a community, form relates to its extent, its boundaries, and the aggregate shape and textures created by its individual parts when viewed from a distance.

A comparative evaluation of mountain community form is twofold: first, whether the composition contains the essential physical features common to ideal communities and, second, the extent to which these components reflect the natural environment. The first question is analogous to a universal language of archetypes; the second, to its translation into a mountain "dialect." Several works on urban design and townscape address the first question,[1] but this book is primarily concerned with the second.

ARCHETYPAL COMPONENTS OF COMMUNITY FORM

Research in urban design has indicated that well-established, cohesive communities have in common certain physical attributes, regardless of differences in landscape context. In some communities, the presence of these traits may be the fortuitous result of a long history, slow growth, and the natural assets of a site. But virtually all of them, even if not consciously created, endure by design.

The following seven physical components are tools of linkage, cohesion, and spirit that reinforce connections among people, place, and time. The patterns in which they are introduced and combined constitute the underlying form of a community and help shape its perceived character.

Boundaries and Edges. A stable community has recognizable boundaries, visually defined by tangible edges such as roads, natural features, and greenbelts.

[1]See in the Bibliography Alexander 1977, 1979; Cullen 1961; Jacobs 1961; Jackson 1984; and K. Lynch 1972, 1976.

These set a community apart from adjacent settlements or precincts of a different character. That is, they confer identity and imply limits.

Boundaries, once intended as a means of protecting the territory within, now function to define the extent of a place. They thus are more a symbol of inclusion and belonging than of exclusion and isolation.

. . . boundaries stabilize social relationships. They make residents out of the homeless, neighbors out of strangers, strangers out of enemies. They give a permanent human quality to what would otherwise be an amorphous stretch of land. . . . [Boundaries] are a way of rebuking the disorder and shapelessness of the natural environment. . . . (Jackson 1984, p. 15)

Gateways. If there are boundaries, there must also be gateways. Defined points of entry to the community that climax an approach sequence of sensory experiences thereby articulate the transition from outside to inside the boundaries.

Landmarks. Historical sites and buildings, monuments, special natural features, parks, panoramic views, and vantage points all function as landmarks to orient people. When visible from a distance, landmarks anchor the community in the landscape, give it an identity, and frequently become symbols of place.

Core. A viable community has a center. Like a magnet, its concentration of higher-density uses pulls people into contact with one another. Physically, a well-defined nucleus is obvious within the community form. From a distance, textures reveal its comparatively greater density and scale. The hierarchy of pathways naturally leads people to it, and landmarks confirm the climax of arrival.

Multilayered Circulation. In ideal communities, cars are controlled, leaving outdoor spaces more conducive to people-oriented activities. Intrusive high-speed, high-volume vehicular traffic should be kept outside the boundaries of neighborhoods and important activity nodes.

A circulation framework that restrains cars compensates with a web of alternative transportation methods and corridors, including pathways for pedestrian and bicycle traffic. It provides adequate and conveniently located parking facilities so that people will willingly leave their cars at the periphery.

In special places, the circulation network is designed to connect sequential experiences and define edges, thus moving beyond functionality to become an instrument of sensory stimulus and a determinant of community form.

Linkages with Nature. In well-designed communities, people are presented with a variety of ways to sense and participate in nature. Visible references to the natural setting are evident in open space throughout the community. Interpretive elements in public spaces call attention to natural values and processes. Transitions from nature to the urban environment of the core and the quality of the edges between them are well modulated.

Public Spaces. Ideal communities offer a variety of functional outdoor spaces: hard and soft, architectural and natural, linear and confined, large and small, boisterous and contemplative. Linked together, they are important to community form because they mark its visible character with a singular pattern and reinforce its connection with nature. In the same way

that evidence of nature within a community connects it to the environment outside, public spaces bind its separate parts together from within.

Translating Archetypes into a Mountain Context

Congruence: a state marked by accord, agreement, consonance, harmony among parts; the quality of coinciding.

—*Webster's Dictionary*

It is not enough to incorporate these archetypal components into a community's physical plan; they must also be relevant to their context. Their siting, form, and distinctive character are established by means of appropriate design. If they fail to evoke the essence of a place, they may provide a functional framework, but they will be devoid of meaning.

When designers take cues from the mountain environment, they use natural forms as the model for community form and natural forces as its rationale. This process translates archetypal concepts into physical components of form unique to a site and fortifies the bonds between the community and the environment.

Creative solutions vary according to values, sensory perceptions, and practical requirements. The following criteria may be used to evaluate them:

Ecological Congruence. Ecological congruence refers to the appropriateness of community form in terms of climate, natural hazards, and development suitability.

1. The community should be sited, oriented, and massed for maximum exposure to winter sun and reasonable protection from wind and temperature extremes.
2. The community should be protected from catastrophic natural events.

3. In its present and projected extent, density, and scale, the community should respect the capability of its site to support it.
4. The distribution of densities over the site should reflect variations in slope gradient and ecosystem values.

Topographical Congruence. Topographical congruence refers to the extent to which topography has been allowed to influence the community's form.

1. The circulation framework required by anticipated densities and activities must be compatible with the terrain's configuration and slope gradients.
2. Natural terrain boundaries should be used to help define reasonable physical limits for the community.
3. The aggregation of building masses and forms should take into account the shape and scale of natural landforms.

Landscape Congruence. Landscape congruence refers to the extent to which the landscape's character is reflected in community form.

1. The community development plan should require only minimal modification of terrain and natural watercourses.
2. Linkages with the natural landscape should be evident in the quality of edges, transitions, and open space.
3. Community form should reflect sensory qualities in the natural landscape. Appropriate responses can be described in terms of compositional unity, textures, and landscape themes in the built environment, as well as in terms of the orientation of the whole to views and special scenery.

TOWN SITE SELECTION: THE BASELINE FOR FORM

The principal determinant of a community's overall form is its site. The selection of one site over another imposes certain patterns on what will be built. The siting of any community reflects many influences, among them topography and other natural factors. Factors unrelated to the environment, such as the objectives of developers and citizens, financial requirements, and property ownership patterns, are often stronger influences on the choice of a site. Of course, unless a site offers adequate developable land, potable water, and economically supportive resources, any other criteria recommending it will be irrelevant. Beyond these essentials, however, physical and ecological differences among prospective sites provide a constructive basis for comparison.

Site Selection Criteria

In the evaluation of prospective sites, selection criteria will help screen out those with physical traits that may constrain the form and layout of a community. The following five townsite selection criteria can also be applied to mountain design issues on smaller scales. Of the five, two—access and the absence of serious natural hazards—are essential.

Ecological Compatibility and Absence of Hazards.

Hazardous areas should be avoided. Although some hazards can be overcome with proper siting and site engineering, the costs of mitigation and the risks to life and property often cannot be justified. A realistic assessment of the dangers of slope failure, seismic events, flooding, and avalanches is basic to the evaluation of prospective sites (see Chapter 5, Natural Hazards and Land-Use Control).

In addition, an ecologically compatible site should offer land sufficient for the projected development without damaging valuable ecosystems and natural watercourses. The site should also have a source of water adequate in quantity and quality to supply the community at its ultimate projected size.

Even if a village, and not a community, is the near-term goal, there should be enough land and water on prospective sites to accommodate any future development of municipal infrastructure and higher densities. If the issue of size is left open-ended, the suitability of the site cannot be evaluated properly.

Tolerable Elevation and Winter Climate.

A high elevation affects community form by reducing acceptable distances for pedestrian movement and forcing the concentration of building masses. And at extreme elevations, the constraints of a high-altitude winter can reach the point of unacceptable severity: Heating and insulation costs may be excessive; outdoor activities may be limited to only the very hardy; and vegetation may be fragile, sparse, and impossible to replace in our lifetime. Relatively small elevation differentials can be significant.

If other factors are generally equal among prospective sites, those lower in elevation will be preferable. Less desirable sites for high-intensity uses are those above the elevation range of forest species, like aspen and lodgepole pine, that are easiest to reestablish on disturbed sites.

Year-round Accessibility.

Topography and distances control accessibility, and access, in turn, determines prospects for growth and economic viability. The relative difficulty and scenic quality of access routes also influence sensory perceptions associated with a destination.

Reasonably convenient access from population centers via good all-weather roads, as well as air (or rail) connections, is essential if a destination resort is ever to be a year-round community. Roads expand the area from which a place can draw supplies, services, labor, and visitors.

Some alpine communities in Europe are accessible only by rail, but they evolved in a society with better rail connections and different attitudes toward the automobile. With the possible exception of Beaver Creek, Colorado, where day skiers are prevented from driving into the village and must use a shuttle bus system for access, there are no comparable towns in the American mountains.

The need for road access does not preclude the concept of auto-free communities in this country; it simply means that access roads have yet to be effectively linked to transfer points and internal circulation networks. In most of the popular mountain resort towns, cars have become a problem. More innovative perspectives on these linkages are urgently needed in order to meet ecological and aesthetic objectives. The solution begins with site selection: The best sites are those whose topography facilitates a circulation layout with multiple means of access and minimal intrusion by cars.

Favorable Topography.

Slope gradients and landform are the principal factors determining the amount of usable land on a mountain site, how it is accessed, and how people will move about within it. Topography is a climatic determinant as well (see Chapter 4, Microclimatic Effects of Variations in Topography). The best sites provide for efficient circulation, maximum winter sun exposure, protection from wind and abnormal cold, and the capacity to contain projected populations without significantly harming the air quality (Figs. 9-1, 9-2).

Topographical integrity, which pertains to the clarity of a site's natural boundaries, is also relevant to site selection. Some landscape units, like an alluvial terrace edged by escarpments, are defined by the terrain. That is, it is clear where they begin, end, and meet other units. They have unity and cohesion, a self-contained integrity, and the distinct edges that more fragmented or unbounded landscapes do not

Figure 9-1. *Perspective sketch (top facing page) is a siting study for the new resort village of Ribbon Creek at Kananaskis, Alberta, one of the facilities built for the 1988 Winter Olympics in Calgary. Drawing by Robert McIlhargey.*

Figure 9-2. *The site analysis for Ribbon Creek (bottom facing page) illustrates some of the motives that influenced the siting decision. Developers, Province of Alberta and Kananaskis Country. Design Workshop, Inc., Aspen, Colorado, planning and landscape architecture.*

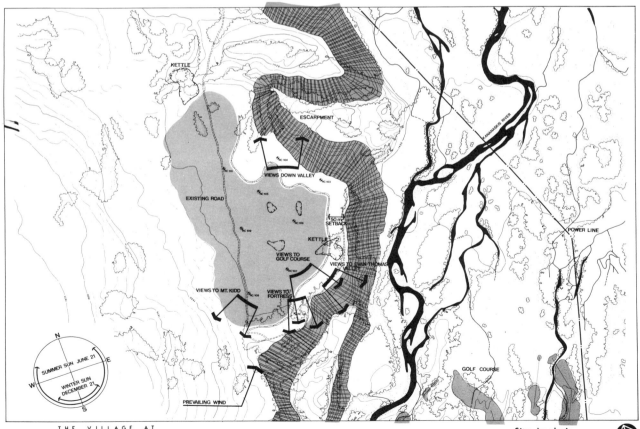

KETTLE

ESCARPMENT

VIEWS DOWN VALLEY

EXISTING ROAD

50 m
SETBACK

KETTLE

VIEWS TO
GOLF COURSE

VIEWS TO EVAN-THOMAS

VIEWS TO MT. KIDD

VIEWS TO
FORTRESS

KANANASKIS RIVER

POWER LINE

GOLF COURSE

N
SUMMER SUN JUNE 21
E
W
WINTER SUN
DECEMBER 21
S

PREVAILING WIND

THE VILLAGE AT
RIBBONCREEK
KANANASKIS COUNTRY

Site Analysis

0   50   100   200   400m

207

have. In regard to community form, they encourage unity of composition and define physical limits to growth.

It is often tempting to view expanses of flat land in the mountains, such as gentler hillsides, larger valleys, and intermountain basins, as the most favorable sites for building. However, topographic constraints can be viewed as an advantage, and not just because flat bottomlands have value for other purposes (agriculture, views). Landscapes without obvious natural limits tempt unfettered and amorphous development, leading too frequently to the growth of communities without a distinctive form or identity.

Special Scenery. A memorable site offers something special: dramatic topography, a landmark natural feature, water, inspiring views, open space that captivates. The mountain landscape offers these in abundance. Choosing a site with scenic attributes is like buying extra insurance for a community's future: not required but exceedingly desirable. But if it is clear that something of high scenic quality would be irreparably damaged by choosing a certain site for development, it obviously would be better to consider other sites.

Changing Priorities. The criteria for choosing a site for a mountain town today are different from those of traditional alpine villagers, whose main need was to live close to the fields and pastures that sustained them. Since World War II, proximity to destination-caliber ski slopes has been by far the most important criterion in the search for new resort sites, and natural factors have too often been discounted. Seasonally depressed pseudovillages frequently have been the disappointing result. Fortunately, the economic and social disadvantages of resort sites chosen on this narrow basis are at last being acknowledged.

There may be few opportunities in the future to plan new resort communities, and even fewer chances to select their sites from among a number of possibilities. The principal requirement for proximity between a ski town and its ski slopes or between a resort town and its scenic resources is unlikely to change, and the number of prime recreation sites available for development as destination resorts is limited.

This seems to suggest that site selection is a phase of diminishing importance in the community design process, a point of view that discourages a thorough evaluation of a site's suitability from a broader community perspective.

Even when a site has already been chosen, it is advisable to test it against desired standards, as this will clarify any handicaps, trade-offs, and unavoidable design constraints. Indeed, the criteria may argue against a site even if it is the only one available.

TOPOGRAPHICAL CONGRUENCE: CIRCULATION

The ideal circulation system is a web of interconnected networks for motorists, pedestrians, bicyclists, skiers, public transit, and service and emergency vehicles. The main arteries in the system determine the community's form and structure.

In a mountain town, the circulation layout is the first priority in site planning, as the need to satisfy functional requirements within the constraints of terrain drives the siting of all other major community and neighborhood components. The single biggest challenge in design on any scale is to fit the armature of roads and pathways to the mountain terrain with minimal visual impacts or functional conflicts.

Conceptual Components. Any circulation plan is a functional network of linked destinations. Although site-specific layouts vary, the necessary components are generally the same: access corridors, parking, entry gateways, hierarchies of streets and pathways, pedestrian zones, activity nodes, and arrival (climax) points.

A circulation plan is a response to questions about the community (or project) and its site: where and by what means people will arrive, how many people will come, where motorists will leave their cars, where the primary in-town destinations (ski lifts, shopping districts) will be in relation to access points, where the zones of heaviest commercial and residential density will be, to what extent these must be accessible by car, and by what other modes to connect them.

Concepts and Adjustments: Vail, Colorado. A diagram of the layout of Vail Village (Fig. 9-3) illustrates a standard sequence of nodes and connections, showing points of transition from vehicular to pedestrian circulation. However, Vail did not always have such a clear sequence.

In Vail's first decade, the streets in the village core were open to auto traffic, and there were large surface parking lots at both ends of Bridge Street, the main thoroughfare (Fig. 9-4). By 1975, however, burgeoning numbers of visitors had created so much congestion that Bridge Street was closed to cars, although service trucks still use it. A free shuttle bus system was initiated, and an 850-car parking structure was built. Its construction, a major factor in reducing the impact of the automobile, precipitated a major

Nothing illustrates the character of an area so well as its influence on the layout itself.
— *Kevin Lynch,* Site Planning

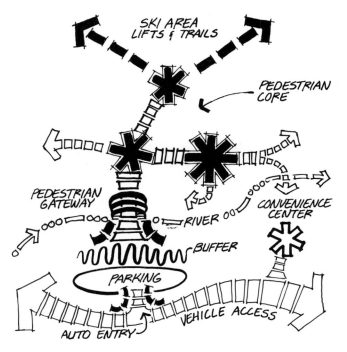

Figure 9-3. *Conceptual layout diagram of Vail Village, Colorado.*

change in the village's character (Fig. 9-5). Bunkered into the edge of Gore Creek's alluvial terrace, the structure is virtually unrecognizable as a garage (Fig. 9-6).

In 1967, a second village core, LionsHead, was opened to the west, about a mile (1.5 km) downstream from Bridge Street, to provide more lodging and another point of access to the ski mountain (Fig. 9-7). Using the same basic circulation sequence, planners laid out a pedestrian mall to funnel skiers from the parking lots to a new gondola. (The two cores are discussed in Chapter 10.)

LionsHead's siting was decided by the location of the lower lift terminals, but the linkages between it and the old village were not of equal priority. A low-density zone separates them and interrupts the flow of pedestrians from the village to LionsHead. To close the void, the town has established a community facilities zone between them, which now includes the hospital, an ice arena, and a public library. A limited-access busway and a creekside bike/pedestrian path now connect the two nodes, creating an increasingly attractive connection (Fig. 9-8).

Figure 9-5. *The same view, after construction of the garage.*

Figure 9-4. *(left) The view toward Vail's ski slopes before development of municipal parking structure. Photo by Royston Hanamoto Beck & Abey.*

209

Figure 9-6. *Illustrative sketch of Vail's transportation center — four levels of structured parking hidden behind a planted slope. Royston Hanamoto Beck & Abey, San Francisco, landscape architecture.*

Figure 9-7. *LionsHead, Vail's second village core, constructed in 1967.*

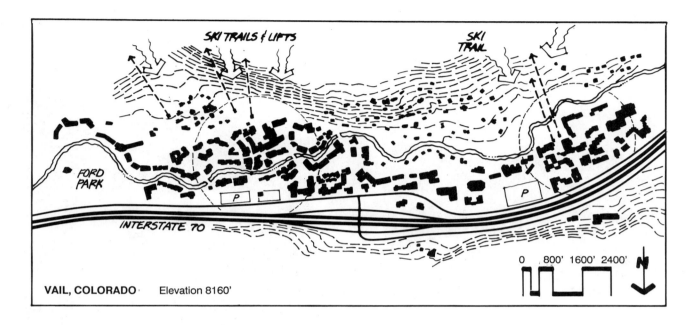

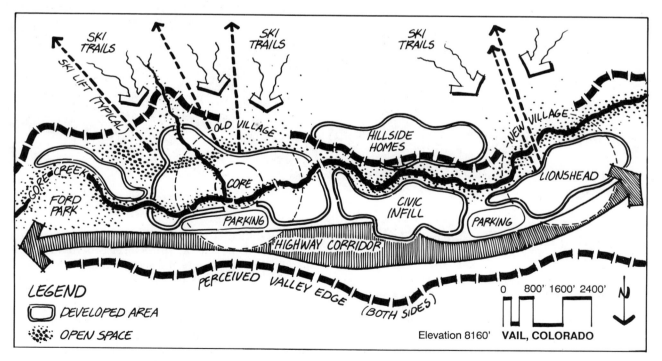

Figure 9-8. *Site plan of Vail, Colorado, elevation 8160 feet (2490 m), clearly shows how town form reflects valley landform (top). Functional diagram (bottom) shows how the town's districts are organized. Site plan drawn by Dennis Anderson.*

Figure 9-9. *Aerial view of Park City, Utah. Photo by Jim Kent.*

Respecting the Dictates of Terrain

Where topography is restrictive, as it is in the mountains, terrain dictates the circulation layout. Yet when translating concepts on paper into projects in the ground, the constraints of mountain topography are often underestimated, and reasonable standards are violated. There are street gradients too steep for safe winter circulation, too much regrading, too many switchbacks, and turning radii that are too tight. Densities are often too dispersed to support a viable public transit system but are too high to avoid congestion.

Despite the obvious problems of coping with cars on slopes, most American mountain towns, whether strictly gridded in the nineteenth-century pattern or in a freer form, are predominantly auto oriented. Of

necessity, their street networks generally conform to the trend of the valley, with long streets running parallel to the contours and shorter cross streets running perpendicularly. The pattern is most obvious in the older gridded towns, like Park City, Utah (Fig. 9-9), where the main street trends in roughly the same direction as the stream course. Lower-traffic streets approximating the contours step up the side slopes, leaving some cross streets with excessive grades.

As long as circulation systems remain tied to the automobile, slope gradient is a serious constraint, and circulation on a sloping site can adversely affect community dynamics.

The Sloping Site: Snowmass, Colorado. Proximity to skiing was the single most important determinant in the siting of Snowmass Village (Fig. 9-10) near Aspen, Colorado, a ski resort that opened in 1967 and

Figure 9-10. *Aerial view of Snowmass Village, Colorado, taken in the early 1970s. Photo by U.S.D.A. Forest Service.*

became an incorporated municipality ten years later.

The original developers, Bill Janss, then the owner of Sun Valley, and D. R. C. Brown, then the owner of Aspen Skiing Company, wanted skiers to have direct access to and from their lodgings. Had they sited the village on the valley floor, access lifts would have been required to compensate for unreliable snow conditions at the lower elevation. Instead, they chose a site for the village nucleus several hundred feet higher on relatively steep (10 to 15 percent), forested north-facing slopes.

In the western states, the hillside siting of Snowmass is an exception. Most forested acreage in the mountains is controlled by the federal government, and because it is mainly the slopes that are forested, private landownership is generally restricted to the valley floors. This, plus the logistical preference for flatter land, means that most American mountain towns avoid the slopes.

The Snowmass site has many pluses: no major natural hazards or constraints to access, exceptional sensory qualities, and expansive downvalley vistas. A small village on the forested slopes at the upper end of the broad alluvial valley would thus appear comfortably contained. The main drawback of the site is its north-facing orientation; the developers assumed that the constraints of slope gradient could be overcome in site planning.

Because direct skier access to lodgings was a fixed program objective, the Snowmass planners chose to make another exception to usual patterns in the layout of circulation. To gain maximum ski slope frontage for the lodge buildings, its main vehicular axis is oriented at right angles to the contours (Fig. 9-11). Although other possibilities were considered, including a switchbacked road and cog

213

railway, this alignment was considered the best of the limited number of options. The decision resulted in a steep grade on the main roadway, which averages 14 percent. In some places, the driveway access to parking lots is over 20 percent. Paving must be electrically heated to keep the road passable in winter.

The plan has had a subtle influence on the village's social dynamics. By separating the pedestrian flow into several short corridors branching across the slope from the main road, it has reduced the vitality of focal spaces. Necessarily aligned with the contours, none of these corridors is oriented to views, and it has been difficult to distinguish the dominant one. The main pedestrian street (Fig. 9-12) is a truncated experience. Sandwiched between parking and the ski slope, it is too short to offer sufficient diversity.

Parking is a problem. Capacity is so strained that a controlled access system has been instituted. Motorists must either pay to drive to the village during the ski season or leave their cars in surface lots midway down the valley and transfer to shuttle buses.

Snowmass was initially envisioned as a small village, the first of several nestled across the slopes,

each with its own inn and retail services and connected to the others by ski lifts. According to this scenario, reminiscent of the Alps, the gradient would have been consistent with desired images and could have been an asset.

Instead, the gradient has become a serious handicap, more so because Snowmass has grown far beyond expectations. Their failure to anticipate the magnitude of future growth allowed planners to site the village where there was not adequate room to respond efficiently. Although development on the scale of a small village might have been appropriate to a sloping site, increased densities have contributed to severe circulation problems and have obscured the site's natural qualities.

With the explosive growth in its visitor-bed base and increasing numbers of permanent Aspen Valley residents, new condominiums and second homes have spread across the hillsides near the village and below it onto the valley floor. Because circulation and parking are restricted by gradient, commercial space within a reasonable pedestrian radius in the village core has not been able to expand commensurately.

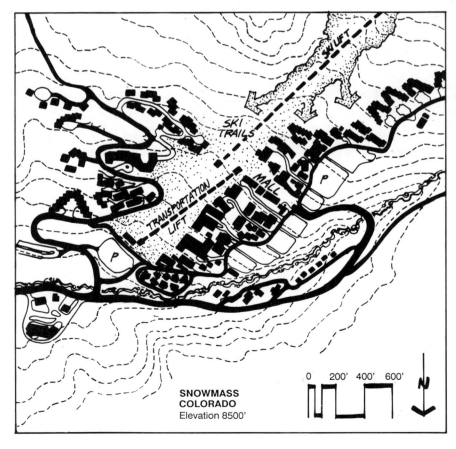

SNOWMASS
COLORADO
Elevation 8500'

0 200' 400' 600'

N

Figure 9-11.

Figure 9-12. *Pedestrian mall, Snowmass Village, Colorado.*

The construction of an auto-oriented convenience center beyond the core at the lower edge of town has relieved the need for some retail services. But Aspen, twenty minutes away, still captures the majority of visitor expenditures on food and shopping, making the county road linking the two towns into a troublesome high-volume corridor. For the Snowmass merchants, winter is still the only good season.

Because they focused on their villagelike vision, the developers did not fully appreciate the logistical consequences of their decisions about siting and layout. In hindsight, densities were not distributed according to land capabilities, and Snowmass has not been able to make a graceful transition from a seasonal resort to a full-fledged community. Had the village nucleus been shifted downhill, at least to the junction of valley and slope, the community would have evolved in an entirely different way.

Escaping the Tyranny of the Car

Topographical constraints argue for reducing dependence on the automobile in mountain site plans. The difficulty of fitting roads into sloping terrain, the sacrifice of valuable flatland for parking, and the propensity for pollution-aggravating temperature inversions in mountain valleys make it imperative. Traditions in town planning and the desire for convenience appear to resist innovation in handling cars, but change must come. Perhaps it will come first in mountain communities, where restrictive topography will force the issue.

Clogged Arteries: Mammoth Lakes, California.
How bad can the problem get? Consider the situation in the Sierran town of Mammoth Lakes, just a few miles down the road from one of America's largest ski areas. Slope gradient is not the problem here. As in many other gridded towns, the real villain is the town's total reliance on cars, which has led to regular bouts with gridlock in peak winter periods. The town also has a massive parking problem: On-street parking makes up the majority of the town's parking capacity, but it is prohibited during the heavy Sierra snowfalls to enable the town to clear the streets.

Settled by miners in the 1850s on a broad, forested terrace, Mammoth Lakes has been a ski center since the 1930s but did not incorporate as a town until 1984. Before then, there was no public entity to focus on municipal problems. Indeed, incorporation came about partly because of the urgency of parking and transit issues.

In the past decade, developers competing for tourist business blanketed the town's two main thoroughfares with shopping centers. With no development controls, rational projections of retail demand, or municipal goals for functional linkage, these projects completely ignored their aggregate impacts on traffic and their combined potential to create a core for their community. The centers are redundant, isolated by parking lots and heavy traffic, and unconducive to pedestrian circulation. Some of them went bankrupt, but not before they had set in place strip development patterns detrimental to the integrity of the town. Transit systems are now being debated, but fragmented landownership and budgetary constraints have thwarted agreement on a plan. The gridded streets of Mammoth are the fabric tying the town together, but they cannot provide the positive linkages that create a sense of community.

Limited Auto Access: Beaver Creek, Colorado.

Reacting to circulation problems like those in Mammoth Lakes, the earliest plans for Beaver Creek Resort near Vail excluded automobiles entirely. All visitors were to be transported by shuttle bus from large surface parking lots near the highway several miles below the village.

Although this is the routine for day skiers, the auto-free concept was relaxed in later planning stages. In the village today, all lodgings have underground parking. Among the reasons for permitting some cars was the projection that the total number of round trips by lodge vans would exceed those of guests arriving by car. A total exclusion might also have deterred prospective buyers.

The experience gained in Mammoth argues that innovation is urgent, but the Beaver Creek decision seems to suggest that the auto-free concept is unworkable. In truth, it only makes it clearer that linkages among circulation modes must be made more convenient in order to make alternative patterns of movement acceptable to the public.

Detaching Tourists from Their Cars.

Keys to making the auto-free concept work are improvements in transportation technology and the existence of mutually supportive circulation networks. With regard to the latter, several design choices are important: the type of alternative transportation modes, the location of points where people can leave their vehicles and make a transfer, the diversity of attractions in pedestrian corridors linking these points to destinations, and the distances between destinations. When these elements are planned as an integrated network, the automobile recedes in

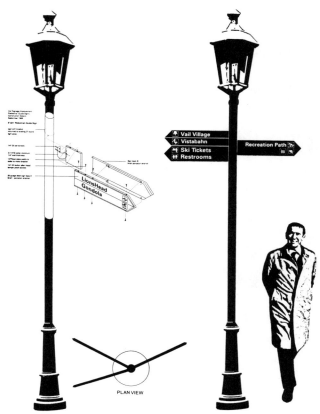

Figure 9-13. *Prompted by its selection as host of the 1989 World Alpine Ski Championships, the town of Vail embarked on a program to improve its public signage. In a style reminiscent of that of European pedestrian villages, directional and informational signs have been standardized according to function. Graphic design Ampersand Studios, Denver.*

importance as a means of transport, and the town gains in appeal.

Resort visitors readily take advantage of a system that offers both convenience and sensory enticement as a reward for leaving their cars behind. Sensory enticement relates to the variety of stimuli that can be enjoyed by those on foot, the diversity of activities along the way, and the number of other people doing the same thing. Convenience depends on the clarity of the circulation system (signage, ability to orient, Fig. 9-13), the ease of access and parking, and the distances that must be traveled on foot between parking or transfer points and in-town destinations.

In regard to these points, Vail is an exceptional model, one of the very few mountain towns in which the sequence of movement is both interesting and convenient enough that people willingly leave their cars outside the core. Of course, motorists have no choice, as the system of restricted auto access is in place, mandated by municipal consensus. But it emphasizes the importance of a viable political process and an adequate local tax base.

Convenience Retail for Residents. The need for convenience auto access to retail and commercial space increases in mountain communities that have a higher proportion of permanent residents, for services in a tourist-oriented pedestrian core typically are neither accessible enough nor particularly suited to their daily needs. The pressures from residents for auto-accessible services are legitimate and inevitable and so should be acknowledged and provided for in ways beneficial to the community as a whole.

In many resort towns, these needs have led to the development of auto-oriented convenience centers near the core, as in Snowmass and Vail. Their primary benefit has been to keep automobile circulation outside pedestrian zones, but there has been concern that they would siphon activity from businesses in the core.

This fear appears not to be warranted where the resident population is sufficiently large to support a variety of services and where the core offers diverse attractions in its own right. Typically, retail enterprises in the core target a visitor market, and those in outlying commercial centers cater to locals. The two can be complementary if their development is properly sequenced with growth and if they are functionally linked in the circulation network.

Public Parking. The siting of public parking areas is critical to community design, particularly in resort communities. It affects not only the public's willingness to leave their cars but also the scenic quality and visual image of a place after development. Parking capacity, proximity to destinations, ingress and egress, and visibility are important design issues, all of which are affected by terrain.

With parking lots, as with roads, an important corollary is how the layout works with the terrain. Excessive regrading or lot size is intrusive and unsightly, and excessive grade is unsafe. At Northstar near Lake Tahoe, for example, parking is broken into lots that step up the slope. Seven hundred cars can be parked in the resort's four curving tiers, which are screened from one another by new and retained trees. The lots are not visible from the arrival point or the village itself, and they are partially screened from the slopes above. The layout works gracefully with the topography and provides convenient auto access to ski lifts and the village core without visual or functional conflicts.

In contrast, vast doughnuts of surface parking surround many mountain resorts, consuming valley acreage and dominating the visitor's initial perceptions of the place. At some point, higher land costs will discourage the continued consumption of buildable land for surface parking. This, combined with the increasing concentration of densities, may make the

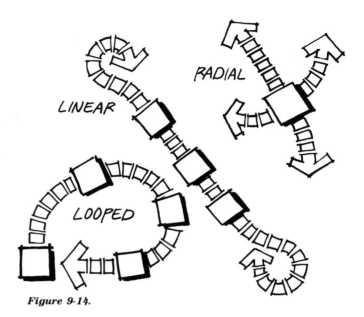

Figure 9-14.

higher cost of structured parking more palatable.

Parking plans need to incorporate room for expansion. In Vail, shortly after the original surface lots were replaced by the first parking structure, another garage, this one for 1200 cars, replaced the surface lots near the LionsHead lifts. Recently, Vail's town council approved the addition of 400 more covered spaces to the first garage, an expansion that had been anticipated in the original design. As a municipality, Vail can use bond financing for these improvements.

Parking plans should also consider the possibilities of shared use. As in Vail's two municipal parking structures, day-skier parking doubles as convenient short-term parking at night.

Building Public Transportation. Even where the topography does not unduly limit roads and parking, a public transit system should be considered in mountain towns if growth is projected beyond acceptable walking distances of principal destinations. To date, buses are the system of choice, although towns differ in the amount of coverage that their bus system provides. In the future, rail and cable systems may be feasible in towns with an adequate taxing and bonding capacity.

The objective in designing a public transit system is to give as many people as possible easy access to stops on the system. This requires a concentration of densities along transit routes. Transit system layouts may be radial, linear, or looped in concept, depending on the topography and how the densities are (or could be) clustered (Fig. 9-14). Scattered development cannot support a cost-effective system.

One of the major considerations in a mountain resort town is how the transit system will handle passenger loads at peak hours when ski lifts open and close for the day. It may not be realistic to purchase enough capacity to satisfy peak demands. If there is only one loop or leg, all passengers will have to ride the same line, regardless of their destination, causing considerable congestion. Peak-load capacity and routing are issues in Vail, for instance, where the town's long, skinny form compounds peak-hour overloading on the one in-town bus route. It is the clustering of densities along that same linear form, however, that makes mass transit feasible at all and that might eventually facilitate a more exotic form of transportation, like a monorail.

Virtually every well-visited mountain town today is experiencing major problems with cars and parking that imperil the environment and the scenic priorities of their recreation-based economies. These problems are the best argument for realistic limits on cars. If all the physical constraints on vehicular traffic in mountain towns were taken seriously, the logical conclusion would be to keep cars out. This is an ideal that may never become a reality in most communities, but it does not justify the failure to try. There is every reason to keep challenging our assumption that it is not practical.

Although public transit may be an expensive proposition for a resort town, its expense must be weighed against the costs of prime land lost to parking and the damage caused by congestion. The real question is not if it is needed but when. The next question is how to phase it in as the town grows.

Beyond Engineering: The Drama of the Journey

Sensory quality is not the predominant influence on the layout of a circulation network, but every site planning decision affects it. Roads and pathways have a profound effect on the way a place is perceived: They function as edges, links, and armatures; they organize, interpret, and orient; they direct the eye to chosen views and landmarks; and they control the

traveler's sequence and pace of experience. And in the volume, velocity, and kind of traffic they carry, they indicate and influence a neighborhood's character.

The Mystique of the Processional. The magnetism of a special destination derives in part from sequential views, changing perspectives, and layered perceptions that build anticipation as one journeys toward it. The path of approach is an interpretive sequence, not just a preamble to the "real" experience, and thus it is a legitimate concern of sensitive design. Every design gesture in the sequence of movement should derive from something specific to a place, revealing clues to its character and building to a climax consistent with expectations.

The approach to a mountain destination has a processional quality. That is, getting there can be as powerful an experience as being there. A mountain journey traces a more exciting sequence than does one through hills or flatlands. It overlays a natural progression in landforms and vegetation: from broad plains upward across gentle inclines to steeper slopes, canyons, and summits, and from plains scrub to the forest species of higher elevations. This natural procession may be dramatic in its contrasts between expansiveness and confinement, breadth and height, sunlight and shadow, moisture and aridity. This is partly why the journeys to legendary mountain destinations, like Banff, Zermatt, New Zealand's Mt. Cook, Aspen's Maroon Bells, or the monasteries of the Himalayas, stand out in memory almost as much as the places themselves.

The three-dimensionality and high surface relief of mountain regions make the design task easier by enabling the manipulation of lines of sight. As the traveler's elevation changes, the ground plane and foreground shift in importance. Distant views of the destination are sequentially revealed, framed, filtered, and contrasted with details nearby. Mountain landforms and the landscapes they compose appear to change as one moves. The cumulative effect is a powerful sensory stimulus.

A dramatic sequence need not be left entirely to accidents of nature. Setting the access road alignment

Figure 9-15.

is an effective means of developing sequences and framing views, but even where it is already set, the route can be embellished. The site planner might clear or plant to open or frame views; carve out places to pause and absorb significant views and natural landmarks; reveal or add foreground details as devices to interpret, describe, or symbolize the character of the vicinity; and highlight the presence of water. To envision these strategies, computer simulation, photos, and models are useful tools.

The processional quality of movement toward a destination is intensified by natural gateways marking progress toward an inner sanctum of high mountains. Gateways can be emphasized by locating places to stop where vistas open, roads crest at a pass, canyons narrow, cliffs rise, or water falls; by making transitions in grade more obvious and taking care where they occur; by making an event out of crossing a stream; by making bridges more visible and tunnels more intriguing; and by erecting signage that explains the historical significance of a stopping point to caravans of another era. The slower the speed, the more impressions the traveler can absorb.

Control of the access corridor is critical to maintaining the spell of the procession. In many mountain towns in America—where land along the access route is in fragmented private ownership and development is less stringently controlled—opportunities to control views and develop a sequence are often lost. Control may be stymied unless a town is buffered from major highways and can restrict commercial signage at its outskirts.

Attention to the quality of the journey also implies control over the elements of a community that first come into view (Fig. 9-16). A dramatic view or a signal feature should capture the approaching traveler's first impressions and should not be overwhelmed by extraneous elements at the fringe.

The Sense of Arrival. The experience of arrival will be more vivid if it coincides with something captivating in the natural landscape: a vantage point that reveals more about the place, a steep slope or abrupt natural edge, a lake or stream. This is what people come to see, the confirmation of arrival that matches expectations.

It is also possible to communicate arrival by means of constructed elements if the buildings' scale and character are consistent with expectations. Large, assertive buildings (like Beaver Creek's Village Hall, Fig. 11-71) and pivotal transportation transfer points (like Snowbird's tram building, Fig. 11-78) are unmistakable arrival points.

The scale of the mountain landscape makes it hard to send messages forcefully through unremarkable constructions. In numerous mountain towns,

Figure 9-16. *One of the traditional gateways to Berne, Switzerland.*

especially those unable to control the approach sequence, entries and arrival points are marked with such elements as flags and pillared arcades, bridges over the access road, and porte cocheres at drop-off points. These may seem anticlimactic without a supportive landscape context and if there has been no intrigue in the journey to that point.

Most resort towns have two arrival points, one for motorists and one for pedestrians. Although the pedestrian sequence may have been constructed with great care, drivers are often left to venture in through the back door. Most people enter a mountain town by car, only to encounter gas stations, congested intersections, parking lots, and frontage roads before they can begin a more interesting sequence on foot.

The cultural history of a landscape sometimes offers opportunities to strengthen the character of the journey and the ceremony of arrival. Taos is a place with this potential. It is imbued with the spirit of three distinct cultures and preserves an indigenous style of building unique to the Southwest. Opportunities to play on these sensory images are immense. People come to Taos to experience its mystique, yet the vision that greets them upon their arrival at Taos Ski Valley makes no reference to it. Instead, the image is faintly Tirolean (Fig. 9-17). The same disconnected imagery permeates ski towns all over America.

219

Figure 9-17. *Taos Ski Valley, New Mexico. Photo by Michael Blake.*

The Sensory Journey: Beaver Creek, Colorado.

When the quality of the access corridor is fully controlled, the journey can be remarkably enticing, as Beaver Creek (Fig. 9-18) illustrates.

The 2-mile journey to this resort village, founded in 1981, begins amid the disorganized development that has engulfed the Eagle River Valley west of Vail (Fig. 9-19). Leaving the interstate highway, visitors proceed by either car or bus across the river and past an alpine-style gatehouse. This, reinforced by the tall gypsum cliffs on one side of the valley, clearly marks a formal entry (Fig. 9-20). From this point on, all the developable land in Beaver Creek, formerly a ranch, is controlled by a single developer, Vail Associates, Inc.

Beyond the entry, the two-lane access road curves past the restored ranch house and climbs up an 8 percent grade to a tight curve at the upper edge of a broad alluvial terrace (Fig. 9-21). The climb is rewarded at the top by a completely new view orientation and a different landscape (Fig. 9-22). This is the clearest edge between the village environs and the valley land below. Its clarity comes from the convergence of signals at a topographical boundary. The vegetation changes, and the first dramatic views up the valley are revealed.

From the lip of the terrace, the access road roughly parallels the creek and the trend of the valley. It defines the edge of a buffer zone along the riparian corridor and directs views to the village above (Fig. 9-23). On the creek side of the road, thick riparian vegetation contrasts with the smooth, pastoral texture of the golf course and the dry slopes above the road.

Figure 9-18. *Aerial view of Beaver Creek, Colorado. Photo by David Lokey.*

Figures 9-19 through 9-24. *The sequence of views leading to Beaver Creek, Colorado.*

Figure 9-19.

Figure 9-20.

Figure 9-21.

Figure 9-22.

Figure 9-23.

Figure 9-24.

Beyond the switchback at the top of the terrace, vacation homes begin to appear, some of extravagant quality and size. To contrast, ranch outbuildings and barns have been preserved along the road, contraposing images of the mountain West's rougher side. There is nothing extraneous, nothing offensive, nothing out of place.

As the distance closes, the village remains the focus, while the perspective on its varied rooflines constantly changes. Marking a less obvious gateway, the golf clubhouse, pillared in a style reminiscent of Lake Tahoe, guards the lower edge of the village. A flattening of the gradient begins to suggest arrival where the road engages the village's larger buildings and the creek. The road forks and arrives at last at a drop-off beside the massive Village Hall complex, a

signal that the journey is at an end (Fig. 9-24).

There are some weaknesses in the sequence because the village is not yet complete. For example, the innermost village boundary is not yet well defined; there are some gaps in the linkages among village buildings; and the daunting Village Hall steps discourage people from proceeding that way on foot. But as the village fills in, some of these shortcomings will be remedied.

The images are contrived, perhaps, but the journey is a pleasure just the same. Indeed, it remains one of the most visually gratifying short journeys to a ski resort anywhere in this country. There could hardly be a greater contrast between the character of what was left behind and the appeal of the place that awaits discovery.

TOPOGRAPHICAL CONGRUENCE: EDGES, MASS, AND DISTANT VIEWS

One reason that traditional mountain villages and hilltowns appeal to us is because in the distant view, their form and composition appear to be outgrowths of the site itself (Fig. 9-25). Convincingly derived from the land, their layouts clearly refer to natural landmarks, sun, and important cones of vision. In the relationship of their buildings and open spaces to the topography, we imagine an intimate, intuitive understanding of the spirit of place.

Topographical congruence is the joining of site and settlement to create compositions in which development is fused with landscape. Today, however, it is not always given credence as a design objective, and too many mountain communities awkwardly impose on the land.

Insufficient sensitivity to the natural landscape is not, of course, the only reason that natural topographical clues are ignored. The tendency to give them short shrift in design is compounded by financial objectives that argue for mass production and density, by the power of modern construction technology to alter landform, and by the common preference for speedier—and therefore more disruptive—modes of transportation. The power of these factors diminishes, however, where there is a respect for place.

The best indications of topographically sensitive community form are the conjunction of town boundaries with natural edges, the correlation between landform and the three-dimensional massing of structures, and the grace with which the whole composition is distributed on the terrain.

Boundaries

A clear line of demarcation with nature is a design imperative in communities surrounded by wilderness. Built edges that reiterate the site-specific lines of topography, vegetation, or water features help create the images that distinguish one place from all others.

The absence of boundaries seems psychologically associated with a loss of control, whether over nature or over the direction and pace of growth. Lack of boundaries is symbolic of instability and imbalance between nature and development, and it prompts the fear that sterility and chaos may prevail.

It is more comforting to draw a meaningful line in the wilderness than to recognize no limits at all. Drawing boundaries is far easier where there are obvious clues in the natural environment. For example, most ski resorts are oriented toward the

Figure 9-25. *Topographical congruence in a traditional hilltown.*

conspicuous topographical edge where the steeper gradient of the ski slopes meets the valley floor. Such a clear edge is magnetic, for one instinctively feels less exposed looking out to the valley with one's back to the slope.

Beaver Creek illustrates the harmony in nearly complete topographical containment. The planners were keenly aware of how the village would be perceived from a distance and so placed the village where the valley flattens, widens, and meets steeper slopes, a siting that seems naturally determined and comfortable. There is a satisfying rationality in the way the village steps up the gentle incline, echoing the horseshoe shape of the valley's perimeter; in the way it embraces but does not infringe upon the creek; and in the way the sideslopes shelter it but are not overpoweringly steep.

Vail is a case in which natural edges compete in the distant view with a particularly abrupt engineered edge (Fig. 9-26). The narrow Gore Creek valley enforces Vail's elongated, linear form. Forested slopes define the town's southern edge. Running parallel to their undulating line, the interstate highway corridor forms an unnatural barrier. Though it is an essential

Figure 9-26. *Vail's highway edge.*

Figure 9-27. *A scheme in the 1973 master plan for the town of Vail proposed using conifer masses to reduce the visual impact of the interstate highway. Royston Hanamoto Beck & Abey, San Francisco, landscape architects.*

pipeline for visitor access, it is also an intrusion of urban proportions.

The highway corridor consumes a broad swath along the foot of the valley's south-facing slopes. Noisy and divisive, it has become a serious impediment to functional connections in the town: In a distance of almost 10 miles, only three highway exits, three underpasses, and one pedestrian overpass penetrate it. In character and attitude, new growth across the highway seems disconnected, although it is within the town's legal boundaries.

The highway has been leapfrogged by development, but little of substance can be done to reduce its stark visibility as an edge. A 1973 master plan for the town of Vail suggested mass conifer plantings sweeping across the highway in fingers (Fig. 9-27), but the

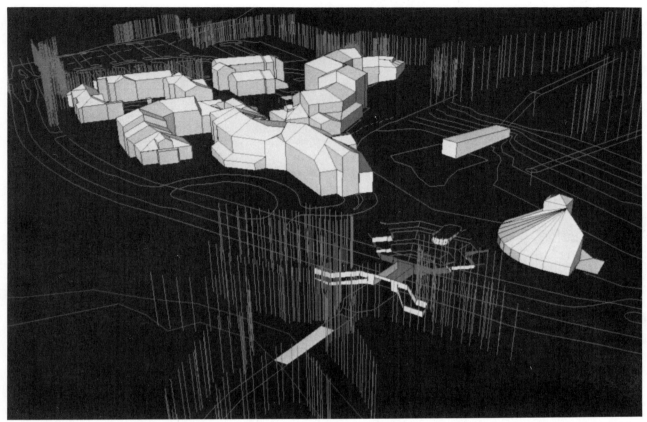

Figure 9-28. *Computer simulation of one alternative for building massing in the village at Blackcomb Bench, British Columbia. Design Workshop, Inc., Aspen, Colorado, planning and landscape architecture.*

practical constraints of climate and economics have dampened local enthusiasm.

When natural edges are soft and feathered, as most vegetative edges are, they offer a natural screen. When they are abrupt, as some topographical edges are, they are dynamic and dramatic. Siting that ignores, obscures, or intrudes on natural edges in incompatible ways has lost an opportunity for congruence. Using edges to align boundaries helps make a community more comprehensible.

Evolution. It is important to establish all the community edges that matter visually and to retain the initial sense of physical integrity as the community grows. Once-clear edges have been breached in town after town, as subsequent development spills out onto outlying land, with little regard for natural restraints or the visual logic of the original site plans. Giving up the defense of initial boundaries will attenuate the sense of place unless new limits are defined. A succession of boundaries will probably need to be established as development proceeds from resort into community.

Developers often try to create a marketable image by erecting boundaries around their projects to distinguish them from the competition. But if cohesive community form is a goal, then individual projects must contribute by reinforcing the linkages within the community's boundaries.

Distant Views: Massing, Textures, and Fit

Correspondence between topography and the three-dimensional form of a community is another means to integrate it with the natural setting. In this sense, community form implies both extent and mass. It is the sum of decisions about siting, form, line, and scale of individual building masses and open spaces. If the sum is a coherent composition inspired by topographical patterns, and if the community as a whole responds to the flow of the terrain, as in traditional villages, it is far more likely to seem compatible with its surroundings.

One way to establish a proper relationship between a community (or any project) and the topography of its site is to visualize the fit from important perspectives. In the early phases of design, visual analysis, sketches, photo and computer simulations, and massing models are helpful.

Simulations of various types were essential to design in proposed new villages at Blackcomb Bench, adjacent to Whistler in British Columbia, at East Fork, and at Mount Crested Butte, both in Colorado. At Blackcomb, building plans were digitized for computer simulation from critical vantage points (Fig. 9-28). At East Fork, digitized topography and forest outlines allowed planners to simulate various ski slope configurations as the cleared areas would be viewed from the village site (Fig. 9-29).

227

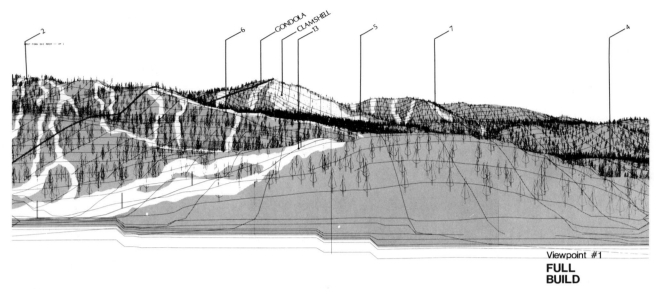

Figure 9-29. *Computer simulation of maximum forest clearing for ski slopes at the proposed East Fork ski area, viewed from the base village. Winston Associates, Boulder, Colorado, planning and landscape architecture.*

At Mount Crested Butte, landscape architects used several techniques to make decisions about building massing, scale, and heights and to define village boundaries. Their objectives were to create a tight village cluster surrounded by open space, to preserve the ridge line as a natural boundary, to frame the view of the village from the access road, to establish a family of building forms and materials consistent with the site, and to locate a focal element within a composition of varied building heights. Sketches and models helped show how different design schemes would look on the site. Weather balloons were even flown to establish acceptable building heights and to mark natural village edges. Figures 9-30 through 9-36 illustrate the process.

Figures 9-30 through 9-36. *A process for siting a village in the landscape: Mt. Crested Butte, Colorado. The approximate village development zone is surveyed on site, and critical building corners are marked with balloons to show actual building heights (Fig. 9-30). A simplified line drawing is made from the site photograph (Fig. 9-31), and a study model of the site and village is constructed (Fig. 9-32). A simple line drawing is made from photographs of the model (Fig. 9-33) and overlain on the line drawing of the site (Fig. 9-34). Working with the composite drawing, the village form is refined (Fig. 9-35) until an appropriate site plan evolves, which is then rendered (Fig. 9-36). Computer simulation has since streamlined this process. Developer, Mt. Crested Butte Resort. Design Workshop, Inc., Aspen, planning and landscape architecture, with William Johnson, Ann Arbor, Michigan.*

Figure 9-30.

Figure 9-31.

Figure 9-32.

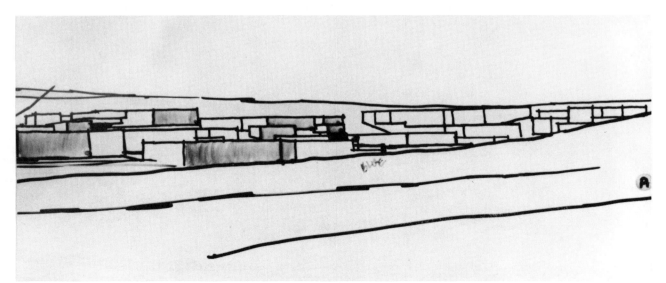

Figure 9-33.

Figure 9-34.

Figure 9-35.

Figure 9-36.

Texture. In the environment, textures are patterns made from the repetition of forms that are somewhat consistent in shape, scale, spacing, or color values. Textural characteristics can be used to describe a community in the landscape, because at a distance, building forms, roofs, and walls are seen as textures. A built environment may seem more compatible with its site when its surface textures are consistent with the natural textures around it.

The angles from which a community is most often seen determine which building elements will be the dominant textures. From vantage points above a town, the roofs dominate, and from the sides and below, facades are more important (Fig. 9-37). Simulation from specific lines of sight thus helps identify which elements will be most significant in the distant view.

Textural impressions are affected by the distribution and scale of building masses. Finer textures are achieved by repeating similar forms of modest scale, by breaking rooflines and facades into smaller segments, by stepping building masses up the slope, by hiding taller and bulkier masses behind smaller-scale structures, and by avoiding bulky masses in critical view lines.

Finer textures conform more nearly to the mosaics of many mountain landscapes and to cultural expectations of what a village should look like.

Historic mountain towns and villages are fine-grained compositions of uniformly small structures, whose fine texture at a distance conveys a sense of intimacy and scale.

Consistent texture often becomes a standard against which people familiar with a place judge subsequent development. If existing textures are associated with images they value, its violation will be a cause for distress. It is thus not surprising that in many older towns, debates are raging over the wisdom of permitting larger structures, in part because they will break with the existing texture of the community fabric.

This issue has also surfaced in newer resort towns that are under pressure for higher densities and larger scales. In Snowmass, for example, an inconsistent texture underlies the dismay with which a recently completed condominium project was received, even though it is not dissimilar in character or height to other buildings in the area. The project, designed to break up the mass by segmenting the roof and facade, apparently exceeded the village's textural norms because its horizontal extent across the contours is so obvious in the view from below (Fig. 9-38).

In Beaver Creek, the handling of textures, along with a closely controlled architectural style (see Chapter 11, The Central Rockies: Regional Revival),

Figure 9-37. *Because Snowmass Village, Colorado, is most often viewed from below, standardized roofing materials and roof pitches could not function as intended to unify the composition.*

Figure 9-38. *Woodrun Place, Snowmass Village, Colorado. William Turnbull Associates, San Francisco, architecture. Design Workshop, Inc., Aspen, landscape architecture. Photo by William Turnbull Associates.*

has been successful in conveying a distant perception of the village as an intimate place, despite the large scale of individual buildings. Sketches from the resort's design regulations illustrate the desired effect (Fig. 9-39). The accompanying narrative emphasizes consistency in building forms as a means to achieve a unified image for the village and a compatible fit with the landscape:

> *At a distance, the Village is seen either from the mountain looking down, or from the entry road upon arrival. Due to vegetation masses, as well as sight lines created by the terrain of the area, the roofs will become the dominant element at this level of perception. At this scale, the Village should be composed of simple understated forms with an overall consistency of materials and color. Roofs shall be simple hip and gable forms. Variety should be a response to changes in topography and exterior spaces. (Beaver Creek 1979, p.2)*

Dominant visual elements, standing apart from overall patterns in building scale and mass, are like compasses, giving people a sense of direction and showing them the place's organization. A backdrop of consistent textures helps make these landmarks visible. Conscious gradations in building heights and scale, reflected in textures, helps clarify transitions and the relative importance of a community's parts. When patterns in massing and textures are chaotic, it may be hard to discern the focus of a composition, giving rise to the suspicion that the community is a maze without a core.

These points are evident in the aerial photo of Park

City, Utah (Fig. 9-9). The older part of town (in the center of the photo) shows an even gradation toward the coarser texture of main street, a consistency lacking in the more recently developed areas (lower right corner).

Every Site Is Unique. Massing is a three-dimensional exercise in composition. Design solutions must always be site specific, organizing masses in ways that relate to landforms, water features, spatial proportions, and visual relationships in the landscape, as well as to climatic, ecological, and programmatic considerations. Sensitive siting, deliberate attention to transitions, terrain- and sun-responsive gradations in height and scale, and clear delineation of edges are the design tools most effective in tailoring a solution to the site.

The Boundless Site: Elkhorn at Sun Valley, Idaho. A development of the Manville Corporation and Bill Janss, Elkhorn (Fig. 9-40) is a satellite resort village whose site was determined not by ski lift locations but by property ownership patterns. At the time the master planning began in the early 1970s, the Elkhorn Valley had already been acquired by the developers, who had been searching for a suitable place to expand the visitor capacity of the venerable Sun Valley resort, opened in 1936 by Averell Harriman and the Union Pacific Railroad. The untouched valley was virtually the only available adjacent land.

232

The Elkhorn Valley is a huge treeless basin in foothill terrain of low to moderate relief. It is separated from the Sun Valley resort and the town of Ketchum, Idaho, by a ring of low, sage-covered hills, which block views of the higher peaks behind them from all but a few points in the valley. There are no streams of any size on the site, but there are some occasionally wet and boggy areas.

This semiarid bowl projects a quality of spaciousness and light but lacks magnetic features, views, or topographical edges to which the site plan might relate. The site's barrenness also precluded using landform or vegetation to knit the village into the landscape. Landforms are gently rounded, and landscape textures are so fine that anything coarser than grass stands out.

Lacking natural reference points or integrative landscape elements, the landscape architects thus envisioned Elkhorn Village as a sculptural counterpoint to the landscape, an isolated architectural statement in keeping with the valley's stark character. The village was to be a compact organism in the middle of the valley floor, separated from the surrounding hills by a permanent golf course buffer (Fig. 9-41). The encircling slopes, deeded as open space in perpetuity, were to be preserved as a backdrop, a constantly visible reminder of the natural landscape.

Figure 9-39. *Image sketches from Beaver Creek Resort Company's Design Regulations illustrating the desired unity of village and landscape. Drawings by Jack Zehren, AIA.*

Figure 9-40. *Distant view of Elkhorn at Sun Valley, Idaho. The SWA Group, Sausalito, California, site planning and landscape architecture. Photo by The SWA Group.*

Figure 9-41. *Conceptual diagram of Elkhorn layout, Sun Valley.*

Figure 9-42. *The entry arcade, Elkhorn at Sun Valley. Photo by The SWA Group.*

This perception of Elkhorn as a gem resting on the landscape is an image of distant views. It requires a contained, unified composition in which architecture is sculpture. The purity of this vision depends on the retention of compactness, defined edges, and unity of form in the architecture; it does not require a natural rationale for form.

In this seemingly featureless, dimensionless landscape, the risk in such a concept was that a village would appear to float, anchorless, in an enormous bowl. If there is any rationale in Elkhorn's siting, beyond functional concerns for access and circulation, it is analogous to water that accumulates in low spots. Like a pond, Elkhorn is cradled at the bottom of its gentle basin, as if gravity put it there. It rests on the ground like a blanket, a modestly scaled, uniformly textured composition of low buildings. A tower marks its center, and entry arcades pierce the boundaries formed by building walls (Fig. 9-42).

In the disconcerting dimensions of dry landscapes,

234

it is extremely hard for most designers to conceive an order for the built environment that evidences a natural rationale and harmony with place. Elkhorn's planners correctly understood the need for textural consistency and a sense of containment for the community. Indeed, the golf course edge is still intact; the surrounding hills are still pristine; and recent buildings maintain a consistent height and scale. However, in choosing to rely on architecture rather than on natural features to "create" a place, they were disappointed, for this is something its placeless architecture cannot do.

LANDSCAPE CONGRUENCE: NATURAL THEMES AND LINKAGES

The natural landscape is among the most potent place-making elements in design. When references to nature in its local forms pervade an inhabited place, they give it a distinctive identity. Working urban patterns into the regional landscape is therefore at the heart of mountain design. Achieving congruence is a matter of choosing appropriate landscape themes and acknowledging natural linkages.

Natural Processes As Themes

In nature, there is a symbiosis between form and process, an inevitability in the way physical forms evolve under given physical conditions. In the mountain environment, the forces of gravity, wind, water, and low temperatures coalesce in the organization, form, and flow of physical features. Landscape design that reveals this relationship between form and causative forces in nature thus has an appeal that cannot be attributed to artistry alone.

Landscape architect Lawrence Halprin calls this elemental relationship the ecology of form (Figs. 9-43, 9-44):

> Since form in nature is perceived by people as right and beautiful, an understanding of the processes of nature is a vital resource for designers—whose primary task is also the making of forms. It is my own feeling that we derive our sense of form from nature because we are biologically and physically part of nature. Our own form—physical and psychological—has arisen through natural processes. Thus natural form is our ultimate criterion for made form. (1979, p. 71)

This is not to say that a successful landscape project in a mountain area must be naturalistic in design; on the contrary, abstractions can make as strong a point and inject a welcome note of urbanity.

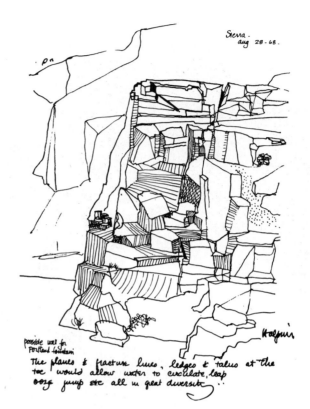

Figure 9-43.

Figures 9-43 and 9-44. *Notebook sketches by landscape architect Lawrence Halprin observing natural processes that he later used in his fountains.*

235

Figure 9-44.

The question is not whether the design *looks* natural but whether it *behaves* in a natural way. It is not a question of copying nature or fitting in with the landscape, but of understanding and expressing nature's processes. According to Halprin, when design reflects nature's inherent forces, "people empathize with the built environment in the same way that they empathize with nature's work" (Chang 1978, p. 145).

Landscape themes are a way of communicating natural processes. They are reminders of context and can elevate the mundane to something affective and evocative. If landscape themes fail to articulate in some way the essence of a place, they will fail to add meaning to experience.

Themes in Vegetation. There is more to using plants in the mountains than merely selecting the right (that is, native) species. The more important question is what one wishes to accomplish by their use (see Chapter 7, Aesthetic Considerations).

Within a community, the preservation of native vegetation is a symbolic act. In higher-density areas, it is rarely possible to preserve a large enough area to retain intact functioning ecosystems. Rather, the real purpose in keeping existing vegetation is to influence urban character and to establish linkages with the natural setting. To that end, what matters is the scale of the effort as well as its overall character.

A native landscape does not always result from using native vegetation. The pedestrian malls in Sun Valley, Idaho, and Aspen, Colorado, for example, are noted for their use of native plants, but both malls put them in a carpet of bluegrass. More important was the intent and the fact that the landscaping was done on an assertive scale.

In Sun Valley (Fig. 9-45), vegetation is a dominant influence on the informal image of the mall, but the composition does not replicate the natural landscape. That the grass is not native is less important than that it is green and vigorous. The vegetation is noticed because it contrasts with the dry native landscape.

In Aspen, spruce and aspen trees in linear beds the length of the mall combine with the period architecture to create a genteel and restrained urban landscape (Fig. 9-46). It is controlled, not wild, nature that one experiences here; the use of native species, though certainly appropriate, is not central to the design goals.

The earth-covered parking structure in Vail Village moves closer to the sense of a natural hillside landscape (Fig. 9-47). There, native vegetation in an enormous, slightly unruly mass completely hides four levels of structured parking, accomplishing an important transition between the urban core and the backdrop of the aspen- and sage-covered slopes

Figure 9-45. Sun Valley mall, Idaho. Photo by Dick Fenton.

Figure 9-46. Linear planting beds define activity areas on the Aspen mall. Photo by Aspen/Pitkin County Planning Office.

Figure 9-47. Native vegetation screens the Vail municipal parking structure (see also Fig. 9-6).

237

behind it. On an irrigated slope of nearly 1 to 1 (a risk that paid off) are small native trees, shrubs, wildflowers, and grasses. One of the lessons in this bold solution is the visual payoff of large-scale plant massing combined with a sloping site.

Vegetation begs to be used in proportions appropriate to the scale of a space. Only then can a balance between hardness and softness in the urban landscape be achieved that is consistent with people's expectation of mountain communities. It is not always how closely a replanted landscape resembles that of the natural context, but whether it contributes to memorable images and spatial character.

Themes in Rock and Water. The presence of water and native rock in a built environment does not guarantee that the composition of which they are a part will feel right for the place or add to its appeal. In the best applications, water and rock appeal to our instincts by involving us in ongoing natural processes (Fig. 9-48). In less adept solutions, these materials are used in weak and incidental ways that contradict the strength of their presence in the mountain landscape (Fig. 9-49).

Consider rock. Like water, it is most effective as a material when its power to influence the organization of the built environment is revealed. For example, at Stillwater Cove, a condominium project on steeply sloping land at the northern end of Lake Tahoe (see Fig. 11-81), practical concessions to a rocky site turned into a design advantage. Gigantic granite boulders were left in place and used as the rationale for siting structures, pathways, decks, stairs, and the swimming pool, where a rock ledge on one side appears to confine the water. The presence of the boulders intensifies the awareness of the natural landscape and signals the subordinance of what has been imposed on it (Fig. 9-50).

Rocks in outdoor art, says contemporary art critic Lucy Lippard, "are symbols of permanence. . . . [They] add new meanings to the old in the midst of our cultural disjunctions . . ." (1983, p. 39). In landscape design, their symbolism is often overlooked. When rock is used in trivial ways, its capacity to connect the built environment with the surrounding landscape cannot be fully exploited, and it becomes just another decorative material.

The same is true for water. Consider, for example, the new fountain in the central public space at LionsHead in Vail (Fig. 9-51). Although it was a needed addition to an oversized space, it was not sited within important axial view lines in the mall. There is little in its composition that makes reference to natural forms or processes. In a public space of a scale that renders lesser efforts unremarkable, it missed an opportunity to use a drop on the site of almost 30 feet

Figure 9-48. *Rocks as a magnetic presence: a play feature on the pedestrian mall, Boulder, Colorado. Everett Zeigel, Boulder, mall architects; Sasaki Associates, Watertown, Massachusetts, landscape architects.*

Figure 9-49. *Rocks as an incidental ornament: highway interchange.*

(10 m) to display all the connective and sensory qualities of water.

If the scale of a feature were the only factor determining its impact, Beaver Creek's central fountain would elicit a stronger response (Fig. 9-52). Taking up a drop of around 15 feet (5 m), this large cascading water feature in front of the Village Hall is made of giant, ragged slabs of native red sandstone. It is the focal element in what will eventually be the main public space in the pedestrian corridor. Although

Figure 9-50. *Rock as the motive force in site planning: Stillwater Cove Condominiums, Crystal Bay, Lake Tahoe, Nevada. Berridge Associates Inc., San Francisco, landscape architecture.*

not a recurring landscape motif, the fountain is, in its isolation and size, an awesome construction, begging for attention in any season.

If there is a problem with the fountain, it is the site development around it. The feature occupies a vexsome space, often in shade. A long run of stairs ascends on both sides of it, disconnecting it from nearby activity areas and leaving insufficient space to linger or sit beside it. (Compare it with the interactive possibilities of the new creekside pocket park at Beaver Creek's bus terminus, Fig. 9-53). The scale is right, but siting consigns the fountain to a role in the urban landscape that falls short of its potential.

Even in more abstract forms, water and rock can still be used as symbols of place, as, for example, in a trio of water features in the formal entry plaza of Vail's Westin Hotel (Fig. 9-54). The central feature is a gusher encircled by huge river boulders in a basin of water-rounded cobbles; flanking it is a pair of right-angled concrete pools. The three are the only elements in a plaza often criticized for the absence of softening vegetation.

The circular fountain is on axis but adrift in the plaza. It is the mountain version of a monument, with the jet as an obelisk and the rocks as totems. The water flows even in winter, creating a summit of ice (but wind sometimes restricts its height in warmer seasons). The boulders at first appear as randomly

Figure 9-51. *Central fountain, LionsHead mall, Vail. Land Design Partnership, Glenwood Springs, Colorado, landscape architecture.*

Figure 9-52. *Village Hall fountain, Beaver Creek pedestrian mall, Colorado. Berridge Associates Inc., San Francisco, landscape architecture; stonework, Gallegos Masonry, Avon, Colorado.*

Figure 9-53. *Beaver Creek entry park. DHM, Denver, landscape architecture.*

Figure 9-54. *Westin Hotel entry courtyard, Vail. ROMA, San Francisco, architecture; CHNMB, San Francisco, landscape architecture.*

Figure 9-55. *Keystone Resort, Colorado.*

placed as rubble from a rockslide, but their massing builds to an apex around the jet, and the concrete circle that contains them restores the sense of control.

In a more abstract expression of control, the concrete-walled reflecting pools have straight edges, corners, smooth textures, and quiet water. Their strict geometry is the one trait they share with the rock

fountain. As a composition, the three features together are consistent with the scale of the space and symbolic of the mountains' presence in a built environment. In a sense, they are a metaphor for the duality of urbanity and nature in this mountain landscape.

A water feature that acknowledges less assertively

Figure 9-56. *Rock fountain at the pedestrian entry to Vail Village. Eldon Beck, Royston Hanamoto Beck & Abey, Mill Valley, California, landscape architecture.*

Figure 9-57. *Fountain, Skyline Park, Denver. Lawrence Halprin, landscape architect.*

the same duality is the artificial lake at Keystone Resort, Colorado (Fig. 9-55), intended as the central organizing element of the village complex. Its perimeter was programmed to support compatible activities: cafes, sitting spaces, lanes for strolling, and boating. In its circumference, there is a carefully detailed transition from the urban edges to the naturalized shoreline: At the far end of the lake,

opposite the urban core, a wetland marsh has been recreated. Though not dramatic, the lake is placid and inviting.

Apart from the creek corridor, it is rare to find instances in mountain communities where the flow of water is used as a dominant motif in the reconstructed landscape of public open spaces. The naturalistic rock fountain by the covered bridge in

Figure 9-58. *Central fountain, Levi Strauss Plaza, San Francisco. Lawrence Halprin, landscape architect. Photo © Peter Aaron/ESTO.*

Figure 9-59. *Levi Strauss Park, San Francisco. Lawrence Halprin, landscape architect.*

Vail is one example (Fig. 9-56). Another will be the Westin complex in Vail. At its completion, a series of physically connected water features fed by a natural spring will lace the site.

Others—not in the mountains but certainly inspired by them—are Lawrence Halprin's cascading fountains in Denver's Skyline Park and in San Francisco's Levi Strauss Plaza. In one of Denver's fountains, stepped concrete forms tinted to match local sedimentary rocks create waterfalls and cascades (Fig. 9-57). At Levi Plaza, an enormous chunk of carnelian granite from the Sierras is enthroned in a pool as a symbol of place (Fig. 9-58), while a stream emerges from another fountain, its serpentine, rock-studded bed the main feature of the adjacent park (Fig. 9-59). In these water features, linkage is the theme; the flow of water is its symbol; and the naturally opposing forces of water and rock are the sensory focus.

Linkages

Linkages between nature and the built environment are tangible assertions of compatibility. They should be evident at every scale of design, from distant views of a community to intimate spaces within it. They can be literal or visual, iterative or interpretive. They are effected through references to nature in built forms and through interconnections of natural and urban zones. Linkage can be achieved through the character of edges that join site and settlement, the natural elements that penetrate the boundaries between them and the views that bridge them, and the reiteration of natural processes in forms and materials.

The Quality of the Edge. Edge character is another word for transition. Whether abrupt or graded, edges can highlight the natural ebb and flow of the landscape. They can incorporate landmarks, revealing them to observers both inside and outside as important symbols of place. They can create gateways that coincide with visually important features or that open up to special views. In the intensity with which they pose contrasts and touch the senses, they can construct a meaningful experience for those passing from one realm to the other.

Views. One means of establishing linkage is using views as reminders of context. This requires respect for important lines of sight in the placement of structures and public open spaces, as in Vail, and it implies a referential site plan oriented to significant natural features, as in Whistler (see Chapter 10 for more on both communities).

Respect for Topography. Lack of facility with grades is a sure way to destroy the sense of linkage. Astute siting is critical. Excessive street gradients and awkward junctions of building and slope are among the first indications that builders were not at one with the site. Linkage can be reinforced in the way that structures meet the ground, tying the composition together horizontally, and in the way that streets and public spaces respond to slope gradient.

Connective Elements. Perhaps the most effective literal connections are landscape features that penetrate boundaries and touch the interior. Remnants of vegetation on the site can be retained as visually prominent, connective components of the urban landscape. Riparian corridors can be woven

through the heart of the community as part of a network of trails and urban green space.

In newer resort communities, these valuable linear connections are being recognized as primary organizing elements in urban design. In Beaver Creek, the creek was identified at the outset as the armature for the village's structure and as the best way to retain the sense of the natural landscape in the core (see Fig. 10-32). In Vail, amenities such as major recreational facilities (Fig. 9-60), nature preserves, and trails are continually being added to the Gore Creek corridor to improve it as a connector, turning it into a major place-making asset. A path along most of the stream frontage through town connects with a 40-mile bike trail over Vail Pass and into the neighboring county.

Very few older American mountain towns availed themselves of the full potential of these in-town connective features. Instead, most of them banished creeks to the backyard edge, built across meadows, cleared forests, and fought topography with their gridded streets. Today, those old towns angling for tourists are trying hard to redress the oversight by restoring natural connections.

At the gateway to Rocky Mountain National Park in Colorado, the historic town of Estes Park has constructed a park at the confluence of the two creeks that flow through town (Fig. 9-61). Stream-flow diversions, sitting places along the banks, and pedestrian bridges and stepping-stones all make the water more accessible. The park reestablishes the confluence as a prominent natural feature in the fabric of the community, a reversal from the years when the business district turned its back on the creek.

For residents of mountain towns, it is not enough just to see the high peaks at the periphery of town; nature needs to be brought closer. Acknowledging that wilderness cannot take the place of urban open space in a mountain town, Park City, Utah, in 1982 commissioned a parks master plan that recommended new recreation facilities, improvements in the town park along the underutilized stream corridor, and the linkage of disparate town-owned development parcels into a cohesive open-space network of parks and trails.

Linkage Despite Density. Even in the areas of greatest density, it is possible to integrate the natural landscape into the built environment. Water and green spaces can still function as a connective motif. Public spaces can be sited at important vantage points, and view corridors can be protected in order to focus on prominent natural features. Building clusters can reiterate the undulations of the land, its vertical scale, angles, colors, and textures. Evidence of geomorphic processes can be preserved and explained. Native materials can be used as unifying

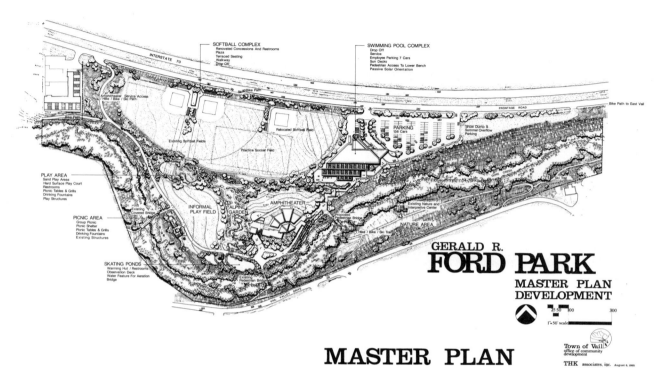

MASTER PLAN

Figure 9-60. *Gerald R. Ford Park is an important component of Vail's open space plan, which focuses on Gore Creek as a connector. THK Associates Inc., Denver, planning and landscape architecture.*

elements and design motifs, and urban forms abstracted from natural forms can interpret natural processes.

The Lost Sense of Place: Copper Mountain, Colorado. Even in the midst of dramatic mountain scenery, it is not as easy as it might seem to retain a sense of the natural place. Where extreme conditions conspire to make building difficult, as at Copper Mountain, it may even be tempting to think that the natural character can be replaced with something more hospitable.

At Copper—a ski resort opened in 1972 just west of the Continental Divide (Fig. 9-62)—the opportunities to use landscape images to lend character to the new community were immense. The site is a dramatically contained alluvial plain wedged between the Gore Range to the north and the Tenmile Range to the east and south. Five peaks soaring to almost 13,000 (4000 m) are embedded in the encircling ring of mountains. At just above 9700 feet (2960 m), Copper is one of the highest resort communities in the country.

Figure 9-61. *New riverfront park and promenade in Estes Park, Colorado, reclaimed the creek edge for pedestrians. Design Studios West, Denver, landscape architecture. Photo by Bob Joseph, Estes Park Urban Renewal Authority.*

245

Major alpine passes control highway access in every direction. Coming from the east, one approaches on the interstate through a narrow canyon; the village, dwarfed by the slopes behind it, is not visible until one is nearly there. After such a journey, the triangular plain is a natural respite. Between plain and slopes, there are grand contrasts in topography and scale. In these and other natural assets were tremendous place-making opportunities.

The gentler, forested slopes at the southern edge of the plain are less intimidating than the Tenmile ridge to the east. Visually, the edge can absorb development of considerable mass. The earliest buildings respected the pull of this edge, but

Figure 9-62. *View to the southwest, Copper Mountain Resort, Summit County, Colorado. Photo courtesy of Copper Mountain Inc.*

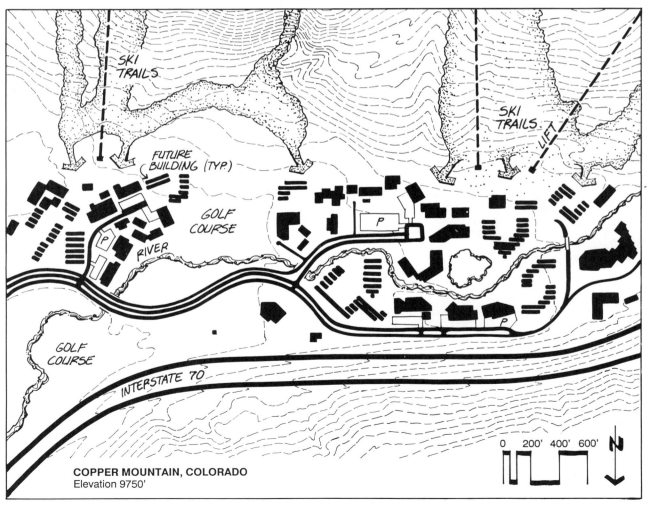

SKI TRAILS

SKI TRAILS

LIFT

FUTURE BUILDING (TYP.)

GOLF COURSE

RIVER

GOLF COURSE

INTERSTATE 70

0 200' 400' 600'

COPPER MOUNTAIN, COLORADO
Elevation 9750'

Figure 9-63.

Figure 9-64. *Copper Mountain's central pedestrian plaza and the view east toward the Tenmile Range.*

subsequent development obscured its magnetism (Fig. 9-63). Neither the siting nor the massing of buildings responds to the alluvial plain as a visual model for form or to the psychological importance of the plain as a place of shelter from the steep terrain.

Little in Copper Mountain's present form or layout reveals an awareness of the site's character. There is no strong reference to important views, sun, or natural features. Edges, other than the highway and the base of the ski slopes, are not apparent. Transitions between nature and the village are missing. Interior roads, unconstrained by topography, lack a natural rationale. Dispersed buildings leave public spaces exposed to the harsh winter climate (Fig. 9-64). Water—which first shaped this wind-swept high-altitude plain—is more ornament than connector.

The west fork of Tenmile Creek once meandered across this valley (Fig. 9-65), combining with the flow of tributary drainages to form ponds and wetlands. A high water table kept the forest on higher ground: Trees on the side slopes stop in a well-defined line just above the valley floor. Today, nothing remains of the original wetlands, for the village layout and the golf course ensured their demise. Yet the severe constraints of high altitude have frustrated efforts to replace them with a different landscape character.

The recently redeveloped Scottish links golf course, seeking identity in a competitive resort market, does not try to resurrect the patterns of the original landscape. To give the terrain some relief, hummocks adorn what once was flat. Ponds have been tidied up; their banks, no longer edged with wetland vegetation, are confined by upright timbers, the signature of the course's designer (Fig. 9-66). Though perhaps a visual surrogate for a wetland meadow, the golf course lacks its biological vitality and sensory interest.

Water in the new valley landscape does not play a connective role and has little amenity value. The meandering creeks were moved out of the way and combined in a new, straighter channel. But since then, management has spent almost a million dollars in an award-winning effort to renaturalize the bulldozed channel, placing thousands of boulders by hand.

Copper's buildings are bulky and dispersed, connected neither to the landscape nor to one another. This is due partly to the fact that the developer exercised little control over (or county officials did not enforce) the sequencing of development. Because of a weak political process, commitments to the intent of the development were left flexible. The first parcels to be developed were not the ones most important to the village core or to a sense of place.

As a result, structures went up with little concern for compactness, spatial connectedness, pedestrian vitality, or critical mass in the center of the village. Their scattered siting and excessively diverse architectural styles, ranging from rustic to brutal,

247

Figure 9-65. Copper Mountain site before development. Photo by U.S.D.A. Forest Service.

Figure 9-66. Tee on the redeveloped golf course at Copper Mountain. Pete and Perry Dye, golf course design.

Figure 9-67. *View south-southwest across the creek and artificial lake toward Copper Mountain's day lodge.*

COPPER MOUNTAIN
VILLAGE CORE CONCEPT SKETCH
OCTOBER 1987

Figure 9-68. *Copper's lake edge will be redeveloped and a major hotel constructed to intensify activity in the village core. Perspective sketch by Craig Schreiber, Land Art, Leadville. Courtesy of Copper Mountain Inc.*

discouraged a unified composition compatible with the landscape and with people's expectations of a sheltering village.

It is ironic that the large scale of buildings in the core did not translate into a concentration of activity. But in such an open, exposed high-altitude environment, roads and landscaping cannot make up for the connections lacking in the architecture and never provided for in the master plan.

Today, Copper Mountain is not yet a village and far from a community. It is the product of an earlier development environment, an agglomeration of visually unrelated, spatially disconnected architectural statements in an unnaturally reconstructed landscape. Had it been built a decade later, it would surely be different today.

The question is where to go from here with a resort that has a magnificent ski mountain. The current management is determined to fill in the village with a better sense of what it takes to make a dynamic place. In a drastically revised master plan, they have taken a fresh look at the original assumptions and have identified new program elements.

Their central objectives are to unify the village and animate the core, visually as well as functionally, by means of infill that brings down the scale, softens the streetscape, and strengthens the linkages. Bus routes and drop-off points will be realigned to reduce their impact on important pedestrian spaces. Memorable landmarks, new facades and landscaping, more work on the stream, design guidelines, consistent and more sophisticated materials, and even nonmetal roofs that hold the snow, are planned. The visual image of the village as a whole is being scrutinized with three-dimensional computer-modeling studies for every undeveloped lot.

One focus of attention is the area around the ice-skating pond in the center of the village. Intended as an activity hub, the pond lies adrift from any natural connection with the stream that feeds it (Fig. 9-67, compare with Keystone, Fig. 9-55). Its edges are uninteresting, exposed to weather and roof avalanches, and oriented away from the best views. In its present form, the pond is a void in the center of the village. Concepts for the area would increase the intensity of activity around the lake. A major hotel and a number of small buildings would be added along the lakeshore, and the visual interest of the edge would be improved by a new connection between the lake and the stream (Fig. 9-68).

In the planning environment of the 1960s, anything seemed possible, and there were fewer regulatory constraints. Today, there is a far better base of planning expertise and much stiffer competition. Visual quality, unique character, and human scale are

more valuable. Copper's new development strategies therefore give it a chance to become a more interesting place for people.

A PROCESS FOR SHAPING COMMUNITY FORM

In the quest for a sense of place, why do so many newer mountain communities disappoint? Although there are surely many contributing factors, one—the process of community design—may be at the root.

Designers can only influence, not control, the process by which a community's form evolves. In most communities, this process represents the interaction of many interest groups over a long period of time, making decisions that can set enduring patterns.

If communities are to develop in patterns sensitive to the needs of people and the values of place, the process by which they do it must be given some thought. Objectives must be articulated and debated, consensus won on ways to achieve them, and mechanisms put in place for their continuing review. Among the many steps and decisions that compose an ideal development process, the following are paramount in creating place-sensitive communities:

1. A statement of intent that embodies a shared vision, an ideal, and a set of goals for the community.
2. Articulated social objectives.
3. Rational projection of the community's maximum size.
4. Impartial analysis of land suitability and capability on sites under consideration.
5. Selection of a community site that accommodates program goals with respect for environmental constraints and that meets economic, social, and aesthetic objectives.
6. Controls on development in the access corridors and on adjacent lands.
7. Protection of important view corridors and natural features.
8. A site-sensitive circulation plan that can expand as the community grows and that incorporates alternative public transportation modes to reduce vehicle impacts.
9. A public open space system.
10. A plan for the community core in which siting, scale, massing, and orientation work together to attract and hold a critical mass of people.
11. Consensus on design guidelines for the community.
12. A legal process for reviewing design proposals and periodically revising community plans.

REFERENCES

Beaver Creek Resort Company. 1979. Design regulations: The village. Avon, Colo.

Chang, Ching-Yu, ed. 1978. *Process: Architecture/Lawrence Halprin.* Tokyo: Process Architecture.

Halprin, Lawrence. 1979. A report on *Taking Part.* Berkeley: College of Environmental Design, University of California.

Jackson, J. B. 1984. *Discovering the Vernacular Landscape.* New Haven, Conn.: Yale University Press.

Lippard, Lucy. 1983. *Overlay.* New York: Pantheon.

Royston, Hanamoto, Beck & Abey, Landscape Architects, and Livingston & Blayney, Planners, 1973. The Vail plan.

Town of Park City, Utah, and Gage Davis Associates, Landscape Architects. 1982. Park City parks master plan.

10
DESIGNING THE COMMUNITY CORE

It has been said that there are landscapes one can walk through, landscapes which can be gazed upon, landscapes in which one may ramble, and landscapes in which one may dwell. . . . Those fit for walking through or being gazed upon are not equal to those in which one may dwell or ramble.
　　　　　—Kuo Hsi (active ca. 1050–1090)

The core of a community is where people come together, a place for the congregation of strangers and friends that reflects the community's social and economic makeup. A typical community core contains restaurants and retail shops, offices and professional services, civic and cultural facilities, entertainment and nightlife, pedestrian amenities and promenades, parks and plazas. There is also a variety of housing within and around it to keep it filled with people.

A mountain community's core may seem an anomaly, an enclave with urban traits in the midst of wild territory. As the point of contact between urbanity and nature, it must provide a stage for concentrated activity without severing its connections with the natural environment. In terms of design, the core is a dilemma, as this is where it is easiest to lose the mountain context.

In any community, the principal design issue in the core is respect for social dynamics. The objective is to promote social vitality, interaction, and commercial exchange through the variables that design can affect: microclimate, sensory quality, scale, and spatial and functional relationships. In mountain communities, the designer must work with these variables in a manner that reveals the mountain context despite the core's greater density.

CATALYSTS OF SOCIAL VITALITY

Archetypal Traits

Community cores that function successfully as magnets share a number of attributes that catalyze human activity. Each of these archetypal traits compounds the potential of a central district to attract and hold people.

Diversity of Activities and Experiences. Thirty years ago, in a lecture on the nature of variety, critic Eugene Raskin noted, "Where the pattern of human activity contains only one element, it is impossible for the architecture to achieve a convincing variety . . ." (Jacobs 1961, p. 225). Diversity in the community core is a prerequisite for dynamism. Without it, monotony and artificiality can barely be disguised. Architecture is not enough, for the core is not just a tighter pattern of buildings and streets. Rather, it is a sequence of activity spaces created by buildings, a composition that derives its vitality not only from the buildings but also from the floor, the sky, the trees, the views, the arrangement of levels, and the people it attracts.

A Central Gathering Place. A viable community core has a focal outdoor place that people recognize as its center. It can be a store-lined street or a public plaza, a park or a promenade. Whatever it is, it has certain attributes that make it attractive to people: It is edged with lively, mutually supportive uses. Breaks in its enclosure may open to intriguing views of what is beyond. Its form at the edges blurs the boundaries between indoors and the outside. It may contain a prominent feature as a symbol of center: a monument, a fountain, public art, or some other attraction that invites congregation around it. It is subdivided into places for flow and places for lingering, eddies and enclaves where people can view the scene from a position of relative calm.

Subordination of the Automobile. Community cores filled with people at ease are not also filled with cars. Socially lively cores, where people linger to talk, stroll, eat, and watch other people, are structured to exclude the chaos of vehicular traffic. Convenient access, nearby parking, reasonable walking distances, and alternative modes of circulation help make the structure work.

Sensory Intricacy. The community core offers a multitude of sensory inducements to participate in one's surroundings. It promises complexities, contrasts, and kinetic qualities. When views, spaces, and experiences are sequentially revealed, the senses are energized, but they shut down when everything is exposed at once.

Meaning and Symbolism. A core that provides several layers of meaning is more interesting to those who live there. Too much clarity is boring, as it leaves no room for discovery.

In imageable communities, buildings and public

spaces add meaning through references to the setting's traditions, cultural roots, and natural history. Without this visual linkage between time and place, the built environment of the core would seem abstract, arbitrary, impersonal, and lacking any sense of the area's underlying character.

A Sense of the Whole. In communities whose core has a strong identity, there is evidence in its diversity of a respect for the whole, a sense of unity, and a clarity of functional organization.

Room for Change. "Leftover" spaces in the core provide room for growth and change without losing the core's established physical character. Room for change blunts the potentially deadening effects of excessive control and instantaneous development.

Individuality. By mandating a certain randomness, eclecticism, and individuality in detailing and ornamentation, a socially vigorous core gives evidence of people's personal involvement in its evolution.

A genuine community core contains a multiplicity

of uses and connections, attractions for all seasons, intriguing edges and spaces, and layers of social interaction and meaning. It evolves over time. Many comprehensively planned resorts, designed for a homogeneous market with limited interests, lack these complexities, but the vision for a resort community need not be this narrow. A vigorous, uncontrived place is an achievable long-term goal, provided that a framework is set up initially to encourage its evolution.

Design Variables: The Dynamics of Space

Dynamics: variation and contrast in force or intensity; the driving physical forces of any area; the pattern of change or growth.
— *Webster's Dictionary*

In the layout and design of the community core, certain dynamic variables—microclimate, sequence, scale, and structure—determine the ability of public spaces to attract people. Each of these is in turn affected by the natural environment in which all of them operate. It is by managing these variables that design is able to promote social vitality in the core.

Microclimate determines the seasonal utilization of important public spaces. It is an important part of what makes the core of a mountain community feel so different from that of other places, but if not managed appropriately, it can inhibit activity.

Sequential experiences contribute to the perception of diversity. Design that uses sequences—of spaces, views, and sensory details—to enhance interest makes the core a more intense and memorable experience. The kinetic and three-dimensional quality of the mountain landscape lends itself to the creation of sequential experiences that are bound to the natural context.

Scale affects the way in which people react psychologically to a place. In the mountains, spaces that have the proper scale and proportion attract people, whereas spaces that feel exposed, unenclosed, barren, or intimidating do not.

The core's structure affects the ebb and flow of movement. In this context, structure does not mean buildings, but the arrangement of buildings, spaces, and streets, which organizes spatial hierarchies and directs circulation. The structure influences the intensity of social activity because it corresponds to the ease of access to the core, the network of connections and their directional clarity, the logic of functional relationships among activities, and the absence of conflict between people and vehicles.

In the core, respect for the mountain environment means something else than it does in broader contexts of design. Here, avoiding hazards and respecting ecological constraints are no longer the dominant environmental concerns. Instead, the main concern becomes one of design opportunities, a search for ways to let the natural qualities of the landscape establish the special character of the core in order to enhance its appeal as a magnet for activity.

HABITABILITY OF SPACE: THE DYNAMICS OF MICROCLIMATE

Design that respects microclimate transforms spaces for human activity into the core's essential connectors. But design that ignores microclimate makes spaces inhospitable, dampens activity, impedes the intended flow through the core, and diminishes the intensity with which it is experienced.

The Objective. The concern for climate in the design of the community core begins with basic decisions about siting, circulation layout, and building massing, and it persists as an issue down to details of form and materials. Throughout the process, the main objective is to make outdoor space and circulation corridors as usable as possible for as much of the year as possible. This requires concern for sun, shelter, and safety.

Criteria for Microclimate Control. The habitability of a mountain community's core can be evaluated according to the utility of public spaces and circulation corridors, particularly in the winter:

1. Major public spaces should be shaped and oriented to reduce their exposure to the full force of the wind. The buildings massed around them should not markedly increase shading or wind velocities.
2. There should be places for people to linger or sit outdoors that are sited for maximum sun, shelter from the wind, and safety from snow and ice falling from roofs.
3. Walkways and steps that connect the pedestrian circulation system within the core should be safe and protected from the elements.

Guidelines for Microclimate Control

Concentrated Site Plans. The site plan for the core should be concentrated and compact. Tight clusters of moderately scaled, medium-density buildings are a better response to a harsh winter climate than dispersed siting, especially when social interaction is a goal and safe circulation a necessity. A concentrated plan minimizes safety hazards, reduces exposure to the elements, and is more energy efficient.

Until recently, the common response to

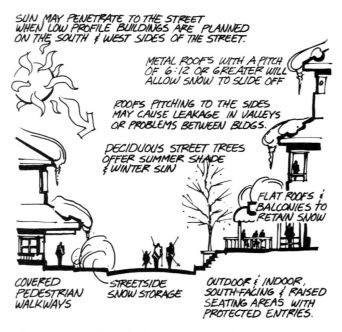

SUN MAY PENETRATE TO THE STREET WHEN LOW PROFILE BUILDINGS ARE PLANNED ON THE SOUTH & WEST SIDES OF THE STREET.

METAL ROOFS WITH A PITCH OF 6:12 OR GREATER WILL ALLOW SNOW TO SLIDE OFF

ROOFS PITCHING TO THE SIDES MAY CAUSE LEAKAGE IN VALLEYS OR PROBLEMS BETWEEN BLDGS.

DECIDUOUS STREET TREES OFFER SUMMER SHADE & WINTER SUN

FLAT ROOFS & BALCONIES TO RETAIN SNOW

COVERED PEDESTRIAN WALKWAYS

STREETSIDE SNOW STORAGE

OUTDOOR & INDOOR, SOUTH-FACING & RAISED SEATING AREAS WITH PROTECTED ENTRIES.

Figure 10-1. *Concepts for protecting pedestrians on the street.*

microclimate in contemporary Alpine and Andean ski resorts was to sidestep the issue by concentrating all social functions in large monolithic structures: "villages" compressed upward, designed with no expectation of activity outside the buildings except skiing (see Chapter 2, Recreation and Rebirth). Although some observers have argued that such villages are a valid response to climate, they violate expectations of social vitality (not to mention scale) by failing to provide, among other things, usable, connective outdoor spaces.

Compact site plans have also not been a consistent response in American ski resort communities. The temptation to spread out is especially strong where the valley's topography is relatively unrestrictive and the land has been divided into parcels for development by separate developers. A number of resorts are fairly dispersed, owing less, perhaps, to creative inadequacies than to the level of planning expertise at the time they were developed. In the most recently founded resorts, like Beaver Creek and Whistler, compact form has been a much higher priority.

Protected Pedestrian Corridors. The intensity of pedestrian activity on a mountain street is partially a function of its alignment, which affects the amount of sun and wind exposure, and the architecture of its edge, which affects the extent to which snow and ice may be a problem. Streets should be aligned and buildings massed to screen the wind, avoid wind

funneling, and admit adequate natural light to populated spaces.

As a general rule, main streets aligned with the trend of a mountain valley funnel the wind. This is often a problem in older mountain mining towns, where the gridded primary streets coincide with the valley trend and give the wind an unobstructed path. Where the access highway is also the town's main commercial thoroughfare, exposure may be even greater because of the road's extra width.

Architectural elements that edge the street can be designed not only to protect people moving along the corridor but also to enable eddies to form in the flow of foot traffic. One street cross section (Fig. 10-1) illustrates some concepts designed to make the street safer and more usable.

Solar Access. In the middle latitudes, street alignment makes a significant difference in the amount of winter sun its frontages receive. Streets or pedestrian corridors running north to south, like Bridge Street in Vail, expose both sides of the street to the sun sometime during each day. In contrast, on a street running east to west, the north-facing side is always in shadow, making it less desirable for outdoor activities and usually creating major problems with ice accumulation on shaded pavements (Fig. 10-2). The solar advantages of a southerly frontage may be sought for individual buildings, but if the appeal of a whole street corridor is at stake, an alignment that relegates one frontage to constant winter shade may be undesirable.

Solar access to public spaces should be protected from subsequent building around them. Urban design guidelines adopted by the town of Vail in 1980, for example, specify that new buildings and expansions in the core not be allowed to change significantly the microclimate in existing public spaces or rights-of-way (Fig. 10-3).

In Beaver Creek, the pedestrian corridor is aligned roughly north northeast to south southwest and, when completed, should get adequate afternoon sun. However, the height (five stories) and mass of the buildings on the uphill (north-facing) edge, combined with the narrow width in some places, may make the street less hospitable to outdoor use at most other times (Fig. 10-4).

Sheltering Building Masses. Even on winter days in a mountain town, outdoor spaces will collect people if there is a sunny place to sit, shelter from the wind, and something to watch. But these spaces don't occur by chance. Building footprints, heights, and massing must be determined with an eye toward the microclimate of the outdoor rooms that their arrangement creates (Fig. 10-5).

Orientation is critical in the middle latitudes.
— *Kevin Lynch*, Site Planning

Figure 10-2. *The main street in Telluride, Colorado, after a heavy snow. Awnings on the right and bigger snowbanks on the left mark the street's east–west alignment. Photo circa 1880s, Denver Public Library, Western History Department.*

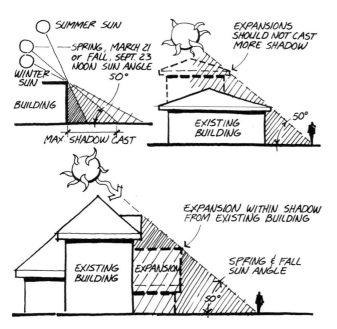

Figure 10-3. *Solar access guidelines from the town of Vail's Urban Design Guideplan. Gage Davis International, Boulder, Colorado, planning and landscape architecture.*

In LionsHead, microclimate control in the pedestrian mall was a victim of excessive building scale, lack of enclosure, and oversized spatial proportions. Aligned in an east–west direction, one side of the mall has a less favorable solar orientation. To counter the problem of icing, heat coils were originally installed under the concrete pavement, but the system, since removed, was unreliable and expensive to operate.

In Vail's 25-year-old core, the challenge now is not so much to create warm outdoor spaces as to protect and utilize those that are already there. As the buildings in the core are improved, wall configurations and interior uses are gradually being rearranged to take advantage of the obvious opportunities outside. The result has been the addition in recent years of sidewalk cafes and sitting areas in sunny spaces previously underutilized. As testimony to the ability of a hospitable microclimate to generate activity, one of the most popular gathering spots in Vail is a terrace cafe added some years later to the south-facing wall of a lodge at the main street's principal intersection (Fig. 10-6).

257

Figure 10-4. Completed portion of Beaver Creek's pedestrian mall.

Snow Removal. The design of outdoor spaces in the core must, despite the density, facilitate snow removal and storage. Otherwise, accumulated snow will become a safety hazard, an impediment to intended patterns of use, and a costly nuisance to remove. Virtually every mountain town suffers from the failure to anticipate where snow will shed from roofs, how it will be cleared, and where it can be stored.

In general, primary circulation corridors should be relatively easy to clear of snow. The siting of places for people to linger or sit should be coordinated with roof configurations so that roof avalanches do not threaten wintertime use. Detailing should reflect a concern for durability (see Chapter 12 for more details).

Special Effects. Outdoor places where people can enjoy the weather (even bad weather) are a special response to climate. The site plan might include sheltered places to watch snow falling, to listen to the rain, to bask in late afternoon light, to catch sunsets, to look at stars, and to warm up while still outside.

Compatible Uses. Careful siting and massing may create an agreeable microclimate, but even the warmest outdoor space will be underutilized unless it is edged with compatible activities and detailed with amenities, like seating, that encourage its use. Some of the most hospitable outdoor spaces along southerly frontages are adjacent to offices, private condominiums, and stores instead of more compatible activities, like restaurants, that could use the spaces to better advantage.

When pedestrian corridors are viewed as a series of usable rooms rather than as negative spaces between buildings, the need for climate control becomes more apparent. In the mountains, the successful management of microclimate requires three-dimensional control of building elevations and massing to produce outdoor spaces that are used year-round. Because habitable outdoor space provides the link with the natural environment that gives a mountain town its unique identity, microclimate must be given top priority.

Figure 10-5. *Sunny plaza in the new resort village of Val Morel, France. Photo by H. Peter Wingle.*

Figure 10-6. *Called the "100% intersection," this sunny crossroad in Vail Village has become a central outdoor gathering spot.*

Figure 10-7. *The pedestrian main street in Whistler Resort Village. Photo by British Columbia Enterprise Corporation.*

DIVERSITY OF SPACE: THE DYNAMICS OF SEQUENCE

Siting and massing buildings to enclose usable outdoor spaces are the first tasks in developing a socially active community core. The next most important task is to assemble the spaces as a connected sequence of interesting experiences that encourage movement through the core. The assembly of this sequence can be described as choreography.

The Objective. Choreography in urban design is concerned with the hierarchy and variety of spaces, the rhythm of their occurrence, the activities and features in and around each space, and the manner in which these are opened to view. The intent in choreographing pedestrian experience is to enhance the core's diversity by making it into a sensory urban journey. Important design decisions in building a sequence are how to connect the spaces, how to clarify their relative importance and function, how and where to punctuate them with attractions, and how to resolve conflicts between pedestrians and vehicles.

Although the concept of choreography is urban in origin, the design context in mountain towns and resorts differs from that of urban settings. Because the core area and the population of a mountain town are so much smaller, the sequence must be more concentrated. Because so many people in a mountain environment are there on leisure time, activities and visual character must reflect not only a different mix of needs and expectations but also stronger images of the natural scenery that people have come to see.

Criteria. The dynamism of the core as a sequence of experiences is measured by the diversity, visual character, level of interest, and continuity of serial attractions.

1. The sequence should establish visual connections between the core and the natural landscape beyond. Important view relationships and lines of sight should be respected and used, where appropriate, to organize the layout of building masses and the enclosure of outdoor spaces. Important spaces should not be so enclosed by buildings that they shut out the natural context.
2. The sequence should incorporate physical connections between the core and the natural environment beyond, using native vegetation, water, and other naturally connective elements in the landscape for structure and theme.
3. The sequence should contain references to the natural context in design motifs, symbols, materials, forms, and themes.

Wherever people are involved, the sensuous quality of a place is as important as cost or shelter or circulation.
— *Kevin Lynch,* Site Planning

Guidelines for Successful Choreography

Lively core areas have some things in common that can be used as guidelines for sequencing: They have subordinated the car to people on foot, and they offer a network of linked spaces that vary in size and character. Through forms, materials, views, and public artworks, the sequence of spaces constantly refers to the natural setting. The spaces contain popular landmarks that have become symbols of place; they are rich with detail; and they support multiple activities. In effect, these commonalities are the recurring urban design objectives that communities everywhere seek to attain in choreographing intensively used, socially dynamic cores.

Absence of Vehicular Congestion. The pedestrian sequence is not designed to be experienced from a car. The speed, noise, congestion and space consumption of automobile traffic defeat the desired quality and scale of a socially vital core. Where the disruptive impact of the automobile has been eliminated from the core, as in Vail, the quality of

Figure 10-8. *Children's fountain and plaza in Vail Village supports a diversity of activity in all seasons.*

public spaces has improved dramatically. Convenient access and proximity to parking are essential to the pedestrian sequence, but the traffic itself should be kept outside.

Diversity of Use. Urban critic Jane Jacobs wrote in her landmark critique of urban streets: "In places stamped with the monotony and repetition of sameness, you move, but in moving you seem to have gotten nowhere. . . . [These places] lack natural announcement of direction and movement . . . and so they are deeply confusing" (1961, p. 223). Without diversity, sequences lack the ability to entice people through them. With it, people come just to be there (Fig. 10-7). "People are most interested in other people. The sight and sound of human beings in action are usually the prominent features of the perceptual form of a place" (K. Lynch 1971, p. 200).

Public space in resort communities is too often envisioned simply as the means to reach lodging and to expose shops and restaurants to those walking by. But this vision sells it short, for there is far more to urban life than shopping. Public open space can by itself contribute much more to the intensity of activity in the core, even if the buildings flanking it add few, if any, other uses. What is needed is a broader perspective on the variety of activity that the urban landscape can sustain and an insistence on more versatile open space. Outdoor spaces with more of the diverse attributes of urban parks—sculpture, fountains and play areas, vegetation and flowers, sitting areas in sun and by water, good views, and places for solitude and for movement—generate activity on their own (Fig. 10-8).

Subdivided and Linked Spaces. People are drawn through a pedestrian zone by the promise that what is around the corner is not more of the same. Thus when the whole of a large space is revealed at once, interest flags. Breaking the zone into hierarchies of interlocking subspaces, clarifying spatial edges, constructing an unbroken chain of visual and physical connections between spaces, and revealing serial views of what is yet to be encountered are techniques that fortify the sequence of experiences.

The three-dimensionality of the mountain landscape can be used to help structure the sequence, define and enclose spaces, locate edges, and introduce different angles of view. In this way, outdoor rooms, although linked, can be differentiated in scale, dimension, and composition to suit desired goals for diversity of use and spatial character (Fig. 10-9).

Meaningful Landmarks. Focal elements are part of any sequence of spaces and experiences, helping orient visitors and distinguishing one space from

261

Figures 10-9 and 10-10. *Image sketches for Beaver Creek pedestrian mall highlight the use of grade changes and focal elements to subdivide and link outdoor spaces. Drawings by Carlos Diniz Associates, Los Angeles, courtesy of Beaver Creek Resort Company.*

another. They mark progress and points of climax and engage people in their environment, thereby encouraging them to react and participate (Fig. 10-10).

The design of focal features carries a responsibility to discern the images and symbols that have meaning for the local area and to be faithful in form to the natural processes that formed the regional landscape. In any locale, feature elements can become imageable landmarks that color the identity of individual spaces, but this is less likely where the object of focus is unrelated to the history, personality, or natural character of the place.

Figure 10-10.

Sensory Details.   Sensory stimulus derives from intricacy, variety, and contrast. It is the finely detailed element that embellishes space with little discoveries, with layered meanings and levels of perception, and with evidence of the context and individuals' contributions (Fig. 10-11).

Ornament and details in public spaces add to visual intricacy and, in the mountains, are consonant with people's expectations of character and spatial intimacy. Sensory qualities in the natural landscape — in the water, rock, native vegetation, views, sounds, and contrasts between sunlight and shadow — are

263

Figure 10-11. *Detail-filled street in the village of Grimentz, Canton of Valais, Switzerland. Photo courtesy of Swiss National Tourist Office.*

abundant and should be used to enrich the urban core.

The embellishment of public spaces depends equally on public policy and individual enterprise. Policies that encourage eclecticism and individual expression are necessary for the sensory quality of public space.

Choreographing Pedestrian Movement: Vail Village, Colorado. The core of Vail (Figs. 10-12, 10-13) illustrates a highly successful effort to develop

an appealing, regionally inspired walking experience. In the town's short history, the pedestrian core has evolved into a lively, visually loaded sequence that reflects its alpine context (in both an indigenous and an imported sense).

The sequence begins at the exit from the earth-covered parking structure (Fig. 10-14), where a panorama of the clocktower against the ski slopes, a favorite of photographers, opens to view. Pedestrians move from the darkness of the garage into the bright

Figure 10-12. *Vail Village pedestrian core. Detail from a watercolor by Stanley Doctor, American Society of Architectural Perspectivists, Boulder, Colorado, courtesy of town of Vail.*

high-altitude light, from confinement into expansiveness, from urban concrete walls into a profusion of native vegetation. Along the stairs descending to a plaza at the edge of Gore Creek, small viewing areas are positioned where people can stop to get oriented and take a picture.

The plaza at the base of the steps is a gathering place outside the gates where arriving visitors congregate. It has places to sit overlooking the creek, sheltered places to wait, and an information kiosk.

The shuttle bus stop here is the main drop-off point for the ski lifts and the center of town. The focal element in the plaza is a fountain of massive local boulders. With its broad, flat rock surfaces, it is a fountain meant to play in, easier to reach than the water in the stream channel nearby.

At the creek crossing, the flow of traffic narrows radically (Fig. 10-15) to cross Gore Creek. The gateway to the pedestrian precinct is a rough wooden covered bridge, an image associated with country

265

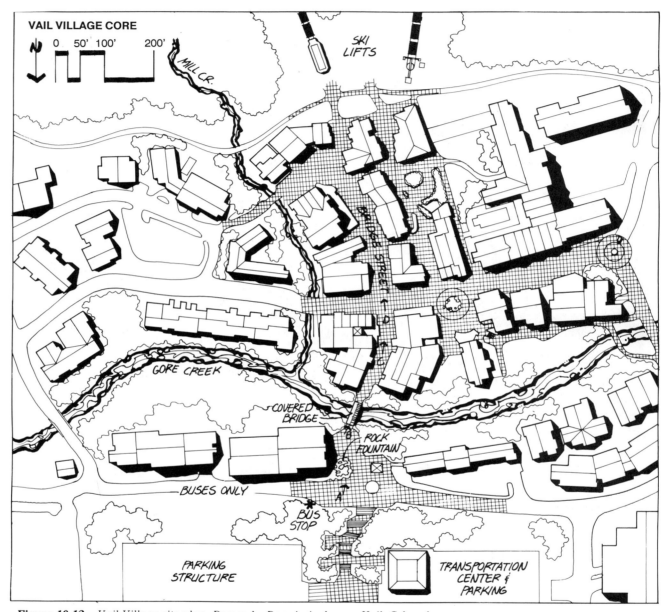

Figure 10-13. *Vail Village site plan. Drawn by Dennis Anderson, Vail, Colorado.*

villages. Although it is not common in the history of these mountains, no one seems to mind. It has become a landmark here, part of the image and ambience of Vail and a symbol of its distinctive character.

Inside the pedestrian core, the streets are lined with retail shops, services for visitors and local residents, restaurants, outdoor cafes, and attractive window displays. Planter boxes are filled with flowers in summer, and public art is sprinkled throughout the zone (Fig. 10-16).

Bridge Street, the main axis, has been the heart of Vail since the town's founding in 1962. An innovative concept for its time, the street was conceived as a small, mixed-use corridor. It ranges in width from 40 to 50 feet (12 to 15 m) and is edged with adjoining mixed-use buildings of no more than three stories, designed in white stucco variations on a Swiss Alpine theme. Running perpendicular to the trend of the valley and counter to the direction of winter storm winds, it is well sheltered. It has a gradual gradient, gaining just over 30 feet (10 m) in elevation in the

Figures 10-14 through 10-17. *Sequence of views through Vail's pedestrian core. Photos are keyed (A) through (D) on the site plan, Fig. 10-13.*

Figure 10-14. (*View A.*)

Figure 10-15. (*View B.*)

Figure 10-16. (*View C.*)

Figure 10-17. (*View D.*)

People like *schmaltz.*
  —*Terry Minger, former town manager, Vail*

quarter mile or so from the creek to the lifts.

The curve in Bridge Street is important to the visual control of the sequence, giving it the magnetism of things promised but not yet wholly visible (Fig. 10-17). Varied building setbacks lead to small sitting nooks and doorways. Second-story overhangs, balconies, and flower boxes hint of other perspectives from which to participate in the activity of the street. As bonuses, three cross-axis intersections along the street frame vistas of the Gore Range to the east.

The buildings that terminate the upper end of Bridge Street, near the ski lifts, are not a strong climax, especially in summer, but improvements are planned, and the continuity of attractions along the axis maintains momentum and moves people to the top of the street anyway.

It is significant to the social vitality of the core and the continuity of the pedestrian sequence that most of the buildings on Bridge Street and its cross axis, Gore Creek Drive, were developed separately as small contiguous parcels. Although a number of developers were involved and the architectural guidelines in the town's earliest years were relatively loose, the buildings of the core are remarkably similar in style and scale, but eclectic enough in storefront detailing to maintain interest along the street.

It is also significant that from the first season, Bridge Street appeared fully formed, although in fact there has been considerable additional development along the street since then. Throughout its evolution, the street's character and texture have remained consistent. As an inducement to building, the town has gradually increased the allowable square footage in the core by over 50 percent. That, combined with the scarcity of undeveloped land and high land costs in the core, has led to a wave of building expansions. Yet even though many of the original parcels have been redeveloped, the human scale of the core has remained virtually unchanged.

In most of the expansions, building mass has been added in the rear of the street-front buildings, where it does not impose on the street, and roofs have been stepped back to preserve solar access to important spaces. View corridors were identified by public consensus and have been zealously protected. For the most part, it has only been at the perimeters of the core—the highway edge and the base of the ski slopes—that taller buildings have been permitted (Fig. 10-18).

As the core has filled in, development along its subsidiary streets has greatly added to the diversity of activity. Additional fountains, sidewalk cafes, shopping alleys, plazas, and improved physical connections with Gore Creek have enriched the pedestrian experience.

Founded as a real estate venture by Vail Associates, Inc., Vail voted four years later, in 1966, for municipal incorporation. During its subsequent growth, it has helped immensely that local residents value the human scale of the original village and

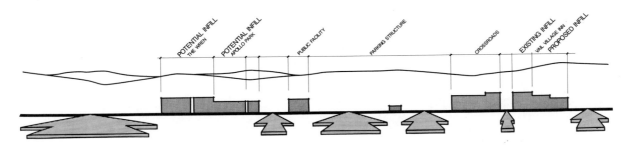

VIEW CORRIDORS (ELEVATION FROM FRONTAGE ROAD)

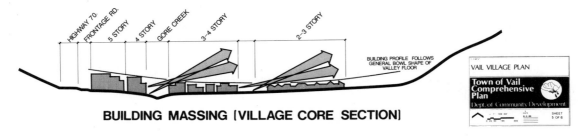

BUILDING MASSING (VILLAGE CORE SECTION)

Figure 10-18. *Building height profiles were included in the Town of Vail Comprehensive Plan (1986) to protect important view corridors and keep large building masses at the highway edge of town.*

269

have actively sought to retain it. Periodic public meetings with design consultants have assisted the town in identifying the physical factors that determine apparent scale and in achieving consensus on the value of controlling them. Without the leadership of a municipal entity to manage change and the active involvement of local residents in setting objectives to preserve the core's character, it is unlikely that Vail Village would have evolved as felicitously as it has.

Sequencing to Revitalize the Grid: Aspen, Colorado. One older mountain town that has so far managed competing growth pressures without sacrificing the character of its original center is Aspen. A typical gridded Victorian mining town, it has come back from hard times since skiing put it in the resort business in the late 1940s. Thirty years later, traffic and parked cars had overwhelmed the business district, seriously detracting from its appeal. (Still a problem, they are a primary focus of municipal planning.)

To reduce conflicts and restore the intensity of people-oriented activity in the core, the town decided to devote to pedestrians one block on each of three adjoining streets in the center of town (Fig. 10-19).

Figure 10-19. *View of downtown Aspen, Colorado, with arrows indicating streets that were converted to a pedestrian mall in 1976.*

Figure 10-20. *View down one segment of the Aspen mall shows how the street was subdivided with linear planting strips. Robin Molny, Aspen, Colorado, mall architect.*

The transformation of the streets into an auto-free mall, completed in 1976, successfully replaced divisive congestion with a congenial sequence of linear activity spaces.

Before the mall was constructed, the streets, including the building setbacks on both sides, were about 70 to 80 feet (21 to 25 m) across. To develop a sequence from these large, undifferentiated spaces, two rows of aspen trees were planted in cobbled drainage swales to subdivide the streets lengthwise (Fig. 10-20). This created a sunny, protected central aisle for sitting and strolling, flanked on either side by narrower shopping lanes against the buildings. In summer, the trees reinforce the sense of enclosure and intimacy, filling spaces that might otherwise be too wide for the two-story height of the buildings. In winter, the leafless trees admit sun to the space all day, and the medians are used for snow storage (see Fig. 12-23).

Each of the three blocks has a distinctive character. Walkways along the store windows are regularly interrupted by protruding arcades and sidewalk cafes, and in some places they flow into recessed entries, cutaway basement spaces, lateral alleys, and small pocket spaces between buildings. Intersections are marked by sculptures, fountains, and views of the ski slopes (Fig. 10-21). The intrigue of the sequence is aided by the fact that the three segments of the mall are at right angles to one another, rather than laid end to end on the same street.

Successful revitalization of the old grid depended partially on the strategic selection of the streets to be closed to cars. Within the pedestrian area, or no more than one or two blocks from it, are most of the assets and symbols that define a real community: the town hall and court house, the historic Wheeler Opera House and Hotel Jerome, the police station, churches, the town park, two movie theaters, and a hardware store. The mall takes advantage of these universally recognized symbols of community to reaffirm the town's identity.

At the time the mall was planned, it was clear that it could not satisfy all the town's commercial needs. Still needed were the high-traffic services that require convenient access by car: a supermarket and a post office, neither of which fit comfortably in the historic district. A subsidiary retail node, containing largely nonredundant services, was developed near enough to the new mall to reduce the pressure of auto congestion in the downtown core without dampening its vitality.

Aspen's new pedestrian core benefits from several features of the town's existing organization. First, the historic commercial district is not on the same street as the highway into town, which is two blocks removed. This made it possible to circumvent major

Figure 10-21. *Downtown Aspen street with ski slopes behind.*

conflicts between pedestrians and cars and to avoid interrupting existing access patterns into town.

Second, the mall is near the primary ski lift but not right at its base, allowing the pedestrian district to develop a life of its own in all seasons. This suggests that the core is more likely to attract a critical mass of people when it is sited at the crossroads to a variety of destinations rather than connected too closely to a single—and seasonal—attraction. The mall's central location out of the shadow of the ski slopes improves traffic for retailers, offers better solar orientation, enhances summertime appeal, and facilitates future adjustments in the core as new activities are added.

In a mountain town, the street begs to be visually complicated. Punctuated by historical architecture and well-crafted ornamentation, the Aspen mall offers a hierarchy of subspaces that are both comprehensible and engaging. Aspen provides what the visitor hopes for: representational imagery, experienced sequentially, that evokes a landscape and a history unique to these mountains.

271

Scale is an elaborate and complex coding system . . . by which things are related to a whole, to each other and to people. The result can be a . . . clear message in which an ordered hierarchy . . . is revealed.
— *Charles Moore,* Dimensions: Space, Shape and Scale in Architecture

PERCEPTION OF SPACE: THE DYNAMICS OF SCALE

No single design factor is more important to the success of an urban project in the mountains than scale. The mass and height of buildings, together with the dimensions of the outdoor spaces they define, control the perception of scale in the built environment. This perception, in turn, controls the level of comfort that people feel in the place. In any community, managing the mass required by increasing densities in the core without overwhelming people by the scale is a pressing development issue. In a mountain town, where the prevailing sense of the region is rural rather than urban, the issue takes on added significance.

Scale is not the same as size. Rather, it is a measure of relative size, the comparison of the size of one thing with that of another. In the mountains, designers must reconcile the scale of the landscape with a scale of human proportions. How they make this transition from vast to intimate scale is a key factor in the vitality and image of any mountain community.

One common mistake in planning a community core is the failure to understand what animates it. The developers of overscaled villages assume that they can generate activity in the core simply by aggregating large-scale, high-density structures around the spot marked center on the master plan, but neither scale nor density guarantees dynamism. Communities instinctively concentrate a diversity of uses in a central area and then grow outward as population expands.

Appropriate scale in the core of a mountain town is to some extent a judgment call, but the decision must relate to the needs and expectations of those people who will spend time there. The most reliable guideline may come from observing how people use existing spaces, for this roughly indicates how they respond to various scales and proportions.

The Objective. The goal in designing a community's core is to create a multichambered container that invites human activity. The scale should be consistent with people's expectations for the core of a mountain community, and the spatial proportions should suit the intensity and kind of intended activities in an amenable microclimate.

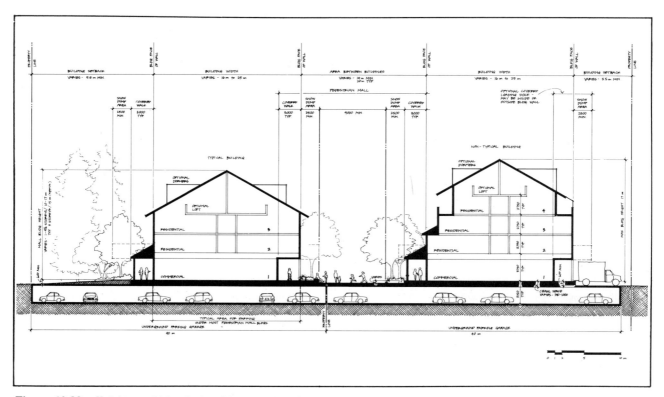

Figure 10-22. *Height-to-width relationships specified for the expansion area in Whistler Resort Village. Eldon Beck Associates, Novato, California, landscape architects; courtesy of British Columbia Enterprise Corp.*

Guidelines for Scale

Buildings of Modest Size. In a mountain community, buildings that avoid the monumental yield many benefits: They enable individuals to express their attachment to place, preserve the community's fabric and spatial texture, facilitate physical connections, tolerate incremental change and infill, enhance diversity, and cast small shadows.

Height-to-Width Relationships. In streets and public spaces, the relationship of the height of building walls to the horizontal extent of public spaces adjacent to them should be appropriate to both use and climate (Fig. 10-22). If the spaces are too wide, they will seem unenclosed and exposed. If they are too narrow and the enclosing walls are too tall, they will seem cold and confining, perhaps even menacing.

Among the variables that affect the perception of spatial dimensions are building massing and scale, facade and roof configurations, varied setbacks, stepbacks of upper stories, variations in grade level, floor plane and wall textures, spatial enclosure, and the presence of elements that break up a space's volume. An important variable is the character and transparency of ground-floor facades, which should exhibit variety in both use and physical form. Microclimate is a variable to the extent that poor orientation to the sun and wind make a space seem larger and more exposed.

Connections with the Natural Context. Views, vegetation, and water features are means to effect transitions between the core and the natural setting. Large building scale and high density can preclude this connection. That is, the core must be porous enough to let something of the natural landscape penetrate, both visually and physically. Porosity in the built environment is related to view-oriented massing and moderation in building scale.

A Study in Proportions: LionsHead at Vail, Colorado. Like Vail Village, the LionsHead mall (Figs. 10-23, 10-24) was conceived as a mixed-use corridor linking parking to ski lifts. The original master plan called for buildings in roughly the same height range as Vail's but somewhat higher in density, with living units above ground-floor shops and restaurants. Problems in the marketplace, however, threatened to leave Vail Associates, Inc., the developer and ski area operator, with operating deficits on its real estate and cost overruns on the new LionsHead gondola. Hoping to use real estate sales to generate cash flow, the densities were

increased, and the building heights were raised to seven or eight stories.

Taller buildings precluded stick-built construction, and so precast concrete was introduced to limit the costs of steel-frame, elevator buildings (see Fig. 9-7). The unadorned architecture makes no reference to place and little to views or landmarks. The only focal feature of note is the gondola terminal's clock tower, which divides the main axis into two segments, neither longer than about 1000 feet (300 m).

The spaces between the buildings do not have congenial proportions. The width of the mall ranges from 70 to 100 feet (20 to 30 m) across, and the two primary public spaces measure roughly 160 feet by up to 250 feet (50 m by 75 m). Before the mall's redevelopment, the spaces were largely undifferentiated, nondirectional, and lacking in sensory details. Landscaping was added to the original plan to soften its stark urban look, but it was ambivalent in character, almost suburban, and made snow removal troublesome (Figs. 10-25, 10-26). It could not by itself help the sense of enclosure or intricacy.

Another factor contributing to the mall's chill was its microclimate. In contrast with Bridge Street's north–south alignment, the main axis in LionsHead's core runs east to west, parallel to the trend of the Gore Creek valley. This decision intensified winter shading and wind funneling, and it also prevented using the creek as an amenity in the core.

LionsHead was not an immediate commercial success. It was perceived as overscaled and uninviting and did not feel as though it were in the mountains. It had trouble attracting a sustained flow of pedestrian traffic. Initial condominium sales were slow, and retailers and restaurants struggled.

In 1972, the LionsHead mall was dedicated to the town of Vail, and in 1980, after extensive public workshops with property owners and merchants, a redevelopment plan for the LionsHead core was prepared. The primary objective of the plan was to reestablish a pedestrian scale, increase visual intricacy, and generally make the place livelier. The concept plan subdivided the mall's large spaces with new steps, ramps, and planting areas positioned to improve the exposure of shops to pedestrian flows.

In 1983, town residents approved a $2.6 million bond issue to fund the improvement program, which was completed in December 1984 (Figs. 10-27, 10-28). Merchants had identified landscaping as important to the mall's ambience; the total planted area was reduced but more purposefully sited, using native stone walls to define the edges. Over 60,000 square feet of new unit paving was installed, along with more seating, cafe spaces, better lighting, and the new fountain.

Figure 10-23. *LionsHead core, Vail, Colorado. Detail from a watercolor by Stanley Doctor, American Society of Architectural Perspectivists, Boulder, Colorado. Courtesy of town of Vail.*

The design team also recommended that property owners make small-scale additions to their first and second stories to narrow the corridor, add storefront variety, and hide the height and scale of larger buildings from street level (Fig. 10-29). Other recommendations that depended on private initiative were new arcades, awnings, patios, and more transparent commercial facades. These changes are proceeding at a slower pace.

The improvements succeeded in some important functional respects: Emergency access was improved; pedestrian flows were reoriented; snow removal concerns were accommodated; and space for large outdoor events was provided. But the main public spaces, now more urban and hard edged, are still too big (Fig. 10-30) and still lack intricacy, variety, focus, and diversity. More needs to be done to achieve an enticing sequence of spaces.

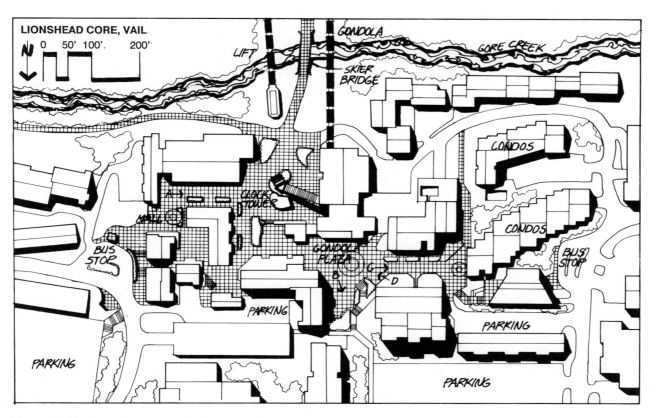

Figure 10-24. *LionsHead site plan. Drawn by Dennis Anderson, Vail, Colorado.*

Figure 10-25. (*View A, before.*)

Figure 10-26. (*View B, before.*)

Figures 10-25 through 10-30. *Sequence of views in the LionsHead core, keyed to the site plan (Fig. 10-24): axial view (A) toward the clocktower before the redevelopment of the mall (Fig. 10-25) and after (Fig. 10-27); view (B) of the mall's central plaza before (Fig. 10-26) and after (Fig. 10-28) redevelopment; view (C) of the western half of the mall, showing extension of retail space into the pedestrian corridor (Fig. 10-29); view (D) of the central plaza (Fig. 10-30).*

Figure 10-27. (*View A, after.*)

Figure 10-28. (*View B, after.*)

Figure 10-29. (*View C.*)

Figure 10-30. (*View D.*)

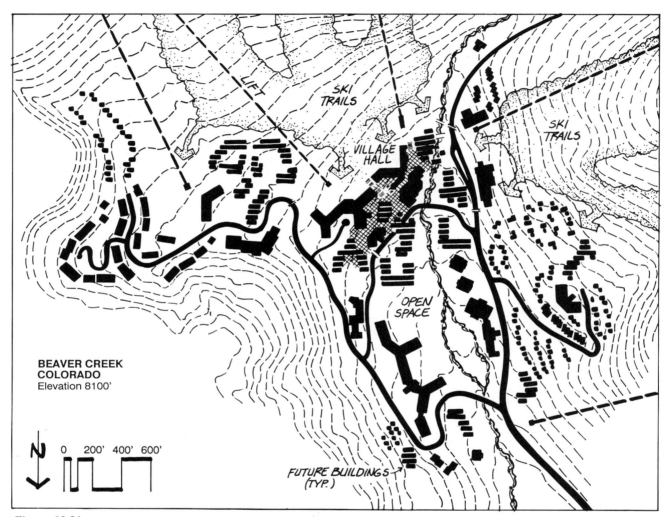

**BEAVER CREEK
COLORADO**
Elevation 8100'

0 200' 400' 600'

LIFT

SKI
TRAILS

VILLAGE
HALL

SKI
TRAILS

OPEN
SPACE

FUTURE BUILDINGS
(TYP.)

Figure 10-31.

**A Study in Scale and Style: Beaver Creek,
Colorado.** In the planning stages of Beaver Creek
(Fig. 10-31), much attention was devoted to image,
scale, and social vitality. The desired image, described
in the resort company's design regulations, was that
of a "remote village with its own identity, an
imaginable place . . ." (1979, p. 1).

Vail Associates, Inc., the developer, recognized that
distant impressions of the village were as important
to this image as experiences within it. So, from a
distance, the village was envisioned as a intimate,
tight composition spanning the valley like a bridge.
Conceptually, it would grace the upper edge of a
meadow within the natural boundaries formed by the
slopes on three sides, and the riparian corridor would
serve as its connective armature (Fig. 10-32). Though
the resort, which opened in 1981, is still in the
developmental stage, these concepts are intact and
have had a positive effect on its emerging identity.

The perception of human scale from a distance is
not always the reality up close, however, as Beaver
Creek's designers were aware. Within the village, they
felt that desired images would be dependent on
architectural styles (see Chapter 11, The Central
Rockies: Regional Revival) and the quality of public
outdoor spaces. The resort company's 1979 design
regulations for the village core make clear the desired
human scale and emphasize the role of buildings in
defining congenial public spaces (Fig. 10-33):

*Within the streets and public spaces of the project . . . ,
the exterior walls become the dominant element,
establishing the overall scale, and defining the public
spaces and pedestrian circulation routes within the
Village. It is important that the sequence of public
streets, walls and plazas be continuous within the
Village, enhanced by minor angular changes with an
avoidance of rigid 90° patterns. The subtle changes*

within wall and street alignments will create interesting streets and walls with constantly changing frontages and points of focus. . . . In order to achieve continuity within the landscape and within the Village itself, it is important to have building-to-building and building-to-public open space connections. . . .

[The] relative tightness of spaces within the commercial core area has been established to create the scale of the pedestrian village. . . . It is important to consider the "void" or exterior spaces between buildings which will provide the public spaces, streets and arcades within the Village. (Beaver Creek 1979, pp. 3, 25)

What is interesting about these statements of design intent is that they were not particularly effective as guidelines for scale. Nowhere in the design regulations is wall height acknowledged as the other essential variable in spatial relationships. "Tightness" of spaces seems to refer only to the distance between walls, but this alone cannot control relative scale or determine how spaces are perceived. And despite the clearly stated intent, it can be argued that the buildings in Beaver Creek's village core, viewed up close, are considerably bigger than human scale (Fig. 10-34).

High land costs and the large size of individual development parcels contributed to the buildings' scale. In the development guidelines for each parcel, heights were limited, but densities were not specified. The developers were thus inclined to put as much bulk on each parcel as possible to recoup their land costs, which led to much bigger building masses than the early concept plans had anticipated (Figs. 10-35, 10-36). Larger building scale was expected to yield economies of scale but instead contributed to extremely high costs per square foot. At four to five stories on the average, buildings were forced into

steel-frame construction, which is not cost effective under around ten stories or so.

Another factor that allowed large-scale structures is the way in which roof height limitations are calculated under the design regulations (Fig. 10-37). Building heights within the village core are restricted to 55 feet (16.8 m) from the finished grade to a point midway between eave and ridge. This works well

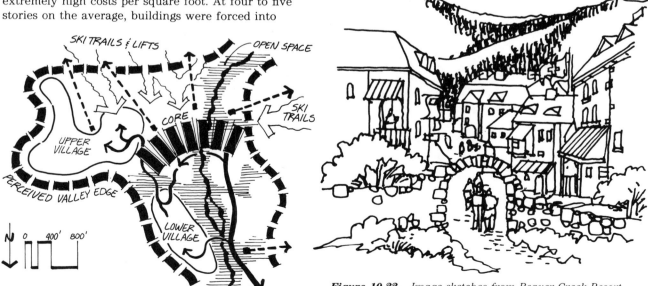

Figure 10-32. *Conceptual diagram of Beaver Creek layout.*

Figure 10-33. *Image sketches from Beaver Creek Resort Company's Design Regulations, illustrating desired character and scale in the pedestrian core. Drawings by Jack Zehren, AIA.*

Figure 10-34. *Beaver Creek Village Hall. Hall Goodhue Haisley & Barker, San Francisco, architects.*

enough where the finished grade is at roughly the same level around the building. However, where there is a considerable drop in grade from the uphill side, the roof can be as much as 100 feet (30 m) off the ground on the downhill side and still comply with the 55-foot limit on mean roof height. Because some of the major buildings in the core are on a slope and are first approached from the downhill side, they appear much larger in scale. Compounding this perception is the fact that the facades facing downhill, the taller ones, also face close to north and cast long shadows.

The core of Beaver Creek today is an aggregation of extremely well-styled, large buildings. It is perhaps too early to tell whether the linkages and comfortably proportioned pedestrian infrastructure that are still lacking will evolve as new buildings fill in the gaps in the core. Indeed, one may question whether it is possible to achieve humanly scaled, connective infill where individual projects are so big. In recent master plan revisions, the resort company scaled down the size of future buildings to respond to perceived changes in the market. Planners are confident that once the village is fully built, they will have successfully translated an alpine vision from sketches into reality.

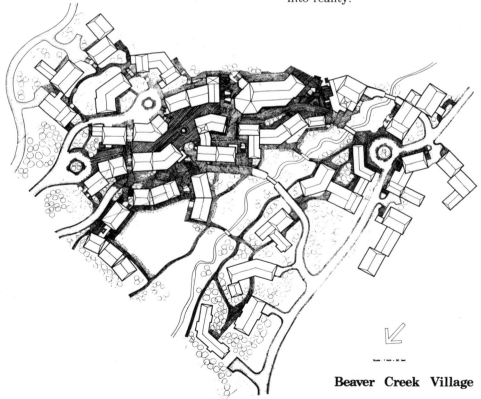

Beaver Creek Village

Figure 10-35. *The earliest conceptual site plan for the core of Beaver Creek Village, done in 1977 by Graeme Woodhouse, Vail Associates, Inc., with Esherick Homsey Dodge and Davis, San Francisco, architecture and planning. Courtesy of Beaver Creek Resort Company.*

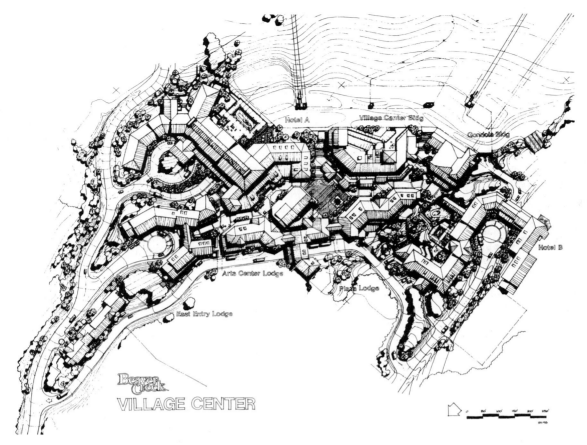

Figure 10-36. *Revised 1978 conceptual village core site plan for Beaver Creek, drawn on the same scale as Fig. 10-35, adheres to the same basic layout as the earlier plan, but individual buildings have grown considerably in size. John Exley Planning and Design Consultants, Inc., San Rafael, California. Courtesy of Beaver Creek Resort Company.*

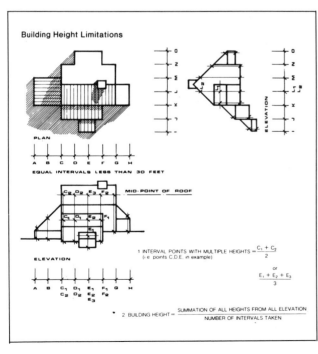

Figure 10-37. *Method of calculating building height limits, from Beaver Creek Resort Company, Design Regulations, 1979.*

LINKAGE OF SPACE: THE DYNAMICS OF STRUCTURE

The structure of the community core refers to the organization of its component parts and systems: the buildings, the spaces, the corridors, and the networks that connect them. Structure is the unifying concept and the outcome of all the decisions about siting, orientation and layout, massing and scale, spatial definition and linkage. Structure is where all the dynamics come together.

The Objective. The organization of space and mass in the core—its structure—is motivated by many factors: intended functions, patterns of access and circulation, microclimate, and, not least, economics. It should also be (but is not often) guided by an intent to reveal the core's functional priorities, clarify direction, define boundaries, mark its center, and communicate its identity and public purpose. These are messages that speak to issues of relationship and the order of importance of component parts. They are conveyed through hierarchies in spaces and scales, through the visual prominence given certain features over others, and through structural elements that separate and differentiate as well as connect and unify.

283

Hierarchies. Gradations in scale of built elements and spaces can be ordered so as to give directional clues and to amplify points of climax in the sequence of experiences in the core. These hierarchical signals help people find the center and, more importantly, reveal community priorities by the importance they assign to the core's various components and functions.

Visual Access. Control of visual access into the core and through its spaces is one of the most powerful tools of urban design. Serial views pull people into the core and lead them from one feature to the next. The framing and sequencing of views help people find the gateways, determine how much they see at one time, and compose the context in which feature elements are viewed and their relative importance is assessed. Visual accessing is a three-dimensional art that goes hand in hand with the control of grade changes and viewing levels.

Structural Elements. If the core is not well located in relation to access routes and destinations, its power

to attract a critical mass of people will be diminished. Circulation systems, open space networks, edges, and gateways are the structural elements that most effectively clarify directional and functional relationships. These elements should be organized to lead people to the core's front door and invite them in. They should ensure the continuity of desired pedestrian sequences by the way they enclose and link spaces, connect related activities, and separate incompatible uses. They are the armature for movement and the signposts for direction in the core.

The Dynamics Come Together: Whistler, British Columbia. In the late 1970s, at the urging of local proponents, the Canadian government undertook the development of Whistler Resort Village as Canada's first world-class destination ski resort. Seventy-five miles (120 km) north of Vancouver at the edge of Garibaldi National Park, the village opened in the winter of 1980–1981 and has become the new hub of a scenic region long popular for skiing and summer recreation.

At an elevation of 2200 feet (675 m), the village is sited on a relatively flat alluvial fan at the base of two adjoining ski mountains, Whistler and Blackcomb (Fig. 10-38). Part of the former floodplain of Fitzsimmons Creek runs along the eastern edge of the site, one of the few environmental constraints. (Another was the inadequate bearing capacity of the alluvial subsoils.)

The concept for organizing the 50-acre first phase evolved from a rigidly axial plan drawn in 1978 (Fig. 10-39) into an organic plan more villagelike in scale and composition. The earlier plan had been an urban solution, laid out to facilitate circulation and parcel subdivision but making little concession to the natural context. The plan that was eventually approved and built (Fig. 10-40), a dense and compact composition of smaller-scale buildings, was derived from the best qualities of the site.

Whistler's planners were determined to create a resort village, not merely a resort. "Excitement, delight and scale," they noted in the plan documents, were the ingredients that would distinguish it from less vibrant places. Accordingly, the concepts that inspired the revised site plan were pedestrian orientation and strong references to the natural landscape.

Implementing the concepts required design commitments to human scale, microclimate control, spatial connectedness, diversity in architectural style, and protection of views. Important view corridors became pedestrian streets. Whistler's curving main axis was aligned to frame the view of Mt. Fissile at the head of the valley. Secondary axes were also oriented to views of peaks.

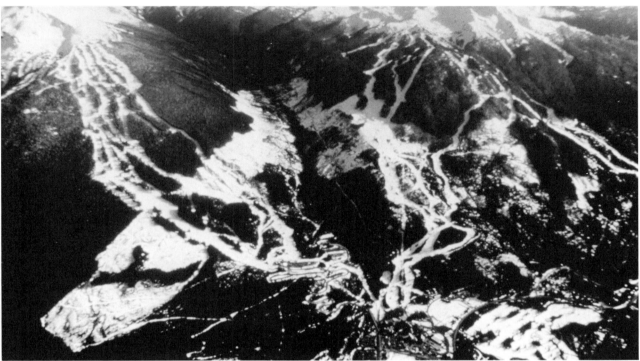

Figure 10-38. *Aerial view of the Whistler resort village site. Whistler Mtn. ski area is on the right, and Blackcomb is on the left. Photo by WLC Dev. Ltd.*

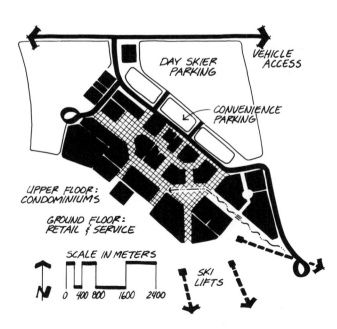

Figure 10-39. *1978 concept plan for Whistler resort village. Redrawn from plan by Waisman Dewar Macdonald, architecture and urban design, and John Perkins Associates, architecture and planning, Vancouver.*

Conceptual priorities were reflected in design controls. Their main purpose was not to unify style but, rather, to ensure that outdoor spaces were properly proportioned, sequenced, and oriented to views and sun. The plan mandated linked buildings, a strategy crucial to visual continuity and spatial control (Fig. 10-41). Massing envelopes, building footprints, and the ridge elevations of roofs were specified for each development parcel in order to protect views and control spatial relationships (see Chapter 11, The West Coast: Mixed Metaphors). Building heights on the south sides of streets and plazas were carefully set for maximum solar access. Taller buildings of greater mass were kept away from street frontages and sited at the base of the mountain. The design intent, in other words, subordinated individual structures to the spatial quality of the place as a whole.

When planning Whistler, the government's focus was the destination resort market; the village core was not designed for long-term residency. This orientation to overnight visitors influenced concepts of circulation, layout, form, and use. However, Whistler's market has evolved somewhat differently from what was projected. Fewer guests come from far away, and more arrive by car from nearby population centers. The local population has grown, giving rise to a

285

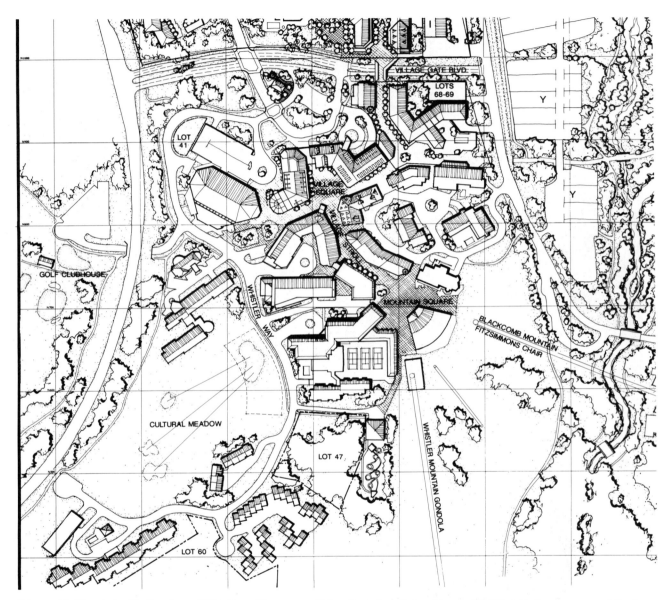

Figure 10-40. *As-built site plan of Whistler village core. Eldon Beck Associates, Novato, California, landscape architecture and land planning.*

separate set of needs. To some extent, this altered population profile has been responsible for unanticipated road bottlenecks, parking shortages, and conflicting priorities between visitors and residents.

These and other needs are currently being addressed in a second phase of planning for Whistler's expansion area, an adjacent 60-acre tract north of the original village core (Fig. 10-42). Program statements for this phase reiterate the original goals, giving highest priority to diversity, a sense of community,

and compatibility with the natural environment. They reaffirm the community's identity as a tourist destination and its desire to create a stable year-round economic base.

In addition to more lodging and tourist-oriented services, the expansion area will include new facilities shared by residents and visitors: improved circulation systems, a town hall and other civic buildings, an events arena, a convenience retail center, parks, and a community recreation center. All are to be connected by an extension of the existing pedestrian axis and by well-landscaped trail corridors (Fig. 10-43). Individual projects will be consistent in form and scale with those of the older village core (Figs. 10-44, 10-45).

One of the foremost objectives in the current planning phase is to inject as much cultural activity into the community as possible. The strategy targets a comprehensive program of activities rather than a single facility to house them. The physical plan has been designed to provide a network of public places with a variety of scale, character, solar orientation, and views that will make possible an equal variety in

cultural and recreational opportunities (Fig. 10-46).

Microclimate control was paramount in the arrangement of buildings. Major plazas at the upper and lower ends of the axis were shaped to enclose south-facing corners in which people could congregate. Secondary activity areas overlooking green space were sited against southern building exposures along the outside perimeter of the core. A continuous covered arcade for protection from rain and snow was made a requirement for all street-front buildings. All guest parking and service entries are underground, and the linkage of buildings gives ample shelter from the wind.

Figure 10-41. *Linked buildings along Whistler's main pedestrian street. Photo by Tom Barratt.*

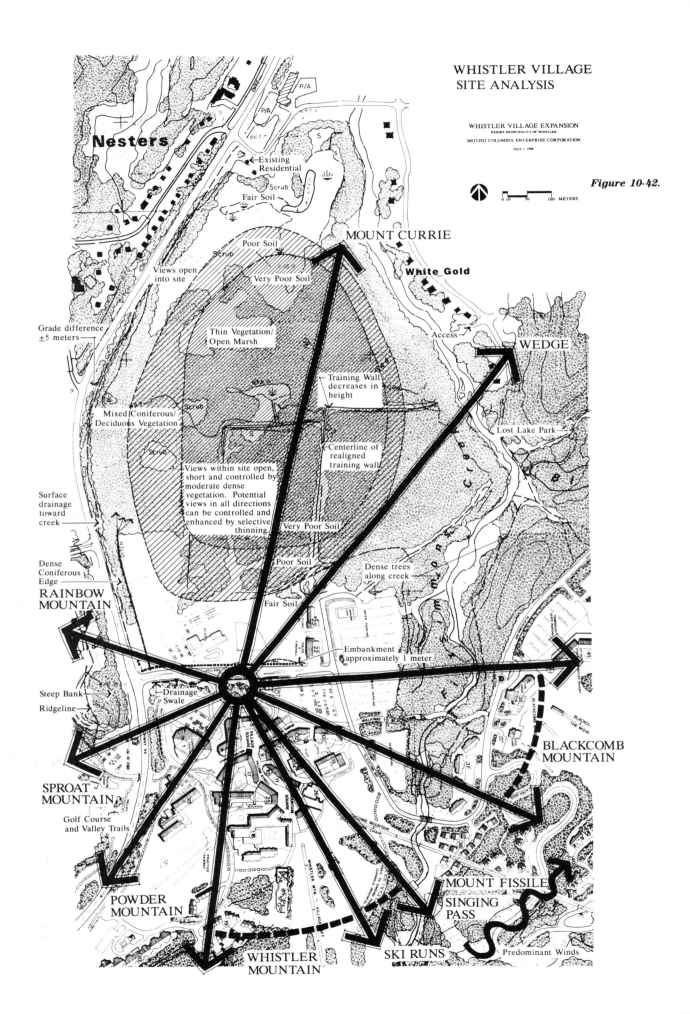

WHISTLER VILLAGE
SITE ANALYSIS

WHISTLER VILLAGE EXPANSION
RESORT MUNICIPALITY OF WHISTLER
BRITISH COLUMBIA ENTERPRISE CORPORATION
JULY 1, 1988

Figure 10-42.

0 10   50   100 METERS

Nesters

← Existing Residential

Scrub
Fair Soil

Poor Soil

Views open into site

Scrub

Very Poor Soil

MOUNT CURRIE

White Gold

Access

WEDGE

Grade difference ±5 meters

Thin Vegetation/ Open Marsh

Training Wall decreases in height

Lost Lake Park

Mixed Coniferous/ Deciduous Vegetation

Scrub

Scrub

Centerline of realigned training wall

Views within site open, short and controlled by moderate dense vegetation. Potential views in all directions can be controlled and enhanced by selective thinning.

Very Poor Soil

Surface drainage toward creek

Poor Soil

Dense trees along creek

Dense Coniferous Edge

Fair Soil

RAINBOW MOUNTAIN

Embankment approximately 1 meter.

Steep Bank
Ridgeline

Drainage Swale

BLACKCOMB MOUNTAIN

SPROAT MOUNTAIN

Golf Course and Valley Trails

MOUNT FISSILE

SINGING PASS

POWDER MOUNTAIN

SKI RUNS

Predominant Winds

WHISTLER MOUNTAIN

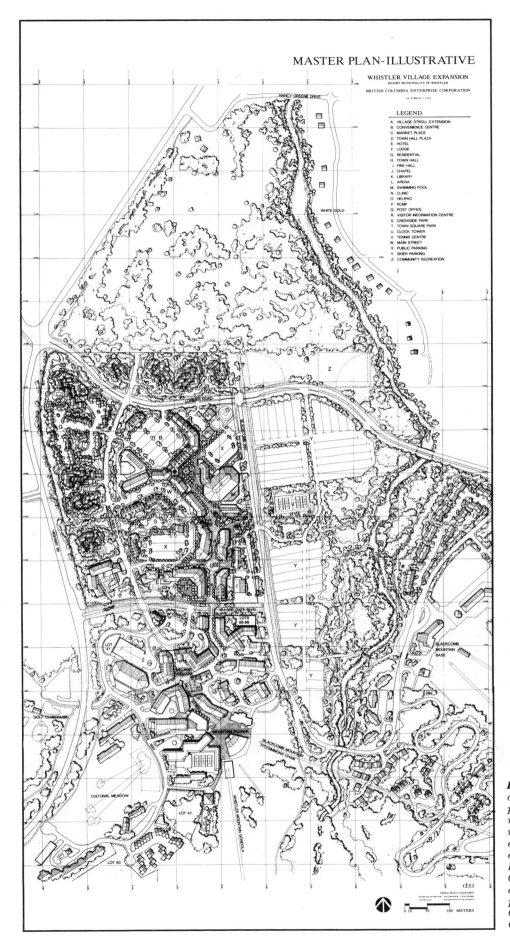

MASTER PLAN-ILLUSTRATIVE

WHISTLER VILLAGE EXPANSION
RESORT MUNICIPALITY OF WHISTLER

BRITISH COLUMBIA ENTERPRISE CORPORATION

OCTOBER 7, 1986

LEGEND

A. VILLAGE STROLL EXTENSION
B. CONVENIENCE CENTRE
C. MARKET PLACE
D. TOWN HALL PLAZA
E. HOTEL
F. LODGE
G. RESIDENTIAL
H. TOWN HALL
I. FIRE HALL
J. CHAPEL
K. LIBRARY
L. ARENA
M. SWIMMING POOL
N. CLINIC
O. HELIPAD
P. RCMP
Q. POST OFFICE
R. VISITOR INFORMATION CENTRE
S. CREEKSIDE PARK
T. TOWN SQUARE PARK
U. CLOCK TOWER
V. TENNIS CENTRE
W. MAIN STREET
X. PUBLIC PARKING
Y. SKIER PARKING
Z. COMMUNITY RECREATION

Figure 10-43.

Figures 10-42 and 10-43. Site analysis and illustrative site plan for the resort municipality of Whistler, including the 60-acre expansion parcel north of the existing village center. Eldon Beck Associates, Novato, California, landscape architecture and land planning. Courtesy of British Columbia Enterprise Corporation.

As the key to keeping the scale in check, development parcels were deliberately kept small, both to reinforce the mandate for smaller buildings and to encourage villagelike architectural diversity. Smaller parcels also gave the residents of the vicinity a chance to participate and decreased the total construction cost of individual projects, thereby reducing the temptation to develop cheaper outlying parcels before those in the core. This also helped ensure that a cohesive core would grow from the center outward. To maintain the economic viability of each project and the diversity of the district as a whole, uses assigned to each parcel were a mixture of retail and rental accommodations.

Although the revised site plan was implemented as proposed, the government's decision to increase densities affected certain design intentions. Taller buildings reduced solar access in places, and additional buildings plugged gaps intended to open views and bring the natural landscape into internal

Figure 10-44.

Figures 10-44 and 10-45. *Image sketches of Whistler's expansion area, illustrating the intended scale and pedestrian character. Drawings by Peter Szasz, San Francisco.*

corridors. More work remains to make the streetscape as intricate and the urban landscaping as reflective of place as the original plan envisioned.

Still, Whistler's linked plan successfully limited development to the human scale of a village, permanently defined its basic physical structure, set up an obvious hierarchy of streets and plaza spaces, and choreographed the pedestrian flow. The controlled scale and connectedness of Whistler's buildings convey a sense of the place as a community and the street as a focus for urban activity.

Whistler's magnificent site, its continued adherence to the spirit of early planning decisions, and its growing municipal activism give this new resort an outstanding chance to become a community in the fullest sense of the word. If home is where the heart is, one might also say about a community that the quality of its heart determines whether it will feel like home.

Figure 10-45.

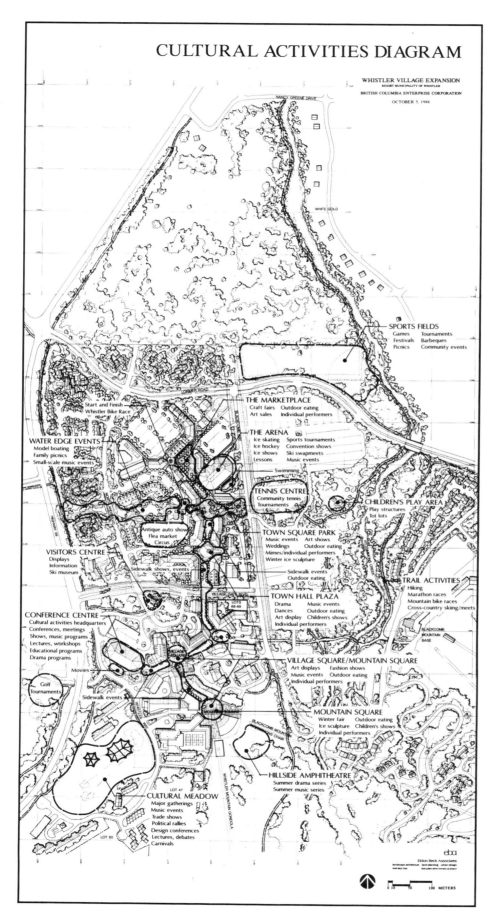

CULTURAL ACTIVITIES DIAGRAM

WHISTLER VILLAGE EXPANSION
RESORT MUNICIPALITY OF WHISTLER
BRITISH COLUMBIA ENTERPRISE CORPORATION
OCTOBER 5, 1988

NANCY GREENE DRIVE

WHITE GOLD

SPORTS FIELDS
Games   Tournaments
Festivals   Barbeques
Picnics   Community events

LORIMER ROAD

Start and Finish
Whistler Bike Race

THE MARKETPLACE
Craft fairs   Outdoor eating
Art sales   Individual performers

THE ARENA
Ice skating   Sports tournaments
Ice hockey   Convention shows
Ice shows   Ski swapmeets
Lessons   Music events

Swimming

WATER EDGE EVENTS
Model boating
Family picnics
Small-scale music events

TENNIS CENTRE
Community tennis
Tournaments

CHILDREN'S PLAY AREA
Play structures
Tot lots

Antique auto show
Flea market
Circus

TOWN SQUARE PARK
Music events   Art shows
Weddings   Outdoor eating
Mimes/individual performers
Winter ice sculpture

VISITORS CENTRE
Displays
Information
Ski museum

Sidewalk shows, events

Sidewalk events
Outdoor eating

TRAIL ACTIVITIES
Hiking
Marathon races
Mountain bike races
Cross-country skiing/meets

VILLAGE GATE BLVD
LOTS 68-69

TOWN HALL PLAZA
Drama   Music events
Dances   Outdoor eating
Art display   Children's shows
Individual performers

CONFERENCE CENTRE
Cultural activities headquarters
Conferences, meetings
Shows, music programs
Lectures, workshops
Educational programs
Drama programs

BLACKCOMB
MOUNTAIN
BASE

Movies

VILLAGE SQUARE/MOUNTAIN SQUARE
Art displays   Fashion shows
Music events   Outdoor eating
Individual performers

Golf
Tournaments

Sidewalk events

MOUNTAIN SQUARE
Winter fair   Outdoor eating
Ice sculpture Children's shows
Individual performers

BLACKCOMB MOUNTAIN CHAIR

HILLSIDE AMPHITHEATRE
Summer drama series
Summer music series

LOT 47

CULTURAL MEADOW
Major gatherings
Music events
Trade shows
Political rallies
Design conferences
Lectures, debates
Carnivals

LOT 60

eba
Eldon Beck Associates
landscape architecture land planning urban design

0 10   50   100 METERS

Figure 10-46. *Cultural activities program for the resort municipality of Whistler. Eldon Beck Associates, Novato, California, landscape architecture and land planning. Courtesy of British Columbia Enterprise Corporation.*

REFERENCES

Beaver Creek Resort Company. 1979. Design regulations—The village. Avon, Colo.

Economic Planning Group of Canada. 1984. Whistler —Development of a resort. Report for the Department of Regional Industrial Expansion, Tourism Canada. Victoria, B.C.

Jacobs, Jane. 1961. *The Death and Life of Great American Cities.* New York: Random House.

Lynch, Kevin. 1971. *Site Planning,* 2nd ed. Cambridge, Mass.: MIT Press.

Town of Vail, Colorado, Community Development Department, and Gage Davis Associates, Landscape Architects. 1980. Urban design guideplans—Vail Village and LionsHead.

11
SEEKING VALID ARCHITECTURE FOR THE MOUNTAINS

Alpine architecture lives in its very own environment which is made up of unusual skies, of intense colds, of the scent of wood and resins, of sweet flowers and impending dangers. . . .

Is there then only one Alpine style? I should like to answer: yes, when a house is built with common sense, using local materials properly and taking into consideration the peculiarities of the site, the climate, the winds, the view and, above all, the use of the building in question.

    —Mario Cereghini, Building in the Mountains

Must everything built in the mountains today carry a label that reads "Imported from the Alps"? Will the public be disappointed when a mountain structure rejects Alpine imagery? We may be quick to answer no, but judging from much of what has been built in the mountains in recent years, some American builders apparently believe it to be true (Figs. 11-1, 11-2).

Few designers would contend that Alpine styles are the only answer for contemporary mountain buildings. If they were, then theme would be the only standard for appropriate mountain architecture. In a setting in which topography and climate are such

Figure 11-2.

Figure 11-1.

Vernacular architecture does not go through fashion cycles. It is nearly immutable, indeed, unimprovable, since it serves its purpose to perfection.
—*Bernard Rudofsky,* Architecture Without Architects

unyielding constraints, theme by itself is not a realistic guideline. Moreover, the architectural choices that individuals make in any landscape are shaped by their own culture, attitudes, ethics, and environmental awareness. Standards for mountain architecture must focus, then, not on style and theme but on context and function.

Architecture is a problem-solving art. It is a design process that provides for human shelter, comfort, and well-being in the physical context of a specific place and the cultural context of a specific community. It is at once an art of practicality, empathy, and vision, an art that affects both human function and human spirit. It is a language of images and symbols that expresses prevailing community values and, in so doing, contributes to the identity of an inhabited place. When architecture is understood in this way, no single stereotype can satisfy all the needs to which today's mountain structures must respond.

In the mountains, the search for appropriate building forms carries a certain urgency. As mountain towns shed their isolation, opportunities to strengthen regional character through architecture are being wasted. Large-scale development pits the desire to preserve local building idioms against the pressure to emulate successful projects elsewhere. Alien building styles, frequently ill suited to the mountain environment, endanger the unity of a neighborhood, just as shoddy reproductions endanger its authenticity. Given growing densities, technological progress, prohibitively expensive craftsmanship, and the cash flow strictures of developers, placeless forms more reminiscent of cities than of nature increasingly intrude, threatening the natural qualities that originally made the mountain site distinctive.

The contemporary challenge for those who design new buildings in mountain communities is to accommodate needs and densities that are becoming more urban than rural without sacrificing the best qualities of traditional mountain architecture: respect for the physical environment, durability over time, and spiritual connectedness with the landscape. A variety of appropriate architectural solutions can emerge if designers refine their understanding of the regional landscape, its history, climate, and hazards, and the expectations of those who will live with their work.

HISTORICAL MOUNTAIN STYLES

Traditional mountain architecture is an eclectic amalgam of historical building styles marked by great respect for nature and climate. Repeatedly copied over the years, the great hallmarks of the genre are virtually inseparable in the public mind from the mountain landscape.

Mountain buildings range from simple log cabins to ornamented farmhouses, from mining mills and ranch homesteads to the timber and stone hunting lodges of the wealthy. In their pragmatic forms and indigenous materials, these diverse types are united by their bond with a wild land. Because the land provided the tools, materials, and inspiration for construction, traditional styles are products of their geography; like Swiss chalets on a treeless prairie, they would be inappropriate in other landscapes.

The oldest mountain building styles are gentle expressions of agrarian life in a rugged climate and remote surroundings. They appear to have evolved as a natural part of their setting. Unpretentious, sturdy, and functional, the most enduring of these styles are pragmatic responses to a difficult environment (Figs. 11-3, 11-4, 11-5, 11-6). At the same time, Old World mountain architecture is the product of a folk artisanry that elevates pragmatism to the level of poetry (Figs. 11-7, 11-8).

Some mountain styles, like the houses and barns of the Alps and the log structures of northern forests everywhere, are products of necessity, tradition, and environmental wisdom acquired over generations.

Figure 11-3. *Traditional wooden buildings in the Alpine village of Wiler in the Lotschen Valley, Valais region. Photo courtesy of Swiss National Tourist Office.*

Figure 11-4. *Thiksey Gompa, Ladakh, India.*

Figure 11-6. *Traditional stucco house in the lower Rhône Valley. Photo courtesy of Swiss National Tourist Office.*

Figure 11-5. *(left) Typical residential building in Srinagar, the capital city of Kashmir, India.*

Figure 11-7. *Grain storage barn built in 1682, Emmental region. Photo courtesy of Swiss National Tourist Office.*

Figure 11-8. *Old farmhouse in Upper Bavaria. Photo courtesy of German Information Center.*

Others, like the homesteads, mining tipples, and early main street commercial buildings of the western American frontier, represent the forces of economic necessity untempered by any emotional connection to the mountain landscape. Still others, like the Adirondack lodges and the rustic style they spawned, reflect the fantasies of a privileged class fascinated by wilderness and unbounded by economic constraints.

That disparate forces produced these varied styles is perhaps less important than their common traits and composite image that define modern expectations of mountain architecture.

Today, nostalgia for these images and their connections to place underlies most attempts to replicate traditional building styles. When mountain builders today borrow from the vernacular, their choices typically have more to do with fashion and fancy than with the physical realities of their site. They borrow the style to borrow the history and create a sense of place, failing to consider that specific physiographic and cultural factors shaped the old forms in their homeland. With this mind-set, it is virtually impossible to determine whether an unaltered traditional form offers a legitimate solution to conditions in a different location.

It is not as superficial themes that historical styles have value for contemporary designers. Rather, their value is in the images of place that they evoke and in their response to local climatic and physical constraints.

From traditional styles, lessons for new mountain architecture can be noted in pragmatic features that counteract the cold, protect from hazards, reduce the discomforts of the long winter season, prolong a structure's useful life, and compensate for the logistical disadvantages of high-relief terrain. An equally important lesson is evident in the aesthetic resonance between traditional buildings and the landscape, a trait that distinguishes any architecture that addresses spirit as well as practicality.

Timbers and Logs As Mountain Archetypes

Among the traditional forms of mountain architecture, the heavy-timbered structure is one of the most ubiquitous images and most enduring archetypes. Its persistence can be traced to both the relatively constant character of the mountain environment and the continuing use of wood for construction in the vernacular architecture of forested northern countries.

In his introductory essay for *Wooden Houses*, architectural historian Christian Norberg-Schulz sees wooden construction as a metaphor for "the Nordic sense of being in the world—a world in which the forces of nature are still strongly felt" (Futagawa et al. 1979, p. 9). The tree, as both the dominant visual element in the landscape and the most easily available material for making things, was the center of the Nordic cosmos.

Two methods of wooden construction formed the basis for the vernacular architecture of northern Europe. In one, the structure has a skeleton of timber posts and beams (Fig. 11-9), and in the other, the structure is made of logs, usually laid horizontally.

Norberg-Schulz observes that "the skeletal structures are found in the 'open,' luminous forests of the west, where deciduous trees were dominant, whereas [log] structures stem from the dark, boundless coniferous forests of the east" (Futagawa et al. 1979, p. 10). Where the two methods were present in adjacent geographic areas, as for example in Bohemia, Norway, and parts of Austria and Switzerland, they tended to mix in various ways.

In the skeletal post-and-beam structures, Norberg-Schulz notes the expression of transparency, the "boundless space of the forest, . . . and the infinite formal richness obtained by the repetition and juxtaposition of slender vertical members." The posts were like "masts, rising from the ground like trees and disappearing in the darkness above." In contrast, log structures, ground hugging and massive, were like "caves of wood, . . . [in which] transparency and skeletal articulation are absent, replaced by enclosure and earth-bound solidity." In both methods, despite the sensory contrast between them, wood was "an omnipresent physical fact, embracing man and giving him a foothold within the unknown expanse of forest and tundra" (Futagawa et al. 1979, p. 9).

That the post-and-beam structure had a spiritual meaning for northern cultures is underscored by the fact that this Nordic wooden prototype almost certainly inspired many later Western architectural forms, including the medieval cathedrals. The lasting practical significance of post-and-beam construction is in its suitability for buildings of larger scale. Its timber skeleton, enabling greater verticality and interior volume than any other method of building in wood, has been used since medieval times for large farm buildings and village halls throughout Europe.

Among wooden structures, the log cabin has the strength of a mountain archetype almost unto itself. Its origins are ancient: Structures predating A.D. 1000 have been traced to the Vikings in Scandinavia and have been found in parts of Japan and Korea. In northern Russia, log construction dominated the vernacular environment. Log farmhouses, elaborate log churches, log bridges, and log towers were prevalent as far east as Siberia by the sixteenth century. The same was true in Sweden and Norway, where medieval rural architecture was characterized by mature log complexes, including not only dwellings but also churches, stables, and barns (Fig. 11-10).

From its Nordic birthplace, log construction spread east and west in two broad bands:

The first extends through the sub-Arctic forests of Sweden, Finland, and central and northern Russia and, since the 17th century, across Siberia to the Pacific, then later to Russian America; the second begins in the French Savoy . . . and reaches through the mountainous spine of Eurasia at least as far eastward as Iran and possibly Kashmir. Included within it are the rugged areas of southern Germany, Switzerland, Austria, Bohemia, the Carpathians, Transylvania, and perhaps Turkey. (Zelinsky 1953, p. 184)

Figure 11-9. *Traditional buildings of large scale and volume used timber post-and-beam construction.*

Figure 11-10. *Medieval Norwegian stave church has been relocated to Oslo, where it is part of the Folk Museum. Photo by Henrik Bull.*

Figure 11-11. *Typical timber-frame buildings.*

Migrating wherever large coniferous forests grew, log construction became the primary identifying feature of most Alpine architecture.

Log construction does not permit much structural variation; only through details and combination with other building methods can variety be introduced. Building size is limited by the length of the logs, although trunks can be joined end to end to create a longer wall, which is stabilized by interior room partitions, corner joints, and doorposts. Window and door openings must be kept relatively small.

Post-and-beam and log construction, though more prevalent, are not the only methods for building in wood; in certain areas, timber-frame construction is also a common technique for building small dwellings. In timber framing, the basic structural unit is the transverse frame, to which a cagelike grid of studs and rails is attached. The spaces between the structural members are filled in with stucco, masonry, or weatherboard, leaving the grid exposed to articulate the structure (Fig. 11-11). Regional variations are expressed in the spacing of the members as well as in details on the facade.

Timber-frame construction was dominant in the architecture of northwestern Europe (northern Germany, Holland, Denmark, and England). Where timber framing migrated to the mountain fringes—in

Figure 11-12. *The First Church of Christ, Scientist in Berkeley, California, designed by San Francisco Bay School architect Bernard Maybeck.*

Switzerland and the southern parts of Germany and Scandinavia—it blended with the other methods, producing, among many variations, the half-timbered houses of central Europe.

Folk architecture in wood symbolizes the relationship between the cultures of the northern forests and their natural environment. But as the old ways of crafting in wood have been gradually replaced by simpler, less costly methods, the articulation of this relationship in structures has diminished. Although wood is unlikely ever again to be so central a character element in buildings, the marriage of post-and-beam construction with new techniques for laminating wooden beams has helped renew interest in its use.

In one of the quiet but consistent themes in twentieth-century architecture, woodcraft has been the signature of a number of modern architects. Frank Lloyd Wright in the early 1900s, Finnish architect Alvar Aalto in the 1930s, and the turn-of-the-century San Francisco Bay School (Joseph Worcester, Bernard Maybeck, Ernest Coxhead, Willis Polk, the Greenes, and Julia Morgan) (Fig. 11-12) all attempted to revive the warmth and expressiveness of earlier wood traditions. Because of this, their work, though not born of mountain landscapes, has strongly influenced contemporary mountain design. The spiritual connection with wood, as Norberg-Schulz writes, runs deep:

> The lesson of wood goes beyond the direct use of wood as a material. First of all, it tells us something about the kind of environment which is meaningful under the Nordic sky. Today we have mostly lost the sense of those values which may give us a sense of belonging and identity, and we build as if we were anywhere. A study of vernacular architecture is important to regain what has been lost, and in the Nordic countries this means to go to its forest roots. (Futagawa et al. 1979, p. 20)

Mountain Archetypes of a Different Sort

Mountain Architecture in Stone. Although the wooden structure is a central archetype and wood the principal building material in traditional mountain cultures, stone is also an integral element. All-stone houses are common in the mountains to the south (Fig. 11-13), and half-timber, half-stone houses are found throughout the northern mountains of Europe (Fig. 11-14).

The Nordic wooden archetype is distinct from stone-based archetypes, in large part because of perceptual differences between the forested alpine landscape and the drier landscape of the more southerly mountains. Explains Norberg-Schulz, "In the north, vegetation forms the continuous 'ground' on which rocks and mountains, as well as buildings,

Figure 11-13. *Traditional stone dwellings of the southern Alps.*

Figure 11-14. *Half-timber, half-stone structures.*

appear. In the dry south, instead, the topographical configurations constitute the background, whereas trees and groves are perceived as relatively isolated 'figures'" (Futagawa et al. 1979, p. 11). These differences in landscape character color the regional vernacular in architecture, reflecting each culture's concept of its relationship to nature.

Flat-Roofed Mountain Structures. Another mountain prototype, the flat-roofed structure, is

301

widely resisted as a model for new architecture, even though there is ample precedent for it in mountain environments. Perhaps because it is foreign to Nordic and Alpine traditions, it seems never to have become part of the Western world's expectations of what a mountain building (particularly a residential building) should look like.

The adobe pueblos of the Southwest are America's only indigenous example of flat-roofed structures in a wintry high-country environment (see Fig. 2-12). Interestingly, individual pueblo dwellings are remarkably similar in form to the high-altitude stone-and-stucco houses in Nepal, Ladakh, and the Tibetan plateau (Fig. 11-15).

In these arid landscapes, where the expansive valleys are visually as dominant as the peaks, flat-roofed buildings mimic the horizontality of the flat valley floor. Aggregations of flat-roofed buildings stepping up a gently sloping mountain flank seem to grow out of the landscape like layered fungi on a decaying tree trunk.

Primitive building methods are one likely reason that the form evolved as it did in the Southwest and the Himalayan cultures, but the natural environment —the dry climate, the intense winter sun, the sparse forest cover—must have been at least as important. The shortage of trees limited the options for

constructing the roof and forced reliance on other building materials for the walls.

Developers of mountain buildings intended for heavy public use have discovered the advantages of flat roofs (Fig. 11-16). When storm winds are strong, flat roofs prevent the problem of imbalanced snow loading that can collapse a peak-roofed structure. And when the winds subside, snow accumulates on the roof and acts as an insulative layer. Flat roofs also offer a functional advantage: Snow cannot avalanche off the roof and endanger pedestrian circulation around the edges of the building. Despite the technical difficulty of perfecting the roof drainage system, it is no coincidence that many buildings recently constructed in the harshest locations, like summit warming houses at ski resorts, have flat roofs.

The aesthetic appropriateness of a flat roof in a natural setting depends not only on climate but also on building height and landscape context. When a flat-roofed building is too tall in relation to its mass and horizontal proportions, it more nearly resembles an urban high rise and loses any visual advantage to be gained from the roofline. In contrast, when building massing is oriented in a compatible way, flat roofs continue the natural line of a foreground landscape that is broad and strongly horizontal (Figs. 11-17, 11-18).

Figure 11-15. *Flat roofs of Leh, the capital of Ladakh, northern India.*

Figure 11-16. *The functional flat-roofed mid-mountain warming house, Mammoth Mountain Ski Area, California. Photo by Tom Johnston.*

Figure 11-17. *The form of this contemporary flat-roofed residence in Summit County, Colorado, is naturally derived from the structure's site at the edge between slope and meadow. Peter Witter, Keystone, Colorado, architect. Photo by Peter Witter.*

Figure 11-18. *Flat roofs of the Aspen Club condominiums are consistent with the aesthetic character of the site and the surrounding landscape. Benedict, Sutherland, Duesterberg, Aspen, Colorado, architects. Fredric Benedict, siting and landscape design. Photo by Marc Schuman.*

Alpine Stereotypes

The images more commonly embedded in our culture's collective vision of mountain architecture are those of traditional Alpine structures. Generally oversimplified and stripped of the visual details needed to draw stylistic distinctions, these generic images have encouraged the notion that Alpine architecture is a unified style with a single stereotype, the Swiss chalet (Fig. 11-19). In reality, however, far more obvious than any overall conformity is the region's stylistic diversity.

Geography has been a decisive factor in the multitude of Alpine building types. Wide variations in topography, elevation, climate, snowfall, and forest vegetation are reflected in local architectural forms and details.

There is a natural logic in some of these adaptations. With increasing altitude, the Alps tend to become more rugged; building forms, in response,

Figure 11-19. *The stereotypical image of Alpine architecture: the Swiss chalet.*

304

In one way or another a house always expresses the builder's knowledge of his environment.
     —*Christian Norberg-Schulz,* Wooden Houses

Figure 11-20. *Stucco structures in the Tirolean style edge the village plaza in the Austrian village of Walchsee. Photo by Alois Sedlacek, courtesy of Austrian National Tourist Office.*

Figure 11-21. *Old farmhouse in the timber-frame style, Koniz, Berne Canton. More elaborate houses like this have a* rundi, *the curvature beneath the roof that covers up the bracing. Photo courtesy of Swiss National Tourist Office.*

become more vertically oriented. At lower elevations, where snowfall is lighter, rain is common, and wintertime low temperatures are not as extreme, dwellings have normal ceiling heights, steeper roof pitches, balconies, and outside stairs. At higher elevations, where snowfalls are heavier and winter temperatures lower, dwellings typically have thicker walls (thicker still and often made of stone on the windward and north sides), lower ceilings, multiple entrances at several elevations, shallower roof pitches to retain snow for insulation, no balconies or terraces, and smaller, deep-set windows with heavy storm sashes (Cereghini 1956, p. 29).

What most of them have in common, regardless of elevation, is a strong orientation to the sun. The broadest facade usually faces south, and the primary living areas inside the house are on that side. The roof axis is most often oriented along a north–south line to expose both sides of the roof to equal amounts of sun.

The varied wooden houses of the Alps are not solely the expression of natural forces; they are also a product of cultural cross currents (Figs. 11-20, 11-21, 11-22, 11-23). The Alps, long a barrier to movement, eventually became the zone of contact between the Mediterranean cultures to the south and the Germanic cultures to the north, with the result that Alpine building styles evolved from numerous sources. The *Einhaus* style (literally, "one house" for both people and animals) came to the Swiss Alps with Germanic tribes from the northwest. Renaissance styles and stonemasonry penetrated from the south. Scandinavian log craft and half-timber styles from medieval cities to the north spread into eastern Switzerland, Bavaria, and the Austrian Tirol.

Superimposed on a varied topography, these culturally based methods of building were isolated and recombined in a mosaic of styles. Wherever homogeneity can be discerned in the vernacular architecture of the Alps, it follows with remarkable consistency the limits etched by mountain valleys rather than by any larger regional or linguistic boundaries (Futagawa et al. 1979, p. 24).

The Swiss Chalet. Among the many Alpine building types, several stand out. One in particular, the Swiss chalet of the Bernese Oberland in west central Switzerland (Fig. 11-24), is universally embraced as the stereotypical dwelling of the mountains.

The large, all-enveloping roof, window-studded southern gable wall, and decorated balconies of the Bernese chalet combine in the same structure a sense of enclosure with a suggestion of openness and a love of the picturesque. Even its name is indicative of the emotions with which the style was long associated in Europe: Derived from the French word for small castle, *chalet* is less a description of its appearance than a hint of the envy with which the free Swiss peasant, liberated from feudal obligations in the thirteenth century, was regarded.

Figure 11-22. *Old peasant home at Ruderswil, Emmental region, Berne Canton. Photo courtesy of Swiss National Tourist Office.*

Figure 11-23. *Tall and narrow wooden structures in this village near Sion are characteristic of the Valais region. Photo courtesy of Swiss National Tourist Office.*

Figure 11-24. *Representative of the authentic Swiss chalet style, the Haus Reichenback was built in 1769 in the Bernese Oberland village of Lauenen (elevation 4100 ft., 1240 m). Its ornamentation is typical of the region. Photo courtesy of Swiss National Tourist Office.*

The Swiss chalet belongs to the Germanic *Einhaus* tradition,[1] in which a typical house had a row of rooms for the family on one or two floors along the south or southeastern exposure, separated by a hall from work rooms and animal stalls along the back side. Like most Alpine houses, the chalet is constructed of logs, generally trunks that have been squared and smooth-cut at the corners.

What distinguishes the chalet from other houses in the *Einhaus* style, writes Norberg-Schulz, is its extraordinary development in width:

> *The chalet is remarkable for its very wide gable wall; the lateral walls are of secondary interest. The steep building sites make a development in depth difficult or impossible. A wide gable wall does not allow for a very pointed roof, and the chalet is therefore distinguished by its relatively flat gable. The general character, thus, is solid and ground-hugging, lending a sense of protection and assurance among the wild forms of mountains. (Futagawa et al. 1979, p. 14)*

Typical of Bernese chalets are the broad, gently sloping roof and the exceedingly wide roof overhang. Supported by cantilevered logs, the huge eaves are a feature of remarkable dynamism and visual dominance. Ceiling heights rarely exceed just over 7 feet (2.25 m). Windows are small but arranged symmetrically in continuous rows on the south-facing side, contributing to the simultaneous feelings of enclosure and welcome. Ornately perforated balcony railings and applied decorations give the gable wall the appearance of a screen, light and airy in contrast with other elements of the structure.

The siting of the chalet is an intrinsic part of the way in which the structure is perceived. Because chalets are generally built on south-facing slopes looking down the valley, they are most often seen from below. Consequently, the openness of the gable wall leaves a stronger impression than does the enormity of the roof. The log construction, which in structures on level ground is such an expressive element, is obscured by shadows from the eaves and likewise becomes subsidiary to the gable wall in determining the perceived character of the structure. The symmetrical positioning of details on the facade "centralizes the frontality and symbolic function of the gable wall, whose proportions are unique to chalet structures. All the expressive energy is concentrated in the direction that these houses face, looking down on valley basins" (Futagawa et al. 1979, p. 34).

[1]Hansen (1971, p. 180) observes that most farmhouses of the Alps are of a common type (what Norberg-Schulz calls the *Einhaus* style) and theorizes that they derive either from the medieval Teutonic styles in northern Europe or from an archetypal form of Celtic house.

Figure 11-25. *South German half-hipped house.*

Other Alpine Variations. North and east of the Bernese region, the terrain becomes somewhat less rugged and the valleys wider. In these valleys, a different variation on the central European *Einhaus* model replaces the chalet. The interior layout is similar, but the rooms are deeper and the immense roofs steeper and half-hipped in typical south German style (Fig. 11-25). If the chalet resembles a gabled screen set across the slope, these houses, with their deeper, elongated forms, have a more pronounced longitudinal axis and reinforce the impression of volume.

Closely related to these south German houses is the Black Forest style of southwestern Germany (Fig. 11-26). These dwellings are equally voluminous, with hipped or half-hipped roofs. The difference is that they are not as symmetrical in their interior layout or in the arrangement of features on the facade.

> *The disposition of the plan is freer. . . . Balconies, entrances, and windows are placed rather irregularly under the large and deep overhangs. The general impression is that of a complex interior which communicates actively with the surroundings but is kept together by the all-embracing roof. Thanks to its combination of strong image and formal freedom, the Black Forest house is one of the truly great achievements of vernacular architecture. (Futagawa et al. 1979, p. 15)*

Many other different models exist in Alpine architecture: the stone-and-stucco houses of the Engadine in eastern Switzerland (Fig. 11-14), the half-timbered houses of the Tirol (Fig. 11-20), and the

307

Figure 11-26. *Black Forest farmhouse near Todtmoos, West Germany. Photo courtesy of German Information Center.*

unadorned, towerlike wooden homes and granaries of the Valais in southwestern Switzerland (Fig. 11-27). They all nonetheless have in common a unity with the natural environment, manifesting ecological wisdom, durability, longevity, and roots. To a great extent, it is these values that have encouraged the spread of Alpine styles.

In contemporary applications, Alpine stereotypes can become a quagmire of design problems. The chalet style may not translate well into different uses, higher densities, and larger scales. The materials are expensive, costly to craft, and, in the case of stucco finishes, harder to maintain where climatic conditions are different from those in the Alps. Without equivalent craftsmanship, the overall effect may be disappointing. However, when the models are adapted to compatible uses and densities, taking into account climate, scale, and quality of finish, it is possible to retain their contribution to the sense of place (Figs. 11-28, 11-29, 11-30).

Figure 11-27. *Wooden houses and granaries typical of the Valais region of Switzerland.*

Figure 11-28. Contemporary interpretation of the tirolean style on a larger scale: Tyrolean Inn, Vail, Colorado. Morter Fisher Arnold, Vail, architects.

Figure 11-29. Interpretation of Alpine style in a development of greater density than the traditional village application: Bishop Park condominiums, Vail, Colorado. Gordon Pierce, Vail, architect; Berridge Associates, Inc., San Francisco, landscape architect.

Figure 11-30. The Poste Montane Inn, Beaver Creek, Colorado, is exquisitely detailed and scaled in the Alpine style. Bull Volkmann Stockwell, San Francisco, architects. In the background, the Centennial, William Turnbull Associates, San Francisco, architects.

American Frontier Archetypes and the Rustic Style

In America, the log cabin, requiring few tools, no nails or glass, minimal carpentry skills, and little time and money, became the prototypical frontier dwelling. It was introduced to the New World after 1640, when Swedish and Finnish immigrants arrived to settle New Sweden (Delaware and southeastern Pennsylvania). America's earliest settlers, mostly of English heritage, had until then been familiar with only timber-frame and brick construction.

Later, log construction accompanied the advancing frontier, appearing wherever Scandinavian influences spread and wherever wood was plentiful. It was carried with the Rhineland immigrants in the early eighteenth century into the Alleghenies of western Pennsylvania and into West Virginia and, after 1740, with Scotch-Irish immigrants into the Virginia Piedmont and through the gaps of the Blue Ridge Mountains into the Carolinas, Georgia, and Tennessee.

Log cabins were the first structures in the mountains of the American West (Figs. 11-31, 11-32, 11-33). By the mid-nineteenth century, the log-building tradition had jumped across the Great Plains to the Rocky Mountain belt with successive waves of fur traders, miners, cattle ranchers, and farmers. Log structures first appeared in Wyoming with cavalry stockades dating from the early 1840s, in Mormon settlements in Utah and Nevada from 1850, and around mining lodes and ranch lands from northern Arizona and Nevada to Montana and the Black Hills after 1860.

Figure 11-31. *The log cabin stereotype of the American West.*

Figure 11-32. *The simplest frontier dwelling: Johnson's cabin, Grayback Gulch, Colorado, date unknown. Photo courtesy of Denver Public Library, Western History Department.*

In America, the log-built form lacked orderly development. Wherever it appeared, characteristic features were brought together in new combinations according to the settler's skill, whims, available tools and materials, origin, and previous experience. By the time it reached the Rockies, it had become impossible to identify log structures in ethnic terms; necessity had become a greater influence than cultural traditions from the Old Country (Weslager 1969, p. 317).

East of the Mississippi, hewn-log houses, which required considerably more skill and time than round-log dwellings, were favored as permanent shelter because the heartwood was less susceptible to decay than the outer layers of bark and sapwood. In the West, however, haste, not permanence, was the main concern, and in the first frenzied waves of settlement, crude round-log cabins went up by the thousands.

By the time more refined, second-generation dwellings were being erected in western mountain mining and ranching towns, lumber mills had arrived on the scene, and the desire to emulate the revivalist styles of more cultured towns seemed to mark the end of the log-building era. Not until the late nineteenth century did log building undergo an American resurgence, albeit under quite different social circumstances. It is a rebirth that continues today (Figs. 11-34, 11-35, 11-36, 11-37).

Figure 11-33. *A more elaborate log cabin: the post office and postmaster's residence near Meeker, Colorado. Photo circa 1880, Colorado Historical Society.*

Figure 11-34. *Log-built clubhouse, circa 1915, at the historic HF Bar guest ranch, Saddlestring, Wyoming.*

Figure 11-35. *In the restoration and expansion of a turn-of-the-century ranch house near Keystone, Colorado, traditional log and stone construction methods were used to retain the structure's rustic character in its new role as a public clubhouse. Backen Arrigoni & Ross, San Francisco, architects.*

Figure 11-37. *(above) Detail, West Ranch, Keystone, Colorado. Backen Arrigoni & Ross, San Francisco, architects. Photo by Backen Arrigoni & Ross.*

Figure 11-36. *(left) To reduce visual and ecological impact, the new log conference center at West Ranch, Keystone, Colorado, was sited at the edge between sage and lodgepole forest. Photo by Backen Arrigoni & Ross.*

Figure 11-38. *Built in the early 1880s by William West Durant and rebuilt after a fire in 1915 by Beaux-Arts architect John Russell Pope, the main lodge at Kamp Kill Kare in upper New York State exemplifies the Adirondack style.*

Log Cabins for the Wealthy. The great camps of the Adirondacks in east central New York State flowered during a brief sixty-year period between the American Civil War (1861–1865) and the onset of the Great Depression in 1929. For decades thereafter, however, these camps influenced American preferences in mountain architecture.

The region around New York's Lake Placid was the site of the earliest concentration of camp development, but later in the period, the camps spread to remote sites throughout the area which is now one of the United States' largest national parks. Built by wealthy eastern families as private summer retreats, the camps adopted a largely indigenous style that by the early 1900s had become the favored expression of mountain architecture throughout the country (Fig. 11-38).

The special character of camp buildings is considered derivative of the Adirondack landscape, although touches of Swiss domestic architecture are occasionally apparent in the broad, shallow-pitched roofs, wide eaves, and overhanging upper floors and balconies.

Consciously sited in remote locations, characterized by the use of logs and indigenous stone, shingled roofs with broad overhangs and porches, and simply-proportioned window and door openings, the building complexes [of the great camps] are among [America's] most original examples of vernacular architecture. Although efforts have been made to link their style to European precedents, and particularly to Alpine chalets, the collective work was in fact a logical and inevitable combination of local craft traditions and readily available materials — the Adirondack style. (Kaiser 1982, p. 2)

Architectural historians have noted that the Adirondack style shares traits with timbered northern regions elsewhere, not only in the Alps, but also in Scandinavia, northern Russia, Japan, and the wetter parts of the Himalayas: all-wood construction, flattened roof pitches to hold snow as insulation against the deep cold, small window and door openings, and stone foundations and chimneys.

That the style flowered in such rustically ornate ways, however, is due to the exacting standards of the wealthy purists who commissioned it. At their

313

Figure 11-39.

insistence, buildings were designed to harmonize with the natural site and to be barely discernible in the landscape. Superficially simple and rough, the camps are in fact a notable logistical achievement, a merger of the clients' romantically naive notions of self-sufficiency in the wilderness with their expectations of a civilized, if not lavish, social life.

Log construction is the single most common trait of the Adirondack style (Fig. 11-39). Although it was time-consuming and expensive, "logs were laid up as walls, framed as trusses, used as supporting purlins for the roof, and peeled as beams and studs. Every detail possessed structural significance. Extensions of log ends, coping of intersecting logs, and crossbracing of poles became decorative elements" (Kaiser 1982, p. 64). The corner notching of logs was elevated to an art form by the region's carpenters, and "rustic work" of small unpeeled logs and branches ornamented everything, inside and out. Aesthetic perfectionism demanded that every material used in the buildings be from the forest; hence, materials such as plaster, wallpaper, and paint were taboo. Even the furniture was made of branches.

Another distinctive tradition in the camps was the construction of individual buildings for separate functions, somewhat analogous to the accretion of structures on a New England farm. This gave the owners some privacy from their legions of guests and servants and prevented the spread of fire through the

complex. The buildings were connected by covered walkways to compensate for the long periods of wet and snowy weather. Other structural details related to the unpredictable climate included large porches as a response to persistent rain, oversized log pillars and roof beams to support heavy snow loads, and extended eaves to prevent the buildup of ice and snow against foundation walls.

Popularization of the Rustic Fantasy. In later camp development, especially around the Saranac Lakes region, the simplicity of the earlier camps gave way to greater luxury. Prominent East Coast architectural firms like McKim, Mead and White were brought in to design elaborate hunting lodges, generating widespread national publicity for what had come to be known as the Adirondack style.

The Adirondack interpretation of rustic living quickly spread to other wilderness settings, from the foothills of the Appalachians to the north woods of the Great Lakes states to the Rockies and beyond. The style became the prototype for grand turn-of-the-century lodges in Yellowstone (Fig. 11-40), Glacier National Park (Fig. 11-41), Yosemite (Fig. 11-42), Grand Canyon, and Jackson Hole. By the time the National Park Service was created in 1916, the style had become synonymous with park architecture, and later, during the Depression years, its rustic details were made part of the campground design standards in the national public works programs of the Works Progress Administration (WPA) and the Civilian Conservation Corps (CCC).

As the best of America's wilderness scenery was opened to the general public, harmony with nature was a recurring theme and the underlying ethic of the National Park Service. "Its struggle to reconcile the tensions between preservation [of scenery] and development [for tourism] have produced some of the most well known elements of Americans' shared architectural heritage, sometimes defining a national park as much as the canyon or geyser" (Myers 1984, p. 42).

The Park Service concept of harmony with nature embraced a spectrum of architectural attitudes, from deference to the landscape to a highly visible and dynamic fusion with dramatic sites. Still, its commissions were uniformly characterized by the use of handcrafting, natural imagery, local materials, and eclectic interior motifs. The collective concern was focused more on the appearance of naturalness than on the preservation of nature unimpaired. Like the Adirondack camps, "early park buildings were romantic fantasies, made possible by the unimportance of labor costs and made handsome by the quality of design and spirit that guided their creation" (Myers 1984, p. 42). The recognition that

Figure 11-40. *The Old Faithful Inn in Yellowstone National Park was designed by architect Robert C. Reamer and constructed in 1903. Photo courtesy of Yellowstone National Park Research Library.*

Figure 11-41. *The Many Glacier Hotel in Glacier National Park, Montana, was designed in the rustic style by St. Paul, Minnesota, architect Thomas D. McMahon and built in 1914–1915 at a cost of $500,000. Photo by W. S. Keller for the National Park Service.*

Figure 11-42. *Yosemite's historic Ahwahnee Hotel, which opened in 1927, was designed by architect Gilbert Stanley Underwood. Photo courtesy of Yosemite National Park Research Library.*

park architecture should respond to regional differences in landscape was slower to evolve and was better expressed in the canyonlands of the Southwest than in the mountains.

Despite increasing criticism of rustic architecture as an artifice to appeal to wealthy tastes, the style remained the hallmark of the National Park Service until the 1950s. As the popularity of wilderness retreats grew to embrace the general public, private landowners and developers throughout the mountain West emulated the style.

As the rustic style spread in the United States, some mountain regions created distinct local variations based on climatic differences or historical singularities. In the Central Rockies, the Adirondack style was reiterated in numerous summer lodges, but with less ornate detail (Fig. 11-43). Throughout the Coast Ranges and the western slopes of the Sierras, overscaled architectural details, proportioned to the huge trees and heavy snowfalls, are typical. In the Lake Tahoe area, the rustic log style of timber taverns and lodges was leavened by the eccentricities and excesses of the lumber barons who built castles around the lake (Fig. 11-44). In the Pacific Northwest,

buildings became slightly more transparent to gain maximum interior light in the rainy climate, and variations in ornamentation appeared that were rooted in Coast Indian traditions. In the Rockies north of Yellowstone, the much grander scale and increasing ruggedness of the mountains are mirrored in architectural proportions and materials. It is as if buildings there were repudiating the fantasies of the rustic style to address the northern region's challenges to survival, among them grizzlies, brutal winters, and remoteness.

The rustic Adirondack style was "not a straitjacket . . . there was considerable room for individualism and artistry—for regional responses to the shapes and scale of the Western landscape and the designs of the American Indians, and for eclectic echoes of English cottage, shingle, Oriental, and Prairie styles" (Myers 1984, p. 42). As a model for contemporary mountain architecture, the Adirondack style is suitable for larger-scale applications, is sensitive to landscape aesthetics and climate, displays artistry with simple materials, and is conscious of the emotional and psychological power of our fascination with mountains (Figs. 11-45, 11-46, 11-47, 11-48).

Figure 11-43. *The Central Rockies' version of the rustic style: Stead's Ranch, Estes Park, Colorado. Photo taken in the early 1900s by L. C. McClure. Denver Public Library, Western History Department.*

Figure 11-44. *Vikingsholm, a Lake Tahoe mansion built in 1929 as a summer home, was designed in the Scandinavian style by Swedish architect Lennart Palme. It has been preserved as part of California's Emerald Bay State Park.*

Figure 11-45. *Soda Springs Station at Donner Summit, California, a rustic mountain lodge redeveloped as condominiums. Ward–Young, Truckee, California, architects. Photo by Ward–Young.*

Figure 11-46. *Contemporary rustic: Chambers Landing, a condominium project at Homewood, California, on Lake Tahoe's western shore. Ward–Young, Truckee, California, architects. Photo Ward–Young.*

Figure 11-47. *A simple cedar-clad vacation cabin, built in 1981 near Lake Tahoe, California, occupies what was for years the owner's family campsite. It was designed to take advantage of mountain views, harmonize with the forest setting, and shed snow away from entries and decks. Its siting preserved all major trees and boulders. Bull Volkmann Stockwell, San Francisco, architects. Photo by Ernest Braun.*

Figure 11-48. *The rustic Snow Park day-skier lodge, built in 1981, is the gateway to Edgar B. Stern, Jr.'s 6750-acre Deer Valley Resort near Park City, Utah. Its generous sloping rooflines, red cedar siding, sandstone base, and massive log columns repeat elements of traditional mountain buildings, but its heavy timber structural system and double-membrane cold roof are direct responses to seismic risk and climate. Esherick Homsey Dodge and Davis, San Francisco, architects. Don Carter, CHNMB, San Francisco, landscape architect. Photo © Peter Aaron/ESTO.*

Rustic Evolution in Canada. The turn-of-the-century resort architecture of the Canadian Rockies was a product of the same fantasies about the wilderness, but eventually it acquired a style of its own. As in the United States, the impetus for Canadian resort development was provided by the railroad, seeking to make its transcontinental line profitable by building hotels in scenic spas along the line. The first of these was the Banff Springs Hotel, begun in 1887.

Designed by American Beaux-Arts architect Bruce Price, the rustic wood-frame hotel reflected the then-emerging concept of buildings as natural extensions of the surrounding environment. Price later refined these design principles for the Château Frontenac in Quebec City, launching the château style that marked Canadian institutional architecture for the next fifty years. The château-in-the-wilderness style had come into full flower by the time the first hotel was demolished in 1912 to make way for the present Banff Springs Hotel, a fourteen-story limestone structure reminiscent of a French baronial fortress (Fig. 11-49). The mountain chalet had been reborn in Canada as a true castle.

Figure 11-49. *The Banff Springs Hotel, Alberta, Canada, begun in 1912 and completed 16 years later, was designed in the Château style by architect W. S. Painter of the Canadian Pacific Railroad. Photo by Rodger Todhunter.*

Boom-and-Bust Architecture: Homesteads and Mines

Historical mountain architecture in the United States has another face. Whereas the trend-setting Adirondack camps were the creation of the wealthy, homestead architecture in the western mountains was shaped by a largely penniless, opportunity-seeking class of frontier settlers.

Although homesteads might be thought of as more genuinely vernacular, they are, paradoxically, far less attuned to their natural setting than is the rustic style originated by eastern urbanites. Yet they have had equal influence on contemporary mountain architecture. To this day, marks of the homestead style can easily be discerned in the restrained architecture of designers native to the central Rockies and intermountain basins.

Parsimonious Architecture. The unpretentious wood-framed houses of miners and homesteaders were expressions of frugality. The architecture is tight and sparse, stripped down to the basics imposed by shortages of craftsmen, money, materials, and time. There is nothing superfluous. Houses were simple in form, minute in scale, meager in comfort and ornamentation, and thrifty in the use of materials (Fig. 11-50).

By the time most homesteaders arrived in the West, the amount of timber and the construction time needed to build a house had been reduced by the spread of sawmills and railroads and by the invention of balloon framing, in which horizontal boards were

Figure 11-51. *Balloon-framed summer cottage built in the 1930s, Colorado Rockies.*

nailed to upright studs (Fig. 11-51). Log structures had come to be seen as wasteful of wood. Indeed, the logs consumed in a one-room cabin, if sawed instead into planks, could provide enough lumber for several dwellings. Settlers could build a framed house in a day; they could even disassemble it and take the timbers along when they moved.

Figure 11-50. *The basic homestead. Photo dated 1897, Colorado Historical Society.*

Figure 11-52. *The Frank Maxwell House in Georgetown, Colorado, was built in 1867 by a Mr. Potter from a picture in a magazine. In 1889, Potter spent $35,000 on an addition to the front, but went broke after the silver crash of 1893 and sold the house to Maxwell, who lived there for 50 years. The house, considered one of the ten finest examples of American Victorian architecture, is on the National Historic Register.*

Borrowed Architecture. "In a mining community, not only the architecture may disappear, but the whole community may disappear. There is no continuity, so therefore no evolution in the buildings and design" (Beer 1986). In those mountain towns that matured, the unadorned clapboard structures of the earliest settlers were replaced by more elaborate homes and public edifices, the more important ones built of stone and brick. True to the idiosyncrasies of small towns everywhere, mining town residents eschewed their nearest frontier models to avoid the stigma of provincialism. They celebrated their survival by borrowing from styles in vogue (or already passé) in the cities of the East, particularly the Victorian-era revivals of Greek, Gothic, Italianate, and Queen Anne architecture (Fig. 11-52). These period revivals were adapted neither to the climate nor to the landscape, but they satisfied a much more pressing desire: the craving for civility, refinement, and permanence in a frontier town.

The quaint Victorian images that remain in nineteenth-century mining towns are part of the heritage of American mountain architecture. They are, however, place specific and difficult to reuse without artifice. Even where these traditions were part of the local history, one can question whether the reproduction of Victorian styles has been any more successful in creating a sense of place than have contemporary structures conforming to the scale, materials, and general form of older buildings. Taken to excess, new Victorians seem contrived, but evoked with sensitivity, Victorian images can contribute to a stronger sense of place (Figs. 11-53, 11-54, 11-55).

In contrast, understated homestead forms are easily translated into contemporary situations (Figs. 11-56, 11-57). They are hard to date, can be adapted to a variety of uses, and can be interpreted in newer materials. Scale and mass can be adjusted upward to a moderate extent. The building cost is frequently lower than the cost of reproducing styles more dependent on craftsmanship for their effect. In its simplicity, homestead architecture expresses a timelessness and humility consistent with a rugged environment.

Figure 11-53. *The restored Inn at Glenbrook, Nevada, a 700-acre first- and second-home community on the eastern shore of Lake Tahoe. Developer, Glenbrook Properties. Backen Arrigoni & Ross, San Francisco, architects. Photo by Backen Arrigoni & Ross.*

Figure 11-54. *Mill Street Plaza, a new shopping mall in downtown Aspen, Colorado, was designed to blend with the Victorian character and scale of the town's historic commercial buildings. Hagman Yaw, Aspen, architecture. Photo by Dave Marlow.*

Figure 11-55. *The 1987 addition to the historic Hotel Jerome in Aspen, Colorado, was carefully detailed and scaled to match the original. Hagman Yaw, Aspen, architects. Photo by Hagman Yaw.*

Figure 11-56. *Coldstream Condominiums in Vail, Colorado, recall the sparse detailing of the homestead style. Developer, Cascade Village Properties. Graeme Woodhouse, conceptual site plan; Morter Fisher Arnold, Vail, architecture; Berridge Associates, Inc., San Francisco, landscape architecture. Photo by Robert Arnold.*

Figure 11-57. *Adjacent to the remains of Old Keystone mining camp (see Fig. 2-15), the Old Keystone Condominiums are unusually faithful to the style and scale of their context. Backen Arrigoni & Ross, San Francisco, architects. Photo by Backen Arrigoni & Ross.*

Figure 11-58. *The Arco mine, Idaho Springs, Colorado, exemplifies the typical geometry of a hillside gold mill.*

Mining Architecture. The domestic vernacular was not the only strong influence of the western frontier on mountain architecture. From the 1850s to the Civil War, mining for precious metals fueled a short-lived, hyperactive wave of industrial building, whose distinct character still colors the western regional idiom (Fig. 11-58).

In contrast with dredging and placer mining, it was lode mining—the exploitation of an underground vein of gold-bearing quartz—that spurred the building of major structures to support its operations (Figs. 11-59, 11-60). After a promising lode was discovered, machinery to excavate a shaft, crush the quartz, and remove the valuable metals had to be brought in and housed. At the top of the shaft, a timber headframe was built to carry the sheaves and pulleys for the hoisting ropes. A processing mill, its size dependent on the promise of the vein and the finances of the mine's backers, was erected nearby. Ore was transported by a variety of devices from the mouth of the shaft to the mill, where it dropped or was fed on mechanical conveyors to the crushing machinery, or stamping shoes. After the rock was pulverized, it passed over a set of amalgamation plates and concentrators, where a chemical reduction process separated the metal from the crushed ore.

Many, though not all, of these stamp mills were constructed on relatively steep slopes below the headframe. Because the processing sequence was a

Figure 11-59. Eureka's huge Sunnyside Mill near Silverton, Colorado, was built in 1917 but burned to the ground two years later. Photo courtesy of San Juan County Historical Society.

Figure 11-60. The Economic Mill at Eclipse, Cripple Creek mining district, Colorado. Photo courtesy of Colorado Historical Society.

Figure 11-61. *Hillside residence in Vail, Colorado, has its stylistic roots in the mining era. Morter Fisher Arnold, Vail, architects. Photo by Robert Arnold.*

linear one, the buildings that followed the slope downhill from the shaft could use gravity and sometimes water power to carry the ore through the process. Also, the mechanical systems that hoisted the heavy iron stamping shoes and kept the conveyors moving required considerable ceiling height. To construct such large buildings on difficult slopes demanded the utmost skill in millwright timbering. The contribution of mining architecture to the regional vernacular of the mountain West thus goes far beyond the superficial idioms of shed roofs and oversized timbers. Rather, its legacy rests on its singular forms and its strength (Fig. 11-61).

Fundamental to the image of mining architecture is a structural system that is well articulated, openly revealed, and extremely durable. The ingenuity with which enormous timbers were assembled to support buildings and machinery of great size is remarkable. Another important trait is the organic combination of geometrically simple forms in a single building, expressing the fusion of site topography and building function. Finally, there is the slope-hugging mass of the mill, which, in reiterating the form of the mountain, defies both gravity and gradient. These old structures anchor a sense of place, not simply because they are historical relics, but because they speak a language of perseverance, practicality, and grandeur of vision in a landscape that appreciates all three.

Traditional Patterns and Contemporary Solutions

Archetypes and historical styles in mountain architecture are instructive as a collection of traits that are functionally and symbolically important to people living in the mountains. As tangible evidence of the forces of nature, most of these models offer valid alternatives for responding to climate and terrain. As the embodiment of human hopes and attachments, all of them offer the means to perpetuate the sense of place that is already so powerful in the mountain landscape.

In our imagination, these historic models merge to create images of ideal mountain habitats: places that offer warmth, shelter, and individuality of craft and that celebrate the presence of people in an untamed and beautiful environment. The challenge today is to apply selectively what they offer, satisfying contemporary needs with the wisdom that comes from sensitivity to place.

CONTROLLING ARCHITECTURAL STYLE

Municipal officials and developers in the mountains today are struggling to codify approaches to architecture that control quality and promote the growth of a strong community identity.[2] One of the major issues in this effort concerns architectural themes and styles: whether (and how) to adapt traditional styles as themes, to encourage regionally specific styles, and to define stylistic guidelines.

The challenge of theme architecture is to identify appropriate local symbols of place and to use them in ways that make the chosen themes feel authentic. In matters of theme, as in matters of siting and scale, there is no single right answer, but the choices made affect how a place is perceived and the population that is attracted to it.

The following examples show how several American mountain resort communities chose to deal with issues of style. Some drew up detailed design guidelines that mandate stylistic conformity; others left the question open.

New England: Obscured Traditions

The New England region calls to mind informal aggregations of white clapboard or shingle-sided

[2]In addition to the design guidelines referred to in this section, see also the Bibliography for references to the following resort communities: Arrowhead, Castle Pines, Crested Butte, and Telluride, Colorado; Sea Ranch, California; and Banff Townsite, Alberta.

houses, barns, and outbuildings in simple geometric shapes (Fig. 11-62). This style, however, is the visual vocabulary of agrarian villages in a different kind of landscape. It is not craggy high-alpine scenery, but leafy forests and gentle, hilly terrain that one sees in these images.

To reinforce their identity as winter recreation centers, many New England ski villages have consequently avoided indigenous regional styles, choosing instead to emulate traditional Alpine architecture. Stratton, Vermont, is a typical example. The Stratton Corporation consciously patterned the architecture in its new village core after Austrian models in order to respond to image expectations and to conform to the Alpine character of the ski area's original 1960s buildings (Fig. 11-63).

In Killington, Vermont, the master plan for a proposed new village center sidesteps the question of theme. There, in a scattered resort currently lacking architectural coherence, the proposed design policy is to seek "individual variety within a satisfying overall continuity. Rather than referencing a particular historical or modern style, the design intent is for the Village Center to explore and develop its own style along certain basic guidelines [emphasizing] simplicity of forms, a conservative palette, and the use of high-quality landscaping" (Robert Burley Associates 1984, p. 36).

Killington's proposed design guidelines focus not on creating a theme but on manipulating form to reduce the apparent scale, bulk, and density of the buildings.

Figure 11-62. *New England vernacular architecture.*

Figure 11-63. *The tirolean-style Village Square was constructed in 1987 as the first phase in a major expansion of Stratton Mountain Village, Vermont. Developer, The Stratton Corporation. Hull-Mozley & Associates, Atlanta, Georgia, master planning; William Cox, Coral Gables, Florida, architecture; The Cavendish Partnership, Ludlow, Vermont, phase I landscape architecture. Photo by Hubert Schreibl.*

Figure 11-64. *With community participation guiding its evolution, new base area development at Ascutney Mountain Resort (background) blends well in style and scale with the existing village of Brownsville, Vermont. Lead consultants: The Cavendish Partnership, Ludlow, Vermont, planning and landscape architecture. Photo by The Cavendish Partnership.*

Certain guidelines for roof shapes (no sheds, hips, gambrels, or flat roofs; gables are preferred), pitch (6 to 10 in 12), roofing material (cedar shingles only), exteriors (only stucco, clapboard, or rough-sawn cedar or redwood), and windows (no double-hung or horizontally aligned) are aimed at a measure of architectural unity.

Although there is nothing in the proposed Killington guidelines that prevents historical and regional connections, there is also nothing that encourages them. Nor is there any sense that the developers understand what kind of place Killington is now or what kind of community they hope to create. In declining to express any expectations of character, the guidelines lack the parameters that engender a stronger identity for the village.

In contrast, Brownsville, Vermont is an atypical case in which historical character has been embraced. In advance of a proposed redevelopment of the contiguous Mt. Ascutney Ski Area, a team of local design and planning consultants helped the townspeople articulate goals for preserving the town's appearance. The resulting consensus on design style stressed the importance of retaining a sense of rural New England. This statement of intent committed the developers to new buildings that are sympathetic to

Figure 11-65. *Model vacation residence in one of the Hawk communities, Vermont. Natural materials blend with the hardwood forest cover, and a multilevel floorplan responds to steep siting. Robert Carl Williams, Pittsfield, Vermont, architect. Photo by Jerry LeBlond, Photiques.*

328

Figure 11-66. *Main pedestrian street in Northstar-at-Tahoe. Developer, Trimont Land Company dba Northstar. Bull Volkmann Stockwell, San Francisco, architecture; EDAW, San Francisco, landscape architecture and environmental planning.*

the natural environment and the existing village (The Cavendish Partnership 1986).

Vernacular Vermont architecture was advocated in form, scale, fenestration, materials, color, and siting. Designers oriented new base area buildings to the surrounding open space, rather than to constructed focal points, to suggest a nineteenth-century farmstead whose interconnected buildings offered protection in winter (Fig. 11-64). The image extended into the landscape design, as special attention was given to retaining existing stone walls, watercourses, hedgerows, and large trees. The new hotel was sited to straddle a watercourse, damming it for a skating pond, and groves of mature native hardwoods were planted to diminish visual impacts.

In a number of New England ski villages (Stowe and Quechee, Vermont; Waterville Valley and Loon Mountain, New Hampshire), as in some residential communities (Fig. 11-65), there are individual development projects that openly refer to their regional origins. However, efforts to express New England roots are not common in mountain communities where the economy emphasizes winter recreation more than regional tourism. The two purposes apparently summon incompatible images: The latter depends on historical character to attract tourists, and the former assumes that only an Alpine identity will satisfy visitors' expectations. Marking a neutral course between the two risks a bland and placeless image.

The West Coast: Mixed Metaphors

New architecture in the Sierras is occasionally reminiscent of regional architectural traditions, but although the rustic style has clearly been a design inspiration for some projects, generally there is little unanimity. In the older ski communities around Lake Tahoe and Mammoth, building styles run the gamut from stucco semi-Swiss to ultradurable, high-tech, high-altitude functionality, an eccentric mélange not unique to the Sierras. Lacking community consensus or shared visions, designers work here according to their own ethic.

Among the mountain resort communities along the west coast, Northstar at Tahoe and Whistler, British Columbia, have taken an active role in setting architectural standards. Northstar, the product of a single developer, is a reclusive composition of modest wooden buildings hidden in the forest landscape (Fig. 11-66).

The developers of Whistler chose a different approach. Familial architecture and unifying themes were not primary objectives; rather, the overriding intent was to build a new Canadian village, with all the diversity, linkages, interaction, and street-front vitality of a real community—and with a real village's ability to absorb occasional design shortcomings.

The product of many designers, Whistler Village is

329

an amalgam of diverse architectural styles, each one contained in a preestablished envelope that controls building height, mass, and footprint (Figs. 11-67, 11-68). This three-dimensional armature was the linchpin of a strategy to control village character by fixing the orientation of streets and buildings to sun, wind, and views; by enforcing streetscape continuity; and by providing the framework for a villagelike hierarchy of spaces and linkages (see Chapter 10).

Design guidelines for Whistler's urban core concentrate on architectural elements that affect use and urban vitality rather than on those that would enforce unity of appearance. These include standards for roof form, articulation of walls and windows, detailing, color, materials, pedestrian amenities, landscaping, and relationships between building functions and outdoor space. Regional influences are allowed expression in a variety of subtle ways through materials, detailing, proportions, and forms.

Given the latitude permitted in style and materials, the guidelines forewarned that the most troublesome architectural element would be (and in fact has been) the junction between buildings. These seams are sometimes awkward, for dialogue, not thematic consistency, was intended to work out the

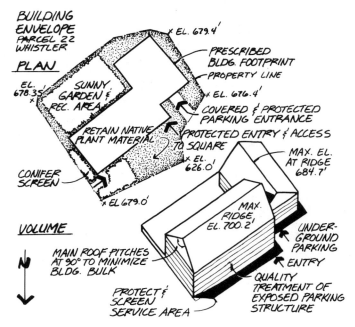

Figure 11-67. Sample of building envelope requirements for development parcels in Whistler. British Columbia Enterprise Corp.

Figure 11-68. Seeking the continuity of a traditional village main street, Whistler's development plan mandated linked buildings but refrained from standardizing the architectural style. Photo by Tom Barratt.

Figure 11-69. *The village core at Keystone Resort, Colorado. Developer, Ralston Purina.*

connections, but the development time frame was too short for perfect coordination.

The design-trained visitor is more likely to notice the imperfections than are those who enjoy Whistler for its liveliness, sensory stimulus, human scale, and comfortable spaces. What is noteworthy about Whistler's architecture is that in its diversity, it projects an exuberance in keeping with the magnificent setting and the western Canadian character.

The Central Rockies: Regional Revival

Several newer mountain resorts in the Rockies have devoted considerable energy to the issue of appropriate themes. At Keystone Resort, Colorado, developed by Ralston Purina, architects made a conscious effort to relate the villagelike complex to place and climate. The effort was less successful in the urban core (Fig. 11-69), whose rigidly rectilinear, flat-roofed buildings are ambivalent in context and origin, but some of the early outlying buildings are softer. In a contemporary idiom, they evoke the settlers' simple architecture of the region: homestead scale and proportions, simple roof shapes, shallow roof pitches, durable base courses to resist weathering at ground level, and small overhangs to protect the wood-clad walls above (Fig. 11-57).

Keystone illustrates several pitfalls in corporate control of architectural design: the difficulty of

attaining the warmth of traditional styles by means of contemporary forms, the risk of monotony when design is too rigidly controlled, and the continuing attention required to retain design consistency over time without exhausting the style's visual power. In more recent Keystone projects, New England saltboxes, Tahoe-like timber structures, and other forms alien to the region have intruded, suggesting that corporate design control has lost its focus on regional themes.

The physical appearance of Beaver Creek, Colorado, is the product of years of theoretical debate within Vail Associates over how to escape Vail's rigidly controlled alpine theme and achieve an American style of alpine architecture. Early in the design process, company planners tried to identify the traits that make a mountain building distinctive. They surveyed architectural styles in European Alpine villages, as well as indigenous American styles that seemed especially sensitive to the natural landscape: the San Francisco Bay School, the early California missions, the Adirondack camps, the East Coast shingle style, and the simple forms of New England farms and Indian pueblos.

They decided that certain traits, independent of local climate and place-specific themes, are essential to the image of mountain architecture. Built forms, they concluded, are consistently simple and unrefined and cannot easily be tagged by period or age. Their essence is expressed in forms and materials, not in

ornamentation or color. Natural materials are appreciated and used for their durability, structural strength, and heat-retentive quality, not as decoration. Their rustic appearance is symptomatic of the weathering force of an extreme climate. Rugged, solid, and massive, buildings communicate their capacity to support heavy snow loads, and they are perceived as metaphors for the weight and bulk of the surrounding mountains.

These common traits formed the nucleus for Beaver Creek's 1979 design guidelines (Fig. 11-70):

The architectural theme for Beaver Creek has been directed at establishing a compatibility between buildings and the natural environment, fulfilling expectations of visitors as a retreat to the mountains, respecting the historic precedent of mountain buildings in both Colorado and Europe, and utilizing energy conservation and solar energy applications. . . .

Major building forms should express a simplicity and directness responsive to the heritage of mountain architecture. . . . Major exterior walls should convey a sense of mass through plaster or rock. Window openings in mass walls shall be relatively small in scale and be used in an informal pattern on the wall, with deep set reveals and varied proportions. Plaster shall have a soft undulating appearance. . . . Vertical wood siding can be used as a sheathing [but] generally, the heavier rock and plaster surfaces shall be below, visually supporting the lighter wood-sheathed elements above. Wall materials should respond to the orientation of the building, with the north closed off (small window openings) and the south open to sun exposure. (Beaver Creek 1979, pp. 1, 12)

The only acceptable building materials in the village core are plaster in warm, off-white colors, wood siding without heavily pigmented stains, flat unglazed roof tiles in grayed tints of blue and green, copper flashings, and rock of approved varieties, laid in random patterns as if dry stacked. Not allowed are fake shutters, volcanic rock, unit masonry, untinted or untextured exposed concrete, aluminum window frames, mirrored glass, asphalt shingles, or metal roofing. The cost of building per square foot is considerably higher than mountain norms, but the resulting quality is exquisite.

These guidelines have given birth to an architectural style for the village that is not derivative of the Rockies in particular but is definitely evocative of mountains in general (Fig. 11-71; see also Figs. 9-24, 10-34, 11-30). Paradoxically, the search for an authentic, simple mountain style mandated levels of

Figure 11-70. *Image sketches from Beaver Creek Resort Company's Design Regulations illustrating desired architectural character and scale. Drawings by Jack Zehren, AIA.*

Figure 11-71. *One of the first buildings to be constructed in Beaver Creek, Colorado, the Village Hall contains lodging, conference facilities, and retail space. Its foreground facade forms one edge of the evolving pedestrian mall. Hall Goodhue Haisley & Barker, San Francisco, architecture; Berridge Associates, Inc., San Francisco, landscape architecture. Photo by Craig Buchanan.*

quality and cost that have made Beaver Creek a modern-day fantasy of another sort. It can be argued that high building costs and large scale have compromised the stated desire for simplicity of form. Nonetheless, the thematic intentions for Beaver Creek provide a rare model for innovative mountain architecture.

In the valley adjacent to Beaver Creek, the developers of Arrowhead also sought an appropriate architectural statement for their planned new resort village. In an attempt to visualize what the buildings might look like, they went through two conceptual iterations, rejecting the first (Fig. 11-72) because it seemed too refined and urbane. The second (Fig. 11-73), woodier, rougher, and more rustic, was nearer the desired image and so will be the basis for graphic guidelines to control building heights, massing,

footprints, and materials (Fig. 11-74). The objective of these tight parameters is not only to unify the architecture but also, as at Whistler, to ensure dynamic outdoor public spaces and linkages.

Architectural guidelines for new resort communities cannot wholly compensate for a short development time frame. In the old European towns and villages that these places seek to emulate, the community and what binds it together physically have traditionally taken priority over the visibility of individual architectural elements, resulting in architectural unity and the evolution of lively social spaces. The gradual pace and continuity of development over time are crucial to contextual consistency and a strong sense of place. The risk in rapidly paced development is that the product will seem more like a movie set than a real place.

Figure 11-72. *Initial architectural image study for the proposed resort village of Arrowhead, near Vail. Developer: Arrowhead at Vail, Edwards, Colorado. Rosall Remmen Cares, Boulder, Colorado, master planning; Communication Arts, Boulder, architectural concepts. Rendering by Stanley Doctor, Boulder, American Society of Architectural Perspectivists.*

Figure 11-73. *Revised architectural image study for Arrowhead. Robert Arnold/Ned Gwathmey Associates, Vail, Colorado, conceptual architecture. Drawing by Robert Arnold.*

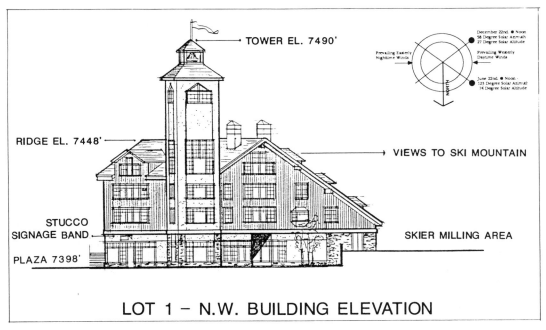

TOWER EL. 7490'

RIDGE EL. 7448'

VIEWS TO SKI MOUNTAIN

STUCCO
SIGNAGE BAND

SKIER MILLING AREA

PLAZA 7398'

LOT 1 – N.W. BUILDING ELEVATION

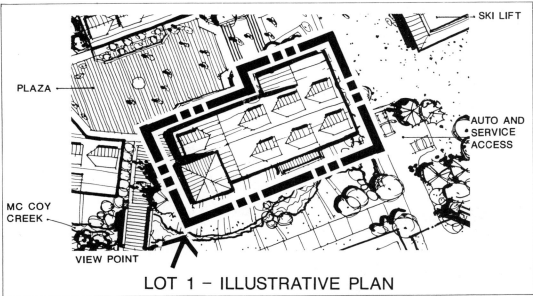

SKI LIFT

PLAZA

AUTO AND
SERVICE
ACCESS

MC COY
CREEK

VIEW POINT

LOT 1 – ILLUSTRATIVE PLAN

Uses Permitted:
Residential - Yes
Commercial - Yes
   Mountain Operations
   Retail Boutiques

Building GSF Permitted:
Residential - 12,500
Commercial - 6,000
Common - 1,500
Total - 20,500

Building Coverage:
Maximum Permitted - 80%

Assumed Floor Elevations:
At Plaza - 7398'
At South - 7403'

Maximum Building Height:
Ridge - 7448'
Eave at South - 7412'
Eave at North - 7431'
Tower - 7490'

Parking:
1.5 cars / D.U.
3.0 cars / 1000 G.S.F. Commercial
Underground parking permitted
with approval of D.R.C.

Roof Requirements:
Dominant Single Gabled
Ridge must run transverse to long axis
of the building.

Exterior Wall Requirements:
Above 7398' - At least 75% stone
masonry and/or wood siding.

Other Requirements:
Stucco signage band at Plaza between
7408' and 7411'
Ambulance Parking

LOT ANALYSIS SUMMARY
LOT 1 DESIGN GUIDELINES - FILING 13

Figure 11-74. *Architectural design guidelines for Arrowhead at Vail, Colorado, specific to each parcel, control the building footprint, volume, materials, roof configuration, and functional linkages with public spaces. Rosall Remmen Cares, Boulder, Colorado, master planning; Robert Arnold/Ned Gwathmey Associates, Vail, Colorado, conceptual architecture.*

The best architecture is that which meets the expectations of the land.

—Henry David Thoreau

CRITERIA FOR APPROPRIATE MOUNTAIN ARCHITECTURE

The wellspring of truly indigenous mountain architecture is the natural environment: its ecological systems, its sensory quality, its climate. Buildings that are wedded to place are those in which form and function have been influenced by the environment in which they are placed. A good mountain building exhibits environmental understanding, delights the senses, and projects the special character of its vicinity. Traditional architectural themes, translated from another place and time, can reinforce the context with symbols of place but cannot, by themselves, make a building right for a mountain site.

New buildings that interpret and respond to the mountain environment may look quite different from one another. Some have little in common with what we traditionally think of as a "mountain" building. Yet they do share certain qualities: sensory and spiritual vitality, references to place, climatic efficiency, functionality, and durability. These traits, which bind them so tightly to their landscape, are the design criteria that we can apply to new architecture in the mountains.

Orientation to the Sensory Landscape. The sensory power of mountain environments demands response in the way structures are sited, oriented, and designed. Good mountain architecture takes into account both the landscape and ecological processes.

Among the ways in which recognition of the sensory landscape can be demonstrated are how comfortably a structure is laid into the topography; how much site disturbance has been necessary; how carefully it is sited relative to significant natural features, views, and sunlight; how well the sequence of approach is controlled; and whether the building forms are consistent with natural processes on the site. Sensitive design makes nature a part of the architectural experience and uses it to enhance the sense of discovery and connectedness with nature (Figs. 11-75, 11-76, 11-77).

One of the most difficult problems for contemporary architects in the mountains is dealing successfully

Figure 11-75. *The Vail, Colorado, public library. Interior spaces are oriented toward the creek on the south-facing side of the building. Snowdon and Hopkins, Vail, architects. Photo by Timothy Hursley, The Arkansas Office.*

Figure 11-76. *The north-facing elevation of the Vail, Colorado, public library is partially earth sheltered. Snowdon and Hopkins, Vail, architects. Photo by Timothy Hursley, The Arkansas Office.*

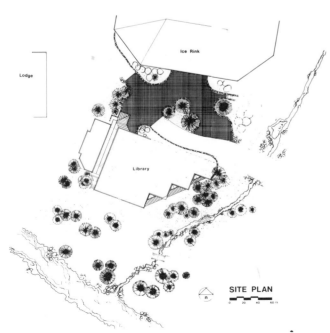

Figure 11-77. *Site plan of the Vail, Colorado, public library. Snowdon and Hopkins, Vail, architects.*

with larger building scales. The massive landforms and expansive vistas of the mountain landscape do not reward timid and fussy efforts. Historical styles cannot simply be enlarged or repeated in cookie-cutter fashion. A better source of inspiration is the landscape itself, for part of its sensory character lies in its scale. Correctly sensing design clues from the scale and form of a dramatic, spacious landscape encourages bolder, more innovative approaches to building scale (Fig. 11-78).

A sensory design evolves from study of the site and the building mass in all three dimensions and from all directions. It tracks the daily and seasonal movements of the sun and uses the kinetic properties of light and shadow on building surfaces. There is a natural rationale in the orientation of spaces and windows: Views become integral character elements indoors, and habitable spaces extend outdoors (Fig. 11-79). There is an obvious kinship between building and setting in scale, forms, colors, textures, and materials (Fig. 11-80). In sum, the building is so clearly a product of its environment that it seems inevitable on its site, a building that one cannot quite imagine erecting in a different place (Fig. 11-81).

337

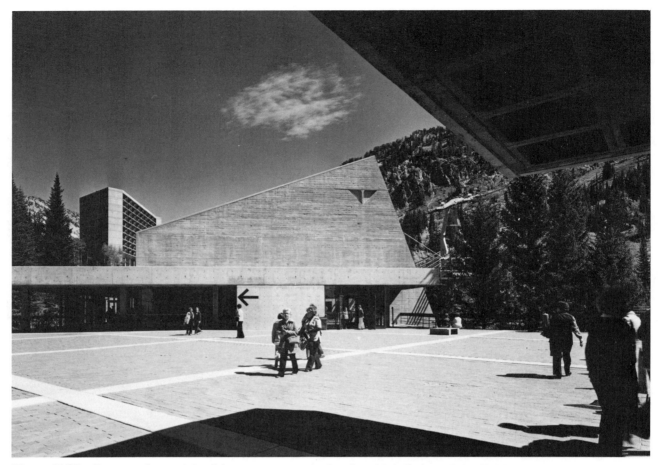

Figure 11-78. *Forms and materials of the tramway terminal at Snowbird, Utah, and the Cliff Lodge behind it respond to the cragginess of the surrounding ridges and to the need to concentrate densities in areas safe from avalanches. Snowbird Design Group, Salt Lake City, master planning. Tram terminal: Brixen and Christopher Architects, Salt Lake City. Cliff Lodge: Enteleki Architects. Photo by Patrick King.*

Figure 11-79. *Contemporary private residence near Aspen, Colorado, echoes the color of aspen bark and the shape of the slope on which it is sited. Hagman Yaw, Aspen, architects. Photo by Dave Marlow, Aspen.*

Perception of the Spirit of Place. The sensory quality of a mountain landscape is mainly a function of nature. The spirit of a place, however, is a more complex fabric in which the natural environment is interwoven with a human dimension and a sense of the passage of time. The spirit of a place is a fusion of the natural context with history and cultural traditions, mythology and accumulated images, communal expectations and human emotions. Spirit infers more than aesthetics, far more than theme (Fig. 11-82).

Indigenous architecture reflects a shared perception of the spirit—and spirituality—of a place, and many new mountain buildings fall short. Slick, irrational forms and placeless styles contradict the spirit of a natural place. True contextual architecture recognizes that spiritual and temporal, as well as natural, lines of force add meaning to design.

Buildings that capture the spirit of place are those that reaffirm context and relationships. Whether traditional or contemporary, they display shared symbols, reinforce connections, and make reference to locally significant features. They refer to their context by means of compatible forms, materials, colors, scale, and methods of construction. They use historical symbols, detailing, and craft as reminders of time and place (Fig. 11-83).

Figure 11-80. *The shingle siding and azure blue shed roofs of the Snowmass Villas mirror the brilliant Colorado sky and the sage-covered hills beyond. Henrik Bull with Ian Mackinlay, San Francisco, architects. Photo by Tom Walters.*

Figure 11-81. *The roofline of this private residence near Sun Valley, Idaho, mimics the slope behind it and sheds snow away from entries. John R. Smith, San Francisco, architect. Photo by Fred Lindholm.*

Figure 11-82. *Reflecting traditional southwestern architecture, condominiums at Quail Ridge Inn, Taos, New Mexico, appear to be a natural outgrowth of the dry, rolling landscape in which they are sited. Antoine Predock FAIA, Albuquerque, architect. Photo by Peter French.*

Figure 11-83. *Stillwater Cove Condominiums take maximum advantage of their rocky promontory overlooking Crystal Bay, Lake Tahoe. Bull Volkmann Stockwell, San Francisco, architects. Berridge Associates, Inc., San Francisco, landscape architects. Photo by Morton Beebe.*

In the specific context of mountains, architecture today is unique because it is predominantly oriented to a recreation-based life-style. In effect, leisure has become part of the spirit of a mountain place. To acknowledge the needs of a seasonal population seeking escape from daily routine, alpine building design operates on the edge of fantasy. Every designer working in the mountains faces the dilemma of delivering on the client's expectations without surrendering to escapist architecture, that is, without copying images from other places and times (Figs. 11-84, 11-85).

Part of the solution is renewed attention to regionally sensitive architecture. In the Rockies, for example, emblems of a regional style are evolving: understated, organic forms; informality in the layout of design elements; passive and active solar features; local materials; openly articulated structural systems; and muted references to regional history.
Taken together, they visualize the spirit of a place that differs in important ways from all others.

Intelligent Responses to Climate. Among the practical criteria for mountain architecture, none is more stringent than how well a structure copes with climatic extremes. The most obvious requirement

Figure 11-84. The street facade of the Hotel Lenado in Aspen, Colorado, was scaled and segmented to fit compatibly in a residential neighborhood of Victorian houses. Harry Teague, Aspen, architect. Photo by Timothy Hursley, The Arkansas Office.

Figure 11-85. Private residence near Aspen, Colorado. The colored stucco of the first level blends into the ground plane, and the wood-clad upper floor, separated from the first by a strip of windows, appears to float above the meadow. Harry Teague, Aspen, architect. Photo by Timothy Hursley, The Arkansas Office.

Figure 11-86. *The residential–office–research facility built for the Rocky Mountain Institute near Old Snowmass, Colorado, is an expression of context and climate. Using local materials, organic forms, and a variety of active and passive systems for energy efficiency, it houses a semitropical "bioshelter" and a year-round growing space for fish and crops. Steven Conger and The Aspen Design Group, architects. Photo by Doug Lee.*

Figure 11-87. *The form and siting of Spruce Saddle, the mid-mountain restaurant at Beaver Creek, Colorado, were decisions in response to winter sun angles, wind, and major views. Bull Volkmann Stockwell, San Francisco, architects. Photo by Wolfgang Herzog.*

imposed by the mountain climate is energy efficiency: warmth and protection from intense ultraviolet radiation in winter (Figs. 11-86, 11-87, 11-88). At the very least, this entails siting and orientation for the least exposure to wind, minimal heat loss, and the best natural light. In the central mountain areas, an amenable climate has elevated passive solar and earth-sheltered construction to the status of regional symbols. Elsewhere, methods of conserving energy include superinsulation, active solar heating systems, double building entries, window configurations determined by solar angles, high-quality construction techniques, and climate-sensitive specification of materials.

The direction of prevailing storm winds and how they affect snowdrifting patterns are important determinants of design. In building orientation, roof configuration, and the location of openings and access points, well-designed structures minimize the problems of ice and snow accumulation.

Less obvious climatic responses in the best mountain buildings include accommodating preexisting snowmelt and site drainage patterns; facilitating snow removal and storage; retaining snow for insulation; protecting sources of natural light

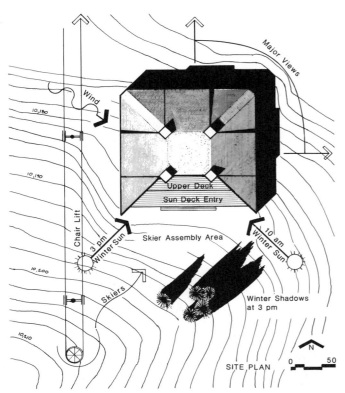

Figure 11-88. *Site plan of Spruce Saddle, Beaver Creek, Colorado. Bull Volkmann Stockwell, San Francisco, architects.*

inside as well as important views outward from accumulating snow; taking advantage of seasonally changing patterns of light, shadow, temperature, and color; using roof overhangs and a durable base course to protect exterior walls from snow and ice; and selecting materials that resist deterioration from weathering.

Mastery of Microclimate. After warmth, another essential microclimatic consideration is light. In temperate mountains and at high altitudes, people's relationship to light is entirely different from that of people living nearer the equator. Farther north, the sun moves in a lower arc and casts longer shadows, even in summer; the sun shines only rarely from directly above. Because winter days are shorter, interior spaces that have a luminous quality are important, especially in coastal mountain climates where cloudier weather prevails. Similarly, in drier mountains, exposure to their strong, pure, concentrated light is an experience that colors the feel of the landscape and should be seen as a design opportunity, not just as a practical exercise in controlling heat gain and glare.

In appropriate architecture, the sizing, height, and placement of windows respond to the sun's seasonal track and the intensity of solar radiation typical of the region. Design elements counteract re-reflection and glare. Colors, fabrics, paints, and building materials are chosen for their ability to stand up longer to ultraviolet radiation. The design of activity spaces blurs the distinction between indoors and outdoors and extends the seasonal periods of use.

Functionality and Timelessness. The best mountain buildings are not just aesthetic additions to a scenic landscape. They are also creative solutions that match uses to forms, scale and density to site constraints, and layout to terrain (Figs. 11-89, 11-90, 11-91). They age well, seem more permanent, and offer the sense of security so important to mountain communities.

Timelessness generally goes hand in hand with a rejection of faddishness and overworked themes, with a relatively simple form and style, and with straightforward construction techniques and durable materials. A larger initial investment in materials and craftsmanship should be expected but can be at least partially offset by the reduced burden of long-term maintenance.

Unity with the Landscape. The marriage of architecture with nature is a concept that views landscape as a metaphor for architecture and architecture as an expression of homage to the

Figure 11-89. *The Gerald R. Ford Amphitheater in Vail, Colorado, offers shelter without losing its vital sensory connections to the mountain landscape. Conceptual site plan, Royston Hanamoto Beck & Abey, Mill Valley, California, landscape architects. Morter Associates, Vail, architects; Glen E. Ellison, Vail, landscape architect.*

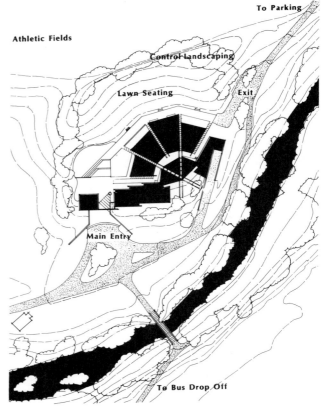

Figure 11-90. *Site plan, Gerald R. Ford Amphitheater, Vail, Colorado. Morter Associates, Vail, architects.*

Figure 11-91. *Vacation house in Carbondale, Colorado, straddles a bench overlooking an alluvial plain. Its north-facing side, pictured here, is windowless; its two-story south-facing side, clad in white clapboard, opens to the expansive views. William Turnbull Associates, San Francisco, architects. Photo © Morley Baer.*

landscape. Whether effected by the subordination of buildings to the landscape or by bold fusions and contrasts, this duality is essential to indigenous architecture in any strong natural landscape. In the mountains, few have mastered it, but most appreciate the symbiosis as a special accomplishment when they see it in place.

REFERENCES

Beaver Creek Resort Company. 1979. Design regulations—The village. Avon, Colo.

Beer, Henry. 1986. Remarks at an American Institute of Architects conference on Rocky Mountain regional design, Denver, May 30.

Cavendish Partnership, Inc., and Douglas J. Kennedy & Associates. 1986. Ascutney Mountain Resort master plan and growth impact analysis. Brownsville, Vt.: Summit Ventures.

Cereghini, Mario. 1956. *Building in the Mountains.* Milan: Edizioni del Milione (English ed. 1957).

Futagawa, Yukio, Makoto Suzuki, and Christian Norberg-Schulz. 1978. *Wooden Houses.* Tokyo: A.D.A. EDITA. (First English ed. 1979, New York: Abrams.)

Hansen, Hans Jürgen. 1971. *Architecture in Wood.* New York: Viking.

Kaiser, Harvey, H. 1982. *Great Camps of the Adirondacks.* Boston: David R. Godine.

Myers, Phyllis. 1984. The Park Service as client I: The early decades of rustic grandeur. *Architecture,* December, pp. 42–47.

Robert Burley Associates, Architects, and the Sherburne Corporation. 1984. Killington Village Center masterplan and development standards. Killington, Vt.

Weslager, C. A. 1969. *The Log Cabin in America.* New Brunswick, N.J.: Rutgers University Press.

Whistler Village Land Company, Ltd. 1980. Whistler Village design guidelines. Whistler, B.C.

Zelinsky, Wilbur. 1953. The log house in Georgia. *Geographical Review,* April, pp. 184ff.

Scene near Mammoth Mountain, California, after a record blizzard in 1969. Photo by Tom Johnston.

12
DESIGNING FOR SNOW AND ICE

Snow is not a wolf in sheep's clothing; it is a tiger in lamb's clothing.

—Unknown outdoorsman

In the mountains or on the flats, a snowy climate by itself defines important parameters for design. Wherever winter means snow, design is inadequate unless it has considered how the accumulation of snow and ice will affect circulation and public safety, snow removal, and the use of outdoor spaces.

SNOW REMOVAL AND STORAGE

Every winter, snow country residents contend with the failure of site planners to anticipate how snow will be cleared from a site and where it will be stored until it melts. Every winter, residential streets revert to paths the width of a snowplow blade. Cars parked along the street are trapped and buried or ticketed and towed away. Parking places disappear under snow banks, not to reemerge until May. Trash collectors can't get to the dumpsters, and it is a struggle to keep fire lanes open. There's no place for the snow to go, but municipalities and condominium associations balk at spending more than $100 an hour for dump trucks to haul it away.

The problem is especially severe in a mountain town's core, where higher-density commercial space and multifamily housing too often are built without regard for where the snow will go. In a recent survey of ski town officials (Birkeland 1988), snow removal and storage, pedestrian safety, and off-street parking were rated the most important factors in ski town functioning. Almost three-quarters of those polled said that because of snow and its impact on maintenance, design standards created specifically for mountain towns should be adopted.

Natural Factors. The ease of snow removal is not a matter of design alone, of course. It is also influenced by weather conditions at the time the snow is deposited (mainly temperature and wind speed), by the amount of snow from a typical storm, as well as its density and moisture content; by the duration of the storm and the periods between storms; by the number of storms in a season; and by the time of day

the storm hits hardest, which determines the amount of interference with traffic and parked cars.

The nature of the snow itself is one of the key variables. Once disturbed, it hardens rapidly, with the rate and amount of hardening dependent on temperature, moisture content, and degree of compaction. Because of this, snow should be removed as soon as possible after it falls; it should be compacted as little as possible before being deposited in a truck or storage area; and it should be handled only once.

It is hard for nonresident designers to comprehend how much snow a mountain site can receive (Fig. 12-1). To get a better picture of actual conditions, it is useful to visit the site in winter, talk to local residents, and obtain as many snowfall data as possible. Helpful statistics include frequency of storms, average and maximum snow depths for a single storm, average amount of snow on the ground at points throughout the season, and average snow moisture and density.

Even with the best statistical support, estimating snow storage requirements is an inexact art at best. If one were planning for only one storm at a time, it might be easier. The area of the surface to be plowed would be measured and then multiplied by the average depth of a typical heavy snowfall to find the number of cubic feet of new snow that will have to be moved. Around 25 to 50 percent of this would represent the volume of snow, after compaction, that has to be stored. Consider how high the snowplow can pile snow, and you will arrive at a rough number for the required area of snow storage space.

Unfortunately, it isn't that easy. In the Rockies, for example, late December to mid-February is the period of the highest snow accumulation and biggest individual storms. The snow that falls during this period remains on the ground, getting deeper, heavier, and harder to move, with the result that snow storage space can be filled up early in the season. From late February until mid-March, it snows a little all the time, so that clearing is easier but storage needs are not eased. By late March, daytime temperatures begin regularly to climb above freezing so that even big snows melt faster. However, freeze–thaw problems mount, and spring snows, notoriously heavy and wet, consume more storage space than do dry mid-winter snows. Not until April and May does the melting begin in earnest.

In effect, there is no reliable way to calculate

Figure 12-1. *House in Mammoth Lakes, California.*

volume requirements for snow storage space. One can only hope to err on the side of excess and provide as much room as possible to store snow.

Mechanical Factors.   The mechanical limitations of the equipment that is used to plow a site should be taken into account (Fig. 12-2). Snowplows come in many sizes, from an 18-inch hand-held portable to 7-foot blades and blowers mounted on front-end loaders, cats, and dump trucks. Their turning radii are generally limited, although some front-end scraper–loaders can easily turn in a 10- to 20-foot radius, or about twice their own width, and bobcats are able to make a 180-degree turn in their own tracks by locking the wheels on one side. None can descend stairs or plow 90-degree corners. Only the bobcats can pull snow out of cul-de-sac spaces. All of them are heavy and easily mired in boggy, thawing soil.

When repeated stopping and reversing direction are required, snow removal equipment operates at less than 50 percent efficiency (Mackinlay and Willis, n.d., p. 15). A snowplow will eventually ruin anything the operator cannot see beneath the snow and anything that restricts its maneuverability. Paving irregularities, corners (sharp or otherwise), and low, sharp-edged curbs are vulnerable to damage from the plow unless they are made of granite. Street-front sidewalks are especially tricky and costly to clear because of safety concerns and because all the randomly placed obstacles, like litter containers, light poles, street signs, and fire hydrants, make them hard to clear

Figure 12-2.   *Bobcat clearing sidewalks, Copper Mountain, Colorado.*

with larger machinery. Small spaces, narrow paths, corners, and stairs must therefore be shoveled by hand, further increasing the cost of snow removal. The costs of clearing will be at least double if the snow has to be trucked away.

Design Responses. Mountain town public works officials agree (Birkeland 1988) that the most constructive site-planning responses to a snowy climate are (1) off-street parking, with surface spaces in excess of normal requirements to allow for snow storage; (2) large, easily accessible snow storage areas; (3) minimal road and pathway gradients in shaded areas and at intersections; (4) a configuration of outdoor spaces, pathways, and landscape accessories (signage, furniture, lighting) that simplifies snowplowing; and (5) a drainage system that effectively handles snowmelt runoff and directs it away from circulation areas.

It is essential to consider snow removal requirements in the early stages of design. Before a site plan is completed, the designer must decide how a development, parking lot, road, or public plaza will be cleared of snow. Snow storage areas must be designated in advance. Otherwise, design intentions for pedestrian circulation and activity areas may be frustrated by snowpiles in areas not originally intended for snow storage.

When devising site plan alternatives, it is important to estimate where snow will accumulate and remain the longest, using massing models of the site (see Chapter 4). Snow accumulation is a function of wind direction and velocity acting in conjunction with landform, building and roof forms, and building clustering. The heaviest accumulation will occur under lee-side roof pitches and in areas shaded by structures and trees. Primary building entries and outdoor spaces intended for winter use thus should not be located in these areas.

To avoid miscommunication and costly long-term maintenance bills, the designer should review site plan alternatives and design intentions with the maintenance manager whose crews will be doing the plowing. Without a constant exchange, snow removers will put the snow where they want to put it. Not all hard-surfaced areas need to be plowed; some less-used pedestrian spaces will be more attractive if left untouched.

Snow removal operations and snow shedding from roofs are constant hazards to plants. Trees and shrubs should be set out from building walls where pitched roofs will shed snow and should not be planted in areas intended for snow storage (Fig. 12-3). (Willows are an exception, as they can bounce back after a winter under heavy snow.) Where snowblowers will be used, evergreen trees should be set back a distance

Figure 12-3.

equal to the throw of the blower (this can be as much as 100 feet along highways), as they may otherwise be defoliated (Fig. 12-4).

Snow Storage Sites. The best places for storing snow have special requirements. Gently sloping ground free of trees is preferable, as flat sites will become too boggy in the spring. Existing meadows, open glades, and gentle south-facing slopes are ideal. Concave surfaces have more storage room than do convex or bermed areas. Snow storage areas in sunny places speed melting in the spring.

In the urban core, only areas that are not of prime visual or functional importance should be designated for snow storage. Snow storage areas should not interfere with pedestrian circulation or visual connections between shoppers and shop windows (Fig. 12-5). Urban spaces designated for snow storage do not have to be devoid of landscaping, even though the palette of suitable plants is limited. Too much bare space may detract from the quality of the place in summer.

Drainage patterns during melting should be a primary consideration, as piles of snow in the wrong places will block meltwater (Fig. 12-6). Snow storage areas will be more efficient if located on unpaved surfaces, which slow the velocity of runoff from snowmelt and allow partial absorption of the meltwater into the soil. If snow must be piled on a paved surface, the ground plane should drain away from the pile. Meltwater from snow storage areas should be redirected or collected before it can cross pedestrian pathways, where it will freeze at night. If this makes a subsurface drainage system necessary,

Figure 12-4. *Snowplow clearing highway in Grand Teton National Park. Photo courtesy of National Park Service.*

Figure 12-5. *Snowbanks along the north-facing frontage of the LionsHead mall in Vail, Colorado, were a constant obstacle to retail traffic before the mall's redevelopment (compare with Fig. 10-27).*

Figure 12-6. *Its access to drains blocked by snowbanks, late winter snowmelt makes a sidewalk impassable.*

catch basin grates should be located in paving that is plowed, so that they can be kept clear. Whether paved or not, major snow storage areas should be accessible by paved path or ramp to keep snowplows from getting mired in mud.

It is better to provide a number of well-distributed, smaller snow dump areas rather than fewer large ones, because wet snow cannot be pushed far before it becomes hard as a brick. Large snowpiles take forever to melt, concentrate meltwater runoff in erosive amounts, and become dirt-encrusted eyesores before they finally melt away.

Even the most intelligent design cannot work without the cooperation of residents and maintenance people. Part of any effective site plan is thus an accepted community plan for snow removal that establishes parking patterns, clearing schedules, and areas off-limits to cars during heavy snow.

GUIDELINES FOR SNOW AND AUTOMOBILES

Safety is the dominant concern in the design of roads in wintry climates, as an efficient design can reduce the hazards to motorists caused by snow accumulation and snowmelt icing. It can forestall conflicts between snow removal crews and traffic or parked cars and reduce the costs of snow removal and ice control. The key factors are gradient, sun, and wind, as the following guidelines suggest.

Roads

1. Avalanche hazards. Known and suspected avalanche runout areas should be avoided in the layout of roads. If this is not possible, then overhead roadway shelters, upslope diversions, and snow-retaining structures might be considered where the avalanche risk is high.

2. Shoulders and rights-of-way. As a general rule, rights-of-way and road shoulders should be more generous in width (the latter at least 15 feet [5 m] wide where the topography allows) to give the fish-tailing or stalled driver some leeway and to leave additional room for snowbanks alongside the road. Where snowfall accumulation is known to be heavy, the shoulder should be widened even more, and the cut slope, if any, should be moved farther back from the uphill edge of the road (Fig. 12-7).

Drainage ditches fill with snow and will be a safety hazard if they are too close to the roadway. The right-of-way may have to be widened to allow ditches to be moved outward, where they can safely increase snow storage capacity along the road.

3. Road configuration. Sharp corners and dead-end streets should be avoided. Right-angle turns at the end of extended straight stretches of road will also be hazardous if the road is icy.

Extremely narrow two-way streets are not good, as they increase the danger of head-on collisions when the pavement is icy. The minimum recommended width is 20 feet (6 m) for driveways other than

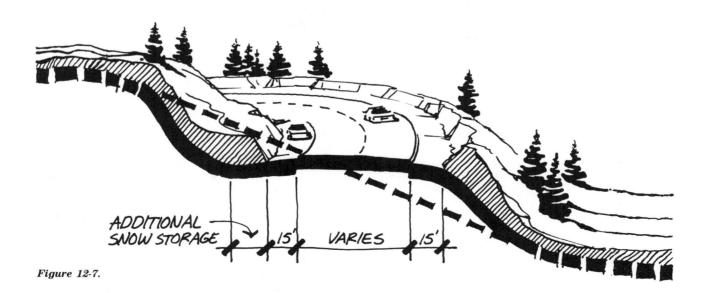

Figure 12-7.

Figure 12-8.

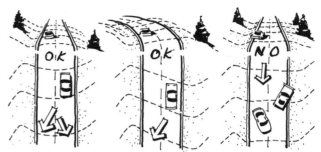

Figure 12-10.

Figure 12-9.

Figure 12-11.

private homes and 25 to 30 feet (7.5 m) for minor access roads.

Divided roads with low median strips can also be dangerous. The median is an added complication for the snowplow and is a driving hazard when hidden by snow. Divided roads should instead be separated by a substantial landscape strip 10 to 20 feet (3 to 6 m) in width (depending on the amount of traffic on the road and its speed), bermed or swaled gently, and marked with trees (if there is sufficient natural water) and guardrails. Boulders or raised planters in the medians can be hazardous to drivers, even at slow speeds, when roads are icy (Fig. 12-8).

In less developed areas, roadway pull-off spots should be provided at regular intervals to give motorists a place to stop out of the way of snowplows and traffic, to put on chains or scrape off windshields. These areas should be on relatively straight sections of roadway where they can be seen clearly by oncoming traffic and where motorists can pull off without sudden movements of the wheel. They require at least a 10- to 15-foot (3 to 4.5 m) extension of the shoulder.

4. Shading. In heavily wooded roadway sections, conifers casting shade on the pavement or shoulder may have to be cleared or thinned to let the sun melt snow and ice (Fig. 12-9).

5. Drainage. Meltwater should be directed to the road edge as quickly as possible. Roads should be crowned to reduce the flow of meltwater across the pavement, and drainage swales or ditches are needed on both sides of the road (Fig. 12-10).

Drainage culverts under pavement will become blocked with ice unless they are sized adequately; 30 inches (1 m) is an acceptable minimum diameter.

6. Wind clearing. The ability of a road to clear itself by means of crosswinds can be exploited by raising fill sections slightly above the surrounding ground. Entrenched roadways should be avoided, as they will drift over (Fig. 12-11).

7. Windbreaks. Obstacles in or near the right-of-way that may cause snow to drift over the road should be removed. Forest or fence windbreaks may be used on the windward side of the road, provided that they are set back far enough so that the resulting drifts will not reach the road shoulder. The Department of Highways for the Canadian province of Ontario has set this distance at a minimum of 75 feet (23 m) for a 3.5-foot (1 m) snow fence (Fig. 12-12).

8. Gradient. Sustained gradients in excess of 6 percent on roads cannot be maneuvered on ice, and even short spurts over 10 percent are impassable in winter without four-wheel drive. Gradients on driveways should not exceed 8 percent unless the pavement is heated with underground coils.

There should not be any high-volume intersections

Figure 12-12.

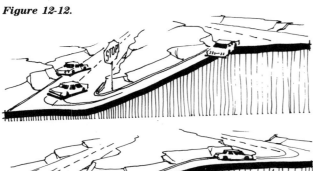

Figure 12-13.

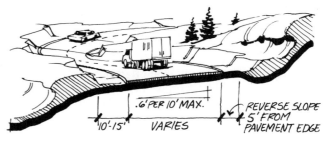

Figure 12-14.

or stop signs on an incline or at the base of a hill or downhill ramp, as drivers will be unable to stop when the surface is icy (Fig. 12-13). The roadway should be flat at driveway–street junctions and at intersections. Visibility at intersections should be unimpaired.

9. Superelevation. The banking of the roadway on turns, or superelevation, should be limited to minimize the risk of sideways sliding. The Ontario Department of Highways uses 0.06 foot per one foot of width (1.8 cm per meter) as its standard. On superelevated sections, the slope of the shoulder on the high side should be reversed 5 feet (1.5 m) from the pavement edge so that snowmelt from slopes uphill drains to the ditch instead of over the road surface (Fig. 12-14).

10. Curbs and gutters. Concrete gutter pans are essential where meltwater runs at erosive levels. Curbs, however, are not always appropriate or necessary. Raised curbs complicate snow removal but in certain areas may be needed to clarify the separation of pedestrian and vehicular circulation. Rolled curbing has been used as an alternative in some mountain towns to facilitate snowplowing without sacrificing the separation.

11. Bridges. Separated grade crossings can be dangerous, as both the bridge and the underpass will ice up. Bridges should be designed with dead-air space under the deck to keep the surface at about the same temperature as the rest of the on-grade road pavement.

12. Signage. Road signs should be set back out of the way of the snowplow and should be high enough that they can be read above roadside snowbanks (10 to 15 ft., 3 to 4.5 m). Crucial road information should be visible on signs that overhang the road. Curves, corners, and intersections should be clearly marked in advance, according to state highway standards.

13. Winter road maintenance. The use of salt to maintain the roadway is discouraged, as it is harmful to roadside vegetation and water quality. Sand and dirt are preferable. To keep sand from blocking sewers, manholes, and catch basins, a settling sump should be added to trap debris. Similar features might be designed into the roadway drainage ditches to allow the highway department to reclaim as much sand as possible after the snowmelt season.

14. On-street parking. In the gridded layout of most older mountain towns, parallel parking on the street has proved to be a major obstacle to snow removal. Even if cars are removed during storms, the parking lane inevitably fills with piles of plowed snow, forcing motorists into the driving lanes to park. Most towns are trying to develop other parking strategies to relieve their dependency on streets for parking space.

Covered Parking

Covered garages are the most effective, but the most expensive, parking solution in snowy mountain climates. The mistake often made with parking structures is to pursue cheaper solutions: to assume that a roof alone, rather than full enclosure, is adequate, when under some circumstances this can cause as many problems as it solves. Even if a parking structure is partially revealed on the downhill side, it is not always practical to leave it sufficiently open to the outside to avoid mechanical ventilation, as snow will certainly drift inside. Partially enclosed, unheated garages can also have problems with persistent icing from daytime meltwater.

If a parking structure is totally underground, soil surveys, groundwater studies, and adequate waterproofing of foundations are essential to protect the structure from seepage. Many of the flat sites large enough to accommodate an underground parking garage are alluvial valleys where high groundwater could be a problem. In these instances, covered parking may have to occupy the ground level instead of the basement, which can detract from the street activity unless the structure's ground-level facade is carefully designed or the perimeter is dedicated to livelier uses.

The uphill walls of structures cut into sloping terrain (Fig. 12-15) must be carefully engineered and reinforced to ensure adequate lateral strength. Bulking up these walls to resist the downward creep of soils, especially when the soils are saturated, is costly. Waterproofing and foundation drainage may also be less effective because of the increased hydraulic head in groundwater accumulating against the uphill wall.

Any parking structure should have positive drainage away from the garage entry, as water that drains inside will be frozen on the floor all winter unless the garage is heated. To prevent icing of the entry ramp, the garage entry should be located on the south or west side. Radiant heating of the pavement is an alternative, but it is expensive and not always reliable.

Carports provided limited protection, but the snow that blows in must be shoveled out by hand. The chore will be lessened somewhat if the carport is oriented so that a solid wall faces the direction of typical winter storm winds.

Surface Parking Lots

1. Siting. Surface lots should be placed on reasonably sunny sites, preferably those that are not already heavily forested. Areas of highly organic or clayey soils should be avoided for paved lots, as frost heaving may ruin the paving.

To avoid excessive cut and fill or massive retaining walls, lots on sloping terrain should be divided into segments that step up the hill.

Buildings adjacent to parking lots should be set back a minimum of 15 feet (4.5 m) to provide for snow storage space without undue buildup near building walls.

2. Capacity. As many as 25 to 30 percent more outdoor parking spaces should be provided than the number normally required by building densities. (Park City, Utah, requires that 10 percent of the parking area be set aside for snow storage, and Breckenridge, Colorado, requires a storage area equivalent to 25 percent of paved surfaces.) This compensates for the loss of parking spaces to meet snow storage needs after a big storm.

3. Snow removal. At the same time the site plan

Figure 12-15. *Beaver Creek, Colorado, Village Hall parking structure runs underneath the lower ski slope runout (see also Figs. 10-34 and 11-71).*

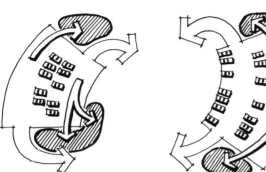

Figure 12-16.

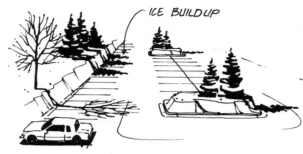

ICE BUILDUP

Figure 12-18.

Figure 12-17.

Figure 12-19.

20'-25'
TREE SETBACK

is done, snow removal for parking lots should also be planned and reviewed with maintenance managers. Two plans work well (Fig. 12-16): In the first, cars are parked in the center of the lot and snow is pushed to the outside, and in the second, cars are parked on one side or the other on alternate days, leaving the opposite side clear to be plowed.

If the lot is to be screened with berms or trees, this will have to be coordinated with the snow removal plan, for neither trees nor berms should occupy spaces dedicated to snow storage. If the lots are small, plan to push snow off the end of the lot, so that effective screening can be placed on the long edges (Fig. 12-17). For parking lots longer than 150 feet (45 m), snow storage areas should be interspersed with trees and berms along the long sides so that snow will not have to be pushed too far. Dead-end lots are unsatisfactory for efficient snowplowing.

4. Vegetation. Heavy planting of new trees is undesirable where the trees will cast shade on the parking lot pavement and allow ice to build up (Fig. 12-18). Some of the existing trees on the south and west edges of parking lots may also have to be thinned and cleared to reduce afternoon shading.

Where snowblowers will be used, new trees should be set back from the edge of the lot at least 20 to 25 feet (6 to 7.5 m) (Fig. 12-19). Trees should not be planted in snow storage areas.

Narrow median planting strips, common in urban parking lots, do not work well in heavy snow

conditions. They complicate the job of clearing the lot, and it is practically impossible for the snowplow to avoid running into them. Instead, a modular system is recommended where blocks of two to four rows of spaces are separated by a landscape strip 10 to 20 feet wide (3 to 6 m), bermed or swaled gently. Snow storage spaces 15 to 20 feet deep (4.5 to 6 m) could also be provided at either end (Fig. 12-20).

5. Drainage. Parking lots should be drained on the surface wherever possible, as catch basins and underground drains are likely to freeze up. It is best to align the lot lengthwise with the contours so that the runoff flows the shortest possible distance across the pavement and the grade change from one end to the other is not excessive (Fig. 12-21). On flatter surfaces, crowning a lot to drain it to the sides is far better than folding it toward the aisles, as this makes movement through the lot messy and hazardous during melting.

Do not surround a lot with uninterrupted curbing, as this will impede runoff. Instead, define the edge in a way that will make it visible to the snowplow driver and resistant to erosion (Fig. 12-22).

Surface runoff should be caught in gutters or rock-lined swales near the edge of the lot. Although they tend to freeze up during snowmelt, gravel drains at regular intervals are helpful in filtering pollutants out of rainwater runoff before it reaches natural drainage courses. Swales revegetated with water-loving grasses and willows act as good natural filters.

GUIDELINES FOR SNOW AND PEDESTRIANS

In environments with severe winters, wintertime concerns for safety and ease of snow removal are top priorities and largely determine which solutions make sense for pedestrian circulation, drainage and grade changes in public spaces, and the detailing of outdoor amenities.

Design embellishments inspired by summertime uses, when outdoor pedestrian spaces come alive with activity, must generally be superimposed on a design concept that works in winter. However, if wintertime standards were the only criterion, appropriate design would be judged by the snowplow alone: Public spaces would be unsegmented and paved, and paths and edges would be straight. But in summer, an urban landscape with eddies and small, linked spaces is part of what creates a desirable ambience. Although these two opposites are hard to satisfy in the same place, creative design and careful detailing can soften the conflict.

Pedestrian Protection

Where ice and snow are regular occurrences, pedestrians need to be protected from exposure to wind and blowing snow, from roof avalanches and falling icicles, from slick pavement, and from sliding vehicles. The variables that the designer has to work with here are sun and shadows, prevailing wind directions, friction coefficients, and slope gradients. Among the ways to control them for the benefit of pedestrians, consider the following:

1. Sun and wind. Wind protection and sun exposure are crucial to the success and safety of pedestrian spaces. The designer thus should orient spaces and walkways so that the sun will melt ice as quickly as possible. Materials that hold heat or reflect radiation to accelerate melting are best. Walls, screens, landforming, and vegetation also can protect important pedestrian circulation corridors from winter storm winds (see Chapter 4, guidelines).

2. Sidewalks. Accumulating piles of snow consume space meant for walking. To compensate, sidewalks should be wider, and street furniture, posts, litter bins, and street signs should be organized in a single continuous strip to permit mechanical plowing of as much of the walkway as possible (Fig. 12-23). To protect pedestrians from cars and to keep walkways free of snow plowed from the streets, the walks should be set back from the street edge.

3. Steps. Steps and ramps should not be located on the north sides of structures or in the perpetual winter shade of trees, for too much snow and ice will

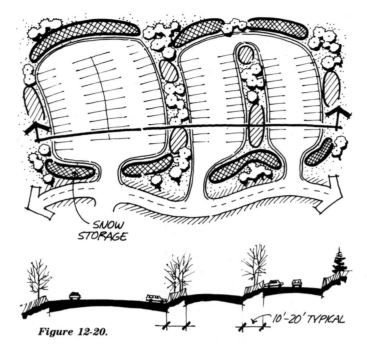

SNOW STORAGE

Figure 12-20.

10'-20' TYPICAL

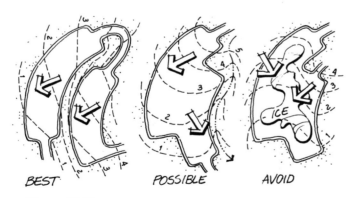

BEST   POSSIBLE   AVOID

Figure 12-21.

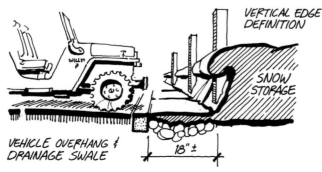

VERTICAL EDGE DEFINITION

SNOW STORAGE

ICE

VEHICLE OVERHANG & DRAINAGE SWALE

18"±

Figure 12-22.

Figure 12-23. *Aspen mall easily accommodates snow storage requirements in winter without deterring pedestrians' use of the space.*

Figure 12-24. *In Copper Mountain, Colorado, sunny lakeshore frontage is made unusable in winter by a roof configuration that endangers anyone walking near the buildings.*

accumulate on them over the winter. When there is no alternative to a shaded location, steps may be protected with a roof overhang or a freestanding shelter to keep off the worst of the snow and ice. Or pairs of handrails could be provided so that pedestrians can hold on to them with both hands when steps are in shaded areas.

4. Roofs. It is extremely dangerous to locate an outdoor space or an important pathway beneath a roof pitching in its direction (Fig. 12-24). Instead, roof extensions or other structurally adequate devices can be used to protect paths, balconies, and on-grade decks from snow and icicles falling from above. (Awnings and arbors are not strong enough.) Shedding

Figure 12-25. *Skier traffic on Bridge Street, Vail Village, Colorado.*

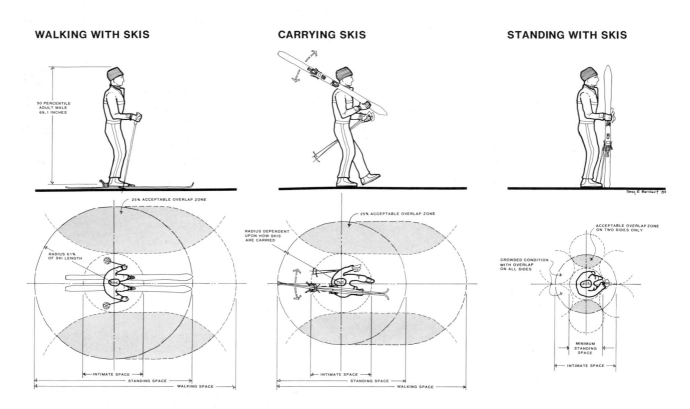

Figure 12-26. *Dimensional considerations in the design of spaces for people with skis. Drawing by Terry R. Barnhart.*

snow and roof drips may be directed into planted areas.

5. Materials. For the best traction underfoot, planed wood and very smooth-textured materials should not be used for paving.

6. People with skis. In the winter, many people in pedestrian spaces are carrying or moving on skis (Fig. 12-25). Therefore, in order to size these spaces adequately, designers need to consider how much space a person with skis requires to maneuver safely (Fig. 12-26).

Grade Changes

The movement of pedestrians in a mountain setting can be greatly complicated by slope gradients. In designing the pedestrian system, care must be taken in designing grade changes and transition points so that they can be negotiated under all but the worst conditions. Even standard maximums for handicapped access (generally 5 percent grade or less) and ramps (8 percent or less) may be excessive if surfaces are icy.

To accommodate ski footwear and to improve footing even when icy, stairs need at least a 16- to 18-inch tread (Fig. 12-27). Do not pitch the treads more than absolutely necessary for positive drainage, for that will make footing feel insecure when steps are icy. Ramps without overhead protection may be difficult to negotiate on foot in winter.

In sum, design features that reduce safety hazards at grade changes include arcades and covered walkways; canopies over shaded flights of stairs (Fig. 12-28); wider treads, shorter risers, and fewer steps in a group; more and sturdier handrails, spaced at closer intervals; and internal circulation networks passing through buildings instead of around them.

Designers might also consider textured metal edges on concrete and wooden steps to make them more durable and metal grating in steps and landings to reduce the amount of snow tracked inside. (Design the area underneath the grates so that it can be kept free of debris.)

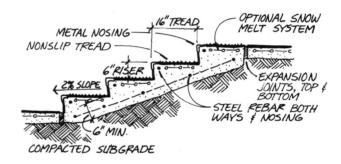

Figure 12-27. *Detail for steps in snowy climates.*

Figure 12-28. *Shaded stairway protected from snow by roof overhang, Copper Mountain, Colorado.*

Snow Removal and Snowmelt

Pedestrian spaces that can support use in winter are among the trickiest design elements because their shape and detailing can make them difficult to plow efficiently and because they are irresistible places to pile snow from sidewalks and streets. When, counter to design intentions, they become snow storage areas, they are lost to other uses for the duration of the winter. To get the most from outdoor spaces and to make them safe, it is essential to consider snow storage requirements, snow removal, and snowmelt patterns.

    1. Snow storage. Planting beds in pedestrians spaces can serve as snow storage areas in winter, provided that the right plants—generally grasses, perennials, and willows—are used. Raised planting areas give plants better protection against snowplows but cannot then be used as easily for snow storage.

    2. Furniture. Movable outdoor furniture makes snow removal easier. Where seating is needed in the winter, try to avoid legs by attaching benches to walls or making retaining walls double as seatwalls. Drain pavement away from permanent seating so that meltwater ponds do not form around it. Face benches toward the south or southwest to speed melting underneath. Avoid creating tight dead spaces under benches that are impossible to clear of snow and debris. Corners of benches protruding into a pathway will inevitably be nicked by snowplows; consider instead inset spaces for bench seating.

    3. Protective curbing. In the detailing of walls and paving, consider adding a concrete edger along the front edge to protect them from snowplow damage (Fig. 12-29). By running the plow blade along the curb, the snowplow operator can avoid getting hung up on irregularities in walls or other small obstacles. To be effective, the edger must mark a straight or broadly curving line.

    4. Fences. Leave enough space for snowpiles between fences or walls and pedestrian areas. Wooden fences cannot stand up under the weight of snow piled against them; open rail fences are better. On solid wood fences, leave space at the bottom to keep the wood from rotting.

    5. Snowmelt and materials. Differences in the thermal and structural properties of materials affect the use and safety of pedestrian spaces. Wood, for example, has a higher specific heat than rocks or concrete. Although slower to heat, wood also holds heat longer and so more quickly melts the snowcover once the sun comes out after a storm. As it is a less durable material, however, wood may not be practical for large uses, and thin lumber dimensions are rarely

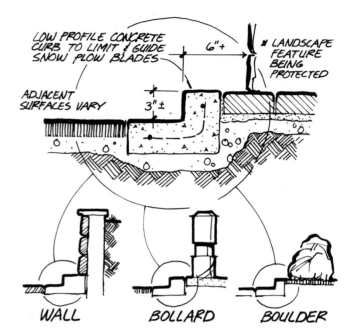

Figure 12-29. *Detail for curb to protect landscape features from damage by snowplow.*

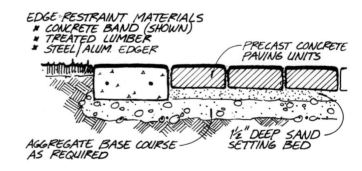

Figure 12-30. *Detail for unit paving.*

tough enough for any outdoor application other than building siding. Wood is also very slippery when wet.

    Asphalt walks melt snow faster than concrete does because their dark color absorbs more heat. As a paving material, gravel is not acceptable for highly used areas, as it makes snow shoveling difficult, and gravel paths get too muddy in spring. High-density unit pavers have proved reliable for use in the extreme mountain climate (Fig. 12-30). They are durable despite continuous freeze–thaw cycles and can be taken up and relaid if the paving surface heaves or subsides.

    6. Drainage. Where gutters or swales are necessary for adequate drainage of pavement, locate them out of main traffic ways, not down the center of a pedestrian space or walkway. Avoid boxing drainage into a paved area within a cluster of buildings. Coordinate the snow removal plan with the drainage plan so that snowpiles do not obstruct the flow of meltwater to drains. Take care to protect areas from standing meltwater where people will be congregating to wait for something, such as at bus stops.

REFERENCES

Birkeland, Robert W. 1988. Ski town circulation design and planning. MLA thesis, University of Washington.
Mackinlay, Ian, and W. E. Willis, n.d. Snow country design. NEA Grant no. A 70-1-15.

13
CHOICES

One of the basic needs of man is to experience life situations as meaningful. . . . The existential purpose of architecture and landscape architecture is to make a site become a place . . . , to uncover the meanings potentially present in the given environment.

—Christian Norberg-Schulz, Genus Loci, Toward a Phenomenology of Architecture

The mountains are not an ordinary landscape. They appeal to us not just because they are beautiful, although that is reason enough. The mountains are also a refuge, a challenge, a place for renewal. They appeal to the senses and the spirit. They are a forceful presence that demands response, participation, and respect. Their grandeur is an expression of the forces of nature and our place in the natural scheme of things.

With modern resources and advances in communications technology, communities of year-round residents are becoming increasingly feasible in the mountains. Where to build, how much, and how to build well in a mountain environment are questions that we cannot afford to submerge in the debate over whether we should build there at all.

Sensitivity in design is not by itself, of course, the solution to these questions. In the debate over how best to utilize and preserve the natural assets of mountain areas, the logical places to begin are regional land-use planning, scenic quality assessment, environmental analysis, and conservation, not design.

Design, however, is the one step in the land-use process that has as a primary objective the infusion of meaning into the built environment. Ideally, it is the one step intended to integrate natural assets with spiritual symbols and cultural values in the satisfaction of human needs. It is by design (and through time) that we build a sense of place. There is no single right answer to the complex challenge of designing in the mountains. There is instead a range of choices, some more appropriate than others. The choices we make on the most important issues will determine whether the places we build in the mountains will enrich our lives.

Uses and Users.   For whom will a mountain place be built, and what purposes will it serve? Will it be purely for recreation, or will it be designed so that it may eventually grow into a community? Is it meant for tourists or for residents, or will it serve both?

Choices regarding the intended population of a place will determine the activities that design must accommodate, and vice versa. Sometimes, however, these decisions are made by default. Without positive

steps to attract permanent residents, a place may forever remain a resort, subject to all the economic vagaries of seasonality. But mountain developments need not start as full-fledged communities; they can progress from resort to community over time, a progression that should be nurtured by design.

This book has argued for a development perspective that encourages the evolution of stable mountain communities, while recognizing that tourism is likely to remain their economic mainstay. Communities need many of the same elements that a resort requires: multiple physical linkages, a core that attracts activity, and the sensory qualities that reinforce connections with nature. But in addition, they need room for community facilities, convenient circulation, variety in housing, and a structure to support gradual economic diversification. It is this perspective on community that inspires sensitive design.

Size and Scale.   What scale is appropriate to buildings and spaces on a mountain site? How much density can a site support and still retain a sense of its natural character?

The factor of scale has an irrevocable impact on the perceived character of a built environment. We have seen that human scale is a central trait in our collective images of mountain buildings and villagelike communities. We have also seen that excessive scale is a common failing in mountain resort communities that are perceived as uninviting and disconnected from nature. In an environment where mountains are the monuments, people seek a humane scale and sociability, not monumentality, in their communities.

Terrain, elevation, and fragile ecosystems pose the greatest limitations to development and growth in the mountains, but most, if not all, successful resort communities have violated realistic natural constraints on size. Environmental data can be acquired in an organized analysis, as outlined in Part II, but if decisions are not derived from a nature-based value system, the constraints indicated by the data are less likely to be respected in judgments about size and scale.

Circulation.   Which framework for movement works best around and within a mountain site? What arrangement of linkages is suggested by the topography? How can the site planner configure roads and parking to reduce the impact of automobiles? Can alternative methods of public transportation work? To what extent can the development be made accessible to people on foot?

No other choices are as important to the long-term functioning of a mountain place as those that set its circulation patterns. No design issue in the mountains

Going to the mountains is going home.

—*John Muir*

is trickier than coping with the automobile. Examples have shown that few decisions can do such lasting damage to the character of a mountain destination.

Choosing among alternative circulation systems and layouts necessitates weighing short-term costs against long-term benefits. In larger contexts, it requires judicious siting and layout of primary uses and control over the concentration of densities, both at the outset and as a community grows. It requires cooperation and consensus. And to accommodate growth, it requires continuing review and adjustment. Even in the smallest projects, circulation design requires understanding the environmental constraints and recognizing that any project still depends on a larger network for access and linkage.

Responding to Climate. Depending on the choices made during the design process, the mountain climate will be either an uncontrollable wild card or a force for which we are well prepared. On every scale, design choices spell the difference between energy-efficient and energy-consumptive habitats, between microclimates that promote activity and those that inhibit it, between human comfort and human distress.

Enhancing the Sense of Place. What elements of the natural site contribute to its essential character? How can designers preserve and reinforce these natural attributes to convey spirit and meaning in a newly built place?

The certain sense of place that animates a well-established community is not just a product of the passage of time, although history can be a powerful enhancement. In some landscapes, nature can be as powerful a place-making influence as time. Given our psychological need for connection with nature, the ageless natural landscape is itself the embodiment of history, offering an anchor in time as well as place. Its contribution to the sense of place can be enriched or obscured by the designs imposed on it.

People are instinctively uncomfortable with placelessness. Most prefer places that respect their context and thereby confer a sense of belonging and pride. Contextual references, visual connections, sensory enticements, regionally specific landscape themes, architectural styles that reflect contemporary needs and physical constraints, and expressive detailing all help create a sense of place in the built environment.

Preserving Design Quality over Time. Which physical elements in a community most influence the design quality of the whole? The examples in Part III suggest that choices regarding preservation of view corridors and landmarks, selection of circulation

modes and corridors, siting and design of public open spaces, protection of important edges and linkages, and restrictions on massing and scale in the core are among the most lasting influences on the quality of a place.

Beyond the basic framework of a community, how should design quality be controlled? If there are design guidelines, what form should they take? How specific should they be? How visual? Consensus on design values is necessary for effective control, but in a heterogeneous community it may be difficult to achieve. The choices made in regard to these issues will depend in large part on the local political process and the participation of residents, property owners, and financial institutions.

It is tempting to control too much in order to ensure a high level of quality. But real places do have the capacity to absorb mistakes, to change, and to tolerate a little randomness in the pursuit of diversity. Within a general framework, there should be room for individual choices.

Attacking the Roots of Poor Design. With time, it is possible to address the causes of inappropriate mountain design. To do so requires involved residents, value-conscious designers and builders, and informed regulatory officials at all levels of government. It also requires sensitivity to environmental limits, to the assets of genuine communities, and to the aesthetic qualities of the landscape.

Environmental understanding is improved through better education regarding natural processes and ecosystems. Community consciousness improves with the maturation of social and economic priorities and with shared experiences that reinforce the benefits of economically healthy, socially interactive small towns. And aesthetic sensitivity improves with broadened personal experiences and cultivated sensory awareness, reinforced by contacts with others who care about special places.

Addressing all three fronts, *Design for Mountain Communities* has synthesized a process and an underlying value system for making choices in design. The process and values can be adapted to mountain projects of any scale, from whole communities to their most isolated component parts, and to projects in any natural landscape. The chapters in this book, if taken to heart, signal a revolutionary approach to building in the mountains.

The book has also attempted to convey the emotional appeal of mountain landscapes, in the hope that their beauty and spirit will infect those who wish to build there. Enlarging the circle of those caught up in the love of these special places may be the best hope for sensitive design in the mountains.

APPENDICES

Appendix A: Vital Statistics on Case Study Towns

Beaver Creek, Colorado

Latitude:	39.5 degrees north
Elevation:	7450 feet (2300 m)
Founded:	1981, by Vail Associates, Inc.
Access:	15 miles west of Vail, 115 miles west of Denver
Status:	privately held corporation
Population:	12 (1988)
Visitor Lodgings:	1000 beds
Area:	2200 acres
No. of Housing Units:	3223 units approved in PUD (half in core; 87 percent multifamily, remainder single-family and duplex)
Densities:	no prescribed limitations in village core; densities limited by lot size and building height
Building Heights:	up to 5 stories
Commercial Space:	277,000 SF planned in core (PUD); 380,000 SF total
Skier Capacity:	n/a
Annual Skiers:	374,000 (1987–1988)
Contact:	Beaver Creek Resort Co. P.O. Box 7, Vail, Colo. 81658 (303) 949-5750

Copper Mountain, Colorado

Latitude:	39.5 degrees north
Elevation:	9600 feet (2925 m)
Founded:	1971, by private developer
Access:	80 miles west of Denver on Interstate 70
Status:	owned by Copper Mountain Inc., a subsidiary of the Horsham Corp., Toronto
Population:	300 (1988 estimate)
Visitor Lodgings:	2800 est.
Area:	PUD approximately 300 acres
No. of Housing Units:	654 condo units (second homes); 210 employee units
Densities:	12 to 32 units per acre
Building Heights:	average 3 to 4 stories; maximum 7 stories
Commercial Space:	80,000 SF built to date of 170,000 SF approved in PUD
Skier Capacity:	12,260 daily
Annual Skiers:	733,000 (1987–1988)
Contact:	Copper Mountain Inc. P.O. Box 3001, Copper Mountain, Colo. 80443 (303) 968-2882

Keystone, Colorado

Latitude:	39.5 degrees north
Elevation:	9300 feet (2835 meters)
Founded:	1969 by Ralston Purina
Access:	75 miles west of Denver
Status:	Keystone Resort is owned by Ralston Purina; areas outside the resort PUD are in unincorporated Summit County
Population:	550 to 600 (in employee housing); 2000 in Snake River Basin planning unit
Visitor Lodgings:	5000 pillows
Area:	PUD 378 acres; private land in basin—11,000 acres

Keystone, Colorado (contd.)

No. of Housing Units:	900 hotel rooms and condos built of 1744 approved in resort PUD; 2390 units in vicinity	**Skier Capacity:**	approximately 12,000 skiers on a peak day
		Annual Skiers:	958,500 (1987–1988)
Densities:	6 to 10 units per acre average	**Contact:**	Keystone Resort, Box 38, Keystone, Colo. 80435 (303) 468-2316, or: Summit County Planning Department, Breckenridge, Colo. 80424
Building Heights:	1 to 7 stories		
Commercial Space:	74,730 SF approved in basin; 67,500 SF built; most is in resort PUD		

Kirkwood, California

Latitude:	38.5 degrees north	**No. of Housing Units:**	130 houses and nearly 300 condo units built of the 1427 approved in master plan (85 percent lodging and multifamily units)
Elevation:	7800 feet (2380 m)		
Founded:	1972 by Kirkwood Associates, Inc.		
Access:	190 miles east of San Francisco; 85 miles west of Reno, Nevada	**Densities:**	about 8 units per acre
		Building Heights:	majority are 2 to 3 stories; maximum 8 stories
Status:	privately owned destination resort	**Commercial Space:**	39,000 SF built of 160,000 SF approved
Population:	approximately 100	**Uphill Lift Capacity:**	15,000 skiers per hour
Visitor Lodgings:	lodging for approximately 1000 visitors	**Annual Skiers:**	380,000 to 400,000 average
Area:	700 acres, plus 2000 acres of skiable terrain	**Contact:**	Kirkwood Associates, Inc. P.O. Box 1 Kirkwood, Calif. 95646 (209) 258-6000

Northstar at Tahoe, California

Latitude:	39 degrees north		
Elevation:	6400 feet (1950 m)	**No. of Housing Units:**	654 condo units built of the 3100 approved; approximately 500 homes built of 600 approved
Founded:	1972 by Trimont Land Co., a subsidiary of Fibreboard Corp.		
Access:	200 miles east of San Francisco; 40 miles west of Reno	**Densities:**	n/a
		Building Heights:	maximum 2 stories
Status:	destination resort owned by Trimont Land Co.	**Commercial Space:**	71,000 SF built (1988) of 116,000 SF approved
Population:	estimated 250	**Skier Capacity:**	n/a
		Annual Skiers:	n/a
Visitor Lodgings:	approximately 230 lodging units (1300 pillows)	**Contact:**	Northstar-at-Tahoe P.O. Box 129 Truckee, Calif. 95734 (916) 562-1010
Area:	2560 acres, including 1700 acres of skiable terrain		

Snowmass, Colorado

Latitude:	39.3 degrees north	**Building Heights:**	vary according to individual PUD provisions; maximum in core typically 5 stories
Elevation:	8220 feet (2505 m)		
Founded:	1967 by The Snowmass Co., a privately held corporation	**Commercial Space:**	101,000 SF retail; 20,000 SF restaurant; 32,000 SF office and service (1988)
Access:	200 miles west of Denver		
Status:	incorporated as a home-rule town in 1977	**Uphill Lift Capacity:**	20,535 skiers per hour
		Skier Capacity:	average day 5000 to 6000 skiers; peak day 14,000 skiers
Population:	1360 (1987)		
Visitor Lodgings:	650 lodge rooms and approximately 950 condo units	**Annual Skiers:**	648,000 (1987–1988)
		Contact:	Planning Department, Town of Snowmass Village P.O. Box 5010 Snowmass Village, Colo. 81615 (303) 923-5524, or: The Snowmass Land Co. P.O. Box 5000 Snowmass Village, Colo. 81615 (303) 923-4500
Area:	2800 acres, plus almost 7000 acres on the mountain, are within the town limits		
No. of Housing Units:	1510 total condo units and 535 single-family houses; village is approximately 85 percent built out		
Densities:	n/a		

Stratton Mountain, Vermont

Latitude:	42 degrees north	**No. of Housing Units:**	720 multifamily; 360 single-family; 90 percent second homes
Elevation:	3875 feet (1180 m)		
Founded:	1961	**Building Heights:**	up to 4 stories
Access:	235 miles north of New York; 140 miles north of Boston	**Commercial Space:**	5500 SF in Village Square
		Skier Capacity:	7000 skiers on an average day
Status:	privately held corporation		
Population:	124 in Stratton, 370 in nearby town of Winhall	**Annual Skiers:**	480,000 in a typical year
		Contact:	The Stratton Corporation Stratton Mountain, Vt. 05155 (802) 297-2200
Visitor Lodgings:	425 units (1 to 5 bedrooms)		
Area:	new Village Square is 20 acres of a 4000-acre resort (not including ski slopes)		

Sun Valley, Idaho

Latitude:	44 degrees north	**Access:**	150 miles north of Boise by road; airport 11 miles south in Hailey
Elevation:	5900 feet (1790 m)		
Founded:	Elkhorn in 1972–1973 by Johns-Manville; Sun Valley in 1936 by Union Pacific	**Status:**	incorporated as a city in 1947

Sun Valley, Idaho *(contd.)*

Population:	approximately 660; around 3000 in neighboring town of Ketchum	**Commercial Space:**	n/a
		Skier Capacity:	uphill lift capacity 24,000 skiers per hour; 3500 to 4000 skiers on an average day
Visitor Lodgings:	approximately 11,000 visitor beds in the vicinity		
		Annual Skiers:	315,940 (1987–1988)
Area:	Elkhorn is 2920 acres within city limits of Sun Valley	**Contact:**	Sun Valley/Ketchum Chamber of Commerce, or: Elkhorn Resort Co. Sun Valley, Idaho 83353 (208) 622-4511 or, The Sun Valley Co. Sun Valley, Idaho 83353 (208) 622-4111
No. of Housing Units:	estimated 5000 units, of which 70–80 percent are second homes		
Densities:	n/a		
Building Heights:	maximum 30 feet in Sun Valley, 35 feet in Ketchum		

Vail, Colorado

Latitude:	39 degrees north	**Building Heights:**	2 to 3 stories in village core and up to 5 stories along highway frontage; 5 to 8 stories in LionsHead
Elevation:	8150 feet (2485 m)		
Founded:	1962 by Vail Associates, Inc., ski area operator		
Access:	100 miles west of Denver on Interstate 70	**Retail Space (1987):**	290,000 SF village core 102,490 SF LionsHead core 109,020 SF outside cores 220,000 SF approved but unbuilt
Status:	incorporated as municipality in 1966		
Population:	4500 (1986 est.)	**Skier Capacity:**	n/a
Visitor Lodgings:	approximately 30,000 to 35,000 beds (1988 est.)	**Annual Skiers:**	1,250,000 (1985–1986)
Area (1986):	3360 acres in the town limits	**Contact:**	Town of Vail, Community Development Dept. Vail Municipal Building, Vail, Colo. 81657 (303) 476-7000, or: Vail Associates, Inc. P.O. Box 7 Vail, Colo. 81658 (303) 476-5601
No. of Housing Units (1980):	5029 units in town (66 percent second homes) of total 11,060 units in county (34 percent second homes)		

Resort Municipality of Whistler, British Columbia

Latitude:	51 degrees north	**Access:**	75 miles north of Vancouver by road
Elevation:	2190 feet (668 meters)		
Founded:	skiing began 1960; village opened 1979–1980	**Status:**	municipal incorporation in 1975
		Population:	2400

Resort Municipality of Whistler, British Columbia *(contd.)*

Visitor Lodgings:	1624 rooms or units; 6250 pillows	**Commercial Space:**	377,000 SF built in Whistler Village (1988)
Area:	31,210 acres (12,630 ha)	**Skier Capacity:**	12,000 (average weekend) to 15,000 (peak) daily
No. of Housing Units:	4484 (1988)	**Annual Skiers:**	1,068,000 skier visits in 1987–1988
Densities:	floor-area ratio in the core averages 1.5 for all uses except residential	**Contact:**	Resort Municipality of Whistler, Planning Dept. Box 35 Whistler, B.C. VON 1BO (604) 932-5535
Building Heights:	maximum in core 17 m (approximately 7 stories)		

Appendix B: Characteristics of Mountain Ecosystems

Central Rocky Mountains

Community: Aspen Forest

Found:	7000 to 10,000 feet. Full sunlight.	**Water:**	Species indicates moist soil conditions; groundwater 1.5 inches to 5 feet below. With long taproot, can grow on dry, rocky sites but will have shrubby appearance.
Dominant Plants:	Aspen over 50 percent (*Populus tremuloides*).		
Growth:	Rapid, from stump sprouts. Pioneer species on burned, clear-cut, or avalanched areas. Cannot reestablish under its own canopy. Succeeded by shade-tolerant species.	**Soil:**	Loams typical, porous, moist; generally deeper and less rocky than soil under conifers.
Diversity and Productivity:	Very high. Improves moisture-holding capacity and organic content of soils. Occurs with wide variety of grasses and forbs.	**Aesthetics:**	Good summer screen; white bark, kinetic leaves; vibrant fall color; color contrast with conifers.
		Problems:	Rapid deterioration after maturity, short life.
Sensitivity to Disturbances:	Moderate. Often indicates prior disturbance or unstable soils. Damage to bark nearly always results in infection of the tree.	**Benefits:**	Fire resistant; good indicator of avalanches and slope instability; fall color, winter bark; good food and cover for wildlife.

Community: Bog

Found:	Nearly level sites over shallow water tables.	**Aesthetics:**	As openings in forest, provide variety and interest, especially at edge.
Dominant Plants:	Water-loving sedges, rushes, willows.	**Problems:**	Restricted, poor drainage; often in flood zone; affected by cold air drainage; areas of heavier snow deposition and drifting at higher elevations; unstable, peaty soils unsuitable for development.
Growth:	Rapid; gradual successional change to meadow.		
Diversity and Productivity:	Moderate.		
Sensitivity to Disturbance:	Low; abundant soil moisture is critical; draining will destroy.		
Water:	Water table 0 to 2 feet below surface.	**Benefits:**	Help absorb flood energy; high water storage capacity; fire-safe; aquifer recharge area; crucial to mountain water quantity and quality.
Soil:	High in organic content, peaty to several feet; subsoils unconsolidated sand and gravel, deep.		

Community: Douglas Fir Forest

Found:	6000 to 10,500 feet (not often above 8500 feet); north-facing slopes; southerly where higher, moist.	**Dominant Plants:**	Douglas fir (*Pseudotsuga menziesii*) 50 percent.

Community:	**Douglas Fir Forest** *(contd.)*		
Associated with:	Ponderosa pine (*Pinus ponderosa*), limber pine (*P. flexilis*), Englemann spruce (*Picea englemannii*), aspen (*Populus tremuloides*), understory of shrubs, forbs, some grasses.	**Water:**	Well-drained sites with water table below 5 feet.
		Soil:	Moderately moist sand and loam likely, low clay content. Biggest trees on deepest soils.
Growth:	Slow.	**Aesthetics:**	Canopy is dense and uniform; good screen but clearing is noticeable.
Diversity and Productivity:	Sometimes in almost pure stands but usually fairly diverse; productivity depends on the site.	**Problems:**	High wildfire hazard. Indicator of cool, shady areas where snow and ice persist later in spring.
Sensitivity to Disturbance:	Temperature–soil moisture balance critical at higher elevations; reestablishment on south-facing slopes difficult. Some shading required for regeneration.	**Benefits:**	Stabilizes snowcover and minimizes avalanches.

Community:	**Greasewood–Saltbush Ecosystem**		
Found:	Any altitude, alkaline soils, shallow water table. Intermountain basins; windy, arid, sunny conditions.	**Soil:**	Extremely alkaline. Presence of low rabbitbrush indicates outer limits of alkaline zone.
		Aesthetics:	Monotonous, unattractive. Cannot screen structures.
Dominant Plants:	Greasewood (*Sarcobatus vermiculatus*), saltbush (*Atriplex sp.*).	**Problems:**	Local flooding potential may be high in intense thunderstorms. Opportunity for improving scenic values is low because conditions limit introduction of other plants.
Growth:	Moderate, stable.		
Diversity and Productivity:	Very limited.		
Sensitivity to Disturbance:	Low. Greasewood sprouts after cutting.		
Water:	Precipitation very low (5 to 10 inches annually), but water table is high.	**Benefits:**	May be only vegetation that can establish cover on these areas. Nesting habitat for birds.

Community:	**Limber–Bristlecone Pine Forest**		
Found:	Small areas from 7500 to 11,500 feet (timberline).	**Dominant Plants:**	Limber pine (*Pinus flexilis*), bristlecone pine (*P. aristata*).

Community:	**Limber–Bristlecone Pine Forest** *(contd.)*		
Associated with:	Englemann spruce (*Picea englemannii*), subalpine fir (*Abies lasiocarpa*).	**Soil:**	Shallow, rocky, coarse, low moisture content, low productivity.
Growth:	Long lived, slow growing, stable.	**Aesthetics:**	Gnarled, striking, fragile, very visible at skyline.
Diversity and Productivity:	Limited. Where ecosystem exists in pure stands, conditions are very harsh.	**Problems:**	Often in avalanche starting zones; severe climate: high winds, heavy snow, lowest winter temperatures.
Sensitivity to Disturbance:	High; very hard to reestablish after disturbance.	**Benefits:**	Cover for high alpine wildlife; wind screen.
Water:	Water table typically deep.		

Community:	**Lodgepole Pine Forest**		
Found:	South- and west-facing slopes, 8000 to 10,500 feet. Best growth 9000 to 10,000 feet. Needs full sun.	**Water:**	Needs well-drained sites. Water table typically deep. Requires more moisture than do lower-elevation trees (ponderosa, Douglas fir) but more sun and warmth than higher-elevation trees (spruce, aspen). Can withstand summer drought.
Dominant Plants:	Lodgepole pine (*Pinus contorta*).		
Associated with:	Most often in pure stands but found (rarely) with ponderosa pine (*Pinus ponderosa*), aspen (*Populus tremuloides*).	**Soil:**	Many types. Takes to dry, rocky, light-textured soil better than do associated species.
Growth:	Slow, long lived; subclimax species (may be climax species where there are no other seed sources).	**Aesthetics:**	Good screen; uniform color and texture. Cuts obvious.
Diversity and Productivity:	Very limited diversity; low to moderate productivity.	**Problems:**	High wildfire hazard. Needs fire and sun to reseed. Disease and windfall possible where clearings are cut. Indicates heavy snowfall; avalanche danger on slopes.
Sensitivity to Disturbance:	Very low; can withstand considerable disturbance by clear-cutting or fire.	**Benefits:**	Controlled revegetation with lodgepole has been very successful in many areas.

Community:	**Meadow Ecosystem**		
Found:	Valley bottoms.	**Associated with:**	Limited shrubs at drier margins: sagebrush (*Artemisia*), cinquefoil (*Potentilla fruticosa*), willows (*Salix*).
Dominant Plants:	Grasses, sedges, forbs.		

Community:	**Meadow Ecosystem** *(contd.)*		
Growth:	Rapid (annual), stable unless drained or overgrazed.	**Soil:**	High organic content and soil moisture; soils overlie unconsolidated alluvial material or glacial till.
Diversity and Productivity:	High in grasses and forbs, low in other species.	**Aesthetics:**	Value in contrast with forest; high interest at edges; low screening potential.
Sensitivity to Disturbance:	Sustained overuse or interference with soil moisture regime will change species composition; otherwise stable and recovers well after disturbance ceases.	**Problems:**	Potential flood zone; potential avalanche runout area; often in cold air sink; heavy blowing, drifting snow.
Water:	Very shallow water table 1 to 5 feet from surface. Soggy and saturated in spring and early summer.	**Benefits:**	Natural fire breaks; highly productive food source for wildlife, critical link in the moisture retention and water production capability of mountain areas. Vital to mountain aquifers.

Community:	**Mountain Grasslands**		
Found:	Broad slopes of all gradients and warmer exposures upland from meadows.	**Aesthetics:**	Screening very difficult except by topography. Transplantation of trees and shrubs into grassland areas not very successful.
Dominant Plants:	Grasses and forbs.	**Problems:**	Erosion prone. Ecosystem usually hard to convert to other species or to agriculture; successional change to shrubs or trees slow to nonexistent. Avalanche hazard. Greater temperature extremes than in forested areas.
Growth:	Limited by short growing season, slow nutrient cycling, high winds, elevation.		
Diversity and Productivity:	Limited; less productive than meadows.		
Sensitivity to Disturbance:	Revegetation often very slow.	**Benefits:**	Natural fire break.
Water:	Well drained; deep water table.		
Soil:	Usually loams, often deep. May have high clay content; slow permeability. Rock content increases on side slopes. Very low soil moisture content, high evaporation rate. Shrink-swell problems.		

Community:	**Mountain Shrub Ecosystem**		
Found:	Southerly aspects; zones of high solar insolation.	**Sensitivity to Disturbance:**	Moderate to good, depending on species. Some sprout from roots after cutting or fire. However, removal will result in new grass–forb ecosystem.
Dominant Plants:	Scrub oak (*Quercus*), chokecherry (*Prunus*), mountain mahogany (*Cercocarpus*), sumac (*Rhus*), bitterbrush (*Purshia tridentata*), and rabbitbrush (*Chrysothamnus*). Also buffaloberry (*Shepherdia*), cinquefoil (*Potentilla fruticosa*), and whortleberry (*Vaccinium*). All are available commercially.	**Water:**	Water table usually deeper than 5 feet.
		Soil:	Usually sedimentary in origin: silts, clays, unstable shales. Often low in permeability, high shrink–swell potential.
Associated with:	Forbs and grasses; occasional aspen and sagebrush.	**Aesthetics:**	Screening potential depends on height and density; can take low structures. High foreground visual interest.
Growth:	Moderate to fast, short lived; stable. Very slow succession to forest in some areas; climax species in others.	**Problems:**	Wildfire; shrink–swell; short life; flash flood zone.
Diversity and Productivity:	Very diverse.	**Benefits:**	Efficient sun energy converter in food chain. Key winter forage. Good zone for solar structures.

Community:	**Pinyon–Juniper Forest**		
Found:	Open woodlands on warm exposures below 8500 feet.		limestones and sandstones. Typically limey and alkaline. Hardpan may be present. May also occur on volcanic, clayey soils.
Dominant Plants:	Pinyon pine (*Pinus edulis*) and juniper (*Juniperus sp.*).		
Associated with:	Dryland shrubs, forbs.	**Aesthetics:**	Provides good screen. Overall distant form is spotty.
Growth:	Slow, stable growth; low productivity.		
Diversity:	Limited. Occurs at the lower limits for forest growth. Openings between trees are often barren.	**Problems:**	Slope instability, shrink–swell, severe fire hazard if understory shrubs are plentiful. May be in flash flood zone. Highly erosive soils. High evaporation, low humidity, hot summers.
Sensitivity to Disturbance:	Very difficult to revegetate if trees are cut.		
Water:	Very deep water table. Precipitation as low as 1 foot annually; light snowfall. Very dry sites.	**Benefits:**	Good wildlife habitat unless abused. Climate in this ecosystem usually not as extreme as in grasslands adjacent to it.
Soil:	Sedimentary origins:		

Community:	**Ponderosa Pine Forest**		
Found:	5000 to 9000 feet elevation on sunny, dry slopes.	**Water:**	Sites generally dry, with deep water table. Species has long taproot. In competition for water, it forms open stands of scattered trees, not dense forests.
Dominant Plant:	Ponderosa pine (*Pinus ponderosa*).		
Associated with:	Douglas fir (*Pseudotsuga menziesii*), white fir (*Abies concolor*), limber pine (*P. flexilis*), aspen (*Populus tremuloides*); substantial shrub understory, grasses, and forbs.	**Soil:**	Wide variety. Erosion prone on slopes over 30 percent in granitic or volcanic soils.
		Aesthetics:	Good screening potential. Careful siting can take advantage of natural forest openings.
Growth:	Slow, long lived, stable except on steep (over 30 percent) south- and southwest-facing slopes.		
Diversity and Productivity:	High; moderately productive where moisture and soil depth are adequate.	**Problems:**	Erosion; forest fire; deep soil freezing because of low average snowcover. Chinooks; low precipitation.
Sensitivity to Disturbance:	Low to moderate except on steep slopes. Regenerates from seed. May convert to shrub, grassland, or aspen ecosystem after fire or logging.	**Benefits:**	Good wildlife habitat. Good pioneer in revegetation.

Community:	**Riparian**		
Found:	Adjacent to aquatic ecosystems in streams and some lakes. Transects wide elevational range.	**Water:**	Very shallow water table, abundant soil moisture.
		Soil:	Highly organic and fine-textured surface soils over alluvial subsoils, which act as aquifers and filters to trap soil erosion from adjacent slopes.
Dominant Plants:	Willow (*Salix*), cottonwood (*Populus*), alder (*Alnus tenuifolia*), aspen (*Populus tremuloides*), blue spruce (*Picea pungens*); variety of rushes, sedges, forbs.		
		Aesthetics:	High visual interest within and at water's edge. Summer screening, fall color. Lots of deadwood.
Growth:	Rapid; short life span, regenerates by sprouting.		
Diversity and Productivity:	Highly diverse and productive.	**Problems:**	Poorly suited for any development of structures or underground utilities. High flood hazard; cold air drainage follows stream gradient.
Sensitivity to Disturbance:	Moderate unless moisture regime is changed. Soil disturbance affects water quality.		

377

Community:	**Riparian** *(contd.)*		
Benefits:	Root mat stabilizes stream banks. Vegetation has positive influence on surface and subsurface water quality. Important food producer for wildlife and fish. Fire barrier.		

Community:	**Sagebrush Ecosystem**		
Found:	Dry slopes.	**Soil:**	Best growth on deep, loamy soils. Usually free of alkali. Some sage species indicate heavy clay with high shrink–swell potential.
Dominant Plants:	Over 20 percent sagebrush (*Artemisia*); also rabbitbrush (*Chrysothamnus*), bitterbrush (*Purshia tridentata*), and saltbush (*Atriplex*). Various grasses and forbs.		
		Aesthetics:	Usually monotonous. Can partially screen low structures that are similar in color.
Interspersed with:	Pinyon–juniper and aspen ecosystems.	**Problems:**	Vulnerable to gully erosion from concentrated runoff. Change to other vegetation types limited by low moisture levels. Sage burns readily. High winds.
Growth:	Moderate, stable.		
Diversity and Productivity:	Low.		
Sensitivity to Disturbance:	Low.	**Benefits:**	Excellent food and cover for wildlife. Regenerates after disturbance.
Water:	Water tables very deep; low precipitation (6 to 20 inches annually, half as snow). High evaporation rates.		

Community:	**Spruce–Fir Forest**		
Found:	8000 feet to timberline; moist slopes, gullies, draws, heavy snow areas, floodplains. Highest and coldest forest ecosystem in western United States.		(*Populus tremuloides*), blue spruce (*Picea pungens*). 9500 feet to timberline: aspen, limber pine, lodgepole (*P. contorta*), bristlecone pine (*P. aristata*). At timberline, grows in form known as *krummholz*.
Dominant Plants:	Englemann spruce (*Picea englemannii*) and subalpine fir (*Abies lasiocarpa*).		
Associated with:	From 8000 to 9500 feet: Douglas fir (*Pseudotsuga menziesii*), limber pine (*Pinus flexilis*), aspen	**Growth:**	Very slow; seedlings take 20 to 40 years to reach 4 to 5 feet.
		Diversity:	Moderate.

Community:	**Spruce – Fir Forest** *(contd.)*		
Sensitivity to Disturbance:	High; very hard to restore after forest is cleared.	**Aesthetics:**	Dense cover and screen. Mature trees often in decline.
Water:	Accessible water table more important than soil properties. Forests often indicate springs and seeps.	**Problems:**	Mass soil movement; wildfire; higher avalanche danger if forest disturbed. Short frost-free period.
Soil:	Wide variety. Stony. Deep humus layer typical over thin loamy surface horizon, with deeper lower horizons, high in clays leached from surface layers.	**Benefits:**	Wildlife cover.

Community:	**Tundra**		
Found:	11,000 to 12,000 feet, timberline and above.	**Aesthetics:**	Landscape of beauty and contrast; very exposed, provides no screening. Highest interest on small scale.
Dominant Plants:	Gnarled, dwarf or prostrate limber and bristlecone pine, subalpine fir; grasses, sedges, forbs; prostrate shrubs. Talus and scree fields mostly barren.	**Problems:**	Avalanche; persisting deep snow cover. High winds.
Growth:	Very slow.	**Benefits:**	Water-producing ecosystem; natural water filter if undisturbed.
Diversity:	Very limited.		
Sensitivity to Disturbance:	Very high.		
Water:	Localized wet areas; permafrost.		
Soil:	Turf and meadow soils thin, immature, low in organic material (some highly organic bog soils). Prone to erosion, mass movement, solifluction, freeze – thaw. Permafrost to 30 inches in bog soils, 8 feet in turf soils.		

Adapted from Dennis L. Lynch, An ecosystem guide for mountain land planning (Ft. Collins: Colorado State Forest Service and Colorado State University, 1974).

Appendix C: Common Erosion Control Methods and Costs

Treatment	Comment	Potential for Erosion Control and Revegetation Success (1 to 10)[a]	Approximate Cost per Acre
1. Seeds and fertilizer broadcasted on the surface, no soil coverage or mulch.	Not very effective except on rough seed beds with minimum slope and erodibility. Should be used only in areas inaccessible to machinery.	1	$280 to $400
2. Same as treatment 1, but seed is buried.	More effective than treatment 1 and worth the extra cost for seed burial.	2	$320 to $450
3. Drill seed (assumes seed is buried and fertilized), no soil preparation or mulch.	Fast and far more cost effective than broadcast methods. Should be used wherever the site is accessible to drill-seeding equipment.	3	$185 to $250
4. Same as treatment 3, but with soil preparation.	Soil preparation is well worth the additional investment.	4 to 5	$225 to $275
5. Hydroseed, fertilize and wood fiber hydromulch at 1600 pounds per acre, using one-step method.	Not worth the cost and should be avoided. Hydromulch alone provides only a minimal effect.	2	$800 to $1000
6. Same as treatment 5 but uses two-step method, no seed burial.	Acceptable method on slopes, tight areas, or for turf and wildflower establishment.	3 to 4	$825 to $1100
7. Same as treatment 6 but seed is buried.	Well worth the cost for seed burial. Slope seedings need all the help they can get. Not feasible on very steep slopes.	4 to 5	$900 to $1200
8. Same as treatment 6. Add organic tackifier at 100 pounds per acre to hydromulch.	Tackifiers[b] are worth the investment on steep slopes, windy or highly erodible sites. No increase in labor or machinery costs.	5 to 6	$1050 to $1350
9. Same as treatment 6, but add plastic soil stabilizer at 30 gallons per acre.	Good for longer-term tackifier requirements. Liquids may be difficult to use in remote areas and in cool weather.	5 to 7	$1200 to $1600
10. Drill seed, fertilize, prepare soil, and dry mulch with hay at 1.5 tons per acre or straw at 2 tons per acre, mulch crimped in.	Use whenever site conditions allow. May be used effectively on slopes 3:1 or steeper. Windy sites may be a problem.	5 to 7	$500 to $800
11. Hydroseed, fertilize, and dry mulch at same rate as in treatment 10. Tack with organic tackifier at 100 pounds per acre and hydromulch at 150 pounds per acre with water at 700 gallons per acre.	Cost-effective method for anchoring dry mulches on relatively steep slopes. High wind sites still a problem. Far less expensive than nettings.	5 to 7	$900 to $1200

12. Broadcast seed and fertilizer, and dry mulch as in treatment 11. Anchor mulch with plastic erosion control netting.	Cost-effective netting technique for noncritical slopes. Green netting may break down too quickly on south-facing slopes. Long-lasting netting has greater visual impact.	5 to 7	$2200 to $3200
13. Broadcast seed and fertilizer, and anchor with excelsior erosion control blanket.	Good weed-free mulch adapted to small areas. Green netting still a problem. May not maintain good soil contact on rocky sites. Possible fire hazard. Moderate visual impact. Double-netted products provide more protection.	6 to 8	$4000 to $6000
14. Broadcast seed and fertilizer, and anchor with straw erosion control blanket.	Mulch and netting are seamed together. Better soil contact. Slightly better erosion protection. Lower visual impact. Possible fire hazard.	6 to 8	$4000 to $6000
15. Broadcast seed and fertilizer, and anchor with jute netting.	Good treatment on rocky sites. Possible fire hazard. Higher visual impact. Smolder-resistant jute available.	6 to 8	$6400 to $7400
16. Broadcast seed and fertilizer, and dry mulch as in treatment 11. Anchor with jute netting.	Same as treatment 14. Dry mulch below jute improves soil contact and often is a good investment.	6 to 8+	$6700 to $7800
17. Broadcast seed and fertilizer, and anchor with double-netted straw and/or coconut erosion control blanket.	Lower visual impact. Good soil contact. Mulch and both layers of straw netting sewn together keep the mulch from moving.	7 to 9	$6000 to $9000
18. Broadcast seed and fertilizer, and anchor with double-netted coconut erosion control blanket.	Cost-effective alternative to protection such as riprap, cobble, and concrete-lined channels, and slope paving. Not permanent: coconut fiber will degrade in 5 to 8 years.	8 to 9+	$8500 to $11,000
19. Broadcast seed and fertilizer, and anchor with erosion control and revegetation mat.	Permanent, nonbiodegradable treatment. Cost-effective alternative to armored protection. Owing to high costs, ECRMs must be used judiciously.	9 to 10	$30,000 to $43,000
20. Backfill soil into 4-inch web structure. Broadcast seed and fertilizer, cover with hydromulch, and dry mulch with tackifier or organic erosion control blankets.	Most complete and effective vegetative erosion control approach on the market. May also be used with rock and/or gravel. Expensive but still a cost-effective alternative to armored protection.	9 to 10	$45,000 to $60,000

Assume double seeding rate whenever broadcasting or hydroseeding.
[a]1 = minimal potential; 10 = excellent probability.
[b]Tackifiers are organically derived glues or binders mixed and applied with hydromulch in a slurry.
This appendix was contributed by Marc S. Theisen. It was originally published in his article, Practical approaches for cost effective erosion control, *Colorado Green* (Spring 1986), p. 19. It has been updated with 1988 costs.

Appendix D: How to Plot Winter Topographic Shadows

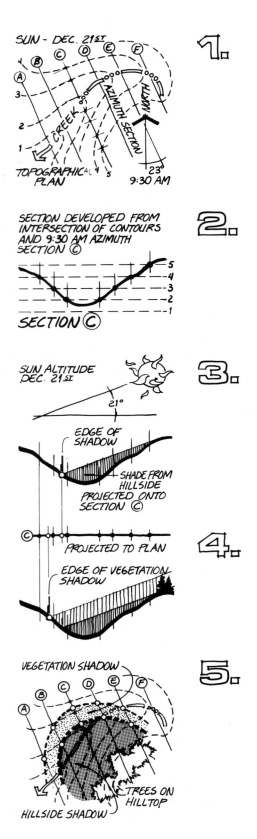

Step 1: Find out the sun azimuths for December 21 at 9:30 A.M. and 2:30 P.M. in your latitude. Draw a series of baselines at a uniform interval on a topographical map of your site, making the lines parallel to the morning and afternoon azimuths.

Step 2: Develop a vertical section for each baseline on your topographical map, using the contour elevations that intersect the lines.

Step 3: Find out the sun's altitude for the same time and place. Project that angle onto the section you drew in Step 2. Areas in shade are those below the sun angle line.

Step 4: If there is mature forest cover on your site, you may want to take its shading into account. Approximate its height and add it to the section with its corresponding shadow. Project the shadow from the section line to a baseline drawn beneath it.

Step 5: Transfer the shadow limits from the baseline under the section to the corresponding baseline on your topographical map. Connect the limit lines to show in plan the area in shadow (Fig. D-5). The smaller the interval between your section lines, the more accurate the result will be.

Bibliography

AESTHETIC AND SOCIAL ISSUES

Alexander, Christopher. 1979. *The Timeless Way of Building*. New York: Oxford University Press.

Alexander, Christopher, Sara Ishikawa, Murray Silverstein, Max Jacobson, Ingrid Fiksdahl-King, and Shlomo Angel. 1977. *A Pattern Language*. New York: Oxford University Press.

Appleton, Jay. 1975. *The Experience of Landscape*. London: Wiley.

Bureau of Land Management, Division of Recreation and Cultural Resources. 1980. *Visual Simulation Techniques*. Washington, D.C.: U.S. Government Printing Office.

Cullen, Gordon. 1961. *The Concise Townscape*. New York: Van Nostrand Reinhold.

Erickson, Kenneth A. 1977. Ceremonial landscapes of the American West. *Landscape* 22, no. 1 (Autumn): 39–47.

Goetzmann, William H., and William N. Goetzmann. 1986. *The West of the Imagination*. New York: Norton.

Graber, Linda. 1976. *Wilderness As Sacred Space*. Washington, D.C.: Association of American Geographers.

Gussow, Alan. 1971. *A Sense of Place: The Artist and the American Land*. San Francisco: Friends of the Earth Library.

Jackson, J. B. 1984. *Discovering the Vernacular Landscape*. New Haven, Conn.: Yale University Press.

Jacobs, Jane. 1961. *The Death and Life of Great American Cities*. New York: Random House.

Keyes, Donald D. 1980. *The White Mountains: Place and Perceptions*. Hanover, N.H.: University Press of New England.

Lippard, Lucy. 1983. *Overlay*. New York: Pantheon.

Litton, R. Burton, Jr. 1968. Forest landscape description and inventories. U.S.D.A. Forest Service Research Paper no. PSW-49.

———. 1973. Esthetic resources of the lodgepole pine forest. Berkeley, Calif.: U.S.D.A. Forest Service, Pacific Southwest Forest and Range Experiment Station.

———. 1984. Visual vulnerability of the landscape: Control of visual quality. U.S.D.A. Forest Service Research Paper no. WO-39.

Lynch, Kevin. 1976. *Managing the Sense of a Region*, 2nd ed. Cambridge, Mass.: MIT Press.

———. 1972. *What Time Is This Place?* Cambridge, Mass.: MIT Press.

Nash, Roderick. 1977. *Wilderness and the American Mind*, rev. ed. New Haven, Conn.: Yale University Press.

Roberts, David. 1979. Alaska and personal style: Some notes in search of an aesthetic. In *The Mountain Spirit*, ed. Michael Charles Tobias and Harold Drasdo. Woodstock, N.Y.: Overlook Press.

Rowell, Galen. 1986. *Mountain Light: In Search of the Dynamic Landscape*. San Francisco: Sierra Club Books.

Rudofsky, Bernard. 1969. *Streets for People*. Garden City, N.Y.: Anchor Press/Doubleday.

Sheppard, Stephen R.J. 1989. *Visual Simulation: A User's Guide For Architects, Engineers and Planners*. New York: Van Nostrand Reinhold.

Steiner, George. 1979. Cairns. In *The Mountain Spirit*, ed. Michael Charles Tobias and Harold Drasdo. Woodstock, N.Y.: Overlook Press.

Tobias, Michael Charles, and Harold Drasdo, eds. 1979. *The Mountain Spirit*. Woodstock, N.Y.: Overlook Press.

Trenton, Patricia, and Peter H. Hassrick. 1983. *The Rocky Mountains: A Vision for Artists in the Nineteenth Century*. Norman: University of Oklahoma Press.

Tuan, Yi-Fu. 1974. *Topophilia: A Study of Environmental Perception, Attitudes, and Values*. Englewood Cliffs, N.J.: Prentice-Hall.

———. 1980. Rootedness versus the sense of place. *Landscape* 24, no. 1: 3–8.

Twiss, Robert H., and R. B. Litton. 1965. Resource use in the regional landscape. *Natural Resources Journal* 5, no. 2 (October): 76–81.

U.S.D.A. Forest Service. 1973. *National Forest Landscape Management Handbook*. vol. 1, no. 434.

———. 1974. *The Visual Management System*. vol 2. no. 462.

———. 1975. *Utilities*, vol. 2, no. 478.

———. 1977. *Range*, vol. 2, no. 484.

———. 1977. *Roads*, vol. 2, no. 483.

———. 1978. *Timber*, vol. 2, no. 559.

———. 1985. *Fire*, vol. 2, no. 608.

———. 1984. *Ski Areas*, vol. 2, no. 617.

U.S.D.A. Forest Service, Rocky Mountain Regional Office, Landscape Architect's Group. 1975. Beaver Creek visual analysis.

ENVIRONMENTAL FACTORS

American Fisheries Society, Western Division. 1980. Position paper on management and protection of Western riparian stream ecosystems. Bethesda, Md.

American Society of Landscape Architects. 1978. Creating land for tomorrow. Landscape Architecture Technical Information Series 1, no. 3. Washington, D.C.: ASLA.

Armstrong, Betsy, and Knox Williams. 1986. *The Avalanche Book.* Golden, Colo.: Fulcrum.

Bailey, R. G. 1971. Landslide hazards related to land use planning in the Teton National Forest, Northwestern Wyoming. Ogden, Utah: U.S.D.A. Forest Service.

Bakker, Elna. 1972. *An Island Called California.* Berkeley and Los Angeles: University of California Press.

Berg, W. A. 1974. Grasses and legumes for revegetation of disturbed subalpine areas. In *Proceedings of a Workshop on Revegetation of High-Altitude Disturbed Lands.* Colorado Water Resources Research Institute. Ft. Collins: Colorado State University Information Series 10, pp. 31–35.

Berg, W. A., J. A. Brown, and R. Cuany, eds. 1974. *Proceedings of a Workshop on Revegetation of High-Altitude Disturbed Lands.* Colorado Water Resources Research Institute. Ft. Collins: Colorado State University Information Series 10 (July).

Billings, W. D. 1978. Aspects of the ecology of alpine and subalpine plants. In *Proceedings: High-Altitude Revegetation Workshop* no. 3. Ft. Collins, Colo.: Environmental Resources Center Information Series 28 (May): 1–17.

Campbell, Russell H. 1980. Landslide maps showing field classification, Point Dume Quadrangle, California. U.S. Department of the Interior Geological Survey, Miscellaneous Field Studies Map no. MF-1167.

Canadian National Research Council, Subcommittee on Snow and Ice. 1964. Snow removal and ice control. Proceedings of a Conference, Technical Memorandum no. 83, NRC 8146, Ottawa, Ontario.

Chronic, John, and Halka Chronic. 1972. *Prairie, Peak and Plateau: A Guide to the Geology of Colorado.* Denver: Colorado Geological Survey, Bulletin no. 32.

Cleaves, E. T., A. E. Godfrey, and O. P. Bricker. 1970. Geochemical balance of a small watershed and its geomorphic implications. *Bulletin of the Geological Society of America,* 81: 3015–3032.

Colorado Department of Highways, n.d. *I-70 in a Mountain Environment — Vail Pass, Colorado.* Report no. FHWA-TS-78-208.

Cook, C. Wayne, Robert M. Hyde, and Phillip L. Sims. 1974. Revegetation guidelines for surface mined areas. Ft. Collins: Colorado State University, Range Science Department, Science Series no. 16.

Cowardin, L. M., V. Carter, F. C. Golet, and E. T. LaRoe. 1979. *Classification of Wetlands and Deep-Water Habitats of the United States.* Washington, D.C.: U.S. Fish and Wildlife Service, Biological Services Program, Report no. FWS/OBS-77/31.

Davis, J. Gary, and Sarah Fowler. 1985. A wetlands assessment and mitigation pre-proposal handbook for Colorado. Boulder, Colo.: Aquatic and Wetlands Consultants.

Dunne, Thomas, and Luna B. Leopold. 1978. *Water in Environmental Planning.* San Francisco: Freeman.

Ellis, Jim. 1984. Snow creep. *Ski Area Management,* May, pp. 102ff.

Gilluly, James, A. L. Waters, and A. O. Woodford. 1968. *Principles of Geology,* 3rd ed. San Francisco: Freeman.

Gray, D. H. 1970. Effects of forest clear-cutting on the stability of natural slopes. *Association of Engineering Geologists Bulletin* 7, no. 1–2 (Fall): 45–65.

Greenland, David E. 1979. Modeling air pollution potential for mountain resorts. Occasional Paper no. 32, Institute of Arctic and Alpine Research. Boulder: University of Colorado Press.

Haeffner, A. D. 1971. Daily temperatures and precipitation for a subalpine forest, Central Colorado. Rocky Mountain Forest and Range Experiment Station, Research Paper no. RM-80.

Hansen, Wallace R. 1975. The geologic story of the Uinta Mountains. *Geological Survey Bulletin* no. 1291. Washington, D.C.: U.S. Government Printing Office.

Hess, M. 1968. Method for determining the effect of land forms on mountain climates. International Congress on Alpine Meteorology. *La Météorologie* 5, no. 10–11 (September): 75–85.

Hill, Mary. 1975. *Geology of the Sierra Nevada.* Berkeley and Los Angeles: University of California Press.

Irwin, Peter A., and Colin J. Williams. 1981. Prevention of excess snow accumulation due to roof mounted solar collectors. Report for Ministry of Municipal Affairs and Housing of Ontario, Toronto.

———. 1983. Application of snow-simulation model tests to planning and design. In *Proceedings, Eastern Snow Conference* 28, June, Toronto, Ontario.

Ives, Jack D., and R. G. Barry, eds. 1974. *Arctic and Alpine Environments.* London: Methuen.

Ives, Jack D., and Michael J. Bovis. 1978. Natural hazard maps for land-use planning, San Juan Mountains, Colorado. *Arctic and Alpine Research* 10, no. 2: 185–212.

Ives, Jack D., and Paula V. Krebs. 1978. Natural hazards research and land-use planning responses in mountainous terrain: The town of Vail, Colorado. *Arctic and Alpine Research* 10, no. 2: 213–222.

Ives, Jack D., Arthur I. Mears, Paul E. Carrara, and Michael J. Bovis. 1976. Natural hazards in mountain Colorado. *Annals of the Association of American Geographers* 66, no. 1 (March): 129–144.

Jenny, Hans. 1941. *Factors of Soil Formation.* New

York: McGraw-Hill.

Jochim, Candace L. 1986. Debris flow hazard in the immediate vicinity of Ouray, Colorado. Denver: Colorado Geological Survey, Department of Natural Resources.

Jochim, Candace L., and William P. Rogers. 1988. Colorado landslide mitigation plan. Denver: Colorado Geological Survey, Department of Natural Resources.

Jorgensen, Neil. 1977. *A Guide to New England's Landscape*. Chester, Conn.: Globe Pequot Press.

Kenny, S. T., ed. 1978. *Proceedings: High-Altitude Revegetation Workshop no. 3*. Environmental Resources Center Information Series no. 28. Ft. Collins: Colorado State University.

Kittredge, Joseph. 1948. *Forest Influences*. New York: McGraw-Hill.

Landsberg, Helmut. 1962. *Physical Climatology*, 2nd ed. DuBois, Pa.: Gray Printing.

Leopold, Luna B. 1974. *Water: A Primer*. San Francisco: Freeman.

Leopold, Luna B., M. Gordon Wolman, and John P. Miller. 1965. *Fluvial Processes in Geomorphology*. San Francisco: Freeman.

Lynch, Dennis L. 1974. An ecosystem guide for mountain land planning. Ft. Collins: Colorado State Forest Service and Colorado State University.

Lynch, Dennis L., and Standish R. Broome. n.d. Mountain land planning. Ft. Collins: Colorado State Forest Service, Colorado State University, and U.S.D.A. Forest Service.

Marsh, William M. 1978. *Environmental Analysis for Land Use and Site Planning*. New York: McGraw-Hill.

Martinelli, M., Jr. 1974. Snow avalanche sites: Their identification and evaluation. U.S.D.A. Forest Service, Agricultural Information Bulletin no. 360.

McHarg, Ian. 1969. *Design with Nature*. Garden City, N.Y.: Doubleday.

McLaughlin, William, and Frederick B. Bevis. 1975. Indian Hills environmental inventory—A citizen's tool for planning. Ft. Collins: Colorado State University.

McPhee, John. 1980. *Basin and Range*. New York: Farrar, Straus & Giroux.

———. 1987. *Rising from the Plains*. New York: Farrar, Straus & Giroux.

Mears, Arthur I. 1977. Debris-flow hazard analysis and mitigation: An example from Glenwood Springs, Colorado. Denver: Colorado Geological Survey Information Series no. 8.

Meiman, J. R. 1974. Water and erosion control in relation to revegetation of high-altitude disturbed lands. In *Proceedings of a Workshop on Revegetation of High-Altitude Disturbed Lands*. Ft. Collins: Colorado Water Resources Research

Institute, Information Series no. 10, pp. 24–30.

Nishimura, John Y. 1974. Soils and soil problems at high altitudes. *Proceedings of a Workshop on High-Altitude Disturbed Lands*. Ft. Collins: Colorado Water Resources Research Institute, Information Series no. 10, pp. 5–9.

Northwest Colorado Council of Governments. 1981. 404 mitigation handbook: Protection of wetlands from development activities. Frisco, Colo.

O'Brien, Robert. 1988. Rehabilitation techniques for gravel-bed channels. Manuscript.

Odum, Eugene P. 1971. *Fundamentals of Ecology*, 3rd ed. Philadelphia: Saunders.

Perla, Ronald I., and M. Martinelli, Jr. 1976. *Avalanche Handbook*. U.S.D.A. Forest Service Agriculture Handbook no. 489.

Price, Larry W. 1981. *Mountains and Man*. Berkeley and Los Angeles: University of California Press.

Reeser, Warner K., Jr., and Lane W. Kirkpatrick. 1975. The air pollution carrying capacities of selected Colorado mountain valley ski communities. Denver: Colorado Department of Health, Air Pollution Control Division.

Retzer, L. J. 1974. Alpine soils. In *Arctic and Alpine Environments*, ed. Jack D. Ives and R. G. Barry. London: Methuen.

Rogers, W. P., L. R. Ladwig, A. L. Hornbaker, S. D. Schwochow, S. S. Hart, D. C. Shelton, D. L. Scroggs, and J. M. Soule. 1974. Guidelines and criteria for identification and land-use controls of geologic hazard and mineral resource areas. Denver: Colorado Geological Survey, Department of Natural Resources, Special Publication no. 6 (reprinted in 1979).

Ronco, Frank. 1976. Regeneration of forest lands at high elevations in the Central Rocky Mountains. In *Proceedings: High-Altitude Revegetation Workshop no. 2*. Ft. Collins, Colo.: Environmental Resources Center, Information Series no. 21, pp. 13–25.

Ryan, B. C. 1978. Influences of winds in mountain terrain. Conference on Sierra Nevada Meteorology, June, pp. 46–52.

Sartz, R. S. 1973. Snow and frost depths on north–south slopes. St. Paul: Central Forest and Range Experiment Station, Research Note no. NC-157.

Schuster, Robert L., and Raymond J. Krizek, eds. 1978. *Landslides—Analysis and Control*. Transportation Research Board Special Report no. 176. Washington, D.C.: National Academy of Sciences.

Soil Survey Staff. 1987. *Keys to Soil Taxonomy*. Ithaca, N.Y.: SMSS Technical Monograph no. 6.

Storer, Tracy I., and Robert L. Usinger. 1963. *Sierra Nevada Natural History*. Berkeley and Los Angeles: University of California Press.

Swanston, Douglas N. 1967. Debris avalanching in thin soils derived from bedrock. Portland, Ore.:

Pacific Northwest Forest and Range Experiment Station, U.S.D.A. Forest Service, Research Note no. PNW-64.

Tahoe Regional Planning Agency. 1978. *Lake Tahoe Basin Water Quality Management Plan.* Vol. II. Handbook of best management practices for control of erosion and surface runoff. Zephyr Cove, Nev.

———. 1982. How to protect your property from erosion: A guide for homebuilders in the Lake Tahoe Basin. Zephyr Cove, Nev.

Tew, Ronald K. 1968. Properties of soil under aspen and herb–shrub cover. Ogden, Utah: Intermountain Forest and Range Experiment Station, Research Note no. INT-78.

Theisen, Marc S. 1986. Practical approaches for cost effective erosion control. *Colorado Green* (Spring): 16–21.

Trefil, James S. 1986. *Meditations at 10,000 Feet.* New York: Macmillan.

U.S. Army Corps of Engineers. 1960. Run-off from snowmelt: Engineering and design. Manual EM no. 1110-2-1406.

U.S.D.A. Forest Service. 1976. Beaver Creek winter sports site environmental analysis report. Minturn, Colo.: White River National Forest, Holy Cross Ranger District.

———. 1987. East Fork ski area draft environmental impact statement. Durango, Colo.: San Juan National Forest, Pagosa Ranger District.

U.S.D.A. Soil Conservation Service. n.d. A guide for erosion and sediment control in urbanizing areas of Colorado (interim version). Denver.

———. 1975. *Soil Taxonomy.* Agriculture Handbook no. 436.

U.S. Department of Transportation, Federal Highway Administration. 1986. Guidelines for slope maintenance and slide restoration. Report no. FHWA-TS-85-231.

University of California, Division of Agriculture and Natural Resources, Cooperative Extension. 1984. Protecting trees when building on forested land. Leaflet no. 21348.

Untermann, Richard K. 1978. *Principles and Practices of Grading, Drainage and Road Alignment: An Ecologic Approach.* Reston, Va.: Reston Publishing.

Vail, Colorado (Town of). n.d. Draft report on water quality.

Way, Douglas S. 1973. *Terrain Analysis*, rev. ed. Stroudsburg, Pa.: Dowden, Hutchinson & Ross.

Weitz, Charles A. 1981. Weathering heights. *Natural History*, November, pp. 72–84.

Whitney, Stephen R. 1983. *A Field Guide to the Cascades and Olympics.* Seattle: The Mountaineers.

Windell, J. T., B. E. Willard, D. J. Cooper, S. Q. Foster, C. F. Knud-Hansen, L. P. Rink, and G. N. Kiladis.

1986. An ecological characterization of Rocky Mountain montane and subalpine wetlands. Ft. Collins, Colo.: U.S. Fish and Wildlife Service Biological Report no. 86.

Zuck, R. H., and L. R. Brown, eds. 1976. *Proceedings: High-Altitude Revegetation Workshop no. 2.* Environmental Resources Center, Information Series no. 21. Ft. Collins: Colorado State University.

Zwinger, Ann H. 1970. *Beyond the Aspen Grove.* New York: Random House.

Zwinger, Ann H., and Beatrice E. Willard. 1972. *Land Above the Trees—A Guide to American Alpine Tundra.* New York: Harper & Row.

MOUNTAIN DEVELOPMENT AND ARCHITECTURE

Abbott, Derek, and Kimball Pollit. 1981. *Hill Housing.* New York: Watson-Guptill.

American Society of Landscape Architects Foundation and U.S. Department of Housing and Urban Development. 1977. *Barrier Free Site Design.* Washington, D.C.: U.S. Government Printing Office.

Arrowhead at Vail Properties Corporation. 1983. Arrowhead design guidelines. Vail, Colo.

Arthur, Eric, and Dudley Witney. 1972. *The Barn.* Toronto: McClelland and Stuart.

Banff, Alberta (Town of). n.d. Banff townsite architectural and environmental guidelines.

Bealer, Alex W., and John O. Ellis. 1978. *The Log Cabin: Homes of the North American Wilderness.* Barre, Mass.: Barre Publishing.

Beaver Creek Resort Company. 1979. Design regulations—Commercial facilities. Avon, Colo.

———. 1985. Design regulations—Pedestrian mall. Avon, Colo.

———. 1979. Design regulations—Single family and duplex residences. Avon, Colo.

———. 1979. Design regulations—The village. Avon, Colo.

Berry, Donald L. 1984. How mountain conditions affect new developments. *Colorado Engineering* 2, no. 6 (March): 10–11.

Birkeland, Robert W. 1988. Ski town circulation design and planning. MLA thesis, University of Washington.

Braun, Thomas A., and Jeffrey T. Winston. 1986. The Vail Village urban design guide plan: A framework for guiding development. *UD Review* 4, no. 4: 12–18.

Bull, Henrik. 1973. The trouble with winter. *Ski Area Management*, Spring, pp. 45–52.

———. 1981. Horse sense energy conservation. *Ski Area Management*, July, pp. 44–45.

———. 1983. Some comments on roofing materials. *Ski Area Management*, May, pp. 84–85.

———. 1986. Lessons from traditional mountain building. *Ski Area Management*, May, pp. 97–99.

Carver, Norman F., Jr. 1979. *Italian Hilltowns.* Kalamazoo, Mich.: Documan Press.

Castle Pines Land Company. 1981. The architectural design guide. Castle Rock, Colo.

Cereghini, Mario. 1956. *Building in the Mountains: Architecture and History.* Milan: Edizioni del Milione (first English ed. 1957).

Chang, Ching-Yu, ed. 1978. *Process: Architecture/ Lawrence Halprin.* Tokyo: Process Architecture Publishing.

Clifford, Peggy, and John M. Smith. 1970. *Aspen/ Dreams and Dilemmas: Love Letter to a Small Town.* Chicago: Swallow Press.

Colorado Historical Society. 1980. Good neighbors, building next to history: Design guidelines handbook. Denver.

Crested Butte, Colorado (Town of). n.d. Design guidelines for architecture and landscape architecture in Crested Butte.

Economic Planning Group of Canada. 1984. Whistler —Development of a resort. Report for the Department of Regional Industrial Expansion, Tourism Canada, Victoria, B.C.

Freudenheim, Leslie M., and Elisabeth Sussman. 1974. *Building with Nature: Roots of the San Francisco Bay Region Tradition.* Santa Barbara, Calif.: Peregrine Smith.

Futagawa, Yukio, Makoto Suzuki, and Christian Norberg-Schulz. 1978. *Wooden Houses.* Tokyo: A.D.A. EDITA Tokyo (English edition, New York: Abrams, 1979).

Hansen, Hans Jürgen. 1971. *Architecture in Wood: A History of Wood Building and Its Techniques in Europe and North America.* New York: Viking.

Hürlimann, Martin. 1938. *Die Schweiz: Bilder Ihrer Landschaft und Kultur* (Switzerland: Pictures of Her Landscape and Culture). Zurich: Atlantis Verlag.

Juul, Tore. 1979. *The Architecture and Planning of Ski Resorts in France.* Norwich, England: Page Bros. (Norwich).

Kaiser, Harvey H. 1982. *Great Camps of the Adirondacks.* Boston: David R. Godine.

Kemp, Jim. 1987. *American Vernacular: Regional Influences in Architecture and Interior Design.* New York: Viking-Penguin.

Kennish, Katharine. 1981. *The Mountain House.* Midland, Mich.: Northwood Institute Press.

Knight, Carleton. 1984. The Park Service as client II: Shifting emphases since World War II. *Architecture*, December, pp. 48–55.

Lawson, Fred, and Manuel Baud-Bovy. 1977. *Tourism and Recreation Development—A Handbook of Physical Planning.* London: Architectural Press.

Lynch, Kevin. 1971. *Site Planning*, 2nd ed.

Cambridge, Mass.: MIT Press.

Mackinlay, Ian. 1967. Building in the deep snow country. Address to the Architect-Researchers Conference, Gatlinburg, Tenn.

———. 1983. The neglected hazards of snow and ice. *AIA Journal*, February, pp. 52ff.

Mackinlay, Ian, and W. E. Willis. n.d. Snow country design. NEA Grant no. A 70-1-15.

Matus, Vladimir. 1988. *Design for Northern Climates.* New York: Van Nostrand Reinhold.

McMahon, Anne. 1980. *The Whistler Story.* West Vancouver, B.C.: A. McMahon.

Merk, Frederick. 1978. *History of the Westward Movement.* New York: Knopf.

Myers, Phyllis. 1984. The Park Service as client I: The early decades of rustic grandeur. *Architecture*, December, pp. 42–47.

Neustadtl, Sara. 1987. *Moving Mountains, Coping with Change in Mountain Communities.* Boston: Appalachian Mountain Club.

Nordhaus, Richard S., Min Kantrowitz, and William J. Siembieda. 1984. Accessible fishing: A planning handbook. Santa Fe: Resource Management and Development Division, New Mexico Natural Resources Department.

Olgyay, Victor. 1963. *Design with Climate.* Princeton, N.J.: Princeton University Press.

Park City, Utah (Town of), and Gage Davis Associates, Landscape Architects. 1982. Park City parks: A parks and recreation master plan for Park City, Utah.

Pearce, Sarah J. 1983. A guide to Colorado architecture. Denver: Colorado Historical Society.

Proksch, Viktor. 1964. *Maisons dans les Alpes* (Houses in the Alps). Innsbruck: Pinguin Verlag.

Rhoades, Robert E. 1979. Cultural echoes across the mountains. *Natural History*, January, pp. 46–57.

Rossbach, Sarah. 1983. *Feng Shui: The Chinese Art of Placement.* New York: Dutton.

Royston, Hanamoto, Beck & Abey, Landscape Architects, and Livingston & Blayney, Planners. 1973. The Vail plan. Vail, Colo.

Rudofsky, Bernard. 1964. *Architecture Without Architects.* Garden City, N.Y.: Doubleday.

San Francisco Museum of Modern Art. 1986. *Lawrence Halprin: Changing Places.* San Francisco: SFMMA.

Sandoval, Judith Hancock. 1986. *Historic Ranches of Wyoming.* Casper, Wyo.: Mountain States Lithographing.

Scully, Vincent. 1972. *Pueblo: Mountain, Village, Dance.* New York: Viking Press.

Sea Ranch Association. 1978. Preliminary design guidelines. Sonoma County, Calif.

Sestini, Valerio, and Enzo Somigli. 1978. *Sherpa Architecture.* Geneva, Switzerland: UNESCO (translated from Italian).

Smith, Duane A. 1967. *Rocky Mountain Mining Camps: The Urban Frontier.* Lincoln: University of Nebraska Press.

———. 1977. *Colorado Mining: A Photographic History.* Albuquerque: University of New Mexico Press.

Snowmass American Corporation. 1972. Snowmass master plan. Aspen, Colo.

Sonnenfeld, Martha, and Frank V. Snyder. 1981. *The Stratton Story.* Stratton, Vt.: Stratton Corporation.

Steadman, Philip. 1975. *Energy, Environment, and Building.* Cambridge, England: Cambridge University Press.

Stilgoe, John R. 1982. *Common Landscape of America, 1580 to 1845.* New Haven, Conn.: Yale University Press.

Stockwell, Sherwood. 1983. Resort construction will cost you. *Urban Land*, October, pp. 12–15. Washington, D.C.: Urban Land Institute.

Stoehr, C. Eric. 1975. *Bonanza Victorian: Architecture and Society in Colorado Mining Towns.* Albuquerque: University of New Mexico Press.

Suzuki, Makoto, and Yukio Futagawa. 1973. *Villages and Towns: #6 Alps.* Tokyo: A.D.A. EDITA.

Telluride Development Corporation. n.d. Design regulations, Telluride Mountain Village. Telluride, Colo.

Thiede, Arthur, and Cindy Teipner. 1986. *American Log Homes.* Emmaus, Pa.: Rodale Press.

Todhunter, Rodger. 1981. Banff and the Canadian national park idea. *Landscape* 25, no. 2: 33–39.

Turner, Frederick Jackson. 1947. *The Frontier in American History.* New York: Holt, Rinehart and Winston (reprinted in 1986, Tucson: University of Arizona Press).

Uphill, Downhill: Deer Valley Resort. 1983. *Architectural Record* 171 (May): 92–97.

U.S. Department of Housing and Urban Development. n.d. *Regional Guidelines for Building Passive Energy Conserving Homes.* Washington, D.C.: U.S. Government Printing Office.

U.S. Department of the Interior, Heritage Conservation and Recreation Service. 1980. A guide to designing accessible outdoor recreation facilities. Ann Arbor, Mich.: Lake Central Regional Office.

U.S. Department of the Interior, National Park Service. 1985. Some important items to consider when providing handicap accessible facilities. Denver: Denver Service Center.

Vail, Colorado (Town of), Community Development Department and Gage Davis Associates, Landscape Architects. 1980. Urban design guideplans—Vail Village and LionsHead.

Watson, Donald. 1983. *Energy Efficient Building Principles and Practices.* New York: McGraw-Hill.

Weslager, C. A. 1969. *The Log Cabin in America.* New Brunswick, N.J.: Rutgers University Press.

Whistler, British Columbia, Resort Municipality of. 1979. Design guidelines, Whistler Village (draft). Vancouver, B.C.

Wirth, Kurt, and David Meili. 1986. *Das Haus des Schweizer Bauern* (Swiss Farmhouses). Berne, Switzerland: Paul Haupt.

Wolgensinger, Bernard. 1981. *Maisons en montagne* (Living in the mountains). Fribourg, Switzerland: Office du Livre.

Zelinsky, Wilbur. 1953. The log house in Georgia. *Geographical Review*, April, pp. 184ff.

LANDSCAPE DESIGN

Allen, Oliver E. 1979. *Winter Gardens.* Alexandria, Va.: Time-Life Books.

Arno, Stephen F., and Ramona P. Hammerly. 1977. *Northwest Trees.* Seattle: The Mountaineers.

Austin, Richard L. 1984. *Designing the Natural Landscape.* New York: Van Nostrand Reinhold.

Douglas, William Lake. 1987. *Hillside Gardening: Evaluating the Site, Designing Views, Planting Slopes.* New York: Simon & Schuster.

Ernst, Ruth Shaw. 1987. *The Naturalist's Garden.* Emmaus, Pa.: Rodale Press.

Evergreen Nursery. The mountain plant guide. P.O. Box 39, Kittredge, Colo. 80457.

Gundell, Herb. 1985. *Complete Guide to Rocky Mountain Gardening.* Dallas: Taylor Publishing.

Kelly, George. 1967. *Rocky Mountain Horticulture*, rev. ed. Boulder, Colo.: Pruett Publishing.

———. 1979. *Shrubs for the Rocky Mountains.* Cortez, Colo.: Rocky Mountain Horticultural Publishing.

Peterson, P. Victor, and P. Victor Peterson, Jr. 1975. *Native Trees of the Sierra Nevada.* Berkeley and Los Angeles: University of California Press.

Robinette, Gary O. 1972. *Plants/People/and Environmental Quality.* Washington, D.C.: U.S. Department of the Interior, National Park Service.

———, ed. 1977. *Landscape Planning for Energy Conservation.* Reston, Va.: Environmental Design Press.

Sunset Magazine and Sunset Books. 1977. *Western Garden Book.* Menlo Park, Calif.: Lane Publishing.

Taylor, Kathryn S., and Stephen F. Hamblin. 1963. *Handbook of Wild Flower Cultivation.* New York: Macmillan.

Thomas, John Hunter, and Dennis R. Parnell. 1974. *Native Shrubs of the Sierra Nevada.* Berkeley and Los Angeles: University of California Press.

Williams, Jean, ed. 1986. *Rocky Mountain Alpines.* Portland, Ore.: Timber Press.

Credits

DESIGNERS

Designers and planners of projects mentioned in the book are listed below in alphabetical order. Figure numbers are parenthesized in italics following the page numbers.

389

Witter, Peter, architect:
House, Summit County, Colorado, 303 (*11–17*)
Zehren, Jack, architect: Beaver Creek Design
Guidelines, 233 (*9–39*); 281 (*10–33*); 332 (*11–70*)

PHOTOS

Photographers and other sources of photos are listed below by page and figure number. Photos not otherwise credited are the author's.

Aaron, Peter/ESTO: 243 (*9–58*); 319 (*11–48*)
Abbot Hall Art Gallery, Kendall, Cumbria, England: 45 (*3–7*)
Armstrong, Richard: 76 (*4–35*); 77 (*4–36*)
Arnold, Robert: 323 (*11–56*); 326 9*11–61*)
Aspen/Pitkin County Planning Office: 237 (*9–46*)
Austrian National Tourist Office: 305 (*11–20*)
Backen Arrigoni & Ross: 312 (*11–35, 11–36, 11–37*); 322 (*11–53*); 324 (*11–57*)
Baer, Morley: 345 (*11–91*)
Barratt, Tom: 287 (*10–41*); 330 (*11–68*)
Baxter, Elmar: 36 (*2–28*)
Beebe, Morton: 340 (*11–83*)
Blake, Michael: 220 (*9–17*)
British Columbia Enterprise Corporation: 260 (*10–7*)
Brooklyn Museum: 3 (*1–1*)
Buchanan, Craig: 333 (*11–71*)
Bull, Henrik: 299 (*11–10*)
Cavendish Partnership: 328 (*11–64*)
Chamberlain, W. G.: 46 (*3–9*)
Colorado Department of Health, Air Pollution Control Division: 65 (*4–16*)
Colorado Geological Survey: 96 (*5–15*)
Colorado Historical Society: 10 (*1–7*); 311 (*11–33*); 320 (*11–50*); 325 (*11–60*)
Cooper, David J.: 150 (*7–10*), 152 (*7–14*), 153 (*7–15*); 164 (*7–25*)
Copper Mountain, Inc.: 246 (*9–62*)
Denver Public Library, Western History Department: 26 (*2–14*); 27 (*2–16*); 28 (*2–17*); 29 (*2–18*); 30 (*2–20*); 46 (*3–8, 3–9*); 257 (*10–2*); 310 (*11–32*); 317 (*11–43*)
Design Workshop, Inc.: 188 (*8–20*)
Fenton, Dick: 237 (*9–45*)
French, Peter: 340 (*11–82*)
French Government Tourist Office: 32 (*2–22*)
German Information Center: 298 (*11–8*); 308 (*11–26*)
Herzog, Wolfgang: 342 (*11–87*)
Hursley, Timothy, The Arkansas Office: 336 (*11–75*); 237 (*11–76*); 341 (*11–84, 11–85*)
Johnston, Tom: 69 (*4–25*); 303 (*11–16*); 346
Joseph, Bob, Estes Park Urban Renewal Authority: 245 (*9–61*)
Kent, Jim: 212 (*9–9*)

King, Patrick: 338 (*11–78*)
Kirkwood Associates: 195 (*8–26*)
LaChapelle, Ed: 74 (*4–30*)
LeBlond, Jerry, Photiques: 328 (*11–65*)
Lee, Doug: 342 (*11–86*)
Lindholm, Fred: 339 (*11–81*)
Lokey, David: 220 (*9–18*)
Marlow, Dave: 322 (*11–54*); 338 (*11–79*)
McClure, L. C.: 317 (*11–43*)
Metropolitan Museum of Art: 19 (*2–5*)
Museum of New Mexico: 24 (*2–12*)
National Park Service: 315 (*11–41*); 350 (*12–4*)
O'Brien, Robert, Inter-Fluve: 110 (*5–29*)
RWDI: 70 (*4–28*), 71 (*4–29*)
Royston Hanamoto Beck and Abey: 209 (*9–4*)
SWA Group: 234 (*9–40, 9–42*)
San Juan County (Colorado) Historical Society: 325 (*11–59*)
Schreibl, Hubert: 38 (*2–20*); 327 (*11–63*)
Schuman, Marc: 304 (*11–18*)
Scrimgeour, Barry: 70 (*4–28*)
Sedlacek, Alois, Austrian National Tourist Office: 305 (*11–20*)
Sheppard, Stephen R. J.: 168 (*7–31*)
Smith, John R.: 34 (*2–25, 2–26*)
Soil Conservation Service: 11 (*1–8*); 126; 127 (*6–1*); 128 (*6–2*); 130 (*6–5*); 132 (*6–7*); 133 (*6–8, 6–9*); 134 (*6–10, 6–12*); 135 (*6–13*); 136 (*6–14*); 138 (*6–15*); 148 (*7–9*)
Sommerfeld, Richard, U.S.D.A. Forest Service: 74 (*4–30*)
St. John, Charles: back cover photo of author
Swiss National Tourist Office: 264 (*10–11*); 296 (*11–3*); 297 (*11–6*); 298 (*11–7*); 305 (*11–21*); 306 (*11–22, 11–23, 11–24*)
Todhunter, Rodger: 319 (*11–49*)
Turnbull, William: 232 (*9–38*)
U.S.D.A. Forest Service: 213 (*9–10*); 248 (*9–65*)
Udall, Mark: 40
WLC Dev. Ltd.: 285 (*10–38*)
Walters, Tom: 339 (*11–80*)
Ward-Young: 318 (*11–45, 11–46*)
Wingle, H. Peter: 33 (*2–23*); 35 (*2–27*); 259 (*10–5*)
Winston Associates: 160 (*7–22, 7–23*)
Witter, Peter: 26 (*2–15*); 303 (*11–17*)
Yellowstone National Park Research Library: 315 (*11–40*)
Yosemite National Park Research Library: 316 (*11–42*)

Index

Page numbers for illustrations are in *italics*.